FEEDING THE PEOPLE

Potatoes are the world's fourth most important food crop, yet they were unknown to most of humanity before 1500. *Feeding the People* traces the global journey of this popular foodstuff from the Andes to everywhere. The potato's global history reveals the ways in which our ideas about eating are entangled with the emergence of capitalism and its celebration of the free market. It also reminds us that ordinary people make history in ways that continue to shape our lives. *Feeding the People* tells the story of how eating became part of statecraft, and provides a new account of the global spread of one of the world's most successful foods.

Rebecca Earle teaches history at the University of Warwick. Her publications include *The Body of the Conquistador: Food, Race and the Colonial Experience in Spanish America, 1492–1700* (2012) and *The Return of the Native: Indians and Mythmaking in Spanish America, 1810–1930* (2007). She has also edited a cookery book.

REBECCA EARLE

FEEDING

— THE —

PEOPLE

THE POLITICS OF THE POTATO

CAMBRIDGE
UNIVERSITY PRESS

CAMBRIDGE
UNIVERSITY PRESS

University Printing House, Cambridge CB2 8BS, United Kingdom

One Liberty Plaza, 20th Floor, New York, NY 10006, USA

477 Williamstown Road, Port Melbourne, VIC 3207, Australia

314–321, 3rd Floor, Plot 3, Splendor Forum, Jasola District Centre,
New Delhi – 110025, India

79 Anson Road, #06–04/06, Singapore 079906

Cambridge University Press is part of the University of Cambridge.

It furthers the University's mission by disseminating knowledge in the pursuit of
education, learning, and research at the highest international levels of excellence.

www.cambridge.org
Information on this title: www.cambridge.org/9781108484060
DOI: 10.1017/9781108688451

First published 2020

Printed in the United Kingdom by TJ International Ltd, Padstow Cornwall

A catalogue record for this publication is available from the British Library.

Library of Congress Cataloging-in-Publication Data
Names: Earle, Rebecca, author.
Title: Feeding the people : the politics of the potato / Rebecca Earle, University of
Warwick.
Description: Cambridge, United Kingdom ; New York : Cambridge University Press,
2020. | Includes bibliographical references and index.
Identifiers: LCCN 2019039285 (print) | LCCN 2019039286 (ebook) |
ISBN 9781108484060 (hardback) | ISBN 9781108688451 (ebook)
Subjects: LCSH: Potatoes – History.
Classification: LCC TX558.P8 E27 2020 (print) | LCC TX558.P8 (ebook) |
DDC 641.3/521–dc23
LC record available at https://lccn.loc.gov/2019039285
LC ebook record available at https://lccn.loc.gov/2019039286

ISBN 978-1-108-48406-0 Hardback

For Matt Western and Lisa Earle

Contents

Figures

CHAPTER 2

CHAPTER 3

CHAPTER 4

CHAPTER 5

CHAPTER 6

CONCLUSIONS

Recipes

INTRODUCTION

CHAPTER 1

CHAPTER 2

CHAPTER 3

Abbreviations

AAA	Archivo Arzobispal de Arequipa, Arequipa
BL	British Library, London
BNE	Biblioteca Nacional de España, Madrid
CIP	International Potato Center (Centro International de la Papa), Lima
FAO	Food and Agriculture Organization of the United Nations
GL	Guildhall Library, London
IYP	International Year of the Potato
LRO	Lancashire Record Office, Preston
McGL	McGill University Library, Montreal
MERLSC	Museum of English Rural Life Special Collections, University of Reading
MP	*Mercurio peruano de historia, literatura, y noticias públicas que da á luz la Sociedad Académica de Amantes de Lima*
RF	Rockefeller Foundation Archives Online
RSA	Royal Society of Arts Archive, London
SAA	*Semanario de agricultura y artes dirigido a los párrocos*
SL	Schlesinger Library, Radcliffe College, Cambridge, MA
TNA	The National Archives, Kew
UN	United Nations
WL	Wellcome Library, London

Pouring Ourselves a Large Gin

WHAT WE EAT IS OUR BUSINESS, OR SO WE GENERALLY believe. We resent being told to consume more vegetables, cut back on salt, and embrace lentils, particularly when the advice emanates from the government. The food writer Diana Henry summed it up: 'When the government tells us to watch our drinking I want to pour myself a large gin.'[1] It's not simply that we are contrary. We also wonder whether such interventions into our private lives violate the underlying principles of democracy. Shouldn't we be allowed to make our own dietary mistakes? New York City mayor Michael Bloomberg learned this to his cost in 2012, when he attempted to ban the sale of extra-large soft drinks. The scheme failed because critics viewed it as an attack on individual freedom. 'New Yorkers need a Mayor, not a Nanny', shouted a full-page advert in the *New York Times*. And when a school near Rotherham, in the north of England, eliminated deep-fried Turkey Twizzlers and fizzy drinks from its cafeteria, outraged mothers rose in protest, insisting that their children had a right to eat burgers, potato crisps and other unhealthy food.[2] Our diets, we feel, are our own concern.

At the same time, we rely on the government to ensure that our food is safe; the pan-European horsemeat scandal focused attention on what can happen when regulatory systems go awry. In January 2013 shocked consumers across the continent learned that their supermarket 'beef' lasagne and chilli con carne might have contained a significant percentage of horsemeat laced with phenylbutazone and other dangerous chemicals. Blame was ascribed in part to reductions in government inspection programmes. We expect the state to help us eat safely and feel let down when it does not. We are also troubled by reports that our

1

fondness for sugar and disdain for exercise is causing a costly crisis in public health and hindering economic growth. British newspapers regularly warn that diabetes and obesity are on course to bankrupt the National Health Service and researchers calculate the economic costs of our collective failure to eat properly. One survey placed the figure at well over fifty billion dollars for the United States alone.[3] Other people, at least, ought to eat sensibly, because their ill-advised consumption habits affect us all.

Our inconsistent attitude towards how much say anyone, and especially the government, ought to have in shaping our diets induces what psychologists call cognitive dissonance – the sense of vague discomfort that results from holding incompatible or contradictory beliefs and values. We'd like to pour a large gin, but fear that if everyone followed that approach the social and economic consequences would be disastrous. Nor is ours the first generation to worry about striking a balance between dietary freedom and public well-being. During the Second World War, deficiencies of the US diet were identified as a threat to national security after a shockingly large number of army recruits were rejected on grounds of ill-health attributed to bad diet. In response, government officials established a wide-ranging programme of dietary reform aimed not only at managing the United States' limited food resources but also at improving public health by changing the nation's eating habits. Yet the very people charged with implementing this programme suspected that it was fundamentally incompatible with liberal democracy. The federal Committee on Food Habits fretted that its own programme was encouraging the sort of submissive rule-following it believed characteristic of totalitarian regimes. Real Americans would, and should, resist such intrusions into their private life.[4]

These tensions between individual choice, public well-being, and the wealth and strength of the nation were born in the Enlightenment. It was in the eighteenth century that everyday eating habits became a matter of state concern. New theories about how to build economically successful states led to new ideas about the relationship between individual diets and national resilience – to the emergence, in other words, of what we might call food security. *Feeding the People* offers a deep history of the concept of food security and a fresh account of how eating became part of modern politics. It also helps explain our own fraught relationship with dietary guidelines by showing how healthy eating became embedded within a neoliberal framework valorising personal responsibility and choice rather than state-led intervention.

Feeding the People tells that story through the history of a food that is emblematic of this transformation: the potato. Today, the potato is a global staple. According to the United Nations, there is not a single country in the world where potatoes are not grown. They are fourth on the list of the world's most important food crops; China is the largest producer, harvesting nearly 100,000,000 tonnes in 2016. Mashed, stewed with cauliflower and cumin seeds, deep fried, made into pancakes, or prepared in thousands of other ways, potatoes are eaten daily around the globe. At present Europeans are the most enthusiastic consumers. Turkmenistan leads the field, at nearly 140 kilos per person per year.[5] Potatoes are an exemplary modern food. Because of their global importance and nutritional merits, the UN declared 2008 to be the International Year of the Potato. (See recipe for Sichuan Stir-Fried Potato Slivers.)

This is a remarkable achievement for a food that was totally unknown to most of humanity before the sixteenth century. Until then the only people who ate potatoes lived along the spine of mountains that runs from the Andes in Bolivia and Chile northwards through the Rockies. These mountains, the homeland of potatoes, were also home to the vast Inca empire, whose overthrow by Spanish conquistadors in the sixteenth century released a whirlwind that blew potatoes to Ireland, India and beyond. The story of the potato's spread around Europe and the world traces out a new history of the relationship between everyday eating habits and the modern state.

According to most scholars, the notion that the population's eating habits affect a state's political and economic security developed between the late nineteenth and mid-twentieth centuries. It was then, explain historians, that individual health ceased to be a private concern and became a matter of public importance.[6] Politicians and officials in many countries became ever more concerned about the impact of poor diet on national efficiency and strength, and responded with a range of

Sichuan Stir-Fried Potato Slivers

More potatoes are grown and eaten in China than anywhere else in the world. Along with chilli peppers, maize and peanuts, potatoes reached East Asia from the Americas over the seventeenth century, and slowly penetrated local foodways. This modern recipe for spicy matchstick potatoes translates several of these new foods into a recognisably Sichuan-style idiom.

Sichuan Stir-fried Potato Slivers
[炒土豆丝 *chao tudousi*]

A. Ingredients
potatoes (250 g.)
spring onion (25 g.)
4 dried chillies
vegetable oil (40 g.)
salt (2 g.)

B. Method
1. Peel and wash the potatoes. Slice into coarse slivers. Steep in cold water and rinse a few times to remove some of the starch, then drain the water. Cut spring onions into 2.5 cm-long sections. Remove the stems from the dried chillies and cut into 2.5 cm-long sections.
2. Add oil to wok and heat to medium-high. First add dried chillies, spring onion and salt – be quick. Once the chillies have turned reddish-brown, add potatoes and stir-fry rapidly until done, remove from the wok and it is ready.

C. Distinguishing features
The potato slivers are crisp. The flavour is slightly spicy. Good for eating with rice or for accompanying alcohol.

innovative new programmes, from state-subsidised school dinners to healthy-eating campaigns. Hunger and malnutrition were transformed from personal misfortune to national emergency, notes James Vernon, because they began to be perceived as threatening 'political stability,

economic production, and racial efficiency' in ways that affected all of
society. They demanded 'not just philanthropic intervention but forms of
statecraft'.[7] The voluminous writings on food security similarly connect developments during the inter-war years to the deepening conviction that adequate diets were essential to national and global
stability. The establishment in the late 1940s of international agencies such as the FAO is usually considered the culmination of this
new conviction.[8]

The belief that effective governance entails effective management
of the population's eating habits is an essential part of modernity.
Developments since the late nineteenth century transformed many
aspects of the state's relationship to food, and politicians and officials have been able to design and implement ambitious projects in
ways unimaginable a century earlier. The degree to which states
accepted responsibility for the population's welfare also changed
significantly. Yet the fundamental modern belief that everyday eating
habits shape a nation's political and economic success emerged not
in the late nineteenth century, but a hundred years earlier, during
the Enlightenment.

This chronology matters. Situating these ideas in their eighteenth-
century context allows us to see the close connections between
enlightened debates about food, political economy, public well-
being and effective statecraft, all of which have decisively shaped
today's world. Everyday eating practices acquired a new political
importance during the Enlightenment because statesmen and scientists, philosophers and philanthropists, became ever more convinced
that there was a correlation between diet and national prowess. The
eighteenth century also saw the emergence of the conviction that the
way to guarantee a well-functioning economy and a secure state was
by enabling people to *choose* the right foods, rather than by requiring
them to do so. The key point, to paraphrase the political scientist
Bernard Harcourt, is that the logic that underpins today's approach
to nutritional governmentality 'was embedded in the first articulations of liberal economic theory'.[9]

We can blame the Enlightenment for our ambivalence about whether
our diets are our business, or everyone's business. Today's healthy-eating

plates, food pyramids and governmental dietary guidelines have their roots in the eighteenth century. So does the hostility to more robust forms of intervention, such as Mayor Bloomberg's soda ban. Following the potato on its journey from the Andes to everywhere is one way of tracing out that history. The history of the potato also opens up alternative vistas for thinking about food security, or, better, about what is often called food sovereignty, which stresses the importance of empowering locals to determine their own eating and agricultural practices. Andean villagers, rather than the Inca state, were the protagonists of the potato's emergence as a South American staple, and early modern peasants and labourers were the pioneers who spread potato cultivation across Europe. Today, UN analysts and agricultural experts increasingly recognise that small farmers hold the key to a sustainable agricultural future.

Following the potato in its travels helps tell this story because it reveals these intersections with particular clarity. Potatoes make visible the ways in which our ideas about eating are entangled with the emergence of capitalism and its celebration of the free market. The potato's story also reminds us that ordinary people make history in ways that continue to shape our lives. Potatoes, in short, are a good way of thinking about the origins of the modern world. *Feeding the People* argues ultimately that we cannot resolve our current concerns about food justice and security without understanding the genesis of the very language and ideas we employ in their analysis.

NOURISHING THE COMMONWEALTH

What ordinary people eat has not always been of much interest to the state. *That* people ate was of course very important. Rulers everywhere have long been concerned about the political consequences of famine. Nothing, declared the Tudor politician William Cecil, 'will sooner lead men to sedition than dearth of victuals'.[10] Attention was usually focused on ensuring an adequate food supply to cities, whose concentrated populations offered the greatest potential for rebellion. Polities in many parts of the ancient and early modern world maintained public warehouses that could distribute grain to urban residents in moments of shortage. The Roman empire for example devoted considerable resources to providing residents of the capital with a reliable supply of grain. The Chinese state was unusual in using its system of state granaries to feed both urban and rural populations. From around the seventh century CE Chinese rulers oversaw a network of grain storehouses located in many parts of the empire whose purpose was to prevent famine and maintain consistent supplies for all their subjects, not only those living in cities. Kings were also alert to the dangers of ignoring the food needs of their own armed forces. In the Andes, the Inca state oversaw an extensive network of storage facilities, which it used to warehouse food and other goods for itself and its troops.[11]

In addition, rulers have long recognised the importance of regulating food prices. The Ottoman empire intervened decisively in the grain cycle to ensure that Istanbul received the hundreds of tons of flour it required daily. Ottoman regulations controlled the prices at which food was sold and at times directly oversaw the transport of grain to urban markets, using a fleet of state-owned ships.[12] Municipal governments in many medieval European cities regulated both the cost and quality of foodstuffs. The guild system also aimed to ensure that foods sold at market conformed to the required standards of healthfulness and quality. Food-suppliers who did not satisfy these expectations were fined. A 1379 English ordinance for example sanctioned London bakers for selling meat pasties containing 'garbage, not befitting, and sometimes stinking, in deceit of the people'.[13] Outlawing such practices was a legitimate, indeed necessary, exercise in governance.

Civic authorities at times also regulated the luxuriousness of meals served at weddings or other festive gatherings. Legislation might prohibit certain dishes or limit the total budget. The Roman *Lex Fannia*, from the second century BCE, restricted the number of courses that could be served at private feasts. Such regulations might in addition detail who was, and was not, permitted to eat particular foodstuffs. Peasants in seventeenth-century Japan were banned from consuming a wide range of foods including tofu and white rice.[14] These sumptuary laws aimed to prevent wasteful expenditure or sinful overindulgence, and also worked to preserve social distinctions. By the sixteenth century European regulations moreover began to reflect a concern that individual or communal gluttony presaged a descent into more general immorality, in ways that threatened the body politic as a whole. The puffy, overfed body of Henry VIII represented for French Catholics both the physical dangers of overindulgence and the moral bankruptcy of Reformation England. The dietary failings of individuals thus influenced, and mirrored, the spiritual state of the country.[15]

Feeding the hungry is furthermore a charitable imperative in most religions. For Sikhs the distribution of food to those in need is a central religious obligation. In early modern Europe and the Mediterranean world a variety of religious charities likewise dispensed food to prisoners, paupers and other hungry folk.[16] These associations between feeding the poor and the larger religious framework helped position governmental attention to the food supply as a matter of ethics. For a prince, insisted the Confucian philosopher Mencius, failing to provide grain in times of famine was the moral equivalent of murder. In pre-Mughal Bengal, kings were likewise expected to distribute rice to those in need. Hunger imposed a moral obligation on rulers, and those who failed to live up to this obligation risked a loss of legitimacy.[17]

For most ancient and early modern states, in sum, ensuring that urban populations had access to a steady and safe supply of food was a recognised component of statecraft. Rulers moreover demonstrated their moral fitness to govern in part through their concern for the well-being of the poor. These multiple involvements with the food supply, observed the historian Charles Tilly, 'did not by any means form a harmonious whole. On the contrary, they virtually guaranteed that food policy would be a matter of bitter political debate.'[18] But as long as the population was not perishing as a result of famine, or unsettling the social order by conspicuous displays of extravagance, or provoking divine wrath through sinful overconsumption, political philosophers did not give much thought to what, specifically, ordinary people had for dinner. Monarchs worried about preventing food riots but not, in general, about the particular features of their subjects' daily diets. Whether their polenta was made of millet or of barley, whether their soups contained cabbage, or whether they baked or griddled their bread possessed no political significance. Such things were the purview of priests and doctors, not statesmen. The only body whose daily diet was of unquestioned political importance was that of the ruler, for whom court physicians designed individualised dietary regimes, and whose robustness was a topic of perennial political anxiety.[19]

Because the diets of ordinary people did not form part of the art of governance, the everyday eating habits of the population do not feature in political treatises from early modern Europe. Niccolò Machiavelli did not find the subject relevant to his discussion of statecraft. Giovanni Botero, whose 1589 *The Reason of State* offered a pioneering and influential analysis of effective governance, took an entirely traditional view of food's importance to this enterprise. He reminded readers that 'experience has shown us, not once but many times' that 'scarcity of bread exasperates the common people more than anything else', and so could lead to rebellion. He noted the importance of food supply in mounting military campaigns, and also lectured rulers on the ethical need for personal restraint in all things, diet included. The particular eating habits of the population, however, did not form part of his model of statecraft.[20] The political philosopher Thomas Hobbes devoted no attention at all to the topic. In his 1651 *Leviathan*, Hobbes addressed eating as simply a basic human need, not as a matter of state.[21] The chapter on 'the nourishment of a commonwealth' does not consider the mundane matter of how people actually nourished themselves. 'Nourishment' instead provides a metaphor for commerce and property rights; for political philosophers such as Hobbes, the 'nourishment' necessary to sustain the body politic was the gold, silver and other commodities that facilitated trade, not bread and pottage.[22] Commerce, the policing of markets and the supply of grain were thus important matters of statecraft, but what people did in their kitchens was not.

By the late eighteenth century, such domestic matters formed part of the art of governance in Europe. In Britain, no less than the prime minister himself addressed Parliament on the need to encourage the population to add more wholegrains and potatoes to their daily bread.[23] This unprecedented interest in such minutiae reflects changes in the understanding of governance. These changes were identified many decades ago by the French theorist Michel Foucault, who described how a new political appreciation of 'the population' emerged in Europe in the late seventeenth century. The new theorists of statecraft viewed the population as a resource to be managed, alongside other endowments such as forests or factories.[24] Together with pro-natalist policies, schemes to extirpate idleness, public health campaigns and other enterprises aimed at improving the population, dietary reform came to form part of the eighteenth-century understanding of how to govern. From the perspective of eighteenth-century political theorists, what people ate on a daily basis was deeply relevant to evaluating the strength and fitness of the polity. By the end of the century the earlier dearth of accounts describing the eating habits of labourers and other ordinary folk had been replaced by myriad commentaries from politically engaged observers eager to assess the overall health of the body politic. The techniques of government, and the modern state, had come to embrace daily diets. The conviction that effective governance requires some scrutiny of the population's eating habits is an essential part of modernity, and this conviction emerged in the Enlightenment.

STATES AND INDIVIDUALS

The new association between the wealth and power of the polity and the energy of the population was addressed by many eighteenth-century writers. The Marquis de Chastellux, a philosophically minded military official who composed an influential treatise on public happiness, maintained that English labourers were healthier than the French because they enjoyed a superior diet. As a result, Britain was stronger than France, regardless of the relative populations of the two countries. The French state therefore had a direct interest in improving the eating habits of French working people.[25] Identifying, and promoting, the foods that would enable this improvement was hailed as a patriotic undertaking. In the view of many writers, potatoes provided an excellent solution to this challenge. A few grains of salt, and a little butter, bacon or milk was sufficient to convert them into a healthful and satisfying meal, observed one French agronomic handbook. 'No plant is as universally useful,' it concluded.[26] French officials before and after the Revolution encouraged potato consumption through prize competitions, publications and exhortation, and they were not alone. Individuals across eighteenth-century Europe experimented with schemes to improve the nutritional health of working people because such projects were believed to increase national prowess. (See figure 1.)

Promotional schemes were all very well, but translating new political convictions into real behavioural change was no easy matter. From the moment that daily diets first attracted the attention of political theorists, debate began over who was responsible for ensuring that people followed these recommendations, and who was to blame if they did not. Eighteenth-century scientists, politicians and social commentators frequently lamented the failure of the working classes to eat properly, and disputed whether blame lay with the fecklessness of the poor, or the economic structures that limited their purchasing power. Peasants, complained the Scottish physician William Buchan in 1776, 'are extremely careless with respect to what they eat or drink, and often, through mere indolence, use unwholesome food, when they might, for the same expense, have that which is wholesome'.[27] Buchan recommended potatoes as a highly suitable and economical foodstuff. Others challenged such criticisms, variously lauding existing working-class eating practices as perfectly healthful, or redirecting blame towards the merchants and officials who pushed food prices to unaffordable heights. More radical voices suggested that the exploitative distribution of power and wealth was the true reason working people so often ate miserable and unhealthy diets.

Disagreements about whether poor diet resulted primarily from 'carelessness' or from poverty persisted. A century after Buchan condemned the eating habits of peasants, the nutritionist Max Rubner critiqued the 'irrational' behaviour of German industrial workers who wasted their limited resources on buttery sandwiches, instead of more nutritious foodstuffs. Others, such as the socialist alderman from Bradford who authored a pamphlet advocating free school meals, blamed unjust economic structures. From York, the philanthropist

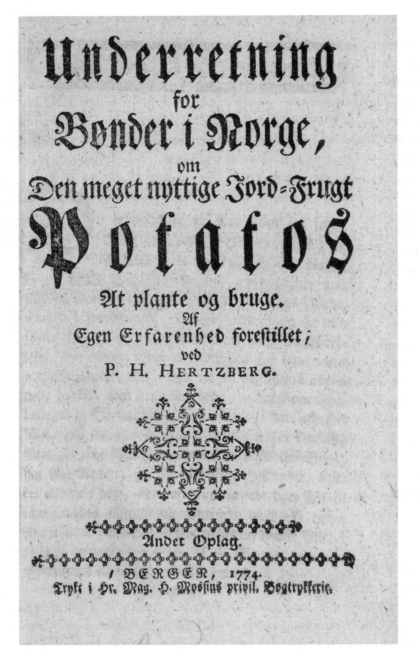

Figure 1 Frontispiece of Peter Harboe Hertzberg's 1774 guide to growing potatoes. This pamphlet provided Norwegian farmers with guidance on cultivating the 'very useful' potato. Similar texts were published across Europe in the late eighteenth century. New ideas linking the health of the population to the wealth and grandeur of the state made nutritious staples such as the potato appealing to political theorists and patriotically minded individuals.

Seebohm Rowntree calculated that many of the city's poor lacked the financial means to eat even a minimally adequate diet. He nonetheless believed that 'some improvement might be effected in their diet, without increasing its cost, if they possessed greater knowledge of the relative value of different food stuffs, and were prepared to profit by such knowledge'.[28] Today's proposals to offer cookery classes to recipients of welfare are the latest instalments in a long-running debate.[29]

What unites these varied opinions is the shared conviction that individual eating habits are not simply a matter of individual concern. Of course, the impact of diet on individual health has long been recognised, and physicians have for millennia offered guidance on what to eat to stay well. Those who failed to comply, doctors warned, were digging their graves with their own teeth.[30] William Buchan and the Bradford alderman, however, perceived a broader, political, risk to such individual failings. Buchan believed that Britain's 'real wealth, the happiness of her people, and the stability of her government' were connected to the everyday eating habits of ordinary people. The Bradford socialist blamed 'under and improper feeding' for the poor physique that rendered 40 per cent of the men who volunteered to fight in the Boer War so puny that they were 'not good enough to be shot at'.[31] When workers made careless or irresponsible dietary choices that affected their health they reduced the nation's security and productivity. Mothers who fed children inappropriate meals were critiqued for weakening both their bodies and their moral fibre, and probably also increasing the likelihood of labour unrest. To counter these evils, eighteenth-century philanthropists published collections of economical recipes that aimed to show poor women 'the way to do much good with little money', and nineteenth-century social analysts recommended that working-class girls be equipped with the basic principles of budgeting, plain cooking and nutritionally informed menu planning. By the twentieth century 'domestic science' had made its way onto the curricula of many state-funded educational systems.[32]

For eighteenth- and nineteenth-century political writers, encouraging the poor to adopt recommended eating habits through such educational campaigns was an appropriate exercise in governance. Most, however, rejected the proposition that the state had an outright responsibility to guarantee a minimum diet.[33] 'To provide for us in our necessities is not in the power of government,' stated the political philosopher and statesman Edmund Burke in 1795.[34] The emergence in the late nineteenth century of welfarist philosophies that ascribed this responsibility to the state marks a new development in political thinking. It does not, however, reflect a new appreciation of the importance of diet to the body politic. The belief that individual health and national strength were connected was born much earlier, in the eighteenth century. The potato's career as an Enlightenment super-food helps tell this story.

PEASANTS AND POTATOES

The South American potato has nourished ordinary people for millennia, doing so long before statesmen in Europe began contemplating its potential to build hearty populations. Wild potatoes were being eaten, from Chile to Utah, some 12,000 years ago. Their domestication probably dates from around 7800 BCE.[35] Villagers along the Andes grew potatoes for their daily sustenance, creating an enormous corpus of agronomic knowledge, and a great variety of potatoes, which were used in diverse ways to provide year-round nourishment. When Europeans and West Africans reached South America's Pacific coast in the 1530s, they instantly identified the potato as an essential staple, the local equivalent of European bread or West African millet, sorghum, or yam porridge. They were the ones who brought potatoes to Europe, thereby initiating its global spread. Colonists moreover associated the potato with the indigenous locals who grew and ate it, and speculated whether a potato-rich diet might in some way explain the distinctive characteristics they believed Andean peoples to possess. Potatoes, and dietary practices more generally, were thus of interest to early modern colonisers, who relied on this sort of medical and ethnographic information to understand and interpret the unfamiliar peoples and polities they aspired to rule.[36] (See figure 2.)

In early modern Europe the potato attracted less attention from representatives of the state. Uninterested as they were in the everyday eating habits of European labourers, few political theorists assessed the novel plant's potential as a foodstuff for Europeans. Those who did complained that the potato was excessively nourishing and so facilitated laziness.

Figure 2 Seventeenth-century drawing of an Andean potato harvest. Potatoes formed the backbone of the Andean diet, alongside other tubers, maize and quinoa. This drawing by the indigenous chronicler Felipe Guaman Poma shows villagers at work harvesting potatoes. The man uses a *chakitaqlla* or foot-plough. Similar tools are still used, as they facilitate the cultivation of steep and uneven land.

Ordinary people, in contrast, embraced the potato, which possessed a number of advantages over existing foodstuffs. Potatoes can produce a prolific harvest even in poor soil, and make a sustaining meal, especially when combined with milk or other dairy products. Moreover, precisely because states were not interested in the everyday eating habits of poorer folk, it took many decades for the potato to attract the attention of tax-collectors and other representatives of the fiscal order. Potatoes thus allowed peasants and labourers to evade some of the less welcome aspects of state control. It is they who are responsible for the potato's entry into the European diet. Chapter 1 tells this history. The central role of early modern peasants and small-scale cultivators in horticultural and dietary innovation has important implications for programmes of agricultural reform today; the Conclusion returns to the contemporary resonance of this earlier period of agricultural and dietary change.

The potato's political invisibility ended in the eighteenth century. The nourishing qualities that had once drawn criticism began to be viewed more positively. As a result, the potato became the object of intense scientific and political interest across Europe. From Norway to Naples, St Petersburg to Geneva, officials, local societies, agronomists, priests, and many other orga-nisations and individuals promoted potato consumption in word and deed. This extensive, pan-European potato investigation and propaganda resulted in the publication of hundreds of texts extolling the potato's potential as a superior staple for working people, one whose greater con-sumption would help ensure the strength and success of the nation. Chapter 2 traces the potato's unprecedented political prominence during the Enlightenment. Its popularity reflected the emergence of the new models of political economy and governance that stressed the importance of a healthy, well-nourished population to the power and wealth of the state. Integrating the slower history of the potato's conquest of European die-taries with its frenetic promotion in the eighteenth century illuminates the central role that food came to play in modern models of statecraft.

Chapter 3 connects eighteenth-century potato-promotion to the new ideas about political economy that were emerging in the same period. Just as Adam Smith believed that allowing individuals to pursue their own interests would ultimately result in a flourishing economy, so potato-enthusiasts (Smith included) argued that the best way to build a robust population was to empower individuals to make sound dietary choices through campaigns of information and exhortation. Enlightened potato-promoters believed the tuber's merits were so overwhelming that self-interest alone provided sufficient motivation for increased consumption. Both markets and public health could thus be left to organise themselves in ways that would result in the optimal outcome for both individuals and the nation-state. Potatoes offer a concrete, everyday example of how this confluence of private interest and public benefit was imagined to occur, at the very moment when these ideas were first theorised.

This history reveals the eighteenth-century origins of the current, neoliberal, insistence that healthy eating is best understood as a form of individual consumer empowerment that at the same time builds a stronger economy and body politic. For the eighteenth-century philosopher Immanuel Kant, determining one's own diet was an essential feature of intellectual maturity, just as characteristic of an enlightened existence as other forms of critical thinking. The ability to think and act autonomously, whether about diet or anything else, remains an essential component of all liberal definitions of freedom. Echoing Kant, the liberal economists Sebastiano Bavetta, Pietro Navarra and Dario Maimone insisted in a 2014 study that 'the highest development of one's human abilities ... results from making autonomous choices', including choices about personal consumption.[37] Making choices leads to greater personal happiness, and that leads to a happier and fairer society, or so it is argued. It is precisely through this sort of idealised convergence that the free choices of individuals have come to form the theoretical foundations of the modern, liberal state. Chapter 3 explores the role of dietary choice within this liberal model of statecraft.

Chapter 4 addresses the potato's global history. The expansion of trade and colonial conquest in the early modern era propelled the tuber around the world, but the processes that made it a global staple reflect not only these forces but also the varied local circumstances that it encountered on its travels. European diplomats, missionaries and colonial officers congratulated themselves on bringing the nutritious potato to the supposedly backward inhabitants of Bengal and Botany Bay, and viewed its adoption as an index of the overall level of civilisation attained

Figure 3 'The Aga and the Potato'. Potatoes travelled all around the world from the sixteenth century. This nineteenth-century illustration depicts a (doubtless apocryphal) scene in which a Turkish governor, or Aga, samples a raw potato found in the luggage of an English traveller.

by locals. For gardeners in Tehran and Māori entrepreneurs in New Zealand, potatoes served other purposes. The transformation of eating habits that followed the global dissemination of American foodstuffs after 1492 was always the result of complex interactions between local environments, patterns of agriculture and landholding, commercial structures and existing foodways. Chapter 4 both explains the place of potatoes within European discourses about imperialism, and also attends to the ways in which ordinary people around the world interacted with this new food. It thus provides a global counterpoint to Chapter 1's attention to the agency of peasants and smallholders in embedding potatoes into local diets. (See figure 3.)

The potato's changing status in China demonstrates well the simultaneously local and global nature of the modern foodscape. For centuries the potato has provided an important resource for villagers in peripheral regions, yet was almost invisible to the state. Since the early 2000s, however, the potato has been incorporated into an extensive national programme aimed at bolstering China's food security. This transformation in the potato's political role coincides with the Chinese state's embrace of the market economy. Consequently, vigorous state promotion of potatoes has emphasised individual choice and personal benefit. 'Let's all be rich potatoes', promises one advertising campaign aimed at encouraging potato consumption. In China, as in Europe, capitalism, individualism, and personal eating practices are closely intertwined with modern forms of statecraft.

These associations between potatoes and political economy born in the eighteenth century endowed the tuber with a powerful political and economic resonance. As a result, potatoes became deeply embedded in nineteenth-century arguments about the merits of capitalism. Chapter 5 charts these debates. Political radicals condemned the tuber as a tool of exploitation. 'We will not live upon potatoes', read a banner unfurled by agricultural labourers in Kent in 1830.[38] These men and women did not object to potatoes per se; their quarrel was with the potato as an ideology. 'Living on potatoes' offered a shorthand for the entire system that the protesters rejected. The potato's contested nineteenth-century status emerges clearly in discussions about Ireland. In the eighteenth century, Ireland had served as an unambiguous illustration of the potato's beneficial role in furthering population and economic growth. By the mid-nineteenth century it had become an alarming illustration of the perils of economic autarky. To successive British governments, the Irish potato facilitated not a flourishing commerce but rather the refusal to enter the modern world. A population of self-sufficient potato-eaters was no longer an attractive proposition when what the nation required was a large pool of proletarianised workers.

At the same time, as urbanisation and industrialisation advanced, the conviction that the population's eating habits had a material impact on the body politic only deepened. The new language of nutrition provided a vocabulary for expressing this relationship. From the mid-nineteenth century the potato's growing importance within the working-class diet attracted not praise but instead the worried attention of nutritionists and statesmen, who condemned the joint effects of 'lazy potato blood' and the lumpen attitudes of potato-eaters: the potato's popularity with working men was blamed for lacklustre economic growth.[39] Talking about potatoes provided a way for working people, scientists, economists and politicians to discuss the enormous changes that were reshaping nineteenth-century Europe in ways that stressed the close connections between economic practices and the everyday eating habits of the population.

The twentieth- and twenty-first-century history of the potato's relationship with the state forms the topic of Chapter 6. From 1900, the potato began to regain its lustre as a political instrument. Developments within the field of nutritional science led dieticians to reverse their earlier condemnations of the tuber as an inferior foodstuff. Their more positive assessments coincided with a substantial increase in the capacity of modern states to influence everyday eating habits. The First and Second World Wars were particularly important in developing the technologies and institutions that made this possible. Concerned to provide for the wartime needs of their populations, European governments actively encouraged potato consumption as a patriotic effort, supported by national agronomic programmes of potato breeding. Some of today's best-known varieties are the result of these state-supported schemes.

Although the commercial breeding and consumption of potatoes thus formed part of national programmes of food security in the twentieth century, the economic development models that emerged in the post-war years paid little attention to potatoes, as part of a larger neglect of small-scale, less commercialised agriculture in the developing world. Only recently has this sort of agriculture been incorporated into international models of food security. Just as the peasant know-how that spread potato cultivation across early modern Europe remained largely invisible, so the smallholder expertise that allowed the potato to preserve its genetic diversity has only begun to be appreciated by international organisations concerned with development. The UN's decision to declare 2008 the International Year of the Potato reflects this new appreciation. Potatoes are now heralded as an essential resource against hunger. They have also become a source of gastronomic pride, and many countries have registered specific varieties as part of their national patrimony. The contemporary history of the potato recapitulates both the eighteenth-century conviction that potatoes could play a role in national security, and also the reality that small farmers, as well as agronomists, possess expertise relevant to building a viable food system.

*

This book explores the genealogy of a particular way of thinking about the relationship between eating and the state. It offers an account of how everyday eating practices became part of modern politics, and argues that ideas born in the Enlightenment influence how we view the relationship between our dietary choices and the strength and economic success of the state. In particular, the roots of our idea that what we eat is at once an individual concern and a matter of public interest lie in the eighteenth century. I am scarcely the first person to observe that in Europe tensions between individual choice and the public good emerged with particular force in the late eighteenth century; these tensions form a central topic of political theory. I am interested here in how our analysis of these tensions is inflected if we consider food alongside the state, politics and the rise of individualism. *Feeding the People* does this without pretending that eighteenth-century modes of thought are identical to ours, any more than eighteenth-century systems of food provisioning, agriculture or political organisation coincide with those of today. Neither do I propose that following the potato is the only way to tell this story. Since this larger story is (I believe) correct, it should be equally possible to trace it out using some other food, or method. Potatoes, however, provide an effective tracer precisely because their penetration into the kitchens of ordinary people does not coincide neatly with their prominence within political discourse. Their sudden elevation within eighteenth-century political discourse throws a spotlight onto new features of modern statecraft. Moreover, because they are such a fantastically successful global foodstuff they allow us to sketch a more global story about the links between everyday diets and the modern state.

Certainly political potato-talk was not everywhere identical; differences in political structures, food systems and many other factors produced both significant variations on a single theme, and, at times, entirely different tunes. Nonetheless, I've sought to identify the under-lying harmonies, where these exist, which allow us to appreciate how 'a certain set of beliefs became common and ... how those beliefs influ-ence our practices'.[40] What is more, the potato's story reminds us of other ways of thinking about the relationship between people, food and the modern state. Since the real work of making potatoes a global food was carried out in large part by ordinary people, rather than political philosophers, a potato-centred history balances out the ebbs and flows of the modern state's interest in what people were eating, with an important *basso continuo* of smallholder innovation and peasant exper-tise. A single object, writes the historian Emma Spary, can possess 'completely distinct meanings and uses in different hands'.[41] The pota-to's dual status as a tool of the modern state, and as an emblem of the historical agency of ordinary people, is a case in point. *Feeding the People* tells the story of how eating became part of statecraft, and provides a new account of the global spread of one of the world's most important food crops.

CHAPTER 1

Immigrant Potatoes

'Potatoes . . . are something like Spanish truffles, aside from being a bit bigger and not as tasty. When dried, these roots are called chuño.'[1]

Vicente de Valverde, 1539

THIS IS THE FIRST WRITTEN DESCRIPTION OF A POTATO. Vicente de Valverde was a Dominican friar who accompanied the fractious and violent expedition led by Francisco Pizarro and several other Spaniards that overthrew Peru's Inca empire in the sixteenth century. Valverde played a prominent (and inglorious) role in the kidnapping and murder of the Inca monarch Atahualpa, who was seized by Spanish troops on Valverde's orders in 1532. After Spanish forces captured the Inca capital of Cuzco, Valverde was named its first bishop, a position he took up in 1538. His prolonged sojourn in Peru familiarised Valverde with the regional foodstuffs, including something he compared to a truffle, or a root: the potato.

Potatoes had for centuries been a staple for the many people living along the Andes. Archaeological excavations suggest that they were cultivated from perhaps 7800 BCE in Peru's Casma Valley, as well as further south, in what were probably separate processes of domestication. Wild varieties were eaten far earlier. Settlers in Monte Verde, in south-central Chile, were gathering wild potatoes thirteen thousand years ago. A site in Utah, along the northern reaches of the same trans-continental mountain range, has likewise yielded evidence of wild potatoes being eaten from as early as 10,900 BCE. Mountain people prepared potatoes in many ways; the Utah potato-eaters seem to have mashed or ground their tubers. At the time Valverde reached Peru, Andeans ate potato soups and stews, together with maize, quinoa, roasted guinea pigs and wild game, dried fish, and a great variety of vegetables, beans and tubers, with or without the addition of chilli pepper to add savour. They also devised an effective method for freeze-drying, which converted tender, rot-prone fresh potatoes into a long-lasting rock-like substance called *chuño*. In their many forms potatoes were an ordinary, everyday food. The Inca state, which had established control over a wide sweep of South American territory in the fifteenth century, viewed them with some disdain, unlike maize, whose cultivation was carefully overseen by an annual calendar of ceremonies and rituals.[2] Potatoes were, however, totally unknown to the rest of the world.

Vicente de Valverde's offhand description of this root was followed by a series of similar reports from other conquistadors, which stressed that the potato was, as they put it, 'the bread of the Indians' – the region's basic foodstuff. The Basque conquistador Pascual de Andagoya, who composed a memoir of his participation in Pizarro's expedition, recorded that 'the foods of those provinces are maize, and some roots that the people there call *papas*, which are like a chestnut, or a nut in shape'.[3] Another Spaniard, Pedro Cieza de Leon, writing a decade after Andagoya, also compared them to chestnuts, or truffles. Within a few years Spanish colonists were collecting them as tribute, alongside maize and anything else of marketable value they could extract from local communities. An English pirate found boxes of them, readied for payment, when he stopped off the Chilean coast in 1587. He described them as 'very good to eat'.[4]

Today the potato is a remarkably successful global food. It ranks just behind wheat, maize and rice in terms of the volume harvested each year, and is the world's fifth most valuable food crop. More potatoes are eaten per capita in Malawi than in Peru itself. Overall, Europeans are now the world's most assiduous eaters of potatoes, consuming on average some 82 kilos per person each year.[5] How did this once-unfamiliar root become part of the European diet?

THE CONSERVATISM OF THE PEASANTS

The standard story about how Europeans learned to eat potatoes goes something like this: potatoes first reached Europe in the late sixteenth century, where they attracted attention as a botanical curiosity, and, very briefly, as a novelty food for elites. They were, however, shunned by everyone else. Resistance to potatoes is ascribed either to 'the conservatism of the peasants', or to fears about the potential health risks posed by this new plant, or to unfamiliarity with the agricultural techniques required to cultivate a plant from tubers rather than seeds. The fact that botanists quickly identified the potato as a species of *Solanum*, the same family as deadly nightshade and the poisonous henbane, is often mentioned as reason for purported suspicion. The tuber's knobbly shape is sometimes said to have inspired anxieties that it might induce leprosy, since the ravages of that disease left its victims with similarly bulbous appendages in place of limbs.[6] As the great historian of the potato Redcliffe Salaman put it:

> The basic trouble lay in the fact that the potato was in every sense a new type of food, the like of which had not been seen previously in Europe. To eat of it, was not merely a venture in dietetics, but an audacious break with common tradition . . . to which should be added the significant fact that . . . definite objection was taken to the potato because it was not mentioned in the Bible, and hence was not a food designed for man by God.[7]

For these reasons, Europeans are said to have ignored the potato's multiple charms for the next two hundred years, with the exception of the Irish, whose early enthusiasm is presented as an anomaly. Not until visionary eighteenth-century elite personages such as Frederick the Great of Prussia championed them did potatoes begin to be consumed more widely, or so runs the story. (See figure 4.)

There is little historical basis for any of these claims. Far from labelling potatoes a botanical oddity that required unfamiliar cultivation techniques, early modern Europeans described them simply as roots, akin to a carrot or a parsnip; a shared subterranean habit was more noteworthy than the fact that one was cultivated from a tuber and the others from seeds. Neither did early modern botanical and horticultural texts linger on this matter. They simply explained how to prepare the seed potatoes and advised on the best methods of planting. As to the suggestion that the potato was rejected because it was a member of the *Solanum* family, the equally unfamiliar chilli pepper, another new-world import,

Figure 4 Frederick the Great inspecting a potato harvest. Frederick II is often credited with convincing sceptical Germans to eat potatoes. This nineteenth-century painting imagines the benevolent monarch chatting with a humble farmer, while his courtiers look on suspiciously. In fact, German farmers had been growing potatoes since the sixteenth century. It was only in the eighteenth century, however, that their activities began to earn the approval of princes and statesmen.

was also identified as a *Solanum*. This proved no impediment to the chilli's quickly becoming – as one writer put it in 1590 – 'a well-known thing', widely consumed across the Iberian peninsula and beyond.[8] The only evidence that potatoes were associated with leprosy derives from a second-hand comment in a 1620 herbal, in which the Swiss author recorded hearing that three hundred kilometres away, in Burgundy, both potatoes and Jerusalem artichokes had been prohibited on these grounds.[9] There is no indication that such a ban in fact occurred, and the herbalist himself was sufficiently confident of the potato's healthfulness to offer several recipes from his native Basle. And the complete absence of cabbages, spinach, oats and many other plants from the Old and New Testaments did not prevent these becoming common foodstuffs across the continent.

What of the claim that peasant conservatism was the main impediment? One authoritative history of the spread of new-world foods opined that 'weaning the peasantry away from tried and true agricultural methods and tried and true foods was perhaps just a matter of time, yet in many cases it was a matter of a very long time'.[10] This chapter suggests otherwise: it did not always take a very long time for potatoes to enter the dietaries of ordinary people; indeed, peasants and labourers were among the first to adopt them. Although we possess much more information about how learned individuals responded to this new plant, working people too cultivated and consumed potatoes. Stories of peasant conservatism do a disservice to these culinary pioneers. Early modern Europeans did not shun the potato because they feared it was poisonous, or because they did not understand how to cultivate it, or because it was unfamiliar. The early modern potato, unsurprisingly, did not replace grains as Europe's principal staple, nor did it reach every corner of the continent, but neither was it met with incomprehension and suspicion until scholars and princes convinced a sceptical populace to eat it.

TIME OUT OF MIND

In 1768 the Cornish parish of St Buryan was engulfed in a dispute over potatoes. St Buryan, which lies about five miles from Land's End, is an ancient settlement; earthworks point to its occupation well before the Norman Conquest. The 1768 dispute concerned historical memory. It arose because the rector of the local chapel believed he was entitled to a larger tithe than he was receiving on the potatoes and other 'garden stuff' grown by several of his tenants. The conventions governing this ecclesiastical tax were extremely complex; where potatoes fit into the evolving edifice of case law and formal regulation was unclear. The defendants argued that they should pay a reduced tithe because the potatoes were intended for their own use, rather than for sale. The case highlighted the murky status of plants grown on a small scale in vegetable gardens rather than open fields, a matter that was not well explained in tithe schedules. The defendants further maintained that, whatever the precise legal status of garden stuff, 'for time out of mind' they had been paying a fractional tax on potatoes and other crops cultivated for domestic consumption, and they petitioned for the continuation of this local practice.[11] The case thus hinged on whether long-standing local custom established a precedent, and also on how long potatoes had in fact been grown in St Buryan. The court found in favour of the defendants, and approved the continued payment of a discounted tithe. In so doing, it endorsed the tenants' assertion that they had been cultivating potatoes for their personal use for many generations.

Tithe disputes offer an alternative history of the potato's spread across early modern Europe. In contrast to stories of peasant conservatism and popular rejection, such records document the diffusion of potatoes into cottage gardens in many parts of Europe, through processes whose protagonists were generally the families of agricultural labourers, husbandmen and artisans, rather than noblemen such as Frederick the Great. Because the titheable status of a crop depended in part on whether it was intended for sale or for personal use, and on how long the food had been cultivated in this way, disputes over potato tithes frequently delved into the history and chronology of potato cultivation in the parish. Sometimes defendants insisted that the potato was too recent an arrival to qualify for tithing; on other occasions they maintained that its alleged exemption from a tithe had been custom and practice for generations. Almost invariably, potato cultivation was understood as an activity undertaken by ordinary people for their own sustenance.

In Britain the earliest such disputes date from the late seventeenth century, and became more frequent in subsequent decades. The timing of when potatoes were first cultivated featured prominently in most cases. In the Yorkshire parish of Kirkby Malzeard for instance an investigation in 1736 explicitly questioned deponents over when potatoes had been introduced. 'Have potatoes been grown or cultivated within the said parish of Kirkby Malzeard time beyond memory of man or do you know or can you remember the time of their being first introduced?', witnesses were asked. Parishioners agreed that potatoes had first been cultivated in open fields some time between 1680 and 1700. Prior to that they had been grown in cottage gardens for domestic use. They credited someone named Buck with the innovation of raising potatoes on a large scale, but were unable to remember a time when potatoes were not planted in cottage gardens.[12] In another case, tenants in the Lancashire villages of Formby, Ainsdale and Raven Meols refused, like the inhabitants of St

Buryan, to pay a newly imposed tithe on potatoes and other garden produce on the grounds that they had long cultivated potatoes without any tithe ever being collected. As they insisted, 'for the preservation of such our rights and properties as the same have heretofore immemorially been held and enjoyed by us ... [we] will not pay'.[13]

Scholars such as Christian Vandenbroeke and Eloy Terrón have traced similar cases in France, Belgium, the Netherlands and Spain, where conflict over the potato's titheable status began to occur in the early eighteenth century. As these scholars note, such disputes do not arise until a crop is fairly well established, so their occurrence in itself indicates a crop's prevalence. These sources suggest that potatoes were being cultivated as garden crops in parts of Flanders, Alsace, Galicia and elsewhere from the 1670s. As in England, parishioners typically claimed that their exemption from the potato tithe dated back to 'time immemorial'.[14] (Clergymen usually countered that potatoes had always been subject to the tithe, even if they had chosen not to exercise their right to collect it.) To be sure, the historical narratives that such cases elicited emerged in a context of legal dispute, in which the date of the tuber's introduction had direct monetary consequences.[15] Nonetheless, the picture of long-standing localised cultivation and consumption is confirmed by a range of other sources. Working people in various parts of Europe turned to potatoes long before eighteenth-century philosophers and kings thought to encourage them.

LEARNING ABOUT POTATOES

Some of the earliest European discussion of potatoes occurs in herbals. Essentially encyclopaedias of culinary and medicinal flora, herbals enumerated the features of interesting or important plants and explained their uses. Hundreds of these often lavishly illustrated texts were produced during the sixteenth century. Entries on potatoes began to appear in the 1550s, alongside other new-world plants such as sweet potatoes, maize and tomatoes. These works described the botanical features of the potato, and attempted to locate it within existing systems of scientific knowledge and classification.[16] Herbals reveal how learned writers responded to this new plant, and also shed light on its broader diffusion across Europe. The Flemish botanist Carolus Clusius, author of a celebrated herbal, for instance, acquired some potato plants in 1587. His potatoes came from Italy, via Belgium, or so he reported. He subsequently shared them with his network of correspondents elsewhere on the continent. The letters exchanged between Clusius and his collaborators show clearly that they perceived no challenge in growing potatoes from the tuber, and also that they did not view them as alarming botanical oddities.[17]

Herbals moreover reveal that potatoes were cultivated not only by botanists, but also in cottage gardens. Clusius, for example, stated that these plants had become quite common in parts of Germany and Italy, although he did not elaborate on the agricultural experimenters responsible for this development. (Experimentation was necessary to adapt these South American tubers to Europe's shorter day-lengths and longer growing season. Recent research has underscored the careful processes of selection and evaluation that would have been required to produce a reliable harvest.[18]) Writing from the Belgian town of Tournai in 1588, another gentleman botanist reported that some years earlier:

> a reputable man of authority, being in my garden and seeing my [potato] plants, asked me if I held them in particular regard. I told him that I considered them to be rarities. He replied that that he had seen great abundance of them in Italy and that some people ate them in place of rape-roots, others cooked these bulbs with lamb, and others used them to fatten pigs, each according to his imagination.[19]

Evidently, in sixteenth-century Italy, the earliest potato-eaters included people who ordinarily ate the humble rape-root, a variety of turnip consumed by the poor. The Swiss botanist Gaspard Bauhin also indicated that people other than botanists were experimenting with potato cultivation. He stated in 1620 that 'many people' preferred to dig them up in the autumn rather than leaving them to overwinter in the ground. A vernacular fund of agricultural knowledge about potatoes was already emerging.[20]

Such accounts make clear that these roots were grown not simply to fatten pigs, but also as food for people. Clusius and his correspondents discussed how Italians prepared them in ragouts, in the same way as one stewed carrots or turnips.[21] Bauhin recorded that in Basle people roasted them with black pepper.[22] The seventeenth-century Roman botanist Tobias Aldini devoted so much attention to their preparation that the author of another herbal complained that Aldini's account appeared more the work of a cook than a scientist. But this critic, the Spanish physician Bernardo de Cienfuegos, agreed with Aldini that there was an infinite number of ways to prepare the potato – roasted; breaded and fried like whitebait; dressed with vinegar, salt and pepper in a salad; sliced and cooked in oil with lemon juice and salt; sautéed like mushrooms with mint; simmered in broth like turnips; made into a casserole ... In his opinion, however, they required a picante sauce, as they were otherwise extremely bland. Cienfuegos also warned that like all root vegetables they provoked wind, and for that reason incited lust.[23] (See figure 5.)

The authors of sixteenth- and seventeenth-century health manuals also discussed the potato. These practical guides to healthy living were produced across early modern Europe, and promised to explain the principles of good health and well-being.[24] Their authors concurred that health was a matter of keeping the body in balance with its larger environment. Eating constituted an open dialogue with the external world and so required particularly careful management lest the body be thrown off kilter. Being thrown off kilter was a perennial risk. All foods were understood to affect the body of the eater in some way, since all had the potential to alter the balance of humours that characterised each person's overall constitution, or 'complexion'. Potatoes, like every other food, thus possessed an inherently medicinal quality. Cienfuegos' comment that potatoes shared both the windy qualities of other root vegetables and their consequent tendency to provoke lasciviousness is typical of this early modern approach to dietetics. In his view, potatoes encouraged the formation of damp humours, and therefore benefited from being prepared with hot, drying spices, which would balance out the potato's moisture. Explanations of how to match potatoes with the appropriate corrective seasonings and cooking methods show that they were amenable to the usual culinary and medicinal techniques necessary to produce a healthful and nourishing meal. These manuals also commented, sometimes at length, on the potato's gustatory qualities, and on which preparation methods produced the tastiest results. An Italian health guide

Figure 5 Drawing of potatoes from Bernardo de Cienfuegos' herbal, *c.*1630. Bernardo de Cienfuegos was a physician from Aragón, and author of a multi-volume herbal that described hundreds of plants. His entry on 'potatoes from Peru' listed many different ways of preparing the roots, and also mentioned that they could be bought at the vegetable market in Madrid. Cienfuegos made clear that he was discussing potatoes rather than sweet potatoes, even though the plant in his drawing resembles the latter.

from 1620 for instance noted that potatoes required quantities of salt and other seasonings, not to render them more healthful, but simply to overcome their bland taste.[25] Then, as now, potatoes provided a blank canvas for the imaginative cook.

YOU SAY POTATO . . .

But what exactly was a potato? Today biologists explain that the 'ordinary', 'Irish', or 'white' potato, *Solanum tuberosum*, is entirely distinct from sweet potatoes (*Ipomoea batatas*) and other American tubers such as the Jerusalem artichoke (*Helianthus tuberosus*), as well as from the African yam (*Dioscorea*). 'White' potatoes are members of the *Solanacea* family, which also includes tomatoes, chilli peppers and aubergines. Sweet potatoes are related to bindweed, the irritating garden pest, but are only distant relatives of the ordinary potato. Jerusalem artichokes and yams belong to different genera altogether. The clarity with which botanical science now distinguishes these plants reflects a classification system quite different from the ones employed in the sixteenth and seventeenth centuries. Although early modern botanists promptly classified the potato as a *Solanum,* this did not render it entirely distinct from other botanically dissimilar plants. The overlapping names for these new roots reflect their multiple interconnections, as well as their links to existing European foodstuffs.

In early modern England, 'potato' might mean either the sweet or ordinary variety, or even the Jerusalem artichoke. When writers wished to distinguish clearly they sometimes referred to sweet potatoes as 'Spanish potatoes', while 'potatoes of Canada' usually referenced the Jerusalem artichoke. 'Virginia potatoes' often meant the ordinary potato, since many English writers believed the plants originated there. All three were, however, considered to be 'potatoes'. The Spanish nomenclature overlapped in similar ways. Spaniards first encountered sweet potatoes in the 1490s in the Caribbean, where these tubers were called 'batatas'. This is the source of the English word 'potato'. Columbus described them as a sort of yam, an African tuber with which Europeans were already familiar. The Spanish invasion of the American mainland added new terms for sweet potatoes to the Iberian lexicon, and also introduced

Europeans to ordinary potatoes, which were known in Quechua, the lingua franca of the Inca empire, as 'papas'. Then as now, Spanish-speakers in the Americas often preserved this distinction between 'batatas' (sweet potatoes) and 'papas' (potatoes), but in Spain itself 'patata' came to refer to either.[26] There, 'batatas' or 'patatas de Málaga' usually meant the sweet potato, which was cultivated on a commercial scale around Málaga from as early as the sixteenth century, while 'patatas de la Mancha' referred to the ordinary potato.[27] A Jerusalem artichoke, in turn, might be labelled a 'pataca'. As in English, in Spanish a similar vocabulary emphasised the interconnections between these different new-world roots. Sixteenth-century German writers also employed a range of overlapping terms: 'Griblingsbaum' (truffle plant), 'Erdäpffeln' (earth-apples), 'Erd Artischocken' (earth-artichokes), 'Tartuffeln' (truffles) and simply 'Knollen', or roots. The semantic link to truffles dates back to the earliest Spanish descriptions, and was common in a number of European languages. Writing in the 1590s, the nobleman Wilhelm IV von Hessen for instance reported that Italians referred to these new roots as 'Taratouphli'; other Italians described them as a kind of 'Tartufole', or truffle.[28] This is the origin of the German term 'Kartoffel'. Scandinavian writers referred to 'jordpäron' (earth-pears), 'jordäpple' (earth-apples), 'artiskocker af Wirginien' (Virginia artichokes) and 'peruvianska nattskatta' (Peruvian nightshade) as well as 'potatoës'.[29] In the late sixteenth century the botanist Clusius and his polyglot network drew on multiple vocabularies in their references to 'taratonfli', 'tartufy', 'papas americanorum', 'papos' and 'papes'.

Overall, early modern authors sometimes differentiated between potatoes, sweet potatoes and Jerusalem artichokes, at times devoting pages to untangling the complex nomenclatures that fostered confusion. On other occasions they moved smoothly from one to the other, simultaneously distinguishing and combining them. William Coles' seventeenth-century botanical handbook first listed a series of recipes suitable for the 'potato', and then commented simply that these recipes worked equally well for 'Virginia potatoes'. As he noted, the 'names and kinds [were] thus mixed together'.[30] As a result of such mixing, there is simply no way of ascertaining whether the ten pounds of 'potatoes' presented by the mayor of Southampton to Lord Hertford in 1593 were sweet or ordinary, since both kinds were already being grown in England.[31] Potatoes, sweet potatoes and Jerusalem artichokes continued to be grouped together in both learned and vernacular taxonomies well into the eighteenth century. A French botanist explained in the 1720s that sweet potatoes were a type of ordinary potato comparable to Jerusalem artichokes; an English traveller in Spain similarly described sweet potatoes as simply another variety of 'the common potato'. Eighteenth-century lexicographers felt no more obligation to differentiate these plants into separate dictionary entries than did travellers or botanists.[32] The commonalities, rather than the differences, are what emerge most strongly from this early modern vocabulary.

Such flexibility is not surprising. All three plants originated in the Americas, and all three travelled around the world as part of the 'Columbian exchange', the world-wide transfer of plants and animals begun in 1492 with Columbus' arrival in the West Indies. There were therefore many reasons to view these plants as deeply interconnected. Their overlapping names remind us of this shared history. If sixteenth-century Europeans failed to distinguish clearly between these different vegetables, this was because they perceived them as similar. All three were new roots from the new world, and all three were eaten by Europeans, who were evidently undeterred by the taxonomic challenges posed by novel tubers lacking biblical provenance.[33]

PARE YOUR POTATON

Readers seeking advice on how to prepare these new roots could turn to the emerging genre of the printed recipe book. The first recipe for something resembling a potato dates from 1581. It appears in a cookbook authored by Marx Rumpolts and published in Frankfurt. Rumpolts worked as personal chef for the wealthy Archbishop-Elector of Mainz. He later went on to cook for a Danish queen. His cookbook offered some two thousand recipes, as well as over thirty sample menus and advice on shopping and table etiquette. Alongside instructions for making a Hungarian tart with many layers and crafting sugar into the shape of an entire Parmesan cheese, *Ein new Kochbuch* included recipes for a number of American novelties such as kidney beans. It moreover explained how to cook typical Spanish dishes such as *olla podrida* (or, as English-speakers called it, *olio*), a complex stew in this case to be prepared with new-world turkey, which had rapidly became a modish banqueting dish in various European courts.[34] Rumpolts was evidently familiar with Iberian cooking traditions, as well as with some of the new ingredients introduced into Europe by the Spanish following their colonisation of the Americas.

His cookbook also printed several recipes for 'earth-apples'. Perhaps by 'Erdtepffel' he was referring to the potato, or perhaps the Jerusalem artichoke, or perhaps something else; we cannot be certain. The recipes for other new-world and Iberian dishes, however, make it plausible that Rumpolts was acquainted with these American tubers. In any event, he instructed readers to 'peel and cut them small. Parboil them in water and press well in a fine cloth. Chop them small and roast with bacon cut into little pieces. Add a little milk and let cook together. This way it is tasty and good.'[35]

Two decades after Rumpolts' earth-apple recipe, a French cookbook explained how to prepare a new kind truffle, or 'tartoufle'. It recommended several different preparations, from roasting them like chestnuts to dressing with butter and sweet wine.[36] From England, the 1596 *Good Huswife's Jewell* offered a recipe for 'a tart that is a courage to a man or woman'. Actually more of a pudding, the tart was a rich dish that included butter, eggs, spices and 'the braynes of three or four cocke-sparrows' alongside a 'potaton'.[37] Sweetened potato tarts of this sort soon became immensely fashionable across Europe; by 1611 Spanish cookbooks were criticising these extravaganzas as culinary abominations to be avoided at all costs. Good advice, since in 1624 Richard Sackville, third Earl of Dorset, died while gobbling up 'a potato pie'.[38] (See recipes for 'Truffles'.)

Like title disputes and herbals, printed and manuscript cookery books indicate that new-world roots were being cultivated on a small scale for domestic use in parts of Germany, England and elsewhere. As one 1651

Four Recipes for 'Truffles'

Mentions of a new kind of 'truffle' started to appear in European sources in the late sixteenth century. Although it is hard to be certain, these are likely to refer to potatoes or some other American tuber. Lancelot de Casteau, a professional chef who worked for several princely households in Liège, offered four different recipes for these 'truffles' in his 1604 cookbook. He also described how to make a cheese-and-herb quiche, leg of mutton in the Irish style, and other up-to-the minute delicacies.

Four Recipes for 'Truffles'

Boiled 'Truffle'

Take well-washed 'truffle', & put it to boil in water, when cooked it must be peeled & cut into slices, melted butter thereon, & pepper.

Another 'Truffle'

Cut the 'truffle' into slices as above, & put it to stew with Spanish wine & new butter, & nutmeg.

Another

Take the sliced 'truffle' & put to stew with butter, chopped marjoram, parsley: then take four or five egg yolks beaten with a little wine, & cast it boiling thereon, & remove from the fire, & so serve.

Another

Put the 'truffle' to roast in the hot embers as one cooks chestnuts, then it must be peeled & cut into slices, put chopped mint, boiled currants on top, & vinegar, a little pepper, & so serve.

cookbook from the Saxon city of Braunschweig noted, 'earth-artichokes or roots ... have become so common that practically every farmer grows them in his garden'.[39] By the early eighteenth century, German cookery books often distinguished explicitly between different new-world tubers, and made clear that in some regions the ordinary potato was 'quite common'.[40] As the century progressed, potato recipes could be found in ever-more published and manuscript recipe collections from many different parts of Europe.[41]

Other sources too indicate that potatoes were cultivated as an ordinary foodstuff far sooner than has been recognised. It is notable that from the early seventeenth century French, Italian and English agricultural manuals began explaining how to grow them. The French horticultural writer Olivier de Serres' 1603 *Theatre d'agriculture et mesnage des champs* described potatoes not as botanical curiosities, but as horticultural plants. The English botanist John Parkinson's 1629 *Paradisi in Sole Paradisus Terrestris* treated the potato in the same fashion. Parkinson, who distinguished carefully between the different sorts of potatoes, reported that 'Virginia' potatoes were 'well knowne unto us' and explained how to cultivate and eat them.[42] He recommended roasting in hot embers, or baking with wine and a little sugar. John Evelyn's 1666 *Kalendarium Hortense* reminded gardeners that in February they should 'sow *Beans, Pease, Radish, Parsneps, Carrots, Onions, Garlick, &c.* and plant *Potatoes* in your worst ground', since they would thrive even in marginal soil. A few decades later a German handbook similarly explained how to cultivate them, noting that they had become very common in parts of Austria.[43]

Customs records and account books also help trace the trajectories of these new roots across Europe, once they had moved from a garden crop raised for household consumption to the status of commodity. In most parts of Europe potatoes remained a garden crop well into the eighteenth century, but new-world roots were traded internationally from the late sixteenth century. Customs records show that as early as the 1570s 'patatas' were grown on a commercial scale in the Canary Islands, from where they were shipped to France and the Netherlands.[44] It is impossible to determine whether these sources refer to potatoes, sweet potatoes, or both, but in any case they indicate that a new-world root was the object of long-distance commercial trade in sixteenth-century Europe. We can in contrast be certain that the new-world roots on sale in Madrid markets in the 1620s were potatoes, since the Aragonese physician Bernardo de Cienfuegos who reported this fact carefully distinguished 'papas del Perú' (Peruvian potatoes) from other types of tuber. He noted that these 'papas' were purchased by both returning colonists and locals. The Peruvian historian and jurist Antonio Leon Pinelo, who travelled to Spain in the early seventeenth century and would have been very familiar with the Andean potato, observed the same thing.[45] Tax records show that something called 'jordpäron', earth-pears, were being imported from Portugal and northern Germany into the southern Swedish province of Småland through the port of Karlshamn from the 1630s.[46] By the late seventeenth century there were specialized potato markets in Lancashire and other northern counties of England, as well as in parts of Scotland and Ireland, and trade legislation detailed the duties owed on this commodity.[47] The potato's shift from subsistence foodstuff to commodity helps explain the increasing number of disputes concerning the potato tithe, since until a potato crop acquired a market value its appeal to tithe-owners was limited. It is likely that the many eighteenth-century conflicts between tenants and clergy over the potato tithe reflect the commodification of the potato as well as an increase in the area under cultivation.[48] Other sorts of economic and legal data too point to the potato's growing status as a commercial crop. Protestants in Ireland for instance claimed monetary compensation for the loss of their potato harvest after the 1641 Catholic uprising against English rule. Such sources further indicate how the potato was incorporated into existing systems of classification and consumption. When officials in the French region of the Vivarais began conducting agricultural surveys in 1690, they listed potatoes together with chestnuts, turnips and other root vegetables, doubtless because all these foods provided a starchy basis for peasant meals.[49] (See figure 6.)

Potatoes, in sum, were present, alongside other new-world tubers, in parts of the British Isles, Spain, Germany, Italy and France within seventy years of Pascual de Andagoya's casual description of these

The Potatoe Man.

Sold by C. Sheppard,

Lambert Hill, Doctors Commons.

1
I am a saucy rolling blade,
I fear not wet, nor dry,
I keep a Jack Ass for my trade,
And thro' the streets do cry,
Chorus, And they're all rare potatoes ho,
      And they're, &c.

2
A Moll I keep that sells fine fruit,
There's no one brings more dy,
She has all things the seasons suit
While I my potatoes cry.

3
A link boy once I stood the gag,
At charing-cross did ply,
Here's light your honour for a mag,
But now my potatoes cry.

4
With a blue birds eye about my squeege,
And a check shirt on my back.
A pair of large wedges in my hoofs,
And an oil skin round my hat.

5
I'll bait a bull, or fight a cock.
Or pigeons I will fly.
I am up to all your knowing rigs,
Whilst I my potatoes cry.

6
There's five pounds two pence, honest weight,
Your own scales take and try,
For nibbing culls I always hate,
For I in safety cry.

Figure 6 An itinerant potato seller, from an eighteenth-century British ballad. Eighteenth-century Britons were familiar with potatoes, and potato merchants. The engraving shows one at work, with his basket of potatoes and donkey. Hawking potatoes on the streets of London is not this potato seller's only source of income. As the ballad explains, he's also a pimp, whose moll sells 'fine fruit' of her own.

chestnut-like roots. In her convent in Ávila, St Teresa ate a gift of 'patatas' she had been sent from Seville in 1577.[50] In the same years satirical literature from England mocked their alleged potential to stimulate sexual appetites.[51] Travellers in Italy and Germany noted the ways in which locals prepared them, and botanists tracked their appearance in cottage gardens. Over the next century cultivation spread further into France through Franche-Comté and Lorraine, into Flanders, and eastward into Brandenburg. In Flanders, they were being raised in such quantities that during the Nine Years War (1688–97) soldiers there were able to sustain themselves 'most plenteously' with potatoes they pillaged from local fields.[52] Such snippets tally with the evidence of tithe disputes and other sources to suggest that by the late seventeenth century potatoes had made their way into the culinary and agricultural practices of many Europeans.

Certainly potatoes were not known in all parts of Europe. There is little evidence for their presence in Russia or Finland before the eighteenth century, and their early introduction as a field crop in Alsace, Franche-Comté and environs was replicated in few other parts of France. Their uneven spread through German lands has been charted in detail by the historian Günter Wiegelmann. David Zylberberg has moreover shown that a local supply of affordable fuel was a prerequisite for the potato to make inroads into English eating habits. Potato consumption, he explains, 'began in peat-burning communities, before spreading to coal-burning ones and was less common in wood-burning regions prior to 1830'.[53] Careful local studies of this sort are necessary to explain the potato's precise trajectory in specific locales. Nor were potatoes eaten as the principal staple. Grains, whether baked as bread or made into porridge, remained the foundation of most meals in most parts of Europe well into the eighteenth century. Nonetheless a picture of blanket rejection prompted by fear and unfamiliarity does not match the historical record. Europeans have been eating potatoes for a long time.

SPREADING POTATOES

It is difficult to identify the people who spread potatoes across early modern Europe. The historian William McNeill hypothesised that Spanish and Basque sailors and fishermen played an important role. These men might well have introduced potatoes to western Ireland, a customary stopping point on fishing voyages back from Newfoundland, for instance. It is also plausible, as McNeill proposed, that Spanish vessels took the potato to Habsburg territories in southern Italy and the Netherlands. Sailors disseminated other novel commodities such as tobacco, together with new consumer practices; there is no reason to suppose they did not play a comparable role with American foodstuffs, but we have little direct evidence.[54] Only exceptionally do sources refer explicitly to the agents of transmission. A Florentine agricultural hand-book composed some time before 1606 stated that potatoes had been introduced into Tuscany by Carmelite monks from Spain and Portugal. Another Italian text from a few years later credits 'the French' with bring-ing potatoes to the Piedmont region. Travelling glassblowers and other artisans from southern Germany reportedly carried potatoes into the north German region of Mecklenburg in the early eighteenth century.[55]

Many decades ago the historian Douglas Hall observed that the reason why the early modern movements of plants are so difficult to reconstruct is that their agents were often ordinary people below the sight lines of contemporary writers.[56] The names and lives of the labourers and small farmers who grew potatoes in their gardens and cooked them like carrots are largely lost to us. Rarely can we do more than note the conclusions of tithe courts such as the one convened in 1766, which determined that in the county of Hainaut potatoes were first cultivated in kitchen gardens by labourers.[57] At that century's end, however, Frederick Morton Eden, second Baronet of Maryland and founder of an insurance company, chose to record the name of the man who first raised potatoes in open fields in Scotland. In the 1790s Eden composed a multi-volume account of 'the labouring classes in England', based on surveys by collaborators, some direct observation, and Eden's extensive reading of British history. Eden was interested in potatoes, which he regarded as an excellent foodstuff. Large-scale cultivation was in his view to be encouraged. According to

Eden, 'Thomas Prentice, a day-labourer' in the Lanarkshire village of Kilsyth, was responsible for this innovation. So great was Prentice's success, Eden noted, that 'every farmer and cottager followed his example, and for many years past it has become a staple article'.[58] I have found no trace of any Prentices in Kilsyth; perhaps Eden's pioneer was the Thomas Prentice born about eight hours' walk away, in Carluke, in 1701.

What is clear is that potatoes spread in an uneven and diffuse fashion, becoming a significant part of the ordinary diet in various parts of Europe by the early eighteenth century. That this was the case in Ireland is well established; potatoes there formed the 'most part of the poors food every one hath his potato garden', according to one writer in the 1650s.[59] In seventeenth-century England too, poor tenants and husbandmen subsisted on 'brown bread and milk, and pease pies and apple pies, and puddings and pancakes, and gruel and flummery and frumenty, yea dry bread and butter and cheese, and cabbages and turnips, and parsnips and carrots, and onions and potatoes, and whey and buttermilk, and small drink', in the opinion of the cleric Richard Baxter.[60] In the eastern Brandenburg town of Frankfurt an der Oder, a naturalist noted in the 1680s that 'around here they have become quite common'.[61]

Baked in cinders or added to stews with cabbages and carrots, potatoes fit easily into the cooking practices of poor families in many parts of Europe, whose meals were usually built around a starchy base, whether provided by oat porridge, rye bread, millet polenta, or a great number of other grain-based dishes invented by the nameless masters of early modern *cucina povera*. Such foods constituted the core of daily diets for the majority of the population. Working men and women hoped to consume something on the order of a pound of bread, or its equivalent, each day. Small quantities of cheese, buttermilk, vegetables, beans and other filling and savoury additions typically accompanied these breads and pottages. Accommodating this cuisine to the potato was straightforward. In soups potatoes were substituted for or used alongside turnips and other roots, or combined with a bit of meat and an onion, whose flavours they would absorb and extend. In areas where fuel was affordable enough to make home baking feasible, potatoes might be baked into farls or other forms of bread. German cookery books described how they were made into salads and eaten cold, and also how to braise them with onions and a splash of vinegar.[62] None of these recipes required unfamiliar techniques or new equipment, and so they could easily enter into everyday cooking practices.

The protagonists of the potato's early incorporation into the European dietary seem to have been the farmers in 1651 Braunschweig who grew 'earth-artichokes or roots' in their gardens, the nameless Italians who planted them in 'great abundance' in the 1580s, and the villagers across Europe who resented handing over their crops of garden stuff to the local priest.[63] These men and women also undertook the experimentation necessary to adapt Andean cultivars to Europe's different day-lengths and growing conditions. It was thus peasants in the Vivarais who, as the historian Madeleine Ferrières put it, 'invented' the potato in that region. Even in areas where potato cultivation began later, in the eighteenth century, villagers and peasants were often the first to raise the crop. This was for instance the case in Galicia, in southern Poland, where potatoes were grown in peasant gardens before they were introduced into the kitchens of landed estates.[64] Just as Europe's artisans developed the new skills necessary to produce the novel commodities desired by early modern consumers, so peasants and small farmers learned to grow new foods. In contrast to craftsmen, however, they were often able to enjoy the fruits of their labours.[65]

Why might potatoes have proved a success with peasants and labourers, beyond their ease of adaption into existing cooking regimes? Their fiscal invisibility was surely part of their appeal. As tithe disputes indicate, parishioners might cultivate this modest root for decades without attracting the attention of the local rector and his agents. In addition, potatoes are an exceptionally efficient way of converting sunlight, soil and water into nourishment. While a hectare of land sown with wheat may yield enough protein to feed seven people over the course of a year, a hectare of potatoes will nourish seventeen. The contrast is even more striking as regards calories: a hectare of land will produce three times the calories if sown with potatoes compared to wheat or oats. Potatoes also require less water than other major crops.[66] The potato is thus an excellent way of feeding more people from the same agricultural inputs. It has further merits, since it flourishes in a range of climates and growing conditions, and is rich in vitamin C and other necessary nutrients. When accompanied by dairy products and a ready supply of fuel for home-cooking, potatoes allowed families to feed themselves far more effectively than virtually any of the available alternatives. In eighteenth-century England, even potatoes purchased at a market provided nearly three times more calories per penny than wheat bread, and about five times as many as meat.[67] Doubtless for these reasons, potatoes proved particularly popular both in Ireland, where English colonisation pushed the rural population onto ever-smaller patches of ground, and regions such as Galicia and Asturias, where peasants enjoyed greater access to land and considerable freedom to plant what they liked.[68]

The anthropologist Robert Netting studied the impact of potatoes on the Alpine village of Törbel, whose peasant inhabitants began to grow them on a significant scale in the eighteenth century.[69] How villagers would themselves have explained their embrace of the potato is a question we are in little position to answer, but Netting was able to show that in Törbel potatoes offered a three-fold improvement over rye, the region's staple, in terms of calories per hectare, and could moreover be grown on lands that were too steep or barren to support cereals. He concluded that potatoes help explain why Törbel's population doubled in the century after their introduction.[70]

In Törbel, potatoes were first cultivated in garden plots, which means they were first cultivated by women. In most parts of early modern Europe maintaining kitchen gardens was a woman's responsibility, as they were considered better suited to the fiddly work of hoeing root crops and other tasks that did not require larger tools such as a plough or scythe. Small-scale potato culture carried out with a hoe fit well into the activities typically undertaken by women, alongside raising chickens and the myriad other tasks required to maintain a farming household. It is therefore likely that in Europe, peasant women, in particular, were in the vanguard of potato cultivation. The 'garden stuff' demanded by the rector in St Buryan was probably grown by that village's women.[71]

Altogether, such features suggest that in early modern Europe potatoes could be classified as 'state evading' – a phrase coined by the political anthropologist James C. Scott to describe crops that enable a degree of autonomy from state control because they can be cultivated on marginal ground and contribute to complex household provisioning systems that are difficult to measure and tax efficiently. Unlike cereals, potatoes do not need to be harvested at a precise moment, and can be left in the ground for weeks or even months. Once harvested, they are cumbersome to transport elsewhere. From a fiscal perspective, the potatoes raised in a kitchen garden are scarcely worth the trouble to tax, and so create, in Scott's words, 'a nonstate space', particularly where there is no established commercial framework for marketing these roots.[72] These qualities surely go some way in explaining their popularity with peasants in Galicia, farmers in Flanders, and poor tenants in England.

Wealthy landowners, in contrast, were less certain of the merits of the potato. Efforts in early eighteenth-century Sweden to encourage potatoes came to nothing because of hostility from landlords, who suspected that the potato's prolific yield would make peasants more self-sufficient, and so less inclined to work for them.[73] Landowners viewed the plant as a costly intrusion into fields that could otherwise produce more marketable commodities. In 1727, an experienced estate manager who had worked for several English dukes recommended that his clients prohibit their tenants from growing potatoes at all, 'except in small quantities for their own use'. Tenants who persisted in planting this crop in open fields should be fined £10 for every acre they wasted on potatoes. They should also be obliged to enrich these fields with an additional load of manure, to compensate for the nutrients that he believed potatoes extracted from the soil.[74] If tenants and labourers wished to eat them, that was their business, but landowners should not countenance the diversion of valuable land to this purpose. Potatoes to him were associated with backwardness and uneconomic practices. He was not alone in this view. Contemplating regional diets in 1740s Sweden, the great botanist Carl Linnaeus, who harboured doubts about the potato's nutritive qualities, wondered why on earth servants 'find it so necessary to go on eating' them.[75] From the perspective of these wealthier men, the potato was a mundane food grown and eaten by ordinary people, which offered little to interest those concerned with the management of great estates, let alone affairs of state.

DEEP-ROOTED INERTIA

Labourers 'blindly repeat what they have seen their fathers and grandfathers do'.[76]

Bernardo Ward, 1779

The peasant is characterised by a deep-rooted inertia; he accepts progress only when someone has forced him out of his inaction by demonstrating the improvement to him dozens of times. Only then will he risk trying it himself. His limited vision inclines him to exaggerate the merits of plants that he has cultivated successfully in the past.[77]

Amédée Dechambre, 1877

It was a long time before people learnt to eat potatoes. In some parts they were ready enough to accept them as cattle-fodder, but not for human consumption. There was stubborn resistance to be overcome. People were afraid that the potato would cause all sorts of illnesses, such as leprosy, glandular disease, tuberculosis or fevers. Because of its resemblance to nightshade, some also feared it was poisonous. Moreover, they did not yet know the best ways of preparing it.[78]

Bernard Hendrik Slicher van Bath, 1960

This chapter has presented an alternative account of how early modern Europeans came to eat potatoes, which accords importance not to experts who patiently demonstrate an improvement dozens of times, but rather to peasants and small farmers. These men and women were raising potatoes long before the root attracted the attention of tithe collectors and other representatives of the state. By 1700 potatoes were grown on a small scale, in kitchen gardens, by villagers, peasants and labourers, in many parts of the British Isles and continental Europe. There is no evidence that the potato's tuberous habit confused farmers any more than it troubled botanists, and Europeans great and small invented many ways of preparing and consuming this starchy root. Insofar as we can detect the direction of transmission, it was the opposite of that imagined by scholars.

It should surprise no one that peasants and villagers were in the vanguard of agricultural and culinary innovation in early modern Europe. These groups were among the first to cultivate maize, another

American import that was to effect an equally dramatic transformation in global diets in the centuries after Spaniards brought it to Europe and West Africa in the sixteenth century. As early as the 1540s maize was growing in the Veneto, where peasants used it in place of millet or other cheap grain to make a new sort of polenta. By the early seventeenth century maize polenta had become the principal food of the region's peasants and the poor.[79] Venetian peasants were evidently unperturbed by maize's novelty or lack of biblical pedigree. Ordinary people in East Anglia were equally willing to adopt the unfamiliar agricultural techniques required to cultivate carrots and other root vegetables when these were introduced by Protestant refugees in the 1550s. Overall, as the historian Philip Hoffman has shown very clearly in the case of France, early modern peasants were by no means opposed to agricultural experimentation.[80] A substantial body of research has moreover established that small farmers in other parts of the world are perfectly capable of innovative agricultural strategies when faced with new plants and new economic situations – a matter to which we will return in the conclusion.

Nor did European agronomic science develop separately from peasant agriculture. Early modern scientific knowledge of all sorts often relied on information, methodologies and theorising produced outside of the community of European savants.[81] The new agronomic practices that made commercial agriculture in seventeenth- and eighteenth-century England and the Netherlands significantly more productive drew on the agricultural practices of peasant farmers. During this period the introduction of new crops and techniques, together with legislative changes that favoured large-scale agriculture, combined to create a new type of agrarian capitalism. This transformation relied in crucial ways on techniques derived from peasant agriculture. A key element of the new agronomy was the use of fodder crops such as lucerne (alfalfa), clover and sainfoin. When ploughed into the earth these plants are an effective means of enriching the soil with nitrogen and other necessary nutrients. The use of such soil-enrichers helped alleviate the need to leave fields to lie fallow to recover lost fertility. Fields could henceforth be cultivated continuously, which dramatically increased the area of land in cultivation. These crops can also be used to feed farm animals, whose manure further enriches the soil. The entire process, however, depended on a reliable commercial supply of seed for these cultivars. The people with the expertise to enable this proved to be Italian peasants, who possessed technical skills and practical knowledge about these plants that were entirely lacking elsewhere. As a result, as the historian Mauro Ambrosoli put it, 'plants grown by the peasantry passed into capitalist agriculture'.[82]

Peasant agricultural expertise most often becomes visible to the historian when it becomes visible to non-peasants. In the case of sainfoin and clover, the importance of these crops to new agronomic practices focused the attention of improving landlords on the Italian peasants who had long cultivated these now-interesting plants. As regards the potato, most sixteenth- and seventeenth-century landlords displayed little interest in its commercial potential, which in part explains the difficulty in charting the tuber's early European history. Only occasionally can we glimpse the traces of its progress across the continent. These suggest that small farmers played a far more important role in its dissemination than has hitherto been acknowledged. Cross-referencing with what we know about peasant practice in other periods and places supports this view. For instance, although scholars sometimes suggest that the potato's excellence as an animal feed demonstrated to early modern peasants that it was 'fit only for animal fodder', this conclusion does not match what we know about farming practice either in Europe or elsewhere.[83] It is a positive advantage for crops to address multiple needs. Farmers in Mexico have long appreciated the maize plant's ability to provide both food and also fodder, fuel and construction material. In Europe itself, wheat's status as an enormously important foodstuff and religious symbol was not undermined by the fact that wheat stalks also serve as bedding for lowly farm animals, or that poultry enjoy its grains as feed. There is no reason to suppose that early modern farmers viewed the potato's versatility any less favourably.[84]

While small farmers were quietly raising potatoes, hoping not to arouse the attention of a tithe-collecting cleric, potatoes were not an object of particular interest among landlords and the owners of large estates. Certainly potatoes were served at the tables of the wealthy. Recipe books explained how to prepare elaborate and expensive dishes such as the potato pie that vanquished the Earl of Dorset, and household records document the purchase of both ordinary and sweet potatoes in great households in Britain, France and elsewhere. They were also raised on a commercial scale in some areas, such as the north of England and Ireland, on occasion on the estates of the nobility. Early modern elites did not spurn the potato, but neither were they particularly interested in it.

Nor were potatoes viewed as an important component of state policy. Extending potato cultivation was not a goal for officials or statesmen, and with a tiny handful of exceptions, no one penned treatises lauding the merits of the potato as a food whose greater consumption would bring widespread public benefits.[85] On the contrary, politically minded commentators lamented the fact that potatoes offered the poor a way to evade the state. William Petty, a philosopher and politician who spent many years in Ireland as a representative of the English colonial government, held precisely this view. Born in England in the 1620s, Petty had an eventful life that took him to France and Holland, as well as Oxford and London, where he taught music and anatomy and helped found the Royal Society. In the 1650s he travelled to Ireland, which had recently been annexed by English forces under the leadership of Oliver Cromwell. Petty worked for many years as a representative of the English colonial state, which aimed to extract as much profit as possible from its new possession. Petty himself acquired several large estates. Petty viewed potatoes as an impediment to Ireland's development as a productive source of revenue for its colonisers. Because it was so easy to live on potatoes, the Irish did not work as hard as Petty would have liked, with the result that the state was able to levy only about half the tax that Petty calculated a more industrious population would have yielded. Potatoes allowed their cultivators too much autonomy from the English state, which in Petty's view would have been better off had the Irish eaten fewer of them.[86]

This attitude was to change dramatically over the course of the eighteenth century. From the 1750s increasing numbers of statesmen, political economists, agronomists, philosophers and landlords championed the potato, arguing that everyone, and in particular the poor, ought to grow and eat more of them. They composed handbooks on potato cultivation, experimented with cooking techniques, and proselytised about the potato's many merits. The next chapter examines the potato's enormous visibility in the eighteenth century, to show how changing ideas about effective statecraft and the importance of building a healthy population shone a spotlight on the hitherto uninteresting eating practices of ordinary people.

The loud voices of these eighteenth-century potato-boosters have resulted in the potato history summarised at the start of this chapter, which asserts that prior to the eighteenth century Europeans did not in general take to the potato, and that peasant farmers were particularly slow to embrace it. Scholars have listened to the eighteenth-century sources, and have rightly heard an eighteenth-century consensus that people ought to eat more potatoes. If we listen carefully we can hear other stories. These tell us both that potatoes were eaten long before eighteenth-century philosophers began to promote them, and also that kitchen gardens are a sensible place to hunt for culinary and agricultural pioneers.

CHAPTER 2

Enlightened Potatoes

'**F**OR SEVERAL YEARS NEWSPAPERS DISCUSSED PRACTICALLY nothing but potatoes.' So claimed the French historian Pierre-Jean-Baptiste Legrand d'Aussy in 1782. Physicians analysed their properties, writers exalted their virtues, and monarchs encouraged their consumption: the potato, Legrand d'Aussy proclaimed, had become the darling of the Enlightenment.[1]

Two features particularly captured the imagination of eighteenth-century potato-enthusiasts. They insisted that potatoes were a healthy and nourishing food that could be eaten with pleasure by everyone. The potato had the triple advantage, announced a French cookbook, of being 'healthful, tasty and very economical', and for this reason was doubtless sent by divine providence itself. The panegyrists of the potato, as one newspaper called them, also noted that the root offered particular benefits to ordinary people. 'What a treasure is a milch cow and a potatoe garden, to a poor man with a large family!', rhapsodised the fashionable Scottish physician William Buchan.[2] All across Europe physicians, statesmen, priests and other members of the republic of letters agreed that potatoes were an exceptional resource for the poor, which would liberate them from hunger and poverty. Inspired by the potato's apparent virtues, monarchs in many parts of the continent issued edicts encouraging their cultivation and countless organisations devised schemes to increase consumption. Perhaps Legrand d'Aussy exaggerated in claiming that this enlightened potato-talk dominated the eighteenth-century public sphere, but it did form a powerful, trans-continental theme for half a century. (See figure 7.)

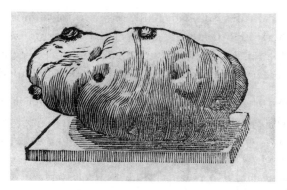

Figure 7 Engraving of a potato from Giovanni Battista Occhiolini's 1784 treatise. The Roman cleric Giovanni Battista Occhiolini's treatise on the 'marvellous American fruit commonly called potato' was aimed at rural labourers. He hoped his explanation of potato-agronomy would encourage them to grow and eat more potatoes.

A venerable body of scholarship credits this eighteenth-century propaganda with the potato's transformation from a despised botanical oddity to the staple it is today. As Chapter 1 noted, the protagonists of this transformation are said to be far-sighted rulers and philanthropists. 'People on both sides of the Rhine tended to believe that you caught leprosy from eating potatoes,' asserts one food historian, who explains that only after a clever promotional scheme patronised by Louis XVI himself did the French begin to accept potatoes.[3] This scheme was supposedly devised by the French scientist and potato-promoter Antoine Augustin Parmentier, who arranged for the tubers to be planted ostentatiously on crown land. As Parmentier's collaborator Julien-Joseph Virey recounted in a posthumous biography of his friend and colleague, when these plants matured:

Parmentier arranged for gendarmes to guard it – but only during the day. His intention was for them to be stolen during the night and the populace did not fail to oblige. Every morning these nocturnal thefts were reported to him; he was delighted, and generously rewarded the informants, who were astonished by his inexplicable joy. But public opinion was vanquished and France from that moment was enriched with an enduring resource.[4]

Nearly identical ruses were, allegedly, required to vanquish public opinion elsewhere in Europe. In Greece, the early nineteenth-century nationalist Ioannis Kapodistrias supposedly convinced sceptical Greeks to embrace potatoes through a very similar stratagem. Kapodistrias:

> ordered that the potatoes be dumped on the docks of Nafplion and placed under guard. Rumors circulated that since the potatoes were so well guarded, they must of be of great value. Before long someone tried to steal some of these 'valuable' potatoes. Since the guards were told to ignore the stealing, it wasn't long before the whole shipment disappeared. The potato continues to be an important part of Greek cuisine today.[5]

These stories have wide currency in European popular culture. I spoke with many people who recounted the tales they learned at school about these potato heroes, and the stubborn resistance they overcame.[6] (See figure 8.)

Figure 8 Votive potatoes left on a plaque to Frederick the Great at Sans Souci Palace, Potsdam. Visitors to Frederick II's palace at Sans Souci who place potatoes on this plaque help perpetuate his reputation as Germany's premier potato-promoter.

These acts of nutritional benevolence are typically presented as ad hoc responses to particular moments of famine or scarcity. In Prussia, recurrent famines from the 1740s are said to have prompted Frederick the Great to issue a series of decrees encouraging potato cultivation. Underpinning such stories is the assumption that state promotion of a favoured food is a natural response to specific episodes of shortage. To be sure, eighteenth-century food shortages focused the attention of the wealthy on the humanitarian and political consequences of hunger. Almost continual warfare during the half-century between 1750 and 1815 placed great strains on the food supply, as did growing populations. These events should, however, be placed in a broader context. The need to raise and equip large armies, investigations into the effect of liberalising the grain trade, the formation of local societies dedicated to disseminating useful agricultural knowledge, hand-wringing over the alcohol consumption of peasants and labourers, schemes to reduce infant mortality, and potato-promotion together formed part of a larger reconceptualisation of the relationship between food and the wealth and strength of the nation. This chapter unravels these associations.

Viewing the eighteenth century's fascination with the potato in this light reveals the connections between individual diets and the new ideas about political economy, public health and effective statecraft that emerged during the Enlightenment. Recognising these connections allows us to make better sense of the historical relationship between food scarcity and state response. Famines had long afflicted Europe; the 'famine' explanation for the enormous eighteenth-century interest in the potato does not explain why it was only in the eighteenth century that states began to respond to dearth by promoting specific foodstuffs. What had changed between the seventeenth century, when famines at times carried off as much as 40 per cent of local populations, and the eighteenth century was not an increase in the incidence or seriousness of famines – scholars tell us that their frequency in fact decreased.[7] What changed was the importance that new models of statecraft ascribed to building a healthy population. The Enlightenment's fascination with the potato reflects the advent not of a new foodstuff or new levels of hunger, but rather of new ideas about the relationship between the health and vigour of the population, and the wealth and power of the state. It was this that lifted the potato from its quiet position in cottage gardens and ships' holds to the treatises of the Enlightenment. The smaller history of the potato thus reveals the larger historical changes that helped make the daily habits of ordinary people visible to the state and its theoreticians.

POPULATION AND THE FOOD SUPPLY

Enlightened discussion of potatoes was inseparable from the eighteenth-century debate over the 'population'. Throughout the century philosophers, *économistes*, officials and other members of the republic of letters engaged in a prolonged examination of the relationship between the number of people inhabiting a territory and its wealth. They considered especially whether a large population was the fundamental motor driving mercantile and commercial success, whether a growing population in itself demonstrated that a country was well governed, and whether it was ever possible for a population to become too large for a given territory. Such questions generated a vigorous corpus of dispute and discussion.

From the late sixteenth century treatises on good government had begun to suggest that states generally benefited from a large population. A larger population provided a larger labour force for agriculture and industry and a wider pool of soldiers. These in turn would increase a prince's hold on power. This interest in the links between population size and state power encouraged the development over the next century of the mathematical fields such as probability and statistics necessary to measure population growth. By the eighteenth century theorists of statecraft had come to view the population not simply as a personal possession of the prince, but as the bedrock of the wealth and power of the state. This conviction prompted a growing number of schemes aimed at protecting the population from disease and death through the draining of marshes, the regulation of hospitals, and other public health measures. Advocates of such ventures stressed not only the powerful humanitarian imperatives that motivated their efforts but also the political importance of preserving the population. A 1750 British *Plan of a Dispensary for Inoculating the Poor* opened with the observation that 'as the strength of the nation is in some measure proportionate to the number of its inhabitants, every attempt to encrease population, by preserving life has a just claim to the regard both of *Patriotism* and *Humanity*'.[8]

These ideas had become commonplace in many parts of Europe by the mid-eighteenth century. Spanish statesmen affirmed that 'the population is the basis of everything', because without people, 'there is neither agriculture, nor industry, nor commerce, arts, power or wealth'.[9] The mathematician Pehr Wargentin, secretary of the Swedish Royal Academy, agreed: 'that a civil society's greatest strength consists of a quantity of good citizens is a saying that is now doubted by almost no one'.[10] This confidence in the merits of a large, and (ideally) densely settled population endured throughout the century. Of course it was possible to theorise situations in which a larger population might be a disadvantage, and not everyone agreed that a large population itself caused economic growth. Advocates of physiocracy, the new economic theory that stressed the centrality of land and agriculture in generating wealth, for instance maintained that a growing population was the result, rather than the cause, of economic success. They nonetheless concurred that it was a positive sign, indicative of a healthy economy.[11]

Contrarian voices began to be raised in the last quarter of the century. Some writers suggested that unlimited growth might eventually backfire, weakening rather than strengthening the polity. The clergyman Thomas Robert Malthus was to become the most influential exponent of this idea. Nonetheless, the dominant vision continued to stress the merits of a large population. In 1795, just three years before the publication of Malthus' *Essay on the Principles of Population*, a correspondent writing to the *Annals of Agriculture*, an influential British journal edited by the agronomist Arthur Young, felt confident in stating that 'the wealth of nations is unquestionably in proportion to its inhabitants'.[12] As late as the 1820s, writers such as James Mill were patiently trying to explain Malthus' ideas in the face of the persistent conviction that a large population was inherently beneficial.[13]

As Michel Foucault argued some decades ago, these population debates signalled the emergence of a new approach to the exercise of power, which stressed the importance of aligning state policies to the larger forces that themselves shaped the vigour, size and productivity of a region's inhabitants.[14] The new science of statecraft was not a simple

matter of ensuring obedience or imposing authority. It entailed managing resources and creating effective systems for their exploitation. 'The
population', in other words, was far more than a miscellaneous collection
of individuals inhabiting a territory. It was an essential resource. Writers
on population constantly stressed that success in managing this vital
resource was a fundamental barometer of a state's effectiveness. An
increase in the number of inhabitants was both an indication, and an
almost inevitable result, of overall public well-being, argued the French
demographer Jean-Baptiste Moheau in an essay on population. For this
reason, population growth, or its absence, 'testifies for or against the
government'.[15]

A large population, however, was not in itself sufficient. A treatise on
how to energise Spain's sluggish economy spelled out what more was
necessary. 'The most fundamental element of any economic system', it
stated, 'is ensuring that men are *usefully employed*.'[16] Its Irish author,
Bernardo Ward, had been commissioned by the Spanish monarch
Ferdinand VI to conduct a study of Spain's agriculture, commerce and
industry, for which he undertook extensive travels across the peninsula.
Ward, who later served as a director of Spain's Royal Mint, had for some
years been thinking about the best way of ensuring that Spain's population was usefully employed. He had earlier devised a plan to intern
beggars and the homeless in an institution where they could be set to
work, 'for the benefit of the State'.[17]

As Ward's attention to vagrancy indicates, a large population was
useless if it was not actively engaged in productive labour. In his report
for Ferdinand VI, which proposed reforms to Spain's management of
both its European and new-world territories, Ward emphasised that the
labour potential latent in the population was an essential resource, and
good governance consisted precisely in unlocking this potential.
Population could be increased 'physically' by augmenting the number
of individuals, but this was not the only, or best, way to develop an
effective population. Converting 'a man who does not work, and who
does not contribute anything useful to the republic' into an industrious
worker was a far greater achievement because it constituted a 'political'
increase in the population.[18] 'When one says that a sovereign's wealth
consists in the number of his vassals, one means the number of *useful*

vassals, since a million idle vagabonds and professional beggars, far from being useful, are an impediment to the state, which would be much better off, and wealthier, without them,' Ward observed.[19] Ward's assessment of the importance of developing a hard-working population was widely shared. If a state's population was not usefully employed in agriculture or manufacturing, it was 'like a treasure that is dead and buried underground', noted the Swedish writer and statesman Edvard Carleson in 1731.[20] *Industrious* inhabitants, not just people in general, lay at the heart of national grandeur and success.

In order to be industrious a population needed to be healthy. Only then would a state be able to prosper. This in turn required not only inoculation schemes and programmes of marsh-drainage, but also an adequate food supply. As the potato-promoter Parmentier observed, 'the type and choice of food greatly influences the population, so it is impossible to take too many precautions when ensuring that the people are well fed'.[21] These ideas were not simply responses to particular moments of scarcity, but rather drew on the growing conviction that a robust population materially increased the power and wealth of a state. Certainly the particular pressures of warfare and shortage focused the attention of officials on the food supply. When the mathematician and bureaucrat Jean-Louis Lagrange designed a 'calculus of nourishment' to estimate the food requirements of the new French republic in 1796, he was motivated by practical concerns as much as by any theoretical curiosity.[22] Well over seven million troops were deployed in the years between 1792 and 1815 in the global warfare that consumed European powers from the outbreak of revolution in France to the aftermath of the battle of Waterloo. This, together with repeated poor harvests, strained food supplies in many countries, yet even during these war years interest in the diets of working people did not reflect only these conjunctural circumstances. Writers consistently stressed the importance of ensuring that 'the lower classes of the people' were adequately nourished because such notions had become commonplace in discussions of the business of governance.[23]

From the late seventeenth century political theorists had begun to identify food as an important component in building a strong state. The polymath German diplomat and political theorist Johann Joachim Becher defined civil society as 'a populous and *well-nourished* community'. The English barrister William Petyt, author of many treatises on governance, drew similar connections between food and the size of the population.[24] As developing a large and active population became ever more central to understandings of political and economic well-being, increasing attention was paid to the political and economic importance of ensuring that the population was well fed. In the 1730s the French lawyer and political philosopher Jean-François Melon embedded the food supply at the centre of his analysis of international trade. In an influential essay Melon offered a series of thought experiments to illustrate the forces shaping commercial exchange. His examination of the trading relations between three hypothetical island kingdoms concluded that a nation's strength was closely correlated with its possessing 'the greatest possible quantity of foodstuffs'.[25] Food was a component of the larger theoretical framework that explained how nations became powerful.

Most important, from this perspective, was ensuring an adequate supply of the sorts of foods suitable for the labouring body. When writers spoke of the need to ensure that the population was energetic and industrious, they had in mind the energy and industriousness of working people. The English philanthropist Jonas Hanway stated this plainly: 'the true foundations of riches and power is the number of working poor'.[26] National strength and wealth thus demanded, in the words of one of numerous pamphlets on the matter, that working people be 'plentifully and cheaply fed'.[27] The interconnections between the bodies of working people, national prowess and a flourishing economy prompted an altogether new interest in the eating practices of labourers.

In connecting the diets of labourers to the body politic these writers drew on ideas that had become increasingly common in a different written genre: health manuals. As noted in Chapter 1, these vernacular guidebooks dedicated to explaining the principles of good living were published in increasing numbers during the seventeenth century. Dietary advice featured prominently, since everyone acknowledged that good health depended fundamentally on consuming suitable foods. In addition to stressing the importance of selecting a diet that matched one's personal constitution or complexion, these books often drew connections between the cuisine of a particular region and the characteristics of the local population. Different diets helped explain both national differences between, say, the English and the French, and the differences that Europeans perceived between themselves and non-Europeans. Amerindians, stated one Spanish doctor, were quite unlike Spaniards in body and character 'because they don't eat the same foods'.[28] Similar points were made by local historians, who likewise sought to account for a region's distinguishing features. Both the melancholy nature of the inhabitants of Wiltshire and the energetic and agreeable personality of people in Glamorganshire were ascribed to the local diet.[29] In this way individual eating practices contributed to moulding regional and national character. These notions helped establish connections between the dietary practices of individuals and the characteristics of the overall population on which eighteenth-century political thinkers could draw.

Many aspects of a nation's well-being were said to be affected by the eating habits of working people. The productivity of industry was one area where observers perceived a clear link. As Adam Smith remarked, 'that men in general should work better when they are ill fed than when they are well fed ... seems not very probable'.[30] In addition, poorly nourished labourers would not engender vigorous children to work in manufacturing and agriculture, and ill-fed soldiers could not be relied upon to protect the kingdom. The two – the health of poor children and the robustness of the military – were in any event interconnected. Imagining the sickly babies born to gin-drinking mothers, the novelist Henry Fielding feared the consequences of 'these wretched infants' becoming 'our future sailors, and our future grenadiers'. He predicted dire results for Britain were it to rely on these enfeebled beings to defend its territory and further its commerce and agriculture.[31] Writers across Europe shared Fielding's concern that the death or debilitation of poor children constituted 'a political loss for the state'. Ensuring that infants grew into healthy and vigorous workers, insisted one of the many texts to consider this matter, was therefore essential for 'the glory and prosperity' of the nation.[32] Books on the topic proclaimed this association clearly in their very titles. *Concrete Causes of Mortality in Foundlings during their Early Years: Remedies for this Serious Evil, and Method for Making them into Useful and Christian Citizens to the Notable Increase to Spain's Population, Strength and*

Wealth, reads the title of one such work from Spain. Its author, a priest and trustee at Pamplona's general hospital, stated explicitly that recovering these doomed babies for the state would increase the population of soldiers and workers: 'how many individuals – which we now lack – would we have for public works! How many labourers! How many honest grenadiers!'[33]

The hospital in Pamplona was one of many institutions that aimed to increase the population of honest grenadiers and labourers by caring for abandoned babies. Food was at the centre of these efforts. The challenges of feeding foundlings were considerable; in the absence of a sufficient number of wet-nurses, mortality rates at orphanages sometimes approached 100 per cent. Precisely because a strong and productive working population depended on its ability to reproduce itself, infant feeding and its links to infant mortality attracted the attention of writers in many parts of Europe. Numerous treatises were composed on the best artificial formulae, and the exceptional importance of infant feeding in general. A number were dedicated directly to ruling monarchs, which hints at the links their authors perceived between the nourishment of poor children and matters of state.[34]

Nowhere were concerns about national security, nourishing food, and working bodies more closely entwined than in the demands of naval provisioning. The British state's efforts to feed the Royal Navy illustrate these interconnections very clearly. Because this 'body of men essential to the existence of the empire' was recognised as requiring a highly nourishing diet, sailors in the Royal Navy enjoyed rations far superior to those on mercantile vessels.[35] Ensuring this was no easy task. Although feeding any branch of the military called for advanced organisation, the special obstacles posed by shipboard life required a more elaborate infrastructure. In the British Isles the monumental task of feeding the Navy was undertaken by the Victualling Board, established in 1683 to oversee all matters related to naval provisions. Its multi-million-pound budget reflects the importance the British state ascribed to the enterprise. Regulations stressed the need for top-quality food; 'the oxen must be fattest and the potatoes, onions and fodder the best that can be procured', noted the 1760 regulations.[36] Official tables stipulated the supplies to which sailors were entitled, again to ensure that the workforce was fit and able to work. The Board's scrupulous records demonstrate that the slightest variation from the regulations was liable to attract an audit, both because it might represent an attempt at defrauding the exchequer and because sub-standard rations undermined the Navy's fighting strength.

Other states lacking the Victualling Board's robust institutional presence shared the conviction that the diet of sailors was a matter of direct importance to governance. Allowing sailors to sicken through poor diet and improper medical attention was an enormous loss to the state, and extremely beneficial to its enemies, insisted the Spanish doctor Pedro María González, a professor at the Royal College of Surgical Medicine at Cádiz.[37] Doctors elsewhere similarly stressed the political importance of providing sailors with nourishing food. When the physician Antoine Poissonnier Desperrières proposed a radical, vegetarian diet for the French navy he framed it within an explicitly political context. Poissonnier Desperrières, author of an earlier text on colonial medicine and member of the Dijon Academy of Sciences, was critical of the reliance on salted meats typical of naval provisioning, which he (like many others) blamed for scurvy, a serious threat to individual sailors and the navy as a whole. In their place he proposed a ration based on rice and legumes, seasoned with ginger and pickled onion. While he admitted that this new diet might unsettle sailors, he insisted that it would create a healthier and more energetic navy. Since it aimed to preserve the health of 'a class of men precious to the nation', he considered his scheme a 'patriotic and economical project'.[38] To think about the diet of working men and women, in short, was a legitimate undertaking for those concerned with politics.

*

Because of the significance that these new models of statecraft ascribed to building a robust population of workers, by the late eighteenth century the quotidian eating habits of ordinary people had become relevant to the overall success of the state. Alongside these new ideas, politicians, landowners, and many others continued to fear the socially and politically destabilising effects of famine and dearth, and philosophers and the clergy continued to lament the suffering caused by hunger. Such concerns were not theoretical, since shortages afflicted ordinary people regularly throughout the century, and on occasion provoked popular action of precisely the sort that had long worried those in power. The devastating famine that struck Naples in 1764 reverberated across the continent, provoking serious riots as far away as Madrid.[39] The food supply, for the eighteenth-century science of the state, was thus both a matter of public order, and also a central component of a larger model of political economy that associated national wealth and greatness with the energy and vigour of the working population.

How, however, to ensure that working people ate suitably nourishing foods? A profound transformation of the economic order to channel more wealth to the working poor was out of the question for all but the most radical political philosophers.[40] Instead, attention focused on identifying inexpensive alternatives to existing dietaries. Writing from Bologna, whose population had only recently recovered from losses in the previous century caused by outbreaks of plague, the agronomist and landowner Pietro Maria Bignami explained that were his homeland to possess an adequate food supply, its population would increase markedly, and if the population grew, industry would be sure to follow. Were that to happen, the region would undoubtedly become 'one of the richest and happiest in all Italy'.[41] To accomplish this, he believed it was necessary to identify 'a new product' able to compensate at least in part for the inadequacy of existing foodstuffs. Perhaps, he suggested, the potato might serve this purpose.

Bignami was not alone in hoping that the potato might address the need for a cheap, population-building staple for working people. All across Europe political thinkers pinned their hopes on the potato as a vehicle to deliver robust working populations. The hardiness and fecundity of long-standing potato-eaters such as the Irish offered a mesmerising vision of pink-cheeked families subsisting on a food they grew themselves. When the Scottish agronomist and printer David Henry lauded the potato's nourishing properties he noted specifically that in addition to being tasty, it had a further quality to recommend it: 'it is favourable to population; for it has been observed, that in the western parts of Ireland, where it is almost the only dyet of the labouring poor, it is no unusual thing to see six, seven, eight or ten, and sometimes more children'. Henry referred approvingly to the 'healthy progeny that crowd the cabins of those mean people'.[42] Others cited the Scottish highlands, whose 'hardy and muscular inhabitants' subsisted largely on potatoes.[43] Potato-eaters in the mountain villages of the Alpes-Maritimes, in southern France, were likewise praised for their 'notable stoutness', a sure indication of robustness.[44] Samuel Engel, president of the Economic Society of Bern, one of the hundreds of patriotic organisations established across eighteenth-century Europe to disseminate useful knowledge, like Bignami composed an entire treatise on the potato's multiple merits, in which he expatiated on the potato's immense potential as a population builder.[45] Ireland was again offered as a convincing illustration of the merits of a potato-based diet. All that was required for the potato to work its magic elsewhere, he believed, was for working people to recognise its potential.

POTATOES AND THE WORKING-CLASS DIET

Unfortunately, the existing dietary practices of ordinary people constituted a mighty impediment to the happy consequences resulting from a large and energetic working population, in the view of many commentators. Unlike the healthy potato-eating Irish, many working people were thought to be crippling themselves through ill-advised, self-inflicted dietary errors. Country people, complained the scientist Antoine-Alexis Cadet de Vaux, committed a catalogue of 'alimentary vices', which were responsible for their terrible physical health.[46] Overconsumption of tea, sugar and white bread was the cause of 'all the evils which affect the labouring part of mankind', fulminated an English author.[47] 'The custom of the common people's drinking great quantities of the most inflammatory and poisonous liquor' came in for particularly frequent criticism.[48] In less hostile tones, philanthropists composed 'friendly recommendations' aimed at showing the poor how to improve their health by reducing food waste, employing more economical modes of cooking, and eating more vegetables.[49] After conducting a remarkable survey of the eating practices of labourers and artisans across England, Frederick Morton Eden, son of a governor of colonial Maryland and identifier of the first Scot to grow potatoes in an open field, concluded that improvidence in 'dress, in diet, and in other branches of private expenditure' played a significant role in exacerbating poverty. With a little attention a labourer could 'reduce the expense of his food one half, without rendering it less palatable, less nutritious, or less wholesome', Eden believed.[50]

The Scottish physician William Buchan composed several books elaborating on this theme. Buchan's career had included a stint as medical officer at an orphanage in Yorkshire, as well as in a private practice in London. These experiences informed his best-selling manual on household medicine, which explained how to treat earache, stressed the need for regular exercise, and reminded students to change their clothing. *Domestic Medicine* also critiqued the eating habits of 'the poor', who in Buchan's view bore some responsibility for their own ill-health. He insisted that 'peasants are extremely careless with respect to what they eat or drink, and often, through mere indolence, use unwholesome food, when they might, for the same expense, have that which is wholesome'.[51] He also blamed sharp business practice by butchers and grocers for the spoiled and adulterated food that often featured in the diet of the poor. These matters, he stressed, should concern everyone, both because spoiled food caused epidemic diseases, and also because 'the lives of the labouring poor are of great importance to the state'.[52]

Buchan expanded on these concerns in his 1797 *Observations Concerning the Diet of the Common People*. This work was composed during the hungry 1790s, when war with France, poor harvests, and government policy combined to create repeated episodes of scarcity in Britain. *Observations Concerning the Diet of the Common People* developed Buchan's earlier interest in improving popular diets, at the same time as it reflected these particular pressures on the food supply. Buchan's aim in both works was to show 'common people' how to live 'cheaper and better' by making superior choices about what they ate.[53] As he explained in *Observations*, most common people consumed far too much meat and white bread, and drank too much beer. They did not eat enough vegetables. The inevitable result, he stated, was ill-health, with diseases such as scurvy wreaking havoc in the bodies of working men, women and children. This, he reiterated, undermined British trade and weakened the nation.

How, however, to ensure that people were well-nourished? What sorts of food would provide a better nutritional base than beer and white bread? William Buchan encouraged a diet based largely on whole grains and root vegetables, which he insisted were not only cheaper than the alternatives, but infinitely more healthful. He was particularly enthusiastic about potatoes. No nation, he believed, had ever been 'very populous' without drawing 'a great part of its food from underground'. Combined with milk the potato provided ideal nourishment: 'some of the stoutest men we know, are brought up on milk and potatoes', Buchan stated. (As was the case with French peasants, stoutness betokened a robust constitution.) Even without milk, potatoes provided a complete meal; Buchan cited a report to the Board of Agriculture by Dr Richard Pearson as evidence for this latter fact.[54] Buchan maintained that it would be easy for landlords to supply their workers with potato gardens, and easy for workers to cultivate them. The benefits would accrue both to the individual workers and their families, whose healthy bodies would be full of vigour, and to the state. He was explicit about the two-fold nature of the improvements that would occur were workers to embrace potatoes, and were landlords to support these new dietary ambitions. 'What a source of real wealth and population!', he insisted. 'Men would multiply, and poverty, unless among the profligate, be unknown.'[55] Potatoes would help make Britain rich and powerful.

This, indeed, was why the British Board of Agriculture and Internal Improvement had published Dr Pearson's report on potatoes in the first place. The Board had been formed in 1793 to investigate and promote innovative agricultural practices. Supported by £3,000 of state funding, it embarked on a heterogeneous programme of research and publication that took in topics from improved millstones and the 'secret of destroying slugs', to the role of salt in manure, and a 'peculiar breed of sheep' with no ears.[56] Its first president, the Scottish agronomist and gentleman-farmer Sir John Sinclair, wrote prolifically on the benefits such information offered the British public. The Board manifested a sustained interest in potatoes and reported regularly on potato-related matters. Its members heard papers on treating potato leaf curl, the manufacture of potato starch, and methods for preserving potatoes by means of desiccation,

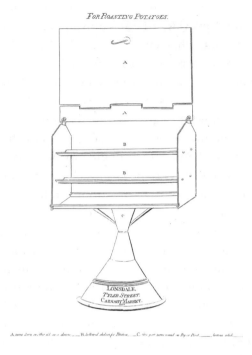

Figure 9 A potato-roaster promoted by the British Board of Agriculture. Members of the eighteenth-century Board of Agriculture dabbled with an impressively varied range of topics, from growing broccoli to raising angora rabbits, but they took a sustained interest in potatoes, which they considered a crop of the first importance to Britain's well-being. This potato-roaster featured in a volume that described their efforts to make a satisfactory bread out of oats, potatoes and other alternatives to white flour.

which the Board believed might be useful for provisioning the Navy.[57] It sought out and arranged trials of new varieties, and commissioned treatises on the results. It offered premiums and placed advertisements to encourage improved cultivation techniques. In 1794 it established a 'Committee on Potatoes', which quizzed bakers on the feasibility of producing potato bread on a commercial scale and answered queries about potatoes from correspondents across Britain.[58] (See figure 9.)

Board members were convinced that potatoes were a sterling crop, providing a reliable, easy and abundant harvest. 'In times of scarcity and distress,' Sinclair stated, 'there is no article comparable to Potatoes.'[59]

The Board's calculations indicted that an acre of potatoes would feed eight to ten people for a year, far more than an equivalent area of wheat. For this reason, 'an increased cultivation of that valuable root, the Potatoe, appears to the Board, to be one of the most important objects, that can possibly be recommended to the attention of British farmers'.[60] The purpose of advising landlords to cultivate more potatoes was to enable ordinary people to eat more potatoes. As the Board explained, their aim was to increase 'regular consumption among the lower classes'.[61] To this end it published a series of pamphlets containing recipes for boiled potatoes, roast potatoes, and, especially, potato bread, a fiddly preparation when made with a high proportion of potatoes. These publications adopted a messianic tone about the potato's merits. In the Scottish Highlands, the Board asserted, the potato was considered 'the greatest blessing that modern times have bestowed on the country'.[62] Like William Buchan, the Board of Agriculture was certain that the potato offered poor people an exceptional opportunity to improve their diet. This, in turn, was a matter 'of great importance in political oeconomy'.[63] Potato consumption, especially by poor people, was a matter of direct political interest.

It is worth recalling that by the 1790s Britons had long been eating potatoes. Already in the 1670s, dictionaries defined the tuber as 'a sort of fruit, coming originally from the West Indies, but now common in English gardens'.[64] A century later its culture 'extended to every county in Great Britain', according to horticultural manuals. Although they were not universally consumed, in areas where fuel was affordable potatoes formed a familiar part of the everyday diet for many working people. The Board itself recognised this in its own publications.[65] Their encouragement of the potato was not based on its absence from the existing food landscape. Rather, their interest in potatoes reflected a new-found conviction that improving the diet of working people was 'of great importance in political oeconomy'.

THE PANEGYRISTS OF THE POTATO

The promotional activities of the British Board of Agriculture were part of an avalanche of potato-enthusiasm that began in the mid-1750s and had engulfed all of Europe by the century's end. Monarchs from Spain's Charles III to Sweden's Adolf Frederick issued edicts encouraging the cultivation of potatoes, in Adolf Frederick's case inspired by experiments on potatoes undertaken at the Swedish Royal Academy of Science.[66] The Neapolitan physician Filippo Baldini and the Swedish merchant Jonas Alströmer composed promotional treatises on their virtues, as did officials in Finland, chemists in France and many others.[67] Newspapers in Copenhagen published testimonial letters encouraging readers to grow potatoes and in England individuals such as the improving landlord and philanthropist John Howard (later famed for his work on prison reform) experimented with new varieties that, Howard hoped, might provide 'great relief & help to a most valuable part of our fellow creatures, the labouring poor in this kingdom'.[68] Priests in Norway and Spain delivered sermons on cultivation techniques and exhorted their parishioners to grow them. Cleric Axel Laurell from Asikkala, in southern Finland, perorated from the pulpit for up to four hours at a time on their merits, and also composed a promotional treatise containing advice on cultivation, as well as a number of recipes.[69] From Turin the physician Antonio Campini reported on the excellent, economical qualities of potatoes, which he proclaimed were:

> one of the best gifts which we have received from America. They provide good, healthy, agreeable and tasty nourishment to country people and their effect is no less favourable to population growth. . . . I saw very few sick soldiers among those who are able to cook potatoes.[70]

Two decades later the Tuileries Garden had been dug up, replaced with potato fields planted on the orders of an enthusiastic Convention Nationale, which hoped thereby to encourage wider cultivation of the root.[71] And in case anyone wondered what to do with all those potatoes, every economical recipe detailed in Hannah More's 1795 *The Cottage Cook; or, Mrs. Jones's Cheap Dishes: Shewing the Way to do Much Good with Little Money* featured the tuber. French readers could consult the equally potato-heavy *Cuisinière républicaine*.[72] (How working people responded to this advice will be probed in the next chapter.)

Certain themes attracted sustained discussion. The best methods of cultivation were a recurrent topic; whether potatoes depleted or enriched the soil was the subject of particular dispute.[73] The related issues of storage and preservation also received attention from agronomists and investigators since the potato's propensity to rot posed practical and technical challenges. Methods ranging from burying the surplus in sand to more complex procedures such as desiccation were evaluated.[74] Regarding the potato's use as an animal food, many investigators concurred that farm animals from horses to chickens thrived on potatoes, and offered recipes for the best mashes.[75] The different ways in which people could consume potatoes were likewise reported. The Irish technique of simmering over very low heat was widely acknowledged as optimal, and pamphlets such as those produced by the Board of Agriculture spelled out how easy it was to prepare tasty and sustaining meals featuring potatoes instead of wheaten bread.[76] Scientists experimented with distilling potato-based spirits, which offered an alternative to grain-based alcohols.[77] Most emblematic of all was the quest for a satisfactory recipe for potato bread. The drive to 'panify' potatoes manifested itself across Europe. The healthfulness and nutritive qualities of such breads were the object of intense, if inconclusive, discussion.[78] Potatoes were moreover declared an excellent artificial feed for infants, and so helped ensure that the population was able to reproduce itself. Ideally, once they were old enough, foundlings could be set to work cultivating their own potatoes on orphanage grounds.[79] (See recipe for Potato Bread.)

Since European countries shared the desire to build strong states that underpinned this new attention to popular diets, interest in the potato transcended national frontiers and languages. Journals and networks of correspondence disseminated this enlightened potato-talk across Europe. The French scientist Antoine Laurent Lavoisier experimented with growing potatoes on his estate in Blois; his findings were promptly reported in Spain by the *Parish Priests' Agriculture and Arts Weekly*, an agricultural journal founded in 1797 with royal support.[80] Both Dublin's Botanical Garden and its Agricultural Society conducted experiments on potatoes on which the newspaper likewise reported.[81] Spain's Charles III moreover funded the publication of an entire book on potato cultivation by the Irishman Henry Doyle.[82] Swiss potato-enthusiasts referenced Swedish agronomists as well

A Spanish Recipe for Potato Bread

In 1797 the parish priest from the Salamancan village of Linares del Riofrío invented a bread recipe that used six pounds of potatoes for every three of wheat. As he explained, his parish grew a great deal of potato but very little wheat; he hoped that a bread requiring less grain would prove beneficial to the poor. The results, he reported, were outstanding. He described the day he first sampled his bread as the happiest in his life. 'It seemed to me,' he recorded, that with the potato 'hunger and poverty would vanish from the face of the earth.'

Potato Bread

'I made an experiment with six pounds of washed, maincrop white potatoes which I cooked until the peels split, which is when they have cooked sufficiently. I then drained and peeled them and crumbled them in a container, breaking them up as much as I could with a strong spatula, but without crushing them so that they remained light. I then added three pounds of wheat flour, as well as a little yeast dissolved in about four ounces of water and a good deal of salt, as potatoes alone are bland. I kneaded it well to combine these substances, and formed a firm dough that did not appear visibly different from a dough made with wheat flour alone. It rose much more and was ready to be placed in the oven just as quickly as a wheat dough. The oven should be a bit hotter than for regular bread.'

as English, French and German treatises on the tuber.[83] English authors translated continental texts on experimental methods of cultivation.[84] The efforts of the Swede Carl Skytte to distil brandy from potatoes were replicated across Europe by enthusiastic amateur chemists, although his surname rarely survived these travels intact.[85]

The potato's advocates made extravagant claims. The Polish writer and statesman Julian Ursyn Niemcewicz declared the tubers to be the 'greatest blessing conferred by heaven', second only to baptism. 'We owe America more gratitude for them than for the precious metals of gold and silver, the fatal implements of greed,' he believed.[86] Claudio Boutelou, head gardener at Madrid's Royal Botanical Garden, agreed that the potato 'is without doubt the most valuable item we have received from the new world', adding that the rest of Europe ought to thank Spain for introducing this botanical treasure.[87] The French scientist Antoine-Alexis Cadet de Vaux likened it to the manna that sustained the Israelites in the desert, likewise sent by a benevolent deity.[88] The editors of a Swiss newspaper described French advances in making potato bread as 'one of the most important discoveries of the century'.[89] And lest anyone imagine such praise was exaggerated, another potato-advocate, the US-born Count Rumford, reminded readers that since schemes to encourage potato consumption aimed ultimately to improve the well-being of the working poor, they were by definition of interest to 'enlightened statesmen'.[90]

Potato-advocates employed a common set of techniques, which typically included premiums, offers of free potatoes, and the dissemination of how-to manuals. Prizes were common. Patriotic individuals and organisations across Europe offered awards for the largest potato crop, the best recipe for potato bread, the most effective remedy for potato diseases. In 1790, Peter Sirkal, a peasant from Lifland, received ten roubles, enough to buy a horse or perhaps two bulls, when he won a competition sponsored by the St Petersburg Free Economic Society for the biggest potato harvest.[91] Similar 'Economic Societies', 'Societies for the Improvement of Husbandry, Manufacture, and Other Useful Arts', and the like, were established in many parts of Europe and its colonial territories from the 1730s, for the purpose of disseminating useful knowledge, particularly about the new agronomic models circulating across Europe that aimed to render agriculture more productive and profitable. (Since these associations rarely included individuals with practical farming experience such as peasants, they tended to reflect the perspective of the landlords, clergymen and officials who comprised the membership. The ambition was usually to disseminate elite knowledge to peasant farmers, rather than the reverse.)[92]

Potatoes attracted the attention of these organisations in many parts of Europe. Members of the society in Erfurt were lectured on how to distil potatoes into alcohol; other German societies published treatises, sponsored competitions, and conducted field trials, all of which revealed the tuber to be an excellent alternative even to high-yielding grains such as buckwheat or rye.[93] In Turku, the Finnish Economical Society energetically encouraged cultivation, distributing seed potatoes free of charge and offering prizes to the most successful potato growers.[94] The Imperial and Royal Academy of Science and the Arts of Brussels, the Monmouthshire Agricultural Society in Wales, the Highland Society in Scotland, and the Royal Economic Society of Aragón did likewise.[95] In 1796, the Aragón Society for instance offered the substantial sum of 300 reales for 'the day labourer who can prove that he and his family have consumed the largest quantity of potatoes'.[96] The Royal Basque Society not only offered prizes but also conducted experiments in potato cultivation and the manufacture of potato bread, and translated a number of agricultural treatises on the potato. As it explained in a 1786 report, the Society had long considered the potato 'one of the most important crops that could be introduced to the benefit of the country'.[97] Far to the east, in the Carpathian mountains, the first Agricultural Society in Transylvania was equally active in encouraging potatoes.[98]

At the heart of these endeavours was a concern with *oeconomy*. *Oeconomy* was the rational management of resources, whether by the individual or the state. It entailed a set of behaviours and values that prioritised restraint and moderation. One could display *oeconomy* in matters ranging from health, personal expenditure and cookery, to the management of a forest. *Oeconomy* linked the actions of individual households – including the foods consumed – to the broader concerns of the polity. It provided a vocabulary for articulating the conviction that even small domestic matters affected the well-being of the state. This is why the

British Board of Agriculture described its promotion of the potato as a matter 'of great importance in political oeconomy'.[99]

To be sure, the potato was not the only plant to attract such attention. Since national well-being required an ample supply of food, individuals and organisations assessed the potential of many other foodstuffs, from the Siberian buckwheat investigated by the Leipzig Economic Society in 1771 to the peanut extract evaluated by the Royal Economic Society of Valencia as a possible substitute for olive oil. Unfamiliar foodstuffs from other parts of the world inspired particular interest; many European states supported programmes of 'economic botany' that aimed to introduce both novel commercial crops and new staple foods into Europe. The botanist Joseph Dombey recommended acclimatising quinoa to France as a substitute for rice. Others championed wild rice, or breadfruits, or sago.[100] The potato, however, was the object of the most sustained and pan-European attention.

According to its advocates, this was because the potato possessed unique virtues. They reported the high yields compared to grains, a point repeated today by the UN and other agencies concerned with world hunger.[101] Cultivation was considered to be straightforward, so that anyone (for instance, Buchan's poor man with a large family) with access to a small piece of ground could easily raise their own. It did not require particularly fertile soil and grew well in all weathers and climates. Promoters insisted it was immensely nourishing, although in the absence of an agreed-upon scientific methodology for assessing a food's nutritive potential, this remained assertion rather than established fact.[102] Proponents emphasised the ease of preparation, and noted that any surplus could be converted into a feed for animals. Children reportedly loved it. Most importantly, promoters stressed that the potato was no novelty, but rather a familiar food eaten regularly by other Europeans. Unlike wild rice or quinoa, potatoes had a long and successful European history, to which potato-promoters specifically alluded. The Scottish merchant Patrick Colquhoun ascribed the success of his London soup kitchen to the fact that it served only familiar foods, including, prominently, the potato. For this reason its users offered 'no complaints on account of [his] introducing a new article of food to which they have not been accustomed'. As he explained, because the potato 'has been long known to many classes of labouring people', there were 'generally few prejudices ... to be combated'.[103] Advocates explained that even if the potato was not eaten in one locality, it was perfectly common elsewhere in Europe. In his many treatises on the potato aimed at French readers, Parmentier for instance carefully explained how it was grown and consumed as an ordinary foodstuff in Holland, Flanders, Lorraine, Alsace, Ireland and Lancashire. The potato's pre-Enlightenment history as an everyday food grown and eaten by labouring peoples thus laid the foundations for its celebration in the eighteenth century as a source of national strength and grandeur.

CONCLUSIONS

The changing status of the potato over the early modern era points to a transformation in the political significance of everyday eating habits. In the seventeenth century the potato's nourishing qualities had annoyed officials and political theorists such as William Petty, who complained that they made it possible for the Irish to get by on only two hours of work a day. 'What need they to work, who can content themselves with potatoes, whereof the labour of one man can feed forty?', he wrote testily.[104] By the eighteenth century this irritating fecundity had become an attraction for 'enlightened statesmen' eager to increase the wealth and power of their nation. The consensus that the well-being of the state depended in part on the health of individuals endowed the eating habits of the working population with political importance.

Writers were explicit about these associations between potatoes, population and political economy. In a treatise published with the support of the Spanish state, the Irish potato-enthusiast Henry (or Enrique) Doyle spelled out the relationship between potatoes and a flourishing economy:

As a population grows and multiplies, so it becomes necessary not only to improve the soil and increase the area under cultivation, but also to take advantage of other roots, plants and vegetables suited to the quality of the land and suitable for ordinary people to eat to sustain themselves, in order to keep commerce in balance at moderate prices at all times. Writers agree that the potato supplies this necessary help both because it is abundant and cheap, and also because it is healthful.[105]

Throughout his oft-reprinted treatise, which by 1804 had swelled to over 250 pages, Doyle stressed that although the potato was eaten with pleasure by the wealthy, its utility lay fundamentally in its potential as a food for working people. He reiterated that it was highly nourishing, and that potato-eaters were 'healthy and robust'. Like many others, he cited the hearty Irish peasant as evidence for the potato's healthful, sustaining qualities. Moreover, because these peasants consumed potatoes, Ireland was able to export millions of pounds of wheat, to the benefit of landowners and the treasury.[106] A working population subsisting on potatoes therefore fuelled agricultural and commercial success, at least from the perspective of the state and large landowners.

The connections between potatoes and a strong state were also demonstrated by the potato's potential as a food for soldiers. Doyle drew attention to the potato's popularity among regimental troops in Madrid. Further adding to its appeal was its ability to promote lactation in nursing mothers, and to provide a suitable substitute for breast-milk. Spain's economic and political well-being, Doyle concluded, depended not only on the government but also on the 'zeal and vigilance of good patriots' who promoted potato consumption by the poor.[107] Doyle's treatise encapsulates the new connections between the robustness of individual members of the population and the overall health and stability of the state and its commerce. In contrast to seventeenth-century political theorists, Doyle and the other eighteenth-century panegyrists of the potato viewed its nourishing qualities as an immense advantage to the state.

*

These links, forged in the eighteenth century, between the daily eating practices of ordinary people and the well-being of the state emerged at a moment when the relationship between all sorts of discrete, disconnected actions and larger impersonal forces was attracting sustained attention. Might the random movements of small physical particles form themselves into meaningful sequences? Could the urgent wishes and desires of the individual be harmonised with the well-being of the larger polity? How should trade and commerce be arranged so as to bring the greatest benefits? Philosophers, mathematicians, botanists and many others were fascinated by such processes of 'self-organization' – the ways in which order emerged out of the seeming disorder of myriad uncoordinated events.[108] The next chapter traces the connections eighteenth-century political philosophers began to perceive between dietary and economic self-organisation. Might the same hidden hand that guided the market also direct the dietary preferences of individuals? By the century's end the conviction that individual eating practices affected the nation's wealth and strength had merged with new ideas about economic self-organisation through market liberalisation. From this merger arose a happy vision of successful dietary self-organisation, in which the very things that led to personal well-being simultaneously proved beneficial to society overall.

CHAPTER 3

Free-Market Potatoes

We cannot practically speak about happiness without considering *whose* happiness it is we mean.[1]

THE CHALLENGES OF HARMONISING INDIVIDUAL FREEDOMS with the public good have long troubled philosophers and political thinkers. This matter lies at the heart of most political theory today, from John Rawls' theory of justice to Charles Taylor's critique of atomism, as he called the 'vision of society as in some sense constituted by individuals for the fulfilment of ends which were primarily individual'.[2] It is also a matter of immediate practical concern to politicians today. Recurrent skirmishes over the regulation of food and drink illustrate clearly that attempts to prioritise public health over individual autonomy usually attract criticism as well as praise. Google 'nanny state' and you will find hundreds of thousands of sites denouncing efforts to influence public health through government regulation. The 'Nanny State Index' for example ranks European nations from 'freest' to 'least free' according to the level of taxation on alcohol, tobacco and vaping. In 2017 it determined that Finland was the 'least free' country in Europe, well ahead of (or depending on your perspective, behind) the UK, which ranked second. The Czech Republic was deemed the freest, as a result of its low taxes on spirits and cigarettes.[3] 'Move over, Big Brother!', urged journalist David Harsanyi in a book on how 'food fascists, teetotaling do-gooders, priggish moralists, and other boneheaded bureaucrats are turning America into a nation of children'.[4] Such commentators, and the voters who share their views, believe that if a choice must be made between letting people eat and drink at will, or limiting their range of options, then the principles of liberal democracy demand that they be left to their own devices. Opponents counter that the consequences will be worse for everyone. Arguing in favour of increased taxation on sugary drinks, an article in the influential *New England Journal of Medicine* for instance enumerated the economic and public health benefits that the United States would derive from a reduction in sugar consumption. The 'escalating health care costs and the rising burden of diseases related to poor diet create an urgent need for solutions, thus justifying government's right to recoup costs', its authors argue.[5] When it comes to individual eating practices, balancing the competing claims of autonomy and the public good is no easy matter.

But what if there were no conflict in the first place? What if the healthiest and most beneficial foods were also the tastiest? This is exactly what advocates of the potato claimed in the eighteenth century. Just as the framers of the new discipline of political economy believed that, ultimately, there was no conflict between allowing individuals to conduct their own economic affairs and the well-being of the larger economic whole, so potato-promoters maintained that the potatoes required to build a strong and prosperous state were the very thing that poor people would themselves choose to eat. All that was needed was an educational campaign and an increase in availability. Potato-promoters accordingly published little pamphlets, and sometimes entire cookbooks, proffering 'hints' on the best ways of eating potatoes and other healthy foods.[6] The many prizes and premiums offered to the labourer who harvested or consumed the largest crop were likewise aimed at enabling, rather than obliging, individuals to act in their own self-interest. To many enthusiasts potatoes provided a concrete example of how self-interest, the proposed motor of a well-functioning economy, dissolved any tensions between individual rights and public good. They represented everything that the proponents of *laissez-faire* and the market advocated.

Potatoes accomplished this by being delicious. The benefits that potatoes were said to bring to the individual thus transcended their ability to suppress hunger. Potatoes, their advocates insisted, produced happiness. This was important since making the population happy was a fundamental duty of the state, according to enlightened theories of governance. That potatoes made people happy was therefore both a motivation for individuals to eat potatoes, and also a way for the state to fulfil this obligation. The potato's happiness potential had political significance.

By presenting the consumption of recommended foods as a matter of individual self-interest, these eighteenth-century debates laid the foundations for today's insistence that personal eating practices should be understood within the framework of informed choice. We, as 'choosing subjects', are expected to make decisions about what we eat based on our own evaluation of what is best for us. Faced with criticism in 2018 that it was encouraging obesity and ill-health through its marketing of sugary snacks, the biscuit manufacturer McVitie's defended itself by explaining that it provided plenty of information about its products, which enabled consumers to make 'informed snacking choices'.[7] Informed choices were precisely what eighteenth-century potato-advocates claimed to encourage.

Ideas articulated in the eighteenth century also helped lay the foundations for the belief that attempts to shape our diets through more direct state intervention are a violation of our right as individuals to direct our own affairs. By paying attention to the economic discourses circulating at the same time as eighteenth-century potato-promotion, we can see more clearly how, from the first, the notion that individual eating practices are of national concern was entangled in disputes about the degree of agency, and responsibility, individuals should have for their own, as we might say today, dietary choices.

This chapter first reviews the personal benefits and pleasures ascribed to a potato-heavy diet, which were considered sufficiently powerful as to motivate individuals to eat potatoes quite independently from the larger political and economic advantages thought to derive from greater potato consumption. The chapter then connects this focus on dietary self-interest to the new language of political economy, which likewise identified the individual pursuit of happiness as the bedrock of national well-being. These connections reflect the fundamental but largely unrecognised importance of eating within eighteenth-century debates over political economy. It is worth recalling that much discussion of free trade focused not on commerce in general, but specifically on the trade in grain, Europe's primary foodstuff. Proposals to liberalise trading regulations, interest in the eating habits of the population, and a rhetoric of choice did not simply run in parallel but were inherently interconnected in the new, eighteenth-century models of individualism and effective statecraft.

CHOOSING POTATOES

The potato, so its eighteenth-century supporters insisted, offered many advantages to the individual at the same time as it strengthened and enriched the state. To begin with, it could end hunger and poverty. With the potato, as a Scottish agricultural text put it, 'the poor can never be said to want food'. William Buchan, the Scottish physician and advocate of potato gardens, encapsulated the happy situation resulting from greater potato consumption: 'men would multiply, and poverty, unless among the profligate, be unknown'.[8] (We will return to the situation of the profligate at a later point.) More than that, potatoes brought pleasure. A consistent feature of eighteenth-century potato-talk was the assertion that potatoes would promote happiness at the same time as they relieved hunger. The improving landlord and potato-promoter Pietro Maria Bignami did not argue only that the potato would make Bologna wealthier. Potatoes would also render it happier, so that his homeland would become the 'richest and happiest in all of Italy'. Writing from the Veneto in the same years, Antonio Zanon, one of the founders of the Society for Practical Agriculture in Udine and author of many texts on economic and agricultural matters, agreed the potato was a source of 'happiness and opulence'.[9] Frederick Eden, writing in the 1790s, summed up this optimistic view of the tuber. The spread of potato cultivation, he wrote, was 'perhaps as strong an instance of the extension of human enjoyment as can be mentioned'.[10] Both the individual and the polity as a whole would benefit from this potato happiness effect. If poor people were to eat more potatoes and other nourishing vegetables, a French cookery book stated, they themselves would be healthier at the same time as their more energetic bodies would better contribute to the glory and prosperity of the state: 'what comfort for them! What happiness for the Nation!'[11]

Potatoes made people happy because they were a pleasure to eat, or so their advocates maintained. For proof one need look no further than the natural inclinations of small children, who adored potatoes, according to the French potato-promoter Antoine Augustin Parmentier. This also showed how well-suited they were to the human digestive system, and moreover spread happiness even more widely from the contented eater to the satisfied onlookers. What pleasure it must accord an impoverished father, mused another potato-enthusiast, to provide his children with a foodstuff that so perfectly matched their dietary needs. Proponents described potato-based recipes as tasty, even luxurious.[12] French writers saluted this 'delicious, prolific and healthful root' as evidence for the existence of a benign deity. Promoters across Europe explained how the most inveterate opponents – usually opinionated labourers – were converted to the tuber once they had been induced to taste it.[13] Rational consideration combined with sensory pleasure should lead everyone, but especially the working poor, to embrace the potato of their own volition. The combination of these individual happiness-inducing choices would in turn lead to a stronger and more successful nation. Self-interest and the interests of the state ran in perfect harmony.

It is no coincidence that these notions emerged at the moment that the tenets of political economy were being developed. The best way to ensure flourishing commerce, its advocates insisted, was to let people look after their own well-being. As Adam Smith argued, if individuals were enabled to do this, the confluence of myriad self-interested actions would form a well-functioning economic system. Writing in 1776, he explained that although individuals generally sought only their own economic advantage, this usually resulted in the population as a whole being 'the happiest and the most comfortable'.[14] Indeed, allowing individuals to pursue their own advantage was more likely than direct interventions to produce such an outcome. In Smith's opinion, 'by pursuing his own interest [a man] frequently promotes that of the society more effectually than when he really intends to promote it'.[15] The individual pursuit of personal advantage thus lay behind a successful economy, which would in turn deliver greater happiness to all. Such ideas began to be expressed in the late seventeenth century, at the same time that theorists began to suggest that a well-fed population was one component in the wealth and strength of the state. The two notions emerged in tandem.

To insist that hunger alone should be sufficient to motivate the poor to eat potatoes reflected the material fact that the potato offered a filling alternative to more expensive grains, at least in those parts of Europe where it was grown in quantity. To affirm that it was a *delicious* alternative implied something more: that individuals might choose to eat potatoes not because they were hungry, but because potatoes were a source of happiness and comfort. Eating potatoes was, in the view of potato-advocates, a pleasant way of advancing one's own well-being while also contributing to the well-being of the nation. On the whole, ordinary people were rarely considered competent to evaluate more weighty matters of state. As the Spanish playwright Nicolás Fernández de Moratín put it, 'ignorant people should know that they are not qualified to make decisions about matters they do not understand, and that when those who have studied these matters speak, they should maintain the most profound silence'.[16] Even such people, however, could probably be trusted to determine whether they enjoyed a particular foodstuff. Gustatory pleasure was an arena where 'ignorant people' were believed to be capable of exercising some judgement, at least when it came to potatoes. The result was a stronger and wealthier state, or so the potato's advocates suggested. 'What comfort for them! What happiness for the Nation!' Here was the dietary equivalent of Smith's invisible hand.

POLITICAL ECONOMY, SELF-INTEREST AND THE SUPPLY OF FOOD

The challenge of marrying self-interest with the well-being of the broader polity preoccupied eighteenth-century economic writers. During the previous century some commentators had begun to suggest that the selfish actions of individuals could prove beneficial if they stimulated commerce or encouraged the invention of new luxuries; Bernard Mandeville's polemical *Fable of the Bees* (1714) presented this argument in the compelling format of rhymed verse. Luxury, he wrote, 'employ'd a Million of the Poor and odious Pride a Million more'. Others proposed that the potentially disruptive forces of individual ambition and avarice would keep each other in check, creating an unstable equilibrium that was ultimately beneficial to the polity. Writing in 1744, the Italian philosopher Giambattista Vico for instance maintained that 'out of the passions of men each bent on his private advantage', divine providence had fashioned a civil order that enabled all to live together in society. 'It turns out that everyone contributes to the general welfare while thinking that he works for his own interests,' stated the French philosopher Montesquieu in 1748. Over the century these ideas, originating largely in the realm of politics, were increasingly employed to analyse the inter-connections between political and economic matters. Montesquieu for instance maintained that the desire for economic gain that motivated international trade worked to reduce political conflict.[17]

Precisely how to align private economic gain with public benefit was a conundrum addressed repeatedly over the century. Particular dispute was provoked by state regulation of trade. A growing number of writers argued that attempts to control commerce through tariffs or other means interfered with the beneficial effects of the individual desire for profit. Not only were such interventions unhelpful, they were perhaps doomed to failure. Victor Riqueti, Marquis de Mirabeau, expressed this view with particular clarity: a prince's role, he stated, was not 'the art of leading men'. Rather, he explained:

> it is the art of providing for their security and for their subsistence through observance of the natural order and physical laws constituting the natural law and economic order, and by means of which existence and subsistence might be assured to Nations and to every man in particular; this object fulfilled, the conducting of men is determined, and each man leads himself.[18]

Riqueti was a follower of physiocracy, the economic model advanced by François Quesnay, physician to Madame de Pompadour and an immensely influential advocate of economic deregulation. Physiocracy offered a theory for explaining economic exchange premised on two beliefs: that humans were governed by an innate desire for personal gain, and that the workings of the economy followed certain fundamental natural laws. These laws could be ignored, but they could not be overturned. The role of the state was, so physiocrats believed, to align its policy with the natural order and allow private interests to operate unhindered, thereby ensuring the good of all. The self-interest of monarchs should therefore lead them to permit qualified individuals to pursue their own economic ambitions unhindered by regulations.[19]

Debate about the merits of market regulation revolved largely around the grain trade.[20] In the view of physiocrats, who stressed that economic growth derived from agriculture alone, the numerous restrictions on the trade in cereals provided the clearest example of the pernicious consequences of departing from the natural laws that governed all exchange. Regulating the food supply, and in particular the grain market, had long been considered a moral obligation of government. The movement of grain and its pricing were often controlled, in the hope of preventing shortages, and the 'hoarding' or speculative buying of grain was frequently banned. City officials also inspected the quality and pricing of food sold at markets. This long-standing system of control over price, movement and quality was premised on the view that the state had a duty to avert sickness and famine, as well as reflecting concerns over the political conse-quences of food shortage. Advocates of the new political economy such as Quesnay insisted that this approach was counter-productive, and likely to provoke the very shortages it aimed to prevent, because it encouraged farmers to produce only the quantity of grain they could be certain of selling. Physiocrats advocated leaving the market to resolve matters of pricing and supply. This, they hoped, would ensure more stable prices and, in the long run, a more reliable supply. They believed, in sum, that the political imperative of ensur-ing a robust economy and population was best managed by allowing individual commercial interests freer rein.

Physiocratic ideas about the importance of supporting agriculture and overhauling the tax system influenced policy in many regions, even if, to the annoyance of physiocrats, their recommendations were often implemented piecemeal. Monarchs from Gustavus III of Sweden, to Charles Frederick, the Grand Duke of Baden, experimented with phy-siocratically inspired legislation and on occasion corresponded directly with important *économistes*, as physiocrats called themselves. In France Quesnay and his followers achieved considerable influence in the gov-ernment of Louis XV during the 1760s–70s, which they used to imple-ment their central aim of deregulating the grain trade. Controls over both the domestic movement of grain and overseas exports were relaxed first in 1763 and 1764, and again in 1774, to disastrous effect, and were on both occasions quickly reinstated. In Spain Charles III replicated these laws in 1765, and, when faced with high prices and public protest, also revoked them. Various Italian states made similar, equally unsuccessful, attempts.[21] These early experiments in *laissez-faire* economics were thus explicitly concerned, not with trade in general, but specifically with the trade in food. Criticism of this approach, such as the influential *Dialogues on the Grain Trade* by the Neapolitan abbé Ferdinando Galiani, similarly focused on the disadvantages of the free trade in grain. Food was central to the debate about political economy, just as it was to the new ideas about governance.

Eighteenth-century writers on economic matters recognised that managing commerce was not separate from the task of building a healthy and happy population. Quesnay for instance was absolutely clear about the connections he perceived between free trade, food, happiness and the wealth of the state. In an influential essay on farmers in the *Encyclopédie*, he maintained that if his ideas were implemented, France's inhabitants would become wealthier, and their increased resources would 'provide them with better food, satisfy their needs, render them happy, increase the population [and] raise the revenue of landowners and the state'.[22] All that was required, in his view, was for governments to cease interfering in the grain trade, and make a few adjustments to the overall system of taxation. In short, interest in the best way of organising economic circulation was powerfully motivated by the specific need to ensure an adequate supply of food, and also by the conviction that an adequate food supply would spread happiness, particularly among the poor. The best way to ensure both was to allow individuals to pursue their own self-interest, or so it was increasingly asserted.

An equivalent emphasis on the rational pursuit of personal well-being shaped discussions of the eating habits of the working people whose alimentary preferences had become a matter of such political concern. At the core of both was the question of whether a system guided by the individual pursuit of happiness and self-interest might prove the most effective way of aligning the disparate members of a polity into a smoothly functioning whole. Labourers might lack expertise to judge their own economic interests, and they surely lacked authority to intervene in matters of state, but they were could probably be trusted to recognise a tasty meal. This, at least, was the claim of many potato-enthusiasts.

THE SOUP OF HAPPINESS

Nowhere is this clearer than in discussions of potato soup. The eighteenth century was awash with recipes for 'economical soup'. These soups combined a starchy base, often provided by potatoes, with a small amount of meat and some pungent seasoning. Stews and pottages had long been staples of the plebeian diet, and often featured in the meals served at poorhouses and other institutions in earlier centuries.[23] As the working-class diet acquired ever-greater political significance over the eighteenth century, stews and soups became not simply commonly eaten foods, but also a subject of public discourse. Cookbooks explained to the home philanthropist how to prepare them for distribution to the poor, and individual cooks copied the details into their personal collections. One such mixture of beef, rice, potatoes, carrots, turnips, leeks, celery, thyme and parsley boiled in thirteen gallons of water was described by the woman who transcribed it into a notebook as 'a wholesome good broth made at a very reasonable rate, to feed the poor in the country'.[24] Newspapers published recipes, and correspondents discussed their merits and offered suggestions for improvement. Governments distributed leaflets explaining how to prepare such soups for either personal consumption or large-scale distribution.[25] Patriotic individuals and institutions established soup kitchens serving charity meals to the deserving poor, and offered premiums for the labourer who could invent 'the most wholesome and nutritious soup, costing not more than 5d. a gallon', which he and his family themselves consumed.[26] Cheap soup had entered the public sphere. (See recipe for A Mess for 25 Soldiers.)

A Mess for 25 Soldiers

In the eighteenth century wealthy Europeans started to take an interest in the starchy soups and pottages that had been sustaining ordinary people for thousands of years. Such nourishing foods would help build a robust population of energetic workers, or so they hoped. This brief recipe for potato-beef soup was copied into a notebook by someone living at the Manor House in Hayes, Middlesex, in the late eighteenth century. They noted that it would feed twenty-five soldiers for a mere tuppence a serving. This recipe was followed by a leek-free variant, and another described as 'a wholesome good broth made at a very reasonable rate, to feed the poor in the country'.

A Mess for 25 Soldiers at 2d each

4 gallons of water
2 qts good split-peas
6 lb brisket of beef
6 heads of celery
6 leeks and 6 onions
parsley & thyme
6 lb of potatoes
pepper & salt
bread

Elite interest in soup kitchens was particularly intense in the last decade of the century, when a combination of war, population growth and poor harvests led to serious shortages. From the 1750s growing populations put increasing pressure on the supply of grain, which had not kept pace with demand. In England, for instance, per capita wheat production fell from 5.9 bushels, in 1750, to 4.6 by 1800. Perturbations in weather caused by the El Niño effect likely exacerbated the situation.[27] Food prices rose significantly. The mobilisation of millions of people during the revolutionary wars of the 1790s moreover removed workers from agriculture at the same time as it increased the demand for wheat and the other staples required to feed the military. The popular dissatisfaction caused by rising food prices combined with the spread of revolutionary sentiments in ways that alarmed governments across the continent. 'The Jacobin papers', warned a British parliamentary committee, were filled with 'the most gross abuse against government, on account of the high price of bread, with a view of instigating the mob to acts of riot, under the supposition that there has been gross misconduct in those who have the direction of public affairs and that they have not taken the necessary precautions to avert this serious calamity'.[28] The establishment of charitable soup kitchens was seen as a practical contribution to ensuring social and political tranquillity. From the Lancashire town of Clitheroe, the antiquarian and curate Thomas Wilson reported in 1800 that 'soup shops have been established in most of the larger towns and good nutritious soup was distributed at a penny a quart. This was certainly a proper mode of providing for the poor.' Wilson complained that the beneficiaries of this largesse were in general ungrateful. They objected that the proffered soup did not agree with them, and that they could ill afford the time it took to fetch the soup home from the distribution centre. Such, Wilson concluded, 'is the difficulty of dealing with the lower orders of people, who are incapable of judging right, and who cannot be convinced that they are wrong'.[29]

Wilson was not alone in claiming that these soups were not always met with the enthusiasm to which their great nutritional merits were thought to entitle them. Writing in 1797, Frederick Eden, historian of the English working classes, recorded sadly that poor people across England's southern counties had an almost insuperable aversion to cheap soup. 'Their common outcry', he reported, was 'this is washy stuff, that affords no nourishment: we will "not be fed on meal, and chopped potatoes, like hogs!"'.[30] In some cities charity kitchens attracted a large clientele – the establishment in Geneva was reportedly serving 1,200 bowls each day, one for every twenty inhabitants – but it is clear that the reception of these soups varied, even during periods of real shortage.[31]

Nonetheless, a loud pan-European chorus insisted that far from being disdained, these soups were eaten with pleasure by their intended consumers. The physician (and nonconformist minister) Theophilus Lobb explained in his 1767 collection of frugal recipes that a dinner of any of the stews and pottages he described 'will be very nourishing, healthful and agreeable to the palate'. A French recipe from the same years noted explicitly that 'our peasants found this soup to be excellent'. Addressing a House of Commons committee in 1800, the agricultural campaigner Arthur Young first explained how to make an experimental soup containing the leanest possible meat, and then stated that this 'made most excellent soup, which the poor relished exceedingly'.[32] Such assertions are not impartial evaluations of the overall popularity of cheap soup. For many consumers, potato soup neither assuaged their hunger nor made them happy, and they demonstrated this through the complaints and agitation that Eden and the curate of Clitheroe recorded. The insistence that these soups were a source of pleasure sought to obscure this reality while at the same time preserving the belief that self-interest would organise individual eating habits into something that supported the state's larger aims. The happiness supposedly provided by potato soup formed part of a larger *political* vision.

That it was the duty of the state to make subjects happy was little short of a banality during the Enlightenment. 'It is undeniable, or at least I have reason to believe that in this enlightened century it is a universally recognised truth, that the first object of any government is to make its people happy,' stated the Marquis de Chastellux in a treatise on happiness.[33] Writers across Europe devoted immense energy to dissecting the nature and sources of happiness, whose pursuit on earth was, in the words of the historian Darrin McMahon, 'the great goal of the century'. It was widely affirmed that promoting public felicity was consistent with, or perhaps constituted, the highest aim of the state. Whether the 'happiness of the people' was enhanced directly by official policies, or indirectly by generalised economic improvement, itself supported by sensible statecraft, philosophers and officials agreed that no state could be successful if it did not pursue this task. Prussia's Frederick the Great insisted that the principal objective of a king must therefore be to augment the 'happiness and felicity' of the people he governed. Concurring voices resonated across the continent.[34] The happiness of the working population, as well as their bodily strength, was thus, in theory, of direct relevance to the power and wealth of the state.

Quite how a state should accomplish this central goal was a topic of sustained discussion. One way to bind individual felicity to *félicité publique* was food. Of course hungry people were likely to be unhappy, as Malthus observed, and unhappy people were liable to be discontented with the political status quo, but the capacity of food to increase both individual and public happiness greatly exceeded the negative potential of food shortages to provoke unhappiness. An ample supply of nourishing food directly increased happiness, and happy subjects were, in Michel Foucault's words, 'the very strength of the state'.[35] This is why the Board of Agriculture described its efforts to increase Britain's food supply as 'laying the foundations for [Britain's] future prosperity and happiness'.[36] Contented eaters were theorised as one component of a set of processes that resulted in a strong, secure state.

The power of this assemblage linking nutritious food, good governance and happiness is reflected in the persistent eighteenth-century efforts to quantify it. Quantification, that 'quintessential form of modern thought', spread rapidly across many areas of eighteenth-century life, from cookbooks, which increasingly included measurements alongside a description of the ingredients and method, to the management of forests. Quantification offered an authoritative new language for analysing the world; presenting the components of happiness mathematically underscored the importance of their interconnections, as well as adding precision.[37] Efforts to create a 'felicific calculus' that linked these factors were common. The Irish philosopher Francis Hutcheson produced a complicated arithmetical formula for measuring the relationship between virtue, evil and happiness, expressed as a series of equations. The youthful Spanish military officer Theodoro Ventura de Argumossa y Gandara proposed in a treatise on political economy that the number of people whom a statesman had made happy, multiplied by the obstacles he had overcome to achieve this, constituted 'the arithmetic expression' of his glory and fame. This quantifying spirit enabled the Marquis de Chastellux to construct an 'index of happiness', which demonstrated that the inhabitants of regions with an abundant supply of wholesome food were the happiest.[38] Plentiful food led, mathematically and philosophically, to happiness, and happiness led to a stronger state. The pleasure derived from potato soup was of direct political relevance.

The century's most famous soup was invented by Benjamin Thompson. Born in Massachusetts in the 1750s, Thompson left North America during the American Revolution, when his support for the loyalist cause made his departure expedient. After a spell working for the British military he served as an adviser to Karl Theodor, the elector of Bavaria. Thompson's brief was extensive. While in Munich Thompson reorganised the Bavarian army and established what he called a 'House of Industry', a sort of internment camp for beggars and the indigent. It was in recognition of these efforts that Karl Theodor awarded him the title of Count Rumford, and the transformation of Bavaria's poor into productive soldier-citizens remained an abiding concern for both Rumford and his employer. Rumford's interests, however, extended far beyond poor relief, to include the design of cannon, experiments into the nature of heat, improved chimneys, soldiers' clothing and more. He was a well-known public figure, whose varied activities inspired the character of General Tilney in Jane Austen's 1818 *Northanger Abbey*.[39] (See figure 10.)

A central element of Rumford's programme for converting the poor into useful Bavarians was food. As he explained, his experience of running the Munich poorhouse provided him with ample opportunity to identify the 'the *cheapest*, most *savoury*, and most *nourishing* Food'. This proved to be 'a soup composed of *pearl barley, pease, potatoes, cuttings of fine wheaten bread*, vinegar – salt and water', boiled together for three hours. Potatoes constituted the core of the recipe, which required two parts of potatoes for every one of barley with dried peas.[40] Rumford calculated the cost of preparing his soup in great detail, but he made clear that simple economy was not his sole focus. The soup also needed to be tasty. Citing Hippocrates, he insisted that 'whatever pleases the palate nourishes'. This was why his soup demanded croutons. Croutons, he explained, required extended chewing. Chewing aided digestion because it generated saliva, but for Rumford its importance transcended

Figure 10 Caricature of Count Rumford in front of his specially designed fireplace. Benjamin Thompson, Count Rumford, was a prolific inventor and famed promoter of potato soups for the poor. He is shown here in front of his thermodynamically improved stove, warming his bottom.

this role in the digestive process. Chewing also increased happiness, because it 'prolongs the duration of the enjoyment of eating, a matter of very great importance indeed, and which has not hitherto been sufficiently attended to'. Seizing the moral high ground, Rumford insisted that most people dismissed the notion that the poor were entitled to happiness, but he did not. 'The enjoyments which fall to the lot of the bulk of mankind are not so numerous as to render an attempt to increase them superfluous', he observed piously.[41] His potato soup, with its croutons, would cheer up even the most miserable of Munich's beggars.

It is pretty clear that the croutons were a way of eking out a small amount of soup (Rumford believed that a twenty-ounce serving provided an ample meal), and it is anyone's guess how much Munich's beggars truly enjoyed his creation. Rumford, however, harboured no doubts. He reiterated that the pleasure derived from this soup was an essential part of its utility, and potatoes played a key role in making his soup a gastronomic success. He alleged that since Munich's poor had at first been hostile to potatoes, he had initially added them to the soup 'by stealth ... to prevent their being detected'. The potatoes, however, so improved his soup that 'the Poor ... testified their approbation of the change ... generally and loudly, and they are now grown so fond of potatoes that they would not easily be satisfied without them'. Of course, he observed, everyone recognised the importance of keeping down costs, but this should never come at the expense of the pleasure of eating, even among the most needy. Fortunately, Rumford reported, the potatoes reduced the cost of his soup considerably, so no such concessions were in fact required.[42]

The gastronomic delights resulting from Rumford's soup are beautifully evoked in an article published in 1800 in Paris in the *Philosophical, Literary and Political Decade,* a periodical closely linked to the French government. Authored by the chemist, colleague of Parmentier, and fellow potato-promoter Antoine-Alexis Cadet de Vaux, the article recounted a conversation between Cadet de Vaux and a gourmandising friend. Cadet de Vaux's friend described the luxurious meal he had eaten the previous night, which included vol-au-vents, several chops, an elaborate assemblage of partridge with truffles, a mackerel, some 'admirable' petits pois and an entire bottle of Volnay. Not surprisingly, this feast was followed by the horrors of digestion and an attack of gout. Cadet de Vaux and his friend agreed that the newly fashionable 'restaurants' that offered such fare were scarcely worthy of the name, since far from restoring health they seriously undermined it.[43]

Cadet de Vaux suggested that they visit a different sort of establishment, a true restaurant, where they could obtain a meal that was at once delicious and genuinely restorative. The following day the Parisians presented themselves at 16 rue du Mail, where they were welcomed by a sign reading: 'Rumford soup. Good for one soup, from mid-day to two o'clock'. The friends entered and sat down to dine, served by the neat and charitable ladies who volunteered at the soup kitchen. On trying the soup Cadet de Vaux's bon vivant companion pronounced it 'not good, but *excellent*'. Over their economical but delicious meal the friends discussed the ways in which it was possible to vary the soup's ingredients to avoid tedium, and concurred that it would be beneficial were such soups served to soldiers in place of the disagreeable food usually dished up. They expressed the hope that rural people would grow more potatoes, barley, and other healthful plants necessary to make such tasty soups, which would also allow them reduce their consumption of bread. That, in turn, would permit France to export more grain and increase its wealth. They concluded their meal praising Count Rumford, whose remarkable soup was able to satisfy the demanding palate of a gourmand, while at the same time contributing to France's economic well-being and strengthening its military might. Cadet de Vaux's parable moved smoothly from an account of the gustatory pleasure afforded by Rumford's soup, to the greater flourishing of the French state. Individual self-interest and the greater good met in a bowl of soup.

Rumford's writings, and his vinegary soup, swept across Europe. His essay on feeding the poor (including the chapter titled 'Of the Pleasure of Eating, and of the Means that May be Employed for Increasing it') was widely translated and reprinted. Individuals from Napoleon to the president of Britain's Board of Agriculture praised his recipes, as well as his patent stove, which facilitated the prolonged cooking his soup required. The war year of the 1790s saw the creation of Rumford-inspired charitable kitchens in many European cities. Rumford himself set one up at the London Foundling Hospital in 1796; by 1800 there were nearly fifty such establishments in the capital alone. More were formed in other German cities beyond Munich, and in Switzerland, Italy, Sweden, Spain and France; in 1802 Paris counted over twenty. When the director of Geneva's Hôpital Général read about Rumford's innovations in a French journal, he travelled to Munich to study the soup distribution in person; on his return he oversaw the establishment of a large kitchen funded by public subscription.[44]

In Spain, the soup attracted the interest of both philanthropic elites and the state. Patriotic organisations translated extracts of Rumford's essays, while the state-funded *Parish Priests' Agricultural and Arts Weekly* provided regular updates on its own experiments with Rumfordesque soups.[45] Charity kitchens were created in various Spanish cities. In Valencia, the local Economic Society, inspired by accounts in the press, determined to set up its own establishment. They carefully compared reports by Rumford's acolytes in different parts of Europe, and charged two members with replicating his methods. Rumford's original recipe was quickly dismissed as excessively bland, so the Society set about adapting it to the Spanish palate. This was accomplished by varying the recipe in several ways that, the Society explained, increased the 'pleasure in eating'. Pleasure was as important as nourishment, in the Society's view. The Society tested its experimental recipes on inmates detained in the city's San Narciso prison. Given the importance they, like Rumford, placed on ensuring that the soup be eaten with pleasure, the Society was delighted to report that their third variant was a success. This version, which proved both the cheapest and the most popular, contained potatoes, barley, beans, onions, oil, salt, mint and hot peppers. It was, in the Society's words, 'best adapted to the local taste, according to the view of the majority of those who tasted it'. The prisoners allegedly loved it, and wanted to eat it every day.[46] (See figure 11.)

The Economic Society in Madrid pursued a similar line of investigation when it determined in 1803 to distribute Rumford soup, in response to that year's poor wheat harvest. Its president, the Marquis

	Rs. ms. vn.
Harina de Cebada. 30 onz. 1	12
Abichuelas. . . . 30 onz.	31
Patatas. . . . . . 6 lib. 1	14
Pan. . . . . 30 onz. 1	9
Sal. . . . . 8 onz. . . .	6
Aceyte. . . . . . 8 onz.	30
Cebollas 3.	2
Hierba buena y pimiento picante . .	2
Agua. 50 libras.	
Leña. 24 libras. 1	
	7 4

Figure 11 Recipe for the Valencia Economic Society's Soup Number Three. Over the autumn of 1800 Valencia's Economic Society pondered the ideal recipe for potato soup. After some experimentation its learned members settled on a version that combined six pounds of potatoes with smaller quantities of barley flour, beans, dry bread and seasonings. The resulting soup was both inexpensive and, in their view, delicious. They served it to inmates of the local prison.

de Fuerte Híjar, formed a commission, which met daily during the autumn to consider the best location for the distribution centre and the ideal composition of the soup. The original German recipe was again rejected as completely unsuited to Spanish tastes. As the president explained, no one, no matter how hungry, could derive 'pleasure, happiness and satisfaction' from a meal that was not suited to the local palate. After some experimentation the Society settled on a recipe that consisted of six parts of potatoes to one part of dried beans, along with smaller quantities of onion, garlic, cumin, sweet and hot paprika, oil, vinegar and salt. The seasonings were to be fried in oil, ground up, and then added along with the vinegar to the previously boiled potatoes and beans. This produced a thick potato soup that cost a paltry seven *maravedíes* per portion. Variant recipes included peas or barley flour in place of the beans, as well as vegetables such as Swiss chard. Potato dumplings could also be added. Like the Valencian society, the Madrid team tested their recipe on increasingly large numbers of the poor, and adapted the recipes in light of the responses. As a result, the Society was confident that its soups 'pleased the Spanish taste'.[47]

Similar pleasure-increasing modifications were effected across Europe. French charity kitchens adapted the soup to the local palate by replacing Rumford's vinegar not with the cumin, paprika and olive oil used in Spain, but rather parsley, thyme, bay leaf and a different type of crouton. French newspapers reported that Rumford himself had inspected Parisian kitchens and personally endorsed these alterations because they improved the soup's taste. In Neufchâtel the potatoes were omitted entirely, 'because the poor preferred rice, barley, peas and pasta'. The Trieste soup was seasoned with *pesto di lardo*, a local speciality.[48] An 1802 guide to establishing a soup kitchen summed up the centrality of pleasure to the success of the enterprise. 'The most important matter', it stated, 'is to ensure that the soup is economical, that it is tasty and that it is healthful.'[49]

In an important investigation of food in eighteenth-century France the historian Emma Spary suggested that soup-promoters assumed that when it came to feeding the poor, 'criteria such as habit or preference could be factored out in alimentary calculations'.[50] Soup kitchens were certainly not sites of gastronomic individualism. Nor did they offer their clientele much opportunity to exercise genuine dietary autonomy. Those who complained were condemned as ungrateful. Nonetheless, habits and preferences, far from being irrelevant, were alleged to be central to a soup's success. Soup promoters took pains to describe the approval supposedly bestowed on their concoctions by the impoverished beneficiaries. The enjoyment with which these soups were consumed occupies a prominent place in descriptive accounts, alongside calculations of cost and techniques for limiting access to the deserving poor. Just as prison inmates were marshalled to endorse the Valencian soup, so descriptions of the economical soups served in the 1760s to hungry Parisians not only included testimonials from wealthy men like the physiocratic Marquis de Mirabeau, but also reiterated that the poor themselves ate these potato-pottages with pleasure. Even the abandoned babies fed by the Parisian Parish of Saint Roch were called upon to bear witness to potato soup's ability to please; these infants, whose innocent palates could scarcely lie, supposedly preferred potato-rice soup to their usual fare.[51]

This insistence on pleasure reveals the inherently political dimensions of these schemes. Happiness rhetoric emphasised individual choice, rather than systemic impoverishment. Nothing, insisted the organisers of one London soup charity, 'can exceed the eagerness with which the industrious poor in every part of the town come forward'. This, they believed, offered proof not simply of the temporary moment of hardship but also of 'the favourable change which has taken place in the habits of the labouring classes'.[52] With a similar focus on voluntary consumption (as well as a de facto admission that these soups were not always popular), a French handbook insisted that the poor should under no circumstances be *obliged* to eat these soups: they must choose to do so of their own accord.[53] Choice, not necessity, was presented as the principal motor driving consumption. 'The catch', as the literary critic Sandra Sherman put it, was that this choice was 'a simulacra'.[54] In reality, the many soup kitchens that appeared in the 1790s reflected worsening economic circumstances, which put pressure on the food supply in a number of European countries. The diet of many working people in late eighteenth-century England, for example, was simply not adequate to sustain the demanding physical labour that they undertook. In Oldham, as the hand-loom weaver William Rowbottom recorded in his diary in 1800, high food prices reduced the poor to 'a most Shocking Situation'. Few could afford 'anything Better than Barley Bread, Barly Pottages Barley Dumpkins'; even potatoes were so expensive that 'the poor cannot by them'. As a result, they were 'in a verey weakly Condition'.[55]

Soup-promoters, however, maintained that the success of charity soup kitchens did not result solely, or even primarily, from poverty. Instead, as Sherman notes, it was said to reflect 'the poor's intrinsic, self-motivated discovery of soup's virtue': poor people, promoters insisted, *wanted* to eat potato soup.[56] In eating as in economics, self-interest was imagined to provide an effective engine for aligning individual happiness with *félicité publique*, in a way that elided tensions between the individual well-being of the poor and that of the economic and political order that required them to enjoy potato soup.

ADAM SMITH AND THE POTATO

It was perhaps inevitable that Adam Smith should particularly recommend potatoes. Smith's enormously admired *Wealth of Nations* (1776) detailed the public benefits of enabling qualified individuals to exercise autonomy in economic matters. As he explained repeatedly throughout the book's cogently argued two volumes:

> the private interests and passions of individuals naturally dispose them to turn their stock towards the employments which in ordinary cases are most advantageous to the society . . . Without any intervention of law, therefore, the private interests and passions of men naturally lead them to divide and distribute the stock of every society, among all the different employments carried on in it, as nearly as possible in the proportion which is most agreeable to the interest of the whole society.[57]

As he emphasised, this would occur 'without any intervention of law'; much of *Wealth of Nations* is devoted to a careful dissection of the pernicious effects of such interventions. Removing the distorting effects of bounties, monopolies and the like would leave each individual 'perfectly free to pursue his own interest his own way'. In consequence, rulers would be discharged from the impossible duty of 'superintending the industry of private people, and of directing it towards the employments most suitable to the interest of the society'.[58] Since each person was in general better able than anyone else to judge their own interests the result would be a wealthier, and happier, nation.

Smith's confidence in the merits of leaving individuals to pursue their own interests was not unlimited. Monopoly organisations such as the great overseas trading companies advanced their own economic gain at the cost of everyone else's, but the flaw lay in the legislation that permitted such institutions to exist in the first place. Neither did Smith imagine that everyone was equally capable of recognising their own true interests. Like many others, he believed that landowners were usually distracted by their easy life from devoting any attention to economic affairs. They were therefore poor judges of what might prove beneficial to their estates.[59] Labourers, the majority the population, lacked 'the necessary information' about economic matters, and even if supplied with it did not possess the time, education and habits required for its interpretation. They were thus poorly placed to advance their own economic interests. This was particularly unfortunate given that the well-being of labourers was 'strictly connected' with that of the society. Smith lamented the 'gross ignorance and stupidity' that benumbed their analytical abilities, and advocated the extension of (largely privately funded) primary schooling to address this.[60]

The *Wealth of Nations* expressed with particular clarity the view that the rational pursuit of individual interest was an effective strategy for organising trade to the benefit of the polity as a whole. Smith argued that this approach would increase the ease, comfort and security of all, and so worked to promote happiness, a desideratum he believed to be deeply embedded in human nature.[61] Smith's theorisation of the free market was premised on the conviction that economic success was possible only when the population was content. No society, he insisted, could be 'flourishing and happy, of which the far greater part of the members are poor and miserable'.[62] Economic growth, he maintained, provided the circumstances for the majority to be happy and comfortable. Growth, in turn, required a plentiful supply of pleasant and nutritious food, and that is what potatoes offered. Not only was the potato far more productive than wheat – Smith calculated that land planted with potatoes would produce three times as much nourishment as land laid to wheat – but it was also easier to cultivate, and, crucially, was an 'agreeable and wholesome variety of food'. As he noted, 'the strongest men and the most beautiful women' in Britain subsisted on potatoes. 'No food can afford a more decisive proof of its nourishing quality, or of its being peculiarly suitable to the health of the human constitution,' he concluded.[63]

Smith linked the personal benefits individuals would derive from a greater consumption of potatoes to a greater flourishing of the economy. If planted with potatoes, agricultural land would support a larger population, and 'the labourers being generally fed with potatoes' they would produce a greater surplus, to the benefit of themselves, landlords and the overall economy.[64] In Smith's vision, as in that of William Buchan, Parisian soup-promoters and countless other potato-advocates, if people chose to eat more potatoes, the benefits would accrue to everyone. Greater potato consumption would increase the nation's wealth at the same time as it augmented individual happiness; no plant, declared the editor of a British encyclopaedia, had 'so decided an influence on the prosperity of mankind as the potato'.[65] The result would be greater happiness all around, and that, in turn, would help build a strong and wealthy state. What the working population ate was thus directly relevant to the happiness and well-being of the nation as whole.

In keeping with the broader understanding of social organisation that underpinned Smith's model of political economy and agricultural improvement, he did not recommend that people be obliged to grow and eat potatoes any more than he favoured restricting an individual's right to truck and barter. Trying to dictate the public's diet was as misguided as trying to control the market. Not by chance did writers who embraced the model of the free market describe any attempt to oblige the public to consume foods they disliked as 'dictatorial'.[66] The very idea of attempting to 'change by law the food of a large part of the community' was, as a House of Commons committee affirmed, 'highly objectionable'.[67] These recommendations for resolving Britain's late eighteenth-century food shortages therefore referred to information and self-improvement, not coercion; 'no one', writes Sherman, '"forces" the poor to change'.[68]

Such discussions of self-interest and choice sit uncomfortably with the reality that the eating practices of the working poor were very largely constrained by coercion. Not having much control over what you ate was almost the definition of poverty. Lack of money and time, as well as the limited range of foodstuffs proffered by charitable establishments and systems of poor relief, functioned every day to restrict their dietary options. The possibility of force and the reality of poverty loomed behind any talk of choice. The inmates at the San Narciso prison who tested the Valencian Society's experimental recipes had few alternatives to Soup Number Three, beyond Soups Number One and Two. Eating charity soup can hardly be viewed as an active choice, but the new models of economic self-organisation encouraged political writers to view it as precisely this.

Potatoes, happiness and the business of statecraft were bound together in the language of political economy. The insistent eighteenth-century promotion of the potato formed part of a new model of statecraft premised on individuals aligning themselves not with the direct dictates of government, but rather the natural laws that governed human and economic behaviour. This is why Adam Smith devoted some pages to their praise. By the century's end, as the historian Keith Tribe put it, 'wealth, liberty, need, and happiness (that is, satisfaction) have become linked in a chain of meaning'.[69] Discussions of how to ensure that people ate the most beneficial foods paralleled the broader principles of the new discipline of political economy, which in turn reflects the mutual connections between food, statecraft, commerce and the management of populations.

CONCLUSIONS

In his 1784 essay 'What is Enlightenment?', the philosopher Immanuel Kant listed three behaviours that he regarded as diagnostic of an immature, unenlightened existence. These were: accepting without question what one read in books, allowing religious authorities to determine one's moral code, and permitting a physician to decide one's diet.[70] Surrendering dietary autonomy was to surrender part of one's freedom. In matters of diet, as in affairs of conscience, Kant held that no outside authority, and certainly not the state, should interfere with the individual's right to decide their own best course of action. The capacity to choose what one ate was as much an element of an intellectually mature existence as the determination to think for oneself about matters of faith.

Kant's moral philosophy, built around an image of individuals as ethically autonomous subjects, diverged in many ways from the principles animating discussions of the new political economy, which viewed the population essentially as socially oriented consumers. For Adam Smith, the drive to consume was deeply embedded in human nature, compelling individuals to strive to obtain the commodities that would bring them esteem in the eyes of their fellows.[71] Kant's free-thinking, enlightened individual was not driven by the same compulsion, but Kant's vision of autonomy likewise posited the freedom to choose as an essential condition of mature humanity. Freedom, he insisted, meant 'independence from being constrained by another's choice'. This was 'the only original right belonging to every man by virtue of his humanity'.[72] Both the philosophical vision of free, autonomous individuals, displaying judgement and self-restraint, and the economic model of society as a community of consumers, situated eating as an activity best understood in terms of an individual's fundamental right to choose one's own actions. Determining one's diet formed part of the Enlightenment's conceptualisation of personal freedom.

In a classic analysis of the rise of liberal economics in eighteenth-century England, the historian Joyce Appleby drew attention to the tensions inherent in any attempt to posit human beings as both free and responsible for their own actions, and also driven by an intrinsic desire for economic self-improvement. Economic writers found it particularly difficult to reconcile these already-conflicting understandings of humanity with the widespread belief that the poor lacked any sort of economic rationality.[73] Could labouring people be either philosophically mature individuals, or sensible consumers? Political economists doubted that either was possible. They were, however, less doubtful of the poor's ability to make wise choices when presented with a toothsome and satisfying foodstuff. Diet was one area in which the labouring poor could be both Kantian autonomous beings and Smithian consuming subjects. Eating provided a space where even the ill-educated could enjoy what the philosopher Samuel Fleischacker called the 'proper pleasure' of exercising judgement in the small, concrete, activities that give meaning to life.[74]

Cross-referencing the modest history of the potato with the larger contours of eighteenth-century economic thinking helps explain the origins of our belief that what we eat is both our business, and also the business of the state. Today the most compelling argument in favour of eating properly is usually that it is in our own self-interest, but that if we all looked after our own well-being then society as a whole would be better off. The same ideas underpinned eighteenth-century explanations of why working people ought to eat the foods necessary to ensure their utility to the state. Potato-advocates stressed the political and economic advantages that would result from an increase in potato consumption, but also insisted that potatoes were a delicious source of healthful nutrition that individuals might happily eat without giving the slightest thought to how much they were benefiting the polity. As the Marquis of Mirabeau put it, 'all the magic of a well-ordered society consists in the fact that each works for others while believing that he works only for himself'.[75] Eating, happiness and the business of statecraft were bound together in the new eighteenth-century language of political economy.

The conviction that governance requires some attention to the dietary habits of local populations trailed along behind the late eighteenth- and nineteenth-century bureaucrats and colonists who set up shop in Batavia, Calcutta and Botany Bay. The potato was also on the move, sometimes travelling in carefully designed boxes intended to transport valuable botanical specimens, and sometimes tucked into the trunks and lockers of nameless seamen. Chapter 4 follows the potato, and the debates about the eating habits of ordinary people, to India, China and beyond.

CHAPTER 4

Global Potatoes

W HO BROUGHT POTATOES TO PERSIA? IN THE EARLY nineteenth century two British diplomats bickered over which of them deserved the credit for this achievement. Sir Harford Jones and Sir John Malcolm served simultaneously as representatives to the court of Shah Fath-Ali in Tehran, in confused diplomatic circumstances that left the men bitter rivals. Among their many disagreements were their competing claims to have introduced potatoes to the region. Both men considered potato-promotion a benevolent undertaking for which they were eager to claim responsibility. Malcolm boasted of having taken great pains to disseminate knowledge about 'this valuable vegetable' across Iran. Over thirty bags of seed potatoes were distributed under his direction, and he also arranged for the circulation of a monograph on the best methods of cultivation. He was therefore irked by reports that the French diplomatic mission had already brought potatoes to Iran a century earlier. 'I desire the good fame of introducing potatoes into Persia,' he recorded in his journal. He was reassured to learn that the 'potato' supposedly introduced by the French was an unrelated (and tasteless) impostor. His good fame was secure. Jones, however, rubbished Malcolm's assertions. 'Much has been said ... of the advantage that the introduction of the potato root into Persia would confer on the inhabitants,' Jones observed, before insisting that none of the glory should adhere to Malcolm. 'Long before Sir John Malcolm visited Persia I gave roots of this plant to several Persians,' he affirmed in his own memoirs.[1]

Now one of the world's most ubiquitous crops, the potato travelled around the globe with the expansion of trade and colonial conquest in the early modern era, but the processes that made it a global staple reflect not only these forces but also the varied circumstances that it encountered on its journey. In Persia, potatoes were by the 1880s 'much grown' by local farmers, alongside spinach, barley and other more traditional foodstuffs. Today, Iranians eat them in salads, and they are sometimes used to add a crusty top to a dish of rice.[2] Whether the potato's adoption by Iranian cooks is due to the activities of Harford Jones and John Malcolm is, however, doubtful. The tuber was already growing on the island of Kharg, the site of a Dutch trading post just off the Persian coast, in the mid-eighteenth century, and the culinary influence of these two self-promoting diplomats was in any event limited.[3] (See recipe for Persian Rice with a Potato Crust.)

Although their contribution to Persian cuisine is uncertain, it is perfectly clear why these men wished to claim credit for the potato's introduction. From the late eighteenth century efforts to promote the consumption of starchy staples in Iran, India, the West Indies and other areas of strategic interest were viewed by European diplomats, missionaries and colonial officers as tangible evidence of their benevolent intentions. Just as potato-promotion in eighteenth-century Europe was framed as a means of increasing happiness among the working poor, so the spread of potatoes around the world formed part of a highly ideological narrative of disinterested European philanthropy. Potatoes were heralded by men such as Harford Jones and John Malcolm as a beneficial foodstuff that removed the threat of hunger and encouraged sound agricultural practices. For these reasons their adoption was claimed to index the overall level of civilisation attained by locals. A failure to embrace potatoes, in contrast, revealed a lamentable recalcitrance. The Andean potato had become evidence of European superiority.

Such narratives show clearly how the agricultural and dietary practices of actual or potential imperial subjects were slotted into broader colonial ideologies, in ways that linked the adoption of recommended foodways to the supposed benefits of formal or informal imperialism and its promise of improvement and progress. We should not take these narratives at face value. Just as the flood of potato-promotion in eighteenth-century Europe was not responsible for the potato's penetration into the European diet, so credit for the potato's global spread cannot be ascribed

Persian Rice with a Potato Crust

Rice pilaff with a crunchy crust is a classic of Iranian cookery. A tahdig *or golden crust can be produced by mixing some of the rice with butter or yoghurt during the cooking process. ('Persian-style' electric rice cookers have a special setting to achieve this.) A* tahdig *can also be formed from other ingredients, including potatoes. Rice has featured in Persian cuisine since at least the eighth century. Potatoes, a more recent addition, help create a new dish that is nonetheless embedded in existing foodways.*

Persian Rice with a Potato Crust

Serves 6

2 cups white or brown basmati rice
2 tablespoons sea salt
4 cardamom pods, crushed
1 tablespoon rose water
6 tablespoons melted butter
1 teaspoon ground saffron dissolved in 2 tablespoons rose water
2 medium potatoes, peeled and cut into ¼-inch slices

Pick over the rice to remove any small particles. Wash the rice by placing it in a large container and covering it with lukewarm water. Agitate gently with your hands, then pour off the water. Repeat 5 times until the water is completely clear. When washed rice is cooked it gives off a delightful perfume that unwashed rice does not have. After washing the rice it is then desirable but not essential to soak it in 8 cups water with 1 tablespoon salt for 2 to 24 hours. Soaking and cooking rice with plenty of salt firms it up to support the long cooking time and prevents the rice from breaking up. The grains swell individually without sticking together. The result is a light and fluffy rice known as 'the pearls of Persian cuisine'.

In a 5-quart, non-stick pot, bring 10 cups water to a boil over high heat. Add 1 tablespoon salt, cardamom, and rose water. Pour the washed and drained rice into the pot.

Boil briskly over high heat for 6 to 10 minutes for white rice (15 for brown rice), gently stirring twice with a wooden spoon to loosen any grains that may have stuck to the bottom. Bite a few grains. If the rice feels soft, and all the rice has risen to the top, it is ready. Drain rice in a large, fine-mesh colander and rinse with 2 or 3 cups cold water.

In a mixing bowl, whisk together 4 tablespoons butter, 2 tablespoons water, and a few drops of the saffron-water mixture, and spread in the pot. Arrange the potato slices in the bottom of the pot. Place a thin layer of rice over the potatoes and press down firmly with your hands. Mound the rest of the rice on top in a pyramid shape. Cover and cook rice for 10 minutes over medium heat to form a golden crust.

Mix the remaining 2 tablespoons melted butter with ¼ cup water and pour over the rice pyramid. Drizzle the rest of the saffron water over the top. Wrap the lid with a clean dish towel and cover firmly to prevent steam from escaping. Cook for 70 minutes over low heat.

Remove the pot from heat. Allow to cool on a damp surface such as a rimmed baking sheet lined with a wet dish towel for 5 minutes without uncovering. This helps to free the crust from the bottom of the pot.

Hold the serving platter tightly over the uncovered pot and invert the two together, unmoulding the rice onto the platter. The rice will emerge as a golden-crusted cake. Serve in wedges.

simply to the promotional activities of imperial agents. Global forces and local circumstances invariably combined. This chapter sketches some of the complex factors that shaped the potato's global transit, to show the diverse ways in which this new food entered into local dietaries, and how its significance changed over time. The potato's meaning was never static, even in its South American homeland.

The potato's changing significance in imperial, Communist and post-Maoist China demonstrates particularly clearly the simultaneously local and global nature of the modern foodscape. The potato reached China some time in the seventeenth century, and has long served as an important source of food for the inhabitants of poor villages in peripheral regions, yet until recently it has been almost invisible to the Chinese state. In the last decades, however, it has become an explicit component of China's programme for achieving food security, and China is now the world's leading producer of potatoes. This transformation in the potato's status reflects the combined impact of market reforms, the provisioning strategies of rural villages, and what the historian Mark Swislocki called 'nutritional governmentality' – the formulation of food policies designed to promote state power and economic success.[4] The close connections between market economies, everyday diets, and the modern state born in the eighteenth century continue to shape contemporary debates about healthy eating and national security.

BREADFRUITS AND BENEVOLENCE

Shortly after assuming the presidency of the newly independent United States, Thomas Jefferson composed a memorandum in which he evaluated his contributions to the nation he had done much to bring into being. Jefferson's 'statement of public service' listed his efforts to end the transatlantic slave trade, his support for religious freedom, and, naturally, the declaration of independence from Britain. He also included his encouragement of commercial rice cultivation. Jefferson was proud of his support for upland rice because 'the greatest service which can be rendered any country is to add an useful plant to its culture'. Such accomplishments were all the more praiseworthy when the useful plant was a bread grain or other dietary staple. Augmenting the supply of starchy foodstuffs was a public service equal to anything a political figure might achieve, or so Jefferson believed. (Jefferson did not meditate on the fact that rice imposed a particularly brutal work regime on the enslaved men and women who grew it, nor did he credit the West Africans whose technical knowledge was essential to new-world rice culture.)[5] From Jefferson's perspective, the spread of rice-growing demonstrated the good intentions, and achievements, of white men such as himself.

Jefferson's conviction that the dissemination of new, starchy foodstuffs constituted a signal service to humanity was shared by his contemporaries. Bryan Edwards, author of an immensely popular history of the West Indies (and owner of several Jamaican plantations with a combined workforce of some 1,500 enslaved men and women) concurred that:

> among all the labours of life, if there is one pursuit more replete than any other with benevolence, more likely to add comforts to existing people, and even to augment their numbers by augmenting their means of subsistence, it is certainly that of spreading abroad the bounties of creation, by transplanting from one part of the globe to another such natural productions as are likely to prove beneficial to the interests of humanity.

Edwards was particularly enthusiastic about Britain's efforts to introduce breadfruit to the Caribbean. Captain William Bligh's success in 1793 in transporting breadfruit from the Pacific to the West Indies marked, in Edwards' assessment, 'an important era in the History of the British West Indies!'[6] The history of the breadfruit's introduction into the Caribbean provides context for the parallel efforts of colonial officials elsewhere to disseminate the potato, so it is worth devoting a little space to that better-known story.

It was only on Captain Bligh's second attempt that he completed this historic endeavour. Bligh had been sponsored by the British government to sail to Tahiti, with the aim of collecting specimens of a tree known as *rima* or *soccus*, or, as the English called it, breadfruit.[7] The intention was to introduce the plants to Jamaica. Bligh's first voyage had ended in the dramatic 1789 mutiny on board the *Bounty*, when his crew took command of the vessel. Anger over the preferential treatment given to the cargo of breadfruits played a significant role in provoking the rebellion. The hundreds of breadfruit plants monopolised the ship's space and water supply, and one of the first actions of the mutineers was to toss the saplings overboard. Bligh and a handful of followers were set adrift in a small boat with minimal supplies or navigational equipment. With grim determination Bligh succeeded in captaining the open boat back to Britain. There he nourished a profound desire for revenge, which he was able to satisfy when the government of William Pitt funded a second breadfruit expedition. This enabled Bligh to complete his mission of transporting breadfruits to Britain's Caribbean colonies, and also to track down and arrest the surviving mutineers.[8]

Bligh's success was lauded by observers on both sides of the Atlantic. Commentators agreed that he displayed remarkable fortitude and expertise during his dramatic voyage back to Britain but the transport of the breadfruit was considered a far greater accomplishment. The new plant was celebrated as a virtually limitless source of nutritious food whose introduction in the Caribbean would transform local diets. The tree and its fruit would be 'of infinite importance to the West India Islands', in the view of writers in both Britain and the Caribbean.[9] The breadfruit's nutritious qualities were presented as the central reason why it merited attention.

In fact, the British government's decision to fund not one but two costly, trans-oceanic expeditions to bring the Tahitian breadfruit to the West Indies had little to do with the actual food requirements of its American colonies. As its name implies, the breadfruit was viewed by botanists as a starchy food somewhat comparable to bread. Who, however, was to eat this bread substitute? The planters such as Edwards who greeted the breadfruit's arrival with applause did not anticipate furnishing their own tables with this exotic import. Neither did the islands' population of enslaved workers need an additional source of starch. As writers at the time acknowledged, the West Indies were already well supplied with starchy vegetables, from sweet potatoes and manioc to eddoes. The enslaved men and women who laboured in colonial plantations would certainly have benefited from an increase in their total food allowance, as well as from additional sources of protein, but a further starch was the last thing they needed. Nor were West India planters generally noted for their attention to the dietary needs of their enslaved workforce in the first place. The majority of arable land was dedicated to producing the lucrative export crop of sugar, rather than to growing food for workers, a task that was often left to enslaved people themselves.[10] For this reason planters displayed limited interest in the trees' dietary potential in the years after their 1793 introduction. 'The fact is', stated the superintendent of the St Vincent botanical garden in 1806, 'planters hate giving it a place on their estates, as they regard it as an intruder on their cane land, and they dislike any other object but canes'.[11] The disregard with which planters soon came to view the tree did not prevent the same superintendent from celebrating George III's support for the enterprise as 'pregnant with benevolence' because it simultaneously increased both 'the comforts and means of subsistence ... [and] the happiness and numbers of mankind'.[12] The fact that no one was eating this peerless food was beside the point.

The tree was less a solution to a provisioning dilemma than a sign of Europe's commitment to its colonies and an emblem of enlightenment. Imperial interest in the breadfruit derived from these associations far more than from practical concerns about food supply in the Caribbean. Indeed, during the same years that it underwrote the breadfruit voyages the British state explicitly rejected claims from planters that its Caribbean colonies were suffering a food shortage.[13] The British state did not fund the transportation of thousands of breadfruits from Tahiti to solve a subsistence crisis whose very existence it denied. Rather, the enterprise was framed as a demonstration of British altruism. As Bligh insisted, 'if a man plants ten [breadfruit trees] in his life-time, which he may do in about an hour', he would instantly fulfil 'his duty to his own and future generations'.[14] That the supposed beneficiaries of this act of nutritional largesse by all accounts shunned the new food demonstrated their ingratitude but in no way undermined the achievements of the mission.[15] (Enslaved workers viewed the breadfruit 'with cold apathy', reported one planter.[16]) The nutritious breadfruit signalled benevolence, regard-less of its actual dietary impact.

Such performances of botanical benevolence were repeated across the British empire during the late eighteenth century. In the same years as the *Bounty* expedition, Robert Kyd, founder of the Calcutta Botanical Garden, was encouraging the introduction of sago palms from the Malay peninsula to India.[17] (Sago, a starchy substance extracted from the stem of a tropical tree, can be used to make a variety of breads, as well as tapioca-like porridges.) Contemplating Kyd's proposal, Joseph Banks, president of the Royal Society and a leading British botanist, mused happily on its multiple advantages. The introduction of sago trees, Banks believed, would provide Indians with an immensely wholesome food. Kyd's plan therefore offered tan-gible evidence of 'the benevolent intentions of government'. As a result grateful Indian beneficiaries would 'revere the name of their British Conquerors'. What is more, Indians would be indebted to the British for delivering them from 'famine, the most severe scourge with which Providence had afflicted them'.[18] Banks' easy progression from the introduction of sago trees, to British benevolence, to the alleviation of famine, to Indian gratitude, reflects well the constellation of ideas associated with the promotion of starchy foodstuffs.

Such schemes were concerned far more with legitimating particular forms of governance than with reducing hunger. Britain's track record in hunger prevention in India was in fact extremely poor. In the decade prior to Banks' self-satisfied comments on sago, Bengal had experienced a devastating famine exacerbated, if not indeed caused, by British poli-cies, in which perhaps ten million people perished. Horrendous famines causing millions of deaths continued to scourge India's inhabitants throughout the period of colonial rule. British policies proved utterly inadequate to the task of alleviating starvation and were in many cases directly responsible for it.[19] Banks' complacent suggestion that famine resulted from the mysterious workings of Providence was entirely disin-genuous. What is more, Kyd's botanical garden occupied lands confis-cated from Indian farmers, whose food crops were cleared to make way for the new specimens. The introduction of sago palms most likely worsened the dietary conditions of locals.[20] Advocates of sago did not believe that this contradicted their claims to be improving the well-being of Indians. As with breadfruits, the sago palm's importance lay not in its actual contribution to resolving food shortages but rather in its perceived ability to symbolise Britain's concern for its colonial subjects. The encouragement of potato cultivation in British India reflects similar convictions, and similar practices. The metaphorical power of food actively shaped political discourse, as well as colonial policy.

ON THE CULTURE OF THE POTATO IN INDIA

The chronology of the potato's early spread across the Indian subcontinent is no clearer than that of its dissemination across Europe. By the mid-sixteenth century, when Europeans first encountered potatoes in the Andes, Portuguese vessels were sailing regularly to Indian ports and had established a settlement in Cochin, on India's western coast. There was therefore ample opportunity to transport foodstuffs such as chillies, potatoes and sweet potatoes from the Americas to India. Quite when these first arrived is uncertain, but by the 1530s chillies were growing along the Malabar coast, and soon established a firm hold on the cuisines of south India. Cashew nuts and other American novelties also entered local foodways in subsequent decades. As to new-world tubers, fragmentary European accounts from the late sixteenth century refer to the widespread consumption of 'batatas', a Caribbean term often referencing the sweet potato, but it seems likely that these were in fact yams, which had long been eaten in India.[21] Edward Terry, who served as a chaplain for the East India Company in the early seventeenth century, reported seeing 'potatoes excellently well dressed' at a banquet in Rajasthan hosted by the Mughal statesman Asaf Khan in 1615. Whether these were yams, potatoes, or sweet potatoes is again uncertain, but since by 1590 the Caribbean pineapple had reached the larders and tables of the Mughal emperor himself, Khan's potatoes could certainly have been either of these American tubers.[22] The first unambiguous evidence dates from the 1670s, when an East India Company surgeon observed their frequent consumption in Karnataka, along the west coast of India. By then potatoes were common enough in the surgeon's home-city of London for us to be confident in his identification.[23] Whenever potatoes first reached India it was surely through the agency of sailors who manned the vessels connecting the silver mines and sugar plantations of the Americas with Europe and Asia, and the Portuguese merchants who settled in the port cities of Goa and Chittagong from the mid-sixteenth century. It is therefore not surprising that the first appearances of new-world tubers were along India's western coast.

Britain's colonisation of India during the eighteenth century prompted British writers to justify these attacks on what they knew to be sovereign states. Undermining the legitimacy of Indian rulers and Indian culture formed a recurrent feature of these efforts. Writers contrasted the state of Indian commerce and society prior to the arrival of Europeans with its current condition, which they found to be much improved, and inventoried the advantages of Britain's 'mild and rational' rule.[24] Agricultural innovations featured prominently in such catalogues. Colonial ideologues maintained that local forms of agriculture were inferior to those of Europe, and that people who persisted in employing inferior agricultural practices abdicated their right to self-government. As John Locke noted in his *Second Treatise of Government*, while God had given the world to all men in common, 'it cannot be supposed He meant it should always remain common and uncultivated. He gave it to the use of the industrious and rational.' From this perspective, sovereignty was linked to certain forms of economically productive agriculture. The industrious and rational British were thus entirely justified in seizing control. What is more, Indians themselves were said to gain from this process, since their inefficient agricultural practices were replaced with improved, European techniques. This notion of 'improvement' provided a framework for presenting colonialism as beneficial not only to the colonisers but also the colonised. It implied, as the postcolonial critic Edward Said put it, 'that certain territories and people *require* and beseech domination'.[25]

When it came to agriculture, India was 'wretched and ignorant', as one journal put it in 1820, while Britain was exceptionally advanced in 'the means of improvement and instruction'. It was therefore fortunate, the journal concluded, that Providence had entrusted Britain with the task of improving Indian agriculture and thereby spreading 'comfort and happiness' among the Indian population. Promoting the 'Interest and the Happiness of the Native Inhabitants' had recently been incorporated into the Charter of the East India Company. Evidently, the dissemination of Britain's agricultural know-how was one way to discharge this obligation.[26] Unsurprisingly, potatoes formed part of this benevolent package of reforms, alongside sago trees and breadfruits. William Tennant, an army chaplain stationed in Bengal in the late eighteenth century, was one of a number of potato-enthusiasts. In the 1790s Tennant composed a series of essays that he subsequently published under the title of *Indian Recreations*. It offered a litany of complaints about tradi- tional agricultural practices, alongside critiques of the irrationality of Hinduism and the cruelty of Indian landlords. Against such inadequacies Tennant juxtaposed the benefits that Indians obtained from colonialism. Prominent among these were the introduction of British agricultural techniques and in particular 'British' plants such as the potato.

Tennant regarded the potato as a particularly powerful contribution to Indian well-being. It was of such singular utility to the poor that, in his view, Britain's efforts in generalising its use in India in themselves atoned for any misdeeds earlier generations of English settlers had perhaps committed during the colonisation of the Americas. Colonial improve- ment in one hemisphere thus compensated for an earlier, less benevo- lent, intrusion in the other. Potatoes were a sort of imperial balm, able to assuage any lingering guilt. Tennant enumerated the plant's merits and recommended that Indian farmers be provided with individual potato plots. This would allow them to substitute potatoes for rice, a fundamental Bengali staple. As far as Tennant was concerned, rice's central position in local foodways was the reason why the region was vulnerable to famine. Tennant stressed that were Indians to eat more potatoes and less rice, they would not only free themselves from the misery of famine, but would also relieve the government of the burden- some obligation to care for them when the rice crop failed, as it had two decades earlier. By linking acceptance of the potato to the extirpation of famine, Tennant intimated that Bengalis would have only themselves to blame if they were to suffer a repeat of the deadly famines of the 1770s. Potatoes, like sago and breadfruit, absolved Britain of any responsibility for future famines, while also demonstrating the superiority of British foods and agricultural traditions.[27]

The Agricultural and Horticultural Society of India, formed in 1820 to effect the 'general amelioration of the agricultural condition of India', was similarly convinced that its own efforts to encourage potatoes demonstrated Britain's kindly intentions towards its Indian subjects.[28] The Society made sustained attempts to promote potato cultivation in Bengal. Its founding prospectus stated clearly that one 'object to be pursued by an Agricultural Society is, *the introduction of new and useful Plants*'. These included food plants, as well as crops of commercial interest. Already, its first president insisted, the promotion of the potato by a few colonists demonstrated the merits of this ambition. How much more, he continued, 'might be accomplished by the joint efforts of a number of persons arduously engaged in the same pursuit!'[29] To this end the Society established an acclimatisation garden in which members grew potatoes alongside tobacco, apples, Seville oranges, nectarines, cherimoyas and avocados. It also imported seed potatoes from Europe and distributed them to members, who experimented with the effect of different manures and soils on the productivity of 'this valuable vegetable'.[30]

The Society's ambitions were not satisfied by such gentlemanly pottering. It wanted Indians to embrace these vegetables as well. Using the same techniques employed in Europe, the Society sponsored prizes for the cultivation by 'native farmers' of potatoes, peas, cauliflowers and other favoured plants. While such incentives were aimed in part at remedying the 'deplorable lack of good produce' in the markets that provisioned their own kitchens, their larger goal was to induce Indians not simply to grow but also to eat potatoes and cauliflowers. The Society therefore conducted questionnaires on the tuber's reception among India's different religious communities, and was pleased when particular villages embraced the potato.[31] A docile and grateful population of Indian potato-eaters was what the Society wanted to encourage. It regarded these enterprises as an uphill struggle against the 'ignorance or mistaken ideas of the natives relative to those things which concern their own interests', but overall it was confident that it was working to increase happiness and improve the well-being of India's rural population. For the Society, such efforts to encourage potato consumption provided vivid evidence of the beneficent intentions of colonists, and also of the obstinate refusal of 'native farmers' to embrace enterprises so clearly in their own interest.[32]

The supposed backwardness of Indian farmers was a source of recurrent comment by the Society. 'The state of agriculture in India', insisted the first president, 'is now more rude than that of England was two centuries ago.' Fields and gardens were disordered and revealed no understanding of horticulture. He bemoaned the complacent attitude of Indian farmers. 'Slaves to custom', they lacked curiosity, as well as proper implements, and were inexplicably untroubled by their own backwardness. Indians, he believed, lived 'in a state of stupid contentment with their present miserable condition'.[33] Members of the Society were therefore uncertain whether their assiduous encouragement of the potato, and of proper horticultural techniques, would find a warm reception among Indian farmers, but they did not doubt that their activities demonstrated a genuine commitment to augmenting 'general happiness', and thereby legitimating British rule.[34]

Celebration of the happiness proffered by potatoes ignored the actual impact of British rule on India's ability to feed itself, which was largely destructive. Export agriculture siphoned off essential staples, and the colonial administration neglected to maintain the complex irrigation systems of the Mughal state. There is little evidence that the well-being of Indians ever trumped the enrichment of the metropolis. Taxes were collected as assiduously as ever during catastrophic famines. Colonial officials fiercely resisted any suggestion that they were responsible for providing Indian subjects with even the minimal subsistence offered by the British poor laws.[35] In India, potato-promotion was a way to blame Indians for hunger and famine, not a practical scheme to improve food security.

The practical impact of the Society's potato-promotion was in any event limited, and the potato's penetration into local dietaries predated their efforts. Commercial potato cultivation, stimulated by demand from British garrisons and colonial residents, developed around Calcutta and the western Deccan in the late eighteenth century, and by the early 1800s the tuber was a familiar ingredient in local cuisine, devoured with 'much avidity and in great quantities'. Over the nineteenth century the potato became embedded in Indian kitchens in many parts of the subcontinent.

It appeared in cookery books and medical manuals, and formed part of the 'familiar and indigenous ways of cooking' within a number of regions. Quite how its production and marketing was organised, and which classes or castes were involved, awaits further research, but today it is an ordinary, everyday food for millions of Indians, and India has become a leading producer.[36] Despite the efforts of colonial ideologues to link the potato to Britain's supposed superiority, it broke free to develop its own local resonances.

By the early twentieth century, anti-colonial writers were themselves promoting potatoes as part of a broader programme to revitalise the Indian population. Nationalists were concerned that their compatriots' largely vegetarian diet weakened their physiques and made them less able to resist British rule. 'Behold the mighty Englishman; he rules the Indian small, because being a meat-eater, he is five cubits tall,' Mahatma Gandhi recalled singing in the schoolground when he was a boy. (Five cubits is about 2.3 metres, or 7.5 feet.) His close friend Sheikh Mehtab agreed that 'we are a weak people because we do not eat meat. The English are able to rule over us, because they are meat-eaters.' Drawing on the latest nutritional science, nationalists focused on the apparent lack of protein in the Hindu dietary, as well as the limited range of nutrients in white rice. More potatoes offered one alternative to this emasculating diet. While nutritionists in Europe were denouncing the potato as inferior in nutritional terms to wheat bread, Indian nutritionists such as Baneswar Singha considered it superior to rice. Potatoes therefore formed part of a larger programme to strengthen the nationalist movement by strengthening Indian bodies. Potato-promotion ran alongside parallel campaigns to demonstrate that vegetarianism was not a religious requirement of Hinduism and to encourage body-building, stick-fighting and the like.[37] The potato that imperialists viewed as a symbol of British superiority became a tool for ending colonial rule.

The potato came to play a role in religious ritual as well. The regular penitential fasting (*upawasa*) practised by pious Hindus requires abstention from foods such as rice or wheat, but does not prohibit the consumption of potatoes, manioc, sago, and a number of other once-foreign foodstuffs. These starches now form the basis of the meals eaten during these fasts.[38] Colonialism and the expansion of European trade in the early modern era brought the potato to India, but these forces alone did not determine the roles it now plays in Indian culture.

CON-CLUEDING THE DAY WITH PURTATERS

The potato's travels to other parts of the world relied in similar ways on a combination of the colonial and mercantile forces that provided the means for the plant to reach a new destination, and the local contexts that shaped its reception. Early modern colonialism greatly accelerated the global dissemination of foodstuffs. In his pioneering works on what he called the 'Columbian exchange', the historian Alfred Crosby made clear that European colonialism of the Americas cannot be separated from the world-wide transfer of plants and animals that it initiated. As Crosby showed, colonists brought their crops and livestock (and diseases) with them when they travelled, and took away unfamiliar plants and animals. These new plants transformed eating habits world-wide, bringing tomatoes to Italy, chilli peppers to India, cattle to the Americas, and myriad other new tastes and flavours to peoples across the globe. Nor were Europeans the only agents of these transformations. West Africans too brought many foodstuffs with them when they voyaged voluntarily or involuntarily to the Americas.[39] The movements of foods from one part of the world to another were motivated by the desire to replicate the familiar and health-preserving foodscapes of home, and to make money through the cultivation of commercial crops such as sugar-cane or coffee. The developing science of botany played an important role in the success of such ventures. Acclimatisation gardens, systematic investigation of agronomic techniques, and the maritime infrastructure necessary to move plants long distances all contributed. Natural history, economic botany, and 'ecological imperialism' – the attempt to recreate European landscapes, cropscapes and foodscapes in colonial spaces – formed part of the larger apparatus of European colonialism.[40]

These forces helped move potatoes around the world, just as they also moved sugarcane to the Americas and tea from China to India. After Portuguese merchants and mariners took the potato to western India, Britain's nineteenth-century colonial infrastructure facilitated its further spread across the subcontinent. In Bengal a commercial potato trade developed specifically along the colonial train routes that linked different villages.[41] In Australia the potato was a component in Britain's larger plan to establish a settler colony, and it performed its role effectively. In the 1780s Joseph Banks supplied the earliest British settlements with seed potatoes, as well as gooseberry bushes, tobacco plants and coffee seedlings, as part of his scheme to create a self-sustaining and commercially productive colonial outpost. Breadfruit Bligh likewise planted potatoes in Tasmania in 1788; by 1817 the island was exporting nearly 400 tons to colonists in Australia.[42] 'Colonisation by gardening' played a similar role in bringing potatoes to French settlements in the Indian Ocean.[43] Potatoes also travelled courtesy of the commercial enterprises that prospered under informal imperialism. The Atkins Sugar Company of Boston boasted of growing Cuba's first potatoes at the botanical garden it established in conjunction with Harvard University in the early twentieth century.[44]

Colonialism likewise helped propel potatoes around the eastern seaboard of North America. Since wild potatoes were eaten in Utah twelve millennia ago, it is possible that they reached the Atlantic coast prior to the arrival of Europeans. If they had, early European settlers did not notice them. The earliest written evidence suggests that they were introduced from Europe, perhaps via colonial settlements in the Caribbean.[45] Just as British settlers in India viewed the potato as part of a superior European culture, so colonists in North America considered the South American potato to be part of their own culinary heritage. In 1685 a resident of the recently established colony of Pennsylvania reported that he had planted '*Irish Potatoes*', which he hoped would yield 'a brave increase to Transplant next year'. Scots-Irish Presbyterians, already familiar with potato cultivation from the British Isles, planted them in New Hampshire in the early eighteenth century. English, Scottish and Irish colonists were likely the first to grow potatoes, but they soon spread far beyond these communities. Swedish settlers in Delaware raised them for personal consumption and sale. French Acadians in Canada and Moravians in North Carolina did likewise. So did Haudenosaunee (or Iroquois) farmers in upstate New York; travellers reported that potatoes grew 'in quantity immense, and in goodness unequal'd' on Senaca lands in the Finger Lakes. By the mid-eighteenth century they were a familiar commercial crop, traded along the Atlantic coast and subject to regulation alongside other commodities.[46]

A great deal of evidence shows that by the eighteenth century they had become a common foodstuff for many of the peoples along the eastern seaboard. 'Purtaters for Sup' was how a New England ship's carpenter fighting in the Adirondacks during the Seven Years War (1756–63) 'Con Clued the Day', according to his diary. Soldiers fighting on both sides of the American Revolution ate them weekly in their rations. Young women carefully transcribed recipes for potato yeast and potato bread into their recipe collections, alongside the details of how to make coconut pudding, almond cheese cake, a remedy for whooping cough, and Mrs Charlston's 'excellent' receipt for curing beef. Recipes for potato-stuffed turkey and rosewater-scented potato pudding featured in the new nation's first printed cookery book, published by a self-proclaimed 'American' in 1796. Its author, Amelia Simmons, described them as being 'in universal use'. And when Benjamin Franklin's grandson was asked to deliver a commencement address at the University of Pennsylvania in 1790, he chose the potato as the theme. Not only were they a peerless food, he proclaimed, but they also conferred on the face 'that lovely white and red which constitute *beauty*'.[47] As in British India, the Andean potato became part of a racialised narrative about Europe's supposed superiority.

The potato's dissemination across Africa likewise owes much to the activities of colonists, colonial bureaucrats and missionaries; the Swahili term for potato translates roughly as 'European root'. Colonial convictions that potato-promotion helped legitimate European rule endured into the twentieth century. French officials in Burkina Faso obliged locals to raise potatoes and other foreign vegetables as part of a larger programme of transformation that aimed to replace West African cultivation practices with supposedly superior European techniques. In 1918 the Local Native Council in British Kenya was likewise distributing seed potatoes as part of its own programme of 'betterment'.[48] In Kenya these efforts to encourage potato cultivation occurred in the context of land seizures by white settlers and the imposition of new farming practices that upended existing gender norms and destroyed the ecological balance maintained by African agriculture. These practices can scarcely be described as improvements, no matter what colonial officials claimed. The coercive nature of these European 'betterment' schemes emerges clearly from oral histories. 'Let me tell you', recalled one elderly Congolese woman in 2017:

> when I was born it was the Belgians who were in power. The *Agronom* would come and measure the men a field. He would measure kilometres, maybe fifteen kilometres and say 'you plough or cultivate this and grow potatoes'. If you didn't finish that you would be arrested.[49]

As in India, colonial administrations repeatedly implemented policies that worsened hunger while simultaneously blaming subsequent shortages on 'native ignorance' and backward agricultural practices.[50]

Everywhere, the adoption of potatoes and other 'European' vegetables was viewed as both an engine and an indicator of Europeanisation. If Tasmanians were to grow potatoes and wheat, opined the *Colonial Times and Tasmanian Advertiser* in 1826, they would soon lose 'their roving disposition and acquire some slight habits of industry, which is the first step of civilization'.[51] Colonial travellers reported approvingly on the potato's presence in the gardens of Christian converts, which in their view were invariably tidier and prettier than those kept by the unconverted.[52] Non-European cultivation habits in turn revealed a larger failure to embrace civilisation. In Iran, observed a nineteenth-century British chargé d'affairs to the Qajar court:

> the potato is in general miserably under-sized, which is owning to the idleness of the gardeners, who deposit the seed almost on the surface of the ground, rather than be at the trouble of scooping or 'dibbing' a hole. Asparagus grows wild in Persia, but the indigenous plant is as inferior to the cultivated as a Hottentot is to a refined European.[53]

Potatoes and asparagus stood as proxies for people, whose capacity for civilisation was writ large in their vegetable gardens.

Shrewish and one-sided as they may be, such reports nonetheless allow glimpses into how the potato entered local foodways. Gardeners in Tehran were evidently growing potatoes in the 1860s, and had developed their own techniques for doing so, no matter how inadequate these appeared to British observers. In New Zealand, where European sailors had planted potatoes in the 1780s, the tubers were quickly adopted into Māori agriculture both as a foodstuff and as a commodity. As a food they supplemented the local staple of sweet potatoes. Unlike sweet potatoes, which were embedded in a pre-existing web of ritual restrictions that limited cultivation, potatoes lacked religious significance and so could be grown in a far wider range of circumstances. For this reason, potatoes were a popular addition to village agriculture and quickly became an important foodstuff, consumed in huge quantities at the *hui* or festive gatherings that punctuated Māori life. They also acquired an economic importance. Together with pigs, they were used as a currency when trading with Europeans for muskets and other iron goods: the European desire for potatoes enabled the Māori to acquire items they valued. By the early nineteenth century Māori farmers were growing the plant on a commercial scale specifically for this international trade. European voyages of exploration and colonisation introduced the potato to New Zealand, but Māori farmers actively managed the trading and diplomatic opportunities it enabled.[54] (See figure 12.)

In sum, the potato's travels around the world were unquestionably initiated by Europe's enhanced ability to launch long-distance pro-grammes of trade and colonisation in the early modern era. Nonetheless, the notion that potatoes were simply 'introduced' by individuals such as John Malcolm or Captain Bligh scarcely captures the complex processes that embedded the potato into certain contexts but not others. Such processes are always specific, which is why potatoes did not spread across the globe at a uniform pace. The botanical features of particular plants – their water requirements, yields, resis-tance to pests, storability, and other qualities – are an important part of the history of plant transfers, as is the extent to which new plants fit into local foodways and systems of land tenure, social organisation and trade. During his travels across the Western Cape in the 1810s the Scottish missionary John Campbell was surprised to meet a South African man dressed in European clothes. Gesturing towards an array of fruit trees, potatoes, cabbages and other vegetables, he announced proudly 'This house is mine! and all that garden!'[55] Perhaps the proud gardener had acquired his potatoes from a local mission, but he had made them his own.

Watikini (Watkins) eating potato, and cleaning the platter 46
Whanganui R.

Figure 12 Māori man eating a potato. Potatoes reached New Zealand thanks to British sailing vessels, but their role in Māori society was determined by local people. The Māori quickly developed potato-growing into a commercial activity that allowed them to trade with passing European ships, and also incorporated the potato into their own culture of communal feasting. Watikini, the man in the drawing, was unlikely to view his potato as exotic, despite its distant origins.

BALANCING THE SCALES WITH THE POTATO

In Peru, the meanings associated with this Andean tuber are exceptionally diverse. The forces of the Enlightenment shaped political culture in Peru and the other outposts of Spain's colonial empire just as they did in Europe. From the second half of the eighteenth century, botanical gardens, astronomical observatories, schools of mining, reforms of primary education, campaigns for street lighting, and other up-to-date enterprises appeared across the hemisphere. Gentlemen scholars drafted reformist treatises that aimed to modernise every aspect of colonial society, and Catholic priests sought to purge religious ritual of irrational folk customs and baroque extravagances. Everywhere colonial officials and local philosophers engaged in the delicate balancing act of celebrating the power of human reason while preserving or even reinforcing existing social, racial and economic hierarchies. This Hispanic-

American Enlightenment shared many features with its European analogues, but it also possessed its own distinctive characteristics.[56]

In Peru, a group of wealthy intellectuals based largely in the vice-regal capital of Lima decided to formalise their shared commitment to enlightened values by establishing an organisation to promote the prosperity and 'civilisation' of their homeland. The Academic Society of the Friends of Lima was founded in 1790, and met regularly for the next four years. It was inspired by the many economic societies formed in Europe and elsewhere in the Americas, and like them it adopted an explicitly patriotic brief. Its principal activity was the publication of a journal, the *Peruvian Mercury*, which discussed literature and philosophy, political economy, scientific and commercial developments, local society, and, especially, ways to foment Peru's economy. Its members enthusiastically embraced the rhetoric of utility and reason, and viewed themselves as spokesmen for enlightenment.[57]

One of the Society's persistent concerns was to counter European criticisms of Spain and its colonies. Spain did not enjoy a good reputation among European *philosophes*, who generally considered it a medieval backwater mired in obscurantism and superstition. Nor were Spain's imperial ventures viewed any more positively. The conquest itself was widely seen as a sequence of massacres that had led solely to the deaths of millions of Amerindians. This view was captured pithily in a 1783 French essay competition that invited contributors to explore whether humanity had gained anything at all from Spain's colonisation of the Americas. The consensus was that it had not. This attitude enraged Spaniards and colonists in the Hispanic world, who disputed the accuracy of particular critiques and offered alternative accounts stressing the multitude of benefits they believed had resulted from Spain's imperialism. The evangelisation of indigenous societies featured prominently in such defences, but their authors did not limit themselves to spiritual matters.[58] For the Peruvian Society the potato too offered an effective rebuttal.

The Society was well aware of the potato's lofty reputation in eighteenth-century Europe. Its members followed European discussions of the relationship between population, political economy and agricultural improvement, and discussed the applicability of these ideas to their homeland. Educated Peruvians spelled out explicitly the potato's contributions to feeding Europe, and thereby to facilitating population growth and economic progress. Spanish writers did likewise, insisting that through the potato Spain had provided nourishment to an ungrateful world. They stressed that it was Spaniards who had brought the potato back to Europe, and were particularly annoyed when Walter Raleigh and Francis Drake were credited with this accomplishment. For such writers, the potato demonstrated the Hispanic world's contribution to universal well-being, and thereby the legitimacy of Spain's vast colonial empire.[59] This potato-based imperial propaganda attracted the ire of the anti-Spanish lobby, which denounced such attempts to diminish the enormity of the conquest by brandishing the potato. 'How dare you try to balance the scales with the cochineal insect [and] the potato?', complained the Scientific Academy of Lyon, which had sponsored the 1783 essay competition.[60]

At the same time, enlightened Peruvians could not have been less enthusiastic about potatoes when it came to eating them. Potatoes had long formed an important part of the Andean foodscape, alongside maize, quinoa and a range of vegetables, and settlers quickly associated the unfamiliar tuber with the indigenous population. As one of the earliest European descriptions stated, the potato was 'a certain food eaten by Indians'.[61] Chroniclers and travellers consistently stressed the centrality of potatoes to the indigenous diet, and described in detail both the ways in which potatoes were consumed and the novel methods employed in making *chuño*, the long-lasting freeze-dried potatoes that formed a staple for the region. These foods, colonial writers agreed, were 'the bread *of the Indians*'.[62]

Potatoes were moreover important within Andean religion, a fact of which colonial writers were well aware. Within Andean cosmology human bodies, plants and the universe were deeply entwined; potatoes were under the particular care of Axamama, the Potato Mother, daughter of the earth goddess Pachamama. In precolonial times potatoes were often presented as offerings to deities, constituting both a gift and a meal. Catholic investigations into the persistence of 'idolatry' revealed that potatoes continued to feature in clandestine religious ceremonies well

after the establishment of colonial rule. Such investigations record offerings of potatoes, alongside coca leaves, llama fat, guinea pigs and other
objects also strongly associated with the indigenous world. These associations endured in both community memories and ongoing agricultural
practices. Writing more than seventy years after the founding of the
colonial state, the Andean chronicler Felipe Guaman Poma de Ayala
was perfectly able to describe the interconnections between the planting
and harvesting of potatoes and the religious rituals of the former Inca
empire. From both a culinary and a cosmological perspective, the
Andean potato belonged to the Amerindian world.[63]

In colonial Peru's hierarchical culture, this was scarcely an endorsement of the potato as a food for reputation-conscious settlers.
Generations of settlers and their descendants reiterated the need to
maintain a European diet, and detailed the risks of eating like an
Indian. To be sure, the realities of life in the colonial Andes meant
that in practice potatoes penetrated deeply into the foodways of the
settler class. Even the pampered nuns at the convents of Santa Teresa
and Santa Catalina in Arequipa regularly consumed potatoes, as their
account books reveal. The colonial diet was inevitably a compromise
between practicality and aspiration.[64] Nonetheless, saddled as it was
with its connections to the unappreciated indigenous world, the potato
lacked the lustre that it possessed in Europe. The *Mercury*'s discussion of
the tuber reflects these associations with poverty and backwardness.
'Paltry' and 'miserable' were the words most closely linked to potatoes
in its pages.[65]

Worse, some Peruvian writers suspected that potatoes were actually
unhealthy. In the thesis that earned him a medical degree from the
University of Montpellier, the Limeño José Manuel Davalos attributed
the ailments typically afflicting the city's residents to their overuse of local
foodstuffs, most notably heavily seasoned pork, manioc and potatoes.
Citing Linnaeus, Davalos noted that the potato 'is a true species of
Solanum, and hence it is easy to judge it to be suspect. If used frequently
it produces a harmful effect even in small quantities.'[66] The *Mercury*
likewise published warnings about the lethal effects of excessive potato
consumption by travellers, especially when accompanied by spicy foods
and alcohol. At best, travellers could expect indigestion, but a fatal

dysentery was more likely.[67] The doctor Hipólito Unanue, one of the founders of the Peruvian Society, agreed that these windy roots, eaten by Lima's poor, tended to turn sour in the stomach, and so were best avoided.[68] Far from promoting potato consumption, Peru's community of patriotic savants discouraged its use. In the discourse of enlightened Peruvians, the celebrated potato whose dissemination provided proof of Spain's contributions to humanity bore little relation to the mundane tuber eaten daily by Amerindians.

Indigenous farmers, whose agricultural knowledge made the Andes so rich in potatoes, gained little from eighteenth-century celebration of the tuber. Few potato-enthusiasts in Europe or the Americas credited them with ending hunger and spreading happiness; indigenous people knew that potatoes most often represented their own stigmatised status. During a quarrel about littering in the Peruvian city of Arequipa in 1819, an angry resident shouted at Lorenza Escudero that she should be ridden out of town 'tied to a llama like a sack of potatoes'. His taunt neatly linked this indigenous woman to her characteristic foodstuff in an insult that cut deeply enough for her to complain about it in court.[69] Potatoes, like the indigenous people who ate them and the llamas that transported them, were lowly things. At the same time, potatoes were much more than a symbol of subordination. They were a significant commercial crop. Grown by indigenous and non-indigenous farmers alike, potatoes were traded up and down the Andes and along the Pacific coast, providing a handsome profit for those able to mount a large-scale trade.[70] They were at once a valuable commodity, a source of daily sustenance, a marker of inferiority, and proof of Spain's contribution to human well-being.

The complex meanings that potatoes possessed in colonial Peru are typical of the global interactions that have shaped eating in the modern world. Global processes of imperialism and trade, and the emergence of new political languages, are always articulated locally. These local articulations are never mere echoes of events elsewhere, but rather possess their own dynamics and internal logics. Thinking about place helps make sense of these multiple, contested experiences that constitute our world. The diverse meanings attached to the potato during the global eighteenth century provide one way to concretise our understanding of the simultaneously mobile and localised nature of modernity, as well as the important role that food, and eating, played in its production.[71]

HAPPY POTATO FAMILY

In China, potatoes have long been viewed as a food of the poor. They probably arrived in the seventeenth century through contacts with Portuguese traders in Fujian or the Philippines, although some scholars postulate a separate introduction through the north-western province of Shaanxi. Other American foodstuffs such as peanuts, sweet potatoes and maize reached China even earlier, also by a variety of routes. It seems that following their introduction potatoes were eaten mostly by the inhabitants of poor mountain villages. There are several reasons why potatoes might have appealed to rural folk. Between 1750 and 1850 the Chinese population more than doubled. This was accompanied by a steady growth in the production of non-food crops such as silk and tea, which greatly reduced the good-quality land available for raising staples. Peasants were pushed onto marginal lands lacking adequate irrigation, and too small in many cases to sustain the household. New foodstuffs that yielded more nourishment from less land were therefore attractive. In some parts of China the sweet potato, together with maize, served this purpose. In some northern provinces, it was the potato. 'The people living in the high mountains make this plant their principal food,' stated one report from early nineteenth-century Shaanxi.[72] The German geologist Ferdinand von Richthofen, who travelled across northern China in the 1860s and 1870s, observed that wealthier people were ashamed to eat them. Potatoes permitted the settlement of mountainous terrains whose climates did not support other crops, and so, like maize, were particularly appealing to poor farmers trying to make a living by diverting part of their land to cotton or other cash crops. Migrants from more heavily populated zones who settled on steep, marginal lands in the northern provinces also found them attractive, especially as they could be cultivated by the smaller number of individuals who typically comprised immigrant households. Their incorporation into local foodways was, one historian explains, 'a revolution wrought from the bottom up'.[73]

During this long period the Chinese state showed little interest in the potato. The Qing dynasty, which governed from the mid-seventeenth century until 1912, *was* concerned about the food supply. 'Nourishing the people' had long been a central component of responsible statecraft. From perhaps the fifth century BCE Confucian scholars and officials had acknowledged the close links between political stability and an adequate supply of food. More than this, the Chinese state developed impressive, and effective, strategies to prevent famine. Government officials monitored the availability of rice and other grains and encouraged the development of a wide-reaching network of granaries to stockpile reserves for distribution at moments of shortage. They opened up new lands for settlement, funded large-scale irrigation projects, and distributed relief in times of famine. The state also attempted to disseminate knowledge about recommended agricultural techniques, again to ensure an adequate supply of grain. By the Qing period, these long-standing structures had helped provide basic sustenance to millions of people.[74]

Qing officials did not, however, encourage changes in the day-to-day eating practices of ordinary people. Qing physicians and statesmen instead focused on the dangers posed by the overly luxurious diets of the wealthy. Such diets sapped the vitality and weakened the bodies of the people they believed most necessary to ensuring China's success: the elite. Effective governance demanded that the emperor and his household be suitably nourished, thereby setting an example to patrician households across the country. It did not require much scrutiny of the specific eating practices of peasants, artisans or other labouring folk. What these people ate was of little political importance.[75]

The growth of nationalism in the first decades of the twentieth century was accompanied by a redefinition of the role of the state in ensuring public health. The global development of the science of nutrition shaped Chinese debates about the relationship between economic and political prowess, and the diets of workers. Nationalist scientists and technocrats, many of whom were trained in the West, increasingly stressed that it was not enough for the population to be fed. Working people required a nutritionally balanced, healthful diet. This began to be seen as an essential component of economic success. The result was the establishment of nutritional institutes, new journals and a growing conviction among scientists and political figures that significant changes in popular diets were necessary for China to become a powerful nation. These ideas acquired all the more salience because the nutritional quality of China's food supply was in fact deteriorating during this period. The mechanisation of rice polishing reduced the price of white rice, enabling urban populations to consume this high-status but nutritionally poor foodstuff to a greater degree than before. The eating habits of the poor became a matter of statecraft in early republican China because new political and scientific notions combined with a concrete deterioration in the availability of nourishing food.[76]

The advent of Communist rule in 1949 deepened the association between nutritive foods and national progress. The historian Sigrid Schmalzer has traced the Communist state's sustained commitment to the investigation and dissemination of modern agricultural practices, which it viewed as essential to economic development. Chemical and biological pest control, fertilisation technologies, the breeding of higher-yielding hybrid varieties of rice and other staples, and much more, attracted government support. Ambitious programmes aimed to connect educated scientists, who were technically trained but ideologically suspect, with 'old peasants', who possessed hands-on practical expertise. The millions of urban youth who were sent out to the countryside during the Cultural Revolution were likewise expected to participate in a nationwide effort to develop the new agricultural techniques that would enable China to feed itself.[77] These practices infused the long-standing Chinese conviction that statecraft demanded 'nourishing the people' with a twentieth-century focus on scientific agriculture, which Chapter 6 will explore in fuller detail.

The focus was primarily on increasing the production of grains. Experimentation and extension work in villages concentrated on developing new varieties of hybrid rice and sorghum. Chinese agronomists did experiment with new sweet potato and potato varieties – by the 1960s there were about thirty research institutes working specifically on potatoes – but tubers did not attract the same attention as the grains that for centuries had constituted the most prestigious, and the most widespread, foodstuffs.[78] Villagers who relied on sweet potatoes and other tubers were at times frustrated by the dominance of rice in research and dissemination programmes, and urged local cadres to investigate these more humble foodstuffs. Farmers in potato-growing regions did their best to ignore state directives to plant more grain. Faced with production quotas for wheat, villagers might continue to cultivate potatoes, but then convert their potato harvest into what they deemed an equivalent quantity of grain. Village officials would report this fictitious grain harvest to regional authorities, in an attempt to honour the quota while continuing to grow potatoes.[79] Potatoes were thus an important local resource but they did not form part of the state's overall strategy for ensuring food security.

On the contrary, potatoes and other tubers to some degree allowed locals to evade the reach of the state. During the terrible 1959–61 famine that resulted from Mao's policies during the Great Leap Forward, when tens of millions of people starved or succumbed to disease, potatoes offered survival precisely because they were not considered important by officials. Although potatoes formed a significant part of the diet in a number of northern regions, statistically they were classified as a supplementary vegetable, not a staple. During the famine the Chinese state requisitioned staple grains, but not vegetables, and therefore not potatoes. An oral history from the northern region of Beidahuang captures their importance in keeping body and soul together. Although Beidahuang as a whole suffered a shocking 18 per cent mortality rate, potato-growing villages did not. Feng, a peasant farmer from one such village, recalled that he and other locals pulled through because 'there were so many potatoes'.[80] Grateful though survivors were, potatoes remain tarnished with famine memories. In today's China, 'I grew up on potatoes' means 'My family was penniless'. Individuals who lived through the famine express little interest in eating more of them.[81]

This poses a challenge to the Chinese state's current ambition to encourage potato consumption. Since the early 1990s China has been the world's leading producer, growing some 22 per cent of the global crop, and both potatoes and sweet potatoes are now identified as important components of the country's overall programme of food security. Potatoes are also seen as a way of improving 'population quality' by providing superior nourishment. In 2013 the Ministry of Agriculture began to develop a strategy to transform the potato from one vegetable among many, into a staple like rice, wheat and maize. Over a hundred institutes currently conduct research into potato breeding and the Chinese state vigorously promotes the development of large-scale potato farms, to supply both fresh potatoes and the raw material for more processed foodstuffs such as potato-flour noodles.[82]

Support for research, and encouragement for commercial agriculture, have been accompanied by schemes to encourage Chinese consumers to eat more potatoes. The so-called nutrition transition characteristic of industrial economies is transforming the nation's eating habits.[83] China's rapidly urbanising, and wealthier, population eats far more meat, dairy products, fresh fruits, and rice than in past decades. None of these are at present produced on the scale necessary to supply the new demand. Government officials hope to meet the nation's food needs by diverting consumption away from such foods towards the potato. By 2015 this had become official policy; Prime Minister Keqiang Li announced plans to increase potato consumption nation-wide. The potato, Ministry of Agriculture officials affirmed, was an 'ideal modern food', a source of healthy nutrition, and a perfect alternative to more environmentally costly grains.[84] In order to accomplish its aim of transforming potatoes into China's fourth staple, officials sought to overturn the potato's reputation as a low-status poverty food. In place of the associations with rural hunger, a new narrative links the potato to upwardly mobile consumers.

The 'Happy Potato Family' campaign captures this ambition perfectly. In one striking advertisement two cartoon potatoes, labelled 'Rich-Potato Brother' and 'Little Sister', cavort alongside a gaily dressed woman identified as 'Sister Potato'. The threesome smile cheerfully, undisturbed by their peculiar cross-species family. (See figure 13.)

'Sister Potato' is the *nom d'artiste* of Feng Xiaoyan, the woman in the advert. Feng is a self-proclaimed peasant from the northern province of Shanxi, one of China's historic potato-eating regions. She has attained national stardom through her enthusiastic promotional songs in praise of the potato. Appearing alongside her cartoon siblings, she represents the ongoing effort to associate potatoes not with dutiful submission to state demands or dire hunger, but with personal wealth. The advert's caption puns off the fashionable term *tuhao*, which refers to the nouveau

Figure 13 'Happy Potato Family'. Feng Xiaoyan, the Chinese singer in this advert, has built a career out of promoting potatoes. The Chinese state plans to double potato production by 2020. This 'happy potato family' hopes to encourage consumers to eat more of them by suggesting that potatoes are part of an upwardly mobile lifestyle. 'Let's all be rich-potatoes' reads the caption.

riche and happens to sound very similar to a word for potato. It translates roughly as 'Join us and let's all be rich-potatoes', or perhaps 'Come make some potato-bling with us'.[85]

Alongside such advertisements, state television programmes disseminate recipes and encourage public discussion about the tastiest ways of preparing potato-based dishes, all as part of an effort to rebrand the potato as a healthful lifestyle choice.[86] A Chinese cookbook published as part of the United Nations' 2008 International Year of the Potato made clear that eating potatoes brought multiple health benefits. The potato, the authors explained:

> is ideal as infant food due to its complete range of nutrients, abundant vitamins and soft texture. It has been reported that fresh mashed potatoes can be externally applied to heal bone fractures. Freshly extracted potato juice is very helpful in controlling ... constipation, gastric ulcers, redundant acidity in the stomach, duodenum ulcers, and nasosinusitis. The potato is beneficial for cancer patients . . . It is also regarded as an anti-senescence food.[87]

This breath-taking array of properties all bring benefits to the individual consumer.

It is no coincidence that this framing of the potato as a source of individual well-being coincides with the Chinese state's embrace of the market economy. Since the death of Mao in 1976 China's leaders have reoriented the economy away from central planning to allow a far greater role for market forces. This has been accompanied by a change in political discourse, which now emphasises self-interest and individual wealth-creation, in place of the focus on collective benefit that characterised earlier rhetoric. Although Maoist-era celebration of 'serving the people' has not disappeared, the valorisation of personal wealth and self-advancement is pervasive.[88] Contemporary potato-promotion is framed within this constellation of values. As in late eighteenth-century Europe, in today's China the potato is conceptualised fundamentally as a way of ensuring food security on a national level, but it is being promoted as a source of individual health and well-being. Personal gain and public good run in harmony, in a dietary analogue to the idealised free market. Potatoes in today's China form part of a market-based view of individuals and the state.

CONCLUSIONS

Globally, the potato's history over the past 500 years is closely linked to the forces of colonialism and overseas trade that drove Europeans and their multiplying array of foodstuffs around the world. For European diplomats, missionaries and officials, growing and eating potatoes formed part of the larger package of European practices that they sought to inculcate. In Indonesia, reported an 1824 issue of the *Asiatic Journal and Monthly Register for British India and its Dependencies*, potatoes, previously unknown:

> have within the last few years been introduced into Sumatra, under the administration of Sir Stamford Raffles, with the most gratifying success. They are thriving in perfection, and not only equal to any procurable elsewhere, but now form an important article of the diet of the population.

In central Sri Lanka, they were growing with equal success. 'Perhaps the most pleasing fact attending this experiment', the paper reported, was that locals too were now cultivating potatoes, a true indication of progress.[89] Potatoes had become fully European. Their embrace by Sri Lankans demonstrated, at least to colonial officials, the beneficent effects of colonialism.

Important though they were to the potato's global spread, colonialism, overseas trade, and Sir Stamford Raffles alone do not explain how or why potatoes entered ordinary diets in Sri Lanka or anywhere else. The arrival of a new food is rarely in itself a sufficient stimulus for local populations to adopt it, no matter how enthusiastically it is promoted. The historians William Beinart and Karen Middleton have analysed the multiple factors that shape the global trajectories of different plant species.[90] Beyond the activities of botanists and officials, the botanical features of each plant and the actions of ordinary people can play a decisive role. Women on wagon trains crossing the Midwest, Afrikaner trekboers, enslaved West Africans, and many others helped move seeds and plants around the world. After reviewing studies of the global spread of many plants, from maize to prickly pears, Beinart and Middleton concluded that it is very hard to generalise about these processes because local circumstances are so important in shaping the reception of any species.

In the case of the potato, the factors that determined its incorporation into particular dietary regimes can be explained only through attention to these local circumstances. For colonial and diplomatic representatives, growing and eating potatoes formed part of the larger package of European practices that they sought to inculcate. For gardeners in Tehran, Māori farmers in New Zealand, Bengali villagers, and peasants in northern China, potatoes served other purposes. In some regions they put down deep roots; elsewhere they remained a supplement to foods such as rice that played a more central dietary role. The availability of land, their commercial potential as a trade good, and their ability to evade the state all influenced the potato's penetration into local foodways.

The potato's global history also demonstrates the importance of colonial spaces to the articulation of new ideas about governance. The potato's colonial origins formed part of Spain's efforts to present itself as a modern, enlightened nation, and the promotion of potatoes helped reassure officials in India of the enlightened aims that, they claimed, underpinned British colonialism. The language of improvement penetrated deeply into colonial discourse, so that both the agricultural and the dietary habits of locals could be read as evidence of growing civilisation, or intransigent barbarism. State-level interest in everyday eating habits manifested itself both in Europe and in Europe's colonial spaces because these were not separate zones.

The efforts of the Chinese state to reposition the potato as a desirable staple recapitulate the history of eighteenth-century Europe, where an uninteresting foodstuff consumed by ordinary folk likewise came to occupy the attention of statesmen concerned to build a strong population. As in Europe, in China interest in the potato coincides with the emergence of a market economy that views consumer choice as an important display of individual agency. The Chinese state hopes that the population will eat more potatoes, but it also hopes that individuals will choose to do so in order to enhance their own well-being. Encouraging the population to eat properly is now an expected part of the apparatus of modern government, as is the expectation that such encouragement will be framed around narratives of personal benefit. It is no coincidence that Chinese potato-boosters stress the financial and health rewards to be gained from greater potato consumption, since economic liberalisation brings with it new attitudes about personal consumption, including food consumption.[91]

Chapter 5 pursues these links between economics and everyday eating habits, to show how potatoes offered a way to discuss the profound social and economic transformations wrought by capitalism.

CHAPTER 5

Capitalist Potatoes

I N DECEMBER 1800, IN THE MIDST OF THE FERMENT PROVOKED BY war with revolutionary France, the *London Gazette* published a letter reportedly sent to the justice of the peace in the Yorkshire town of Wakefield. The letter warned that unless the needs of the poor were addressed, 'this town will soon be In Ruins'. It continued: 'if you do stint us to a quartern loaf take care of your life damn King George the third and Billy Pitt may hell be their Portion for ever and ever damn your Red herrin[g]s Potatoes and you and all that have any thing to do with it'.[1] Threats against the monarch and prime minister were not taken lightly. The concerned authorities offered a substantial reward for information leading to the arrest of the author.

The intense potato-promotion of the late eighteenth century endowed the tuber with a powerful symbolic resonance. Insistently recommended to the working poor as a source of happiness, personal well-being and health, potatoes had become closely associated with the move to a market economy, and the dissolution of older models of social organisation. By singling out potatoes for hostile comment, the Wakefield letter-writer identified, and rejected, the larger political and economic model of which he or she, together with potatoes, formed a part.

Over the nineteenth century potatoes became deeply embedded in arguments about the merits of capitalism. For those suspicious of these new models of governance, the potato came to represent nothing less than a tool of exploitation. 'We will not live upon potatoes', read a banner unfurled in Kent in 1830.[2] Living on potatoes expressed in pithy form the reduced existence they perceived in the new manufacturing economy, which threatened to condemn them to a diet of little more than potatoes and endless toil.

By the 1820s the confident eighteenth-century conviction that a large, energetic population ensured a flourishing commerce was fading. Thomas Robert Malthus' dismal vision of catastrophic population increase encapsulated these shifts in understandings of political economy. With this came pessimism about the potato's capacity to contribute to national well-being. Far from increasing trade and boosting economic exchange, the potato became an obstacle to modernity, because it helped sustain precisely the sectors of the population that capitalism aimed to eradicate. The potato-eating Irish cottier exemplified that obsolete world. During the nineteenth century the sad example of Ireland was held up by writers in many European countries as an illustration of the potato's tendency to stifle enterprise, industry and economic prowess. Peasants who ate potatoes were now an impediment to, not models for, an economically successful state.

States across Europe instead focused on the food needs of the urban proletariat. The people whose diets mattered were now the growing numbers of industrial workers. The connections between urban malnutrition, social unrest and national efficiency attracted the worried attention of scientists and statesmen concerned to ensure the strength of national industry. The new language of nutritional science, with its calories, albuminoids and fats, provided a powerful way of correlating the eating habits of ordinary people with the nation's economic well-being, and once again the dietary habits of working people were identified as an impediment to economic success. Now, however, the problem was that they ate too many potatoes, not too few. Experts believed that high potato consumption typified the eating habits of less productive workers. From these uneconomic, nutritionally inferior potatoes, to the Wakefield letter-writer's damned potatoes and red herrings, talking about potatoes was a way of making concrete the connections binding the lives of individual men and women to the spread of the market economy, and of expressing an opinion about its impact. Talking about potatoes, in short, provided a way to talk about capitalism.

DAMN YOUR POTATOES

As the Wakefield letter-writer intimated, by the turn of the nineteenth century the English poor associated potatoes with an unwelcome transformation towards capitalism and the impersonal market. The potato soups and other 'squashy stuff' recommended so insistently to the poor formed part of a new model of political economy that was replacing the older bonds of mutual obligation and paternalism. A number of scholars have argued that for this reason English working people flatly refused to eat potatoes.[3] In reality, working people in early nineteenth-century England gladly ate potatoes. They grew them in cottage gardens, purchased them at market, and prepared them in a variety of fashions. Working people showed their appreciation of potatoes by appropriating them during food riots, alongside meat, butter and other desirable comestibles. During an uprising in May 1800 a Birmingham crowd commandeered the stocks in potato warehouses, which they then sold at what they deemed a just price. In Manchester in the same year several people were trampled in a rush on the potato market in a similar uprising. Hungry people also helped themselves to potatoes when they were able to find them in the gardens of their wealthier neighbours. In 1801 Devon, landowners determined that since 'several Gardens cultivated Lands and orchards within this Parish have been frequently robbed and plundered of Cabbages Carrots Potatoes Turnips', they would establish a fund to prosecute offenders.[4] Potatoes in short were a valued component of the working-class diet when eaten alongside other foods. Together with bread, cheese, butter and meat, they constituted the '5 principel Things that poor Peple want to bye', as an anonymous letter posted in Lewes in 1800 put it.[5]

What many working people objected to was the suggestion that potatoes should be eaten as a substitute for wheat bread, their principal staple. The Wakefield letter-writer's excoriation of potatoes and red herrings responded to the enthusiastic attempts by elite politicians and self-proclaimed philanthropists to promote such foods not simply as healthful additions to the diet, but specifically as alternatives to bread.

Convincing the working poor to eat potatoes in place of bread was precisely the aim of many eighteenth-century potato-promoters.

Population growth, together with the century's new ideas about state-craft, fuelled the quest for more productive alternatives to the low-yielding grains that underpinned ordinary diets across Europe. Potatoes had emerged as the clear front-runners. Potatoes, so their advocates alleged, made a perfect substitute for bread grains. They could even be eaten in the form of bread. The challenge of converting low-gluten potatoes into a yeasted loaf fascinated curious home-experimenters and trained scientists in many countries. Recipes purporting to produce a good result had circulated since the 1750s, and advocates persistently recommended potato breads as both pleasant and nourishing. The scientifically minded likewise experimented with the manufacture of potato starch, which could be used in place of wheat starch to powder wigs, and with distilling potatoes into brandy or aquavit, again to reduce pressure on the supply of grain.[6]

By the 1790s, episodic recommendation was replaced by organised promotion. As military conflict engulfed the continent, and several years of poor harvests reduced grain supplies, finding alternatives became a political priority. In Britain, the assizes of bread, which for centuries had regulated the composition of commercially produced loaves, were modified in 1795 to permit the inclusion of potato, rye, barley, oat and maize.[7] The government-funded Board of Agriculture established a 'Committee on Potatoes', which devoted sustained attention to the manufacture of mixed breads containing potatoes alongside cheaper grains such as barley. The Committee engaged several London bakers to conduct experiments on the feasibility of producing these on a commercial scale. 'The public advantages which may be expected from such a discovery', it stated, 'will immediately occur to the board without any suggestion'.[8] Motivated by similar concerns, comparable programmes were launched in other European countries.[9]

Gentry families were exhorted to set a good example by banning white bread from their tables. Consuming whole-wheat bread, or bread made with mixed grains and potatoes, became a patriotic act. 'I have forbid the use of any [other] flour in my family for the present,' the agronomist and politician Lord Sheffield reported proudly from his estate in Sussex in 1795.[10] Behind such actions was the assumption that since the lower classes naturally imitated the behaviour of the more wealthy, the sight of the nobility consuming mixed breads should be sufficient to encourage every-one to do so. 'All the Lower Classes will comprehend it. They will admire and venerate it . . . and many of them will gradually imitate it,' insisted the Tory politician Lord Auckland. By 1795, noted the historians Beatrice and Sidney Webb, 'we find almost every public body, whether vestry or statutory commissions, town council or quarter session, right up to the Privy Council and Parliament itself, voluntarily agreeing, by formal resolution, to restrict their personal consumption of wheat'. The fictional characters in the didactic novels of the political propagandist Hannah More did likewise.[11] A letter published in *The Times* in 1795 summarised well the advice offered to 'the rich': set a good example by reducing consumption of superfluities and by eating more whole grains, vegetable soups, oats and potatoes.[12]

The real targets of such admonitions, however, were working people and the poor. Bread was a structural element of the diet of ordinary people, and the well-to-do worried that a scarcity of bread would provoke exactly the sort of upheaval threatened in Wakefield. Events across the Channel provided a particularly worrisome model. These worries were not unreasonable; poor harvests meant that the cost of wheat doubled between 1794 and 1795 and working people found it increasingly difficult to afford even the most modest diet of barley bread and cheese. Potatoes were often out of the question. Organised groups of men and women in many parts of the country intercepted grain shipments and requisitioned foodstuffs from merchants, often so that these could be sold at lower prices. Incidents of arson and other disturbances also increased steadily from April 1795.[13] The author of the 1795 *Times* letter referred specifically to these concerns. He urged the poor to take heed of the dreadful example of revolutionary France by not rioting, exercising 'some economy', and embracing a diet based on oats, barley and potatoes. Similar suggestions were offered by none less than the prime minister William Pitt, who assured Parliament that potato and maize breads were both 'pleasant and nutritious', and recommended them to the nation.[14] (See figure 14.)

Abundant evidence indicates that the poor baulked at eating such breads. Dismayed members of the gentry reported from across the coun-try on the recalcitrant behaviour of the poor, who were 'too fine mouthed' to eat mixed loaves.[15] The Reverend William Butts lamented that the 'daintiness' of working people around the Suffolk village of

Figure 14 Satirical cartoon showing recommended 'substitutes for bread'. William Pitt and his ministers feast in a room decorated with notices that warn of impending famine. One sign lists some substitutes they might consider in lieu of bread: venison, roast beef, turtle soup, champagne. In front of the banqueting lords is a small basket of potatoes, labelled 'potato bread to be given in charity'. The cartoon lampoons the efforts of the wealthy to encourage the poor to eat potatoes as a patriotic response to the shortage of wheat.

Glemsford led them to reject anything other than white bread.[16] Farmers in Essex condemned the 'wanton extravagance' of cottagers who insisted on wheat flour.[17] Writing from Stockport, the attorney Holland Watson complained that:

> a very liberal subscription has been entered into for the purpose of distributing oatmeal and other provisions among the poor at reduced prices – this measure, I am sorry to say, gives little satisfaction to the common people, who are still clamorous and insist on having wheaten bread; although every assurance has been given them that it cannot be obtained.[18]

Unsatisfied by such assurances, the locals in Stockport had rioted. Such behaviour exasperated landlords. Sir Charles Willoughby, chairman of the Oxfordshire quarter sessions, complained that he had been able to induce his labourers to eat whole-wheat bread only by providing them with subsidised wheat 'on condition that they made good brown bread and only had the very coarse bran taken out'.[19]

Working people did not favour white bread because they wished to emulate the consumption practices of the gentry. As such complaints indicate, the failure of efforts to encourage emulation was a source of considerable disappointment to successive British governments, as well as landlords and the chairs of quarter sessions. Rather, working people believed white bread to be the most nourishing. As one London baker explained in 1767, 'every pound of the fine flour taken is near half of it the nourishment and therefore the poor where I live prefer the fine and say the best is the best cheap [i.e. cheapest]'. Adding potatoes and other bulking materials to bread simply diluted the quantity of nourishment encompassed in the loaf. Such breads also provoked 'bowelly complaints', as the residents of the Lingford Poorhouse put it. Falling wheat prices in the first half of the eighteenth century had helped the urban poor to access this more nutritive food and they were loath to relinquish it.[20]

It was in the face of these mixed-bread campaigns, together with the promotion of cheap soups discussed in Chapter 3, that working people such as the Wakefield letter-writer denounced potatoes, red herrings and the other components of the new dietary recommended to them by the more wealthy. Potatoes, from this perspective, were not inherently objectionable. When eaten together with meat, they formed part of a welcome move away from a monotonous bread-based diet. When eaten instead of bread, and in the absence of anything else other than a sliver of herring, they were deemed inadequate.[21] In this context, the refusal to endorse potatoes as a replacement for bread amounted to a political act. The encouragement to eat potatoes formed part of a larger ambition to transform the economic landscape into one filled with individual proletarianised workers, each responsible for pursuing their own well-being. 'Damn your Red herrin[g]s Potatoes and you and all that have any thing to do with it,' they replied.[22]

Nowhere is this association between potatoes and the new capitalist dispensation clearer than in the writings of William Cobbett. Cobbett was a political activist, farmer, journalist and, at the end of his life, MP for Oldham. Although Cobbett initially endorsed the overall programme and anti-Jacobin focus of Pitt's government, from the early nineteenth century he grew dissatisfied with its fiscal policies and, increasingly, with its lack of attention to the dismal situation of rural workers. Real wages were deteriorating, and the loss of access to common land and prohibitions against gleaning and other traditional subsistence practice reduced the ability of households to feed themselves, while the terms of agricultural employment were becoming ever more precarious. In 1802 Cobbett began editing a weekly newspaper, *The Political Register*, which by 1816 was outspoken on the need for parliamentary reform, universal male suffrage, higher wages for agricultural workers, lower taxes, and overall greater political engagement with the needs of rural labourers. Cobbett identified deeply with agricultural workers and artisans in the south of England, through which he travelled both to hear the opinions of 'gentlemen, farmers, tradesmen, journeymen, labourers, women, girls, boys' and also to lecture to the large crowds who turned out to listen to him. He was sharply critical of the transformation in rural life wrought by commercial agriculture, mechanisation, and the focus on profit that he witnessed. He wrote extensively in praise of traditional rural culture, and never entirely abandoned the hope that it might prove possible to reconcile the needs of farmers and their workers, and so restore the harmony that he believed had once existed in the countryside.[23]

Cobbett despised potatoes. They were the root 'of slovenliness, filth, misery, and slavery'.[24] The potato-eating Irish peasant offered a particularly terrifying vision of the future for British workers. Potatoes, Cobbett believed, kept the Irish alive to be exploited by landowners. The enthusiasm for potatoes among English landlords formed part of an attempt to 'bring English labourers down to the state of the Irish, whose mode of living, as to food, is but one remove from that of the pig, and of the ill-fed pig too'.[25] The differences between the Irish and the potatoes that (barely) sustained them were slight as far as Cobbett was concerned. Both were filthy, uncivilised and brutish. He painted a dismal picture of life in an Irish cottage, whose inhabitants 'scratch [potatoes] out of the earth with their paws', tossed them unwashed into a pot and then ate them off a dirty wooden board alongside their farmyard animals.[26] Overall, he was certain that the 'misery and degradation of the Irish were chiefly owing to the use of the potatoes as the almost sole food'.[27]

Cobbett lamented that in England potatoes and tea had replaced healthful beer, bacon and bread in the working man's diet.[28] He moreover linked potatoes to the mumbo-jumbo of Methodism and other religions that in his view encouraged the poor to reform themselves rather than society. Beware 'the sleek-headed Methodist thief that would persuade you to live upon potatoes', he warned.[29] The promise of happiness that lay at the heart of the new liberal ideology struck him as particularly dishonest. Farmers, he complained, presented the potato plot as a 'blessing to all the lower classes of the community' but in fact it allowed them to keep wages low.[30] Denouncing proposals to weaken the poor laws that for centuries had provided a safety net for the infirm, unemployed and necessitous, Cobbett pointed specifically to the fiction that such changes would lead to greater happiness. As the 1834 Parliament debated the wholesale revision of England's system of social relief, Cobbett railed against the bill's claim to promote happiness, which he denounced as 'the impudence of all impudence'. It was, he wrote:

> the impudence of all impudence to support this bill under the pretence that it would make the lives of the working people *more happy*, when there lie the instructions to the barrister who drew the bill, stating, 'THAT IT IS DESIREABLE TO BRING THE WORKING PEOPLE TO LIVE UPON COARSER FOOD THAN THEY NOW LIVE UPON'. Of all the impudence that the world ever witnessed, the impudence of supporting the bill upon the grounds that it will make the working people *better off*, is the greatest.

The bill's true aim, he believed, was to force the working people of England to live upon 'potatoes and sea-weed', while pretending that this dismal diet would make them happier.[31]

Potatoes, for Cobbett, were overall an inferior crop that exhausted the soil and produced no straw for farm animals. They were a nutritionally empty foodstuff, especially when consumed together with tea. Most centrally, they were associated with the proletarianisation and immiseration of working people. 'It is an undeniable fact', he stated, that 'in the proportion that this root is in use, as a substitute for bread, the people are wretched'. Cobbett insisted that any employee bringing a potato into his own household would be dismissed on the spot.[32]

The Captain Swing uprising of 1830 provided Cobbett with a particular opportunity to emphasise the links between potatoes, agrarian capitalism and rural poverty. The upheaval, which mobilised thousands of rural workers and terrified landlords, many urban residents and the state, was essentially a protest against the transformation of English agriculture into a fully capitalist system. By the 1820s, many rural labourers, as the historians Eric Hobsbawm and George Rudé put it, had become 'not merely a full proletariat, but an underemployed, pauperised one'.[33] Protesters complained of falling wages, unemployment and parsimonious payments of poor relief. A particular target was equipment such as threshing machines that reduced demand for labour. Large groups of (mainly) men marched through the countryside in over twenty counties, demanding increased wages and the destruction of threshing machines, and on occasion setting fire to barns and farmhouses. Sometimes these demands were preceded by threatening letters signed by the rebels' fictional leader 'Captain Swing', who gave the events their name. The uprising was particularly intense in the south and east, areas sharply affected by the agricultural boom and dissolution of older social ties between farmers and labourers, but most English counties experienced some unrest.

Cobbett had not only predicted the Swing riots, but also travelled across the southern counties during the uprising, lecturing to village halls packed with agricultural labourers. His endorsement of their demands earned him an arrest on the charge of inciting violence, although the trial subsequently collapsed. For Cobbett, the potato symbolised the pitiable conditions against which the rioters rose. Country labourers, to their credit, had 'resolved not to be reduced to potatoes'. 'In order to preserve themselves from this state of terrible degradation', they had marched and agitated. Being 'reduced to potatoes' was a shorthand for the entire system that Cobbett condemned.[34]

For rioters too, potatoes encapsulated the impoverished conditions they and their families endured. 'We will not live upon potatoes', proclaimed a banner held aloft by marchers in the Isle of Thanet, in Kent. In the Sussex village of Pulborough, a group of between thirty and forty labourers gathered in the vestry room of the church to explain to the farmers who had come to listen that they had been 'starving on potatoes long enough, and there must be an alternation'. They asked for, and obtained, an increase in wages. When a group of labourers in Ringmer, in East Sussex, met with the local landowner to explain their grievances, they likewise complained of their monotonous potato diet. 'Have we no reason to complain that we have been obliged for so long a period to go to our daily toil with only potatoes in our satchels, and the only beverage to assuage our thirst the cold spring', they enquired, before asking for an increase in wages and the immediate dismissal of the governor of the local poorhouse.[35] To be living on potatoes summarised effectively the misery of the rural poor in the new capitalist economy.

This did not mean that protesters refused to eat potatoes. Although Cobbett viewed the potato, like the tea-kettle, as a malevolent interloper in the labourer's cottage, this opinion was not shared by most rioters. Labourers who had fired a barn near the Kentish village of Orpington observed cheerfully that 'we only want some potatoes; there is a nice fire to cook them by'. Villagers in Wiltshire expressed the hope that in the future their children could sleep with 'a belly full of tatoes instead of crying with half a belly full'.[36] Joseph Arch, founder of Britain's first union for agricultural workers, was a little child in Warwickshire during the period of the uprising. Potatoes, he recalled, were a desirable commodity. They were in short supply and the one man who grew them 'hoarded them up' for his own use.[37] Indeed, William Cobbett's exasperated threat to dismiss any labourer found in possession of potatoes acknowledged that the tuber was popular with the very rural workers whom he hoped to protect from a demeaning potato diet.[38] Labourers aspired to continue eating potatoes, but under circumstances more of their own choosing. What they rejected was not potatoes, but being reduced to potatoes.

Being reduced to potatoes continued to provide a powerful shorthand for the immiseration of the working classes within the capitalist economy. The labourers who actually grew Britain's food should be able to afford something more than 'POTATOES AND RAGS', insisted petitioners in 1838.[39] Elite recommendations that the poor could subsist happily on potatoes, of the sort common in the previous century, were increasingly labelled as cynical subterfuges. Cobbett was not alone in denouncing such claims as impudent. When Robert Bullock Marsham, Warden of Merton College, Oxford, suggested during the harsh winter of 1842–3 that if workers could not afford to buy bread, they at least 'rejoiced in potatoes', he was widely pilloried.[40] For critics of the abstract market, potatoes encapsulated its heartlessness.

WHAT PROGRESS CAN ONE EXPECT FROM A PEOPLE WHO EAT POTATOES?

While Cobbett castigated the potato as a tool of capitalist exploitation, capitalists took a different view. For them, the potato was an obstacle to market discipline, not its enabler. Advocates of liberal capitalism looked forward to a bright future of rational economic practice and the sensible exchange of labour as one commodity among many. From this perspective the prolific potato enabled too much autonomy from the market. Just as William Petty, the seventeenth-century political philosopher, believed that potatoes allowed the Irish to lead a life of idleness, so nineteenth-century liberals complained that potatoes facilitated exactly the sort of uneconomic behaviour that they hoped to eradicate. Cobbett and the liberals thus disagreed profoundly on whether the potato enabled or impeded the spread of capitalist market relations. All, however, concurred that Ireland provided the clearest illustration of their divergent analyses.

During the eighteenth century Ireland had often been heralded as the premier example of the potato's beneficent power to increase the population of healthy, industrious workers. During his travels around Ireland in the 1770s, the English agricultural writer Arthur Young praised the potato as a nutritious food that encouraged population growth and general good health. The fact that it insulated Irish labourers from the market was a further attraction. English workers, Young observed, were at the mercy of grain prices, as most purchased their food rather than growing it themselves. In Ireland, in contrast, 'the poor have nothing to do with prices, they depend not on prices, but crops of a vegetable very regular in its produce', namely the potato. 'Which therefore is the best off?', Young asked: the Englishman, or the Irishman with his potato bed and cow.[41] For Young, the answer was clear.

By the 1820s, the potato's capacity to sustain families independent of market conditions looked less attractive to some observers. As the historian David Lloyd has argued, this transformation reflects changes in the British economy and in statecraft. As Britain's economy moved from a fundamentally agrarian model towards a more industrial, capitalist framework, the eighteenth-century emphasis on building a self-sustaining labour force was replaced by the conviction that wealth and power derived from a smoothly functioning economic system, not simply from a larger population of diligent workers. The market economy demanded not merely healthy people, but a particular organisation of society around specific forms of waged labour and relations between employers and the workforce, and the dominance of the market in setting prices and wages. Potatoes, Lloyd noted, were increasingly associated with 'moral and political as well as economic characteristics that are recalcitrant to capitalist development'. The autonomous, potato-eating Irish labourer praised by Young had become 'a scandalous and potentially destabilising alternative to the economic and political forms that the reproduction of capital requires'.[42]

The writings of Thomas Robert Malthus are a barometer of this change. Malthus, who was born in 1766 in Surrey, spent most of his adulthood as the professor in history and political economy at the East India College, an institution intended to educate future colonial administrators. A minister in the Church of England, he also delivered sermons at the College, and over his life published a series of provocative and widely discussed works on economic and political matters, which reflected both his moral convictions and his thoughts on the nature of economic organisation. By the 1830s his ideas were sufficiently influential to underpin the substantial reduction in entitlement to poor relief enshrined in the 1834 New Poor Law, which limited parish relief to a narrowly defined group of 'deserving' poor – the bill that Cobbett had denounced as an impudence to end all impudences.[43]

The work that attracted the most fame was Malthus' essay on population, first published in 1798 and repeatedly printed, with substantial revisions, in subsequent decades. The *Essay on the Principles of Population* captured well the growing doubts about the potential of a healthy population alone to generate economic growth. Malthus' desire to write the essay was apparently prompted by conversations with his father about human society's capacity for happiness, a matter on which the younger Malthus took a gloomy view. His overall aim was, in the words of the historian Alessandro Roncaglia, 'to assert the uselessness of any attempt at improving the situation of the great mass of the workers'.[44] Malthus maintained that since the size of the population was limited by the supply of food, any effort to ensure that working people were amply fed would result in unsustainable population growth, and would lead inevitably to some sort of collapse. The poor laws, he explained, 'may be said therefore in some measure to create the poor which they maintain'. Their abolition would discourage the poor from having children, and thereby 'promote the happiness of the great mass of mankind'.[45] The essay's popularity, measured by the number of subsequent editions, as well by Malthus' later success in shaping public policy, reflects its ability to crystallise new ideas about the relationship between political stability, economic success and the size of the population.

Unsurprisingly, Malthus was unenthusiastic about potatoes. Because the potato was so much more productive than wheat, it enabled an unprecedented rate of population growth, but unlike eighteenth-century writers Malthus did not view this as an advantage. He believed that the increase in the Irish population enabled by the potato system would find its natural limit; an abundant supply of food guaranteed not a robust population but rather an impending catastrophe. A failure in the potato crop, which he regarded as highly probable, would result in circumstances 'beyond all comparison, dreadful', he wrote in 1803.[46]

Like Cobbett, Malthus associated the potato with degradation. The potato, together with the 'ignorance and barbarism of the people', had combined with squalid living conditions, inadequate clothing and poor hygiene to maintain the Irish population in a depressed and miserable state. Were the same system extended to England, 'the rags and wretched cabins of Ireland would follow'. An increase in potato consumption, and the spread of potato grounds would constitute 'the most cruel and fatal blow to the happiness of the lower classes of people in this country, that they had ever received'.[47] In various essays he dissected the 'radical evils of the use of potatoes' as a staple, and linked their widespread consumption to the backward and degraded state of the Irish labourer (although he by no means held the potato uniquely responsible). The cultivation of potatoes by Catholic labourers led to unsustainable population increase, but did nothing to keep down the price of other commodities, and so prevented rural workers from purchasing any of the other goods that they needed to live a commodious life. For Malthus, potatoes were bad for the Irish, and they set an ominous precedent for people in other countries. Nothing good could possibly come of an increase in their consumption.[48]

The dismal effect of Ireland's reliance on potatoes and its existing system of land tenure was expressed with equal clarity by the Scottish economist John Ramsay McCulloch, a disciple of Malthus' friend and fellow economist David Ricardo, in an entry in the 1824 *Encyclopaedia Britannica*. McCulloch's aim in his entry on the 'Cottage System' was to demolish the suggestion that English labourers might benefit from access to land on which to grow potatoes or raise a cow. In McCulloch's view such a proposal was totally misguided, since the result would be to reduce England's economy to the condition of Ireland, or rural France. In those places, he observed, the irrational division of labour and capital among a multitude of minute landholdings stifled any spirit of industry and suffocated the desire for self-improvement that was essential for economic growth. Citing Ireland in particular, McCulloch noted that the result was 'to approximate man to the state of the savage', since rural workers were obliged to supply all their wants by their own labour. Lacking contact with the stimulating forces of the outside world, the stagnant rural labourer 'sinks into a state of apathy, and of sluggish and stupid indifference'. Isolation and ignorance impeded the formation of the arts, and prevented the rural population even from recognising their miserable condition. Consequently, he noted, 'they cannot act collectively, and must, therefore, submit themselves with less resistance to the yoke of the oppressor'.[49] The autonomy enabled by potatoes was no autonomy at all.

The dreadful famine that struck Ireland in the years between 1845 and 1849 following successive failures of the potato harvest proved, to the satisfaction of the British government, that a form of agriculture that its own policies had done much to encourage was in fact unsustainable. From 1845 an infestation of late blight devastated potato harvests in many parts of Europe. On the continent the loss of the potato crop caused tens of thousands of deaths, particularly in areas such as the Netherlands and Prussia where the rye and wheat harvests were also affected. In Belgium, the 1845 potato harvest was 87 per cent lower than usual, while the 1846 rye harvest was reduced by 50 per cent. Some 40,000 people died as a result.[50] The scale of the disaster in Ireland was, however, of another order.

In Ireland, as Young, Malthus and many others observed, the potato's superlative power to convert earth and light into calories made it possible for rural families to live on the minute patches of land onto which they were squeezed as commercial wheat, dairy and meat production expanded under Britain's colonial rule. By the 1840s some 40 per cent of the population subsisted almost entirely on potatoes, or potatoes with a bit of buttermilk if they possessed enough land to pasture a cow. Poor men in rural Ireland ate between three and five kilos of potatoes a day and little else. The ready availability of peat for cooking, together with the potato's very high yields in the moist Irish soil, allowed entire families to subsist on Cobbett's miserable potato diet.[51] While a single valley in the Andes might contain over a hundred different types of cultivated potato, most of the potatoes grown in nineteenth-century Ireland were a single yellow-fleshed variety known as Irish Lumper. Reliance on a single cultigen greatly increases vulnerability to disease. When the crop failed in 1845, and again in 1846, 1848 and 1849, over a million people died. Ireland's population of eight million was devastated by the combined effects of the famine and the resultant emigration of another million to the Americas.[52]

The famine was triggered by the arrival of late blight, but the magnitude of the calamity was greatly increased by the response of the British government, which viewed the crisis as a welcome opportunity to reshape Irish society. In the opinion of officials such as Charles Trevelyan, chief administrator at the Treasury in London, Ireland's entire economic structure was an affront to modern capitalist practice. Heir to substantial government compensation following the abolition of slavery in the British West Indies, Trevelyan studied under Malthus at the East India College in the 1820s. He served for a number of years as a colonial official in India, before taking the position at the Treasury. He exercised a powerful influence on the government's approach to the famine. The collapse of the potato economy would, he hoped, propel Irish small-holders off their tiny plots of land and into the ranks of the proletariat. This, Trevelyan believed, would be an enormous improvement, well worth the 'transient evil' of a famine. It would also sweep away the inefficient and listless class of Irish landlords, whom the British held responsible for the catastrophic humanitarian crisis. The last thing the British government should do, from his perspective, was prop up this archaic system with aid to the stricken Irish. For liberals such as Trevelyan, the potato was an obstacle to modernity, a roadblock on the march towards economic rationality. It was the enemy of the state. 'What hope is there for a nation which lives on potatoes?', he exclaimed in disgust.[53]

Trevelyan was explicit about the beneficial consequences of the famine. How, he asked, were Irish labourers to support themselves in the future? He saw only one possibility: 'the position occupied by these classes is no longer tenable and it is necessary for them to live by the wages of their labour'. The Irish would no longer subsist on potatoes that they grew themselves, but rather on grain, 'which they will purchase out of their wages'. In other words, they would become a rural proletariat. They would continue to live from agriculture, but 'agriculture conducted according to new and very improved conditions'.[54] The famine, as Trevelyan and many other British liber-als agreed, thus provided a 'glorious opportunity' to transform Ireland away from a society of autarkic potato-eaters into one where the Irish consumed 'a higher kind of food' and developed the neces-sary 'habits of industry and improvement' that would allow them to purchase that food. 'Even in the most afflicting dispensations of Providence there was ground for consolation, and often even occasion for congratulation', as one MP put it in 1846.[55] The potato famine, viewed from the perspective of Westminster, usefully obliged the able-bodied Irish to join the rural proletariat. The potato, in contrast, had enabled and represented their earlier failure to enter the modern world.

Writing in London in the early 1850s, capitalism's greatest theorist, Karl Marx, drew on these notions when he likened the politically inert French peasantry to potatoes in a sack. The French nation, he stated in his *Eighteenth Brumaire of Louis Napoleon*, consisted of little more than a disparate mass of disconnected peasant families, much as an aggregation of individual potatoes constituted a sack of potatoes. Neither could be considered to possess any larger collective identity. Like McCulloch, who believed that the isolation created by the Irish agricultural system meant that cottiers 'cannot act collectively, and must, therefore, submit themselves with less resistance to the yoke of the oppressor', Marx maintained that the autarkic existence of peasant smallholders isolated them one from another, and also from the modern world. Since each farm was essentially self-sustaining, smallholders had no opportunity to develop any sort of class consciousness. In consequence, they were unable to recognise, let alone advance, their own interests, and so remained on the sidelines of political life, trapped in an archaic and damaging mode of life and prey to the blandishments of tyrants and demagogues. 'They cannot represent themselves, they must be represented', he observed. Little wonder that the metaphor Marx selected to describe this state of isolation from the modern world was the potato.[56]

Marx scarcely needed to travel to London to absorb this image of the potato as an impediment to progress. In many parts of Europe the potato had by mid-century come to epitomise a stagnant world devoid of sociability and consumer desires, and characterised by the persistence of pre-capitalist forms of production. 'What progress can one expect from a people who are content to eat potatoes?', asked the French physician and journalist Amédée Dechambre. 'Extreme sobriety', he observed, was as damaging to national progress as excessive consumption.[57] While in the seventeenth century writers such as Petty disliked the potato because it enabled Irish peasants to evade the reach of the state, by the nineteenth century its crime was to facilitate an evasion of economic reality. (See figure 15.)

Figure 15 Potatoes and capitalist rationality. When the free-trade magazine *The Struggle* wanted to explain the destructive effect of tariffs it turned to potatoes. The 1843 cartoon shows seven men inside a cage that represents a Britain deprived of affordable food imports. In the event of a bad harvest the more wealthy remain unaffected, but the less well-off are obliged to eat more potatoes and less beef and bread. Man No. 5, the caption explains, 'is a labouring man; he drops bread, and takes chiefly to potatoes'. If working people resisted the free market, the magazine implied, they had no one to blame but themselves if they were reduced to a diet of potatoes.

LAZY POTATO BLOOD

Across Europe, the idea that potatoes impeded the discipline of capital-ism advanced in tandem with industrialisation and urbanisation, both of which more than doubled over the nineteenth century in the United Kingdom and France, with Germany not far behind.[58] These changes in the nature of work and the organisation of society provoked anxieties about their impact on morality, social cohesion and the health of the body politic. Attention focused on the strength and vitality of the indus-trial workforce. Of particular concern was the fear that the flesh-and-blood bodies of urban workers would not be able to sustain the relentless labour that industry demanded. 'Fatigue' emerged as the great enemy of national efficiency and economic success. Food, the fuel that powered the human motor, was crucial to maintaining the bodies of workers in good order, and thereby ensuring the competitiveness of national industry.

From the second half of the century, scientific investigation into thermodynamics resonated with growing industrialisation to create an understanding of the human body as a sort of motor. Labour, explained the Italian politician and economist Francesco Nitti, 'is nothing but heat transformed into mechanical energy'. Heat, in turn, 'can only be produced by the combustion of food-stuffs' within the human worker. Consequently, 'countries which are badly dieted are those where the working energies are slight'.[59] As the historian Anson Rabinbach has shown, by mid-century scientists and politicians concurred that understanding the fuel needs of this motor was essential to a nation's economic and political success.[60] Investigators such as Carl von Voit, Wilbur Atwater and a great many others devised a range of ingenious experiments into food chemistry, which allowed them to correlate food inputs with energy outputs. The invention in the 1870s of the calorie expressed concisely this connection between food and work: the calorie measured the amount of energy that a specific food enabled its eater to expend. This, together with the emergence of a scientific consensus about the physiology of human digestion, made food chemistry an effective language for expressing the relationship between the diet of workers and their productivity. The quantification of food's nutritive value through the calorie and other numerical measures resonated with ongoing nineteenth-century efforts to establish mathematical methods to measure work, which further refined the links between food inputs and labour outputs. As a result, the overall nutritiveness of a dietary regime, in the form of its caloric value and chemical constituents, could be correlated mathematically with the health and vigour of eaters, which in turn affected economic efficiency. The long-standing conviction that the dietary practices of workers materially affected the economic and military success of the nation was thus greatly strengthened by the emergence of a mathematical and scientific language for expressing this relationship.[61]

Experiments in food chemistry usually focused explicitly on the energy requirements of industrial workers, soldiers and other people viewed as particularly important to national success. Armand Gautier, professor of physiology at the University of Paris, for instance worked to calculate the food energy that both groups needed to carry out a range of tasks. The Prussian physician Wilhelm Hildesheim likewise focused on the nutritional adequacy of military diets in his 1856 study.[62] Where eighteenth-century writers had contented themselves with asserting a general connection between the abundance and healthfulness of the food supply and the wealth and power of the state, nineteenth-century scientists were able to demonstrate precise numerical correlations between the chemical components of different foodstuffs and the thermodynamic work they enabled.

The influential German physiologist Max Rubner, who advised the Prussian government on military provisioning and prison diets and served as a director of its Imperial Health Board, wrote prolifically on the importance of nutrition to national well-being. First as a professor at Marburg and Berlin, and then as founding director of Berlin's Kaiser Wilhelm Society for the Advancement of Science, he stressed the imperative of ensuring that Germany's population of urban workers was well fed. Nutrition, he believed, was 'the foundation of the individual's physical and mental performance, and thus the foundation of national productivity and public health'.[63] The health and diets of urban workers were of direct economic and political interest to the state. Rubner, like Gautier and many others, was particularly interested in the nutritional needs of the urban proletariat and soldiers, and he devoted sustained attention to analysing the dietary practices of these crucial groups. He consistently stressed the destructive impact of the modern diet on the worker's body, and published both scientific and popular works aimed at explaining the principles of rational nutrition. Through such activities Rubner and his colleagues helped establish the political, economic and social importance of this new nutritional paradigm.

Its findings were not encouraging as regards the potato's contribution to industrial efficiency. The nineteenth century witnessed a steady increase in the scale of commercial potato cultivation as the tuber made ever-greater inroads into the diets of many Europeans. Potato production increased thirteen-fold in Prussia; total production in tonnes vastly outstripped the combined yield of grains by 1850. Labourers in

Upper Silesia and elsewhere were said to be subsisting on potatoes, black bread and schnapps. Writing in 1854, the physician Friedrich Tiedemann made similar observations about the diet of the lower classes in central and southern Germany.[64] By mid-century potatoes were grown, along with rye, on virtually all smallholdings in Flanders, and occupied up to 20 per cent of all agricultural land in the Dutch provinces. Potatoes were 'the most general and the most important foodstuff for the lower and even for a part of the middle classes in the Netherlands', according to the minister of the interior in 1845. Labourers in Utrecht ate them three times a day.[65] In the Danish region of Mid Jutland, they were reported to form the core of the diet of poor peasants, along perhaps with a spoonful or two of boiled cabbage. In Sweden, potatoes by the 1840s constituted nearly 40 per cent of the total harvest in terms of volume.[66] Rural Russians reportedly consumed 185 kilos each year in the 1880s. 'The food of the peasants is terribly uniform,' noted one observer. 'Day in and day out rye bread, potatoes, cabbage; the remaining foods are merely a sort of seasoning for these three.'[67] In England, where potatoes had long formed an important part of the diet of ordinary people, commercial cultivation grew markedly, so that potatoes covered as much as 25 per cent of the arable land. Potatoes, reported the British Association for the Advancement of Science in 1881, were 'easily the [population's] most important vegetable food'. As elsewhere, they featured particularly prominently in the diet of working people.[68] (See recipe for Baked Potatoes.)

The spokesmen and -women of the new science of nutrition were largely unenthusiastic about the potato's growing ubiquity. It was truly lamentable that potato consumption had increased so markedly among the lower classes, wrote Tiedemann in 1854, since this nitrogen-poor root was single-handedly responsible for the yearly growth in cases of rickets and tuberculosis, as well as the notable increase in the numbers of 'cripples and idiots'. The potato-heavy diet of German workers would lead inevitably to degeneration and a decade-by-decade decline in both physical and intellectual capabilities, according to another German physician. He predicted catastrophic consequences for the fatherland.[69] Far from being the

Baked Potatoes

Elena Molokhovets' enormously popular A Gift to Young Housewives *was first published in St Petersburg in 1861. This cookery book, which went through some twenty editions, aimed to help wealthy women run a household, manage a team of servants and address the other expectations of bourgeois sociability. Many of the dishes call for ingredients far beyond the reach of most Russians; Molokhovets' almond kulich or Easter bread requires seventy eggs. A few, however, reflect the more humble foods eaten on a daily basis by the majority of the population. This simple recipe for potatoes baked in ashes is from the 1897 edition.*

Baked Potatoes

'Wipe off the potatoes without washing them. Bury them in the coals of a Russian stove or bake in the oven, turning frequently so that they do not burn. Serve for breakfast and pass salt and butter separately.'

nourishing powerhouse that eighteenth-century promoters had perceived, the potato was increasingly condemned as a nutritionally inferior foodstuff. Laboratory analysis revealed it to be low in protein compared to meat, and nutritionists argued that its chemical components were a poor match to those of the human body. A diet heavy in potatoes left its eater sluggish, enfeebled and unsuited to the demands of modern labour. A mere fourteen days of subsisting on potatoes was all that was required to render a labourer unable to work at all, in the view of the Dutch physician and politician Jacob Moleschott.[70] Moleschott gained a degree in medicine from the

University of Heidelberg in 1845, and subsequently lectured at various universities in Switzerland, Germany and Italy, before taking Italian citizenship and from 1876 serving as a senator in Rome. Moleschott's varied compositions on scientific and policy matters stressed the importance of eliminating poverty and ensuring that working people could afford the nourishing food that would allow them to live with a measure of dignity. He also stressed the centrality of food to industrial productivity and national progress. Like many other food chemists, Moleschott believed that a large quantity of protein, together with phosphorus, was essential to good nutrition, and for this reason he regarded the potato as a poor substitute for meat. It was therefore unfortunate, in his view, that it so often performed precisely this role in the diet of ordinary Germans.[71]

Moleschott insisted that a potato-heavy diet led inevitably to illness and infirmity. It provided inadequate nourishment for the workers who so often relied on it. 'Lazy potato blood, how can it give muscles the strength to work, or the brain the stimulating impulse of hope?', he asked in his 1858 *Lectures on Food*. Reliance on potatoes moreover explained Ireland's poverty, and condemned it to permanent subservience to Britain. The chemical properties of potatoes generated 'powerless despair' in the Irish constitution. In contrast, the energising blood of meat-eaters coursed through the veins of their British colonisers. 'Poor Ireland, whose poverty begets poverty,' he sighed, 'you cannot win!' National strength and economic success were fatally impeded, not advanced, by a potato diet.[72]

Like Moleschott, other influential nutritionists too viewed a potato-heavy diet in a dim light. His pioneering nutritional experiments into nitrogen and protein convinced the German chemist Carl von Voit that bread should form the bulk of a worker's diet, with potatoes and other vegetables making up no more than 30 per cent.[73] Voit's calculations indicated that the human motor required at least 118 grams of protein per day in order to function efficiently, and many other nutritionists endorsed this 'Voit standard' as a minimum.[74] Insofar as the low-protein potato replaced more nourishing meat in the worker's diet, its consumption was positively dangerous. Francesco Nitti was certain that the rapid progress made by Belgian industry was due primarily to the shift from a potato- to a meat-based diet by industrial workers. He noted that between 1853 and 1891, their monthly per capita meat consumption had climbed from 15.920 kilos to 20.770, while potato consumption fell from 22.573 kilos to 17.866. A shift from potatoes to meat likewise explained why Irish workers, who in their homeland were 'idle, weak, whimsical', were transformed into energetic and productive workers on emigration to the United States.[75]

The new nutrition thus provided a powerful framework for comparing the industrial productivity of different nations. Nitti believed that the high consumption of meat explained the greater productivity of US and British industry, while the high consumption of potatoes and other 'hydrocarbonates' was responsible for the inferior performance of German and French workers. He produced a series of comparative charts that showed the close correlation between diet and the robustness of soldiers and industrial workers.[76] The German academic and social critic Gerhart von Schulze-Gävernitz came to similar conclusions in his careful comparative study of the cotton industry in Germany and England. Schulze-Gävernitz's family was itself in the business of cotton-printing; his grandfather had undertaken an apprenticeship in Manchester. The young Schulze-Gävernitz travelled across northern England in the 1880s, visiting cotton mills and examining the details of manufacturing. Diet formed an important part of his analysis. He quizzed operatives in Oldham and other parts of Lancashire on their weekly budgets and listened to their opinions about how working and dietary practices had changed over the last half century. His studies convinced him that English workers enjoyed a far higher standard of living, and that their superior diet was both a cause and a reflection of this advantage. Workers in the English cotton industry ate meat and wheat bread every day. German workers, in contrast, lived off rye bread and potatoes. As a result, English operatives were between two and three times more productive than their German analogues, or so he calculated.[77] The potatoes that Frederick the Great (and the British Board of Agriculture) had so enthusiastically championed a century earlier were now identified as reason why Germany lagged behind Britain in economic output and national prowess.

CONCLUSIONS

During a stop in Blackpool the young Gerhart von Schulze-Gävernitz fell into conversation with an elderly man who resided at a lodging house where the travelling German took dinner. Over a meal of tea, ham, and mutton with potatoes and peas, the old man, a former cotton operative, conveyed his life story. His parents had been handloom weavers in Lancashire, and his childhood in the 1820s had been one of abject poverty. From his earliest years he worked in a spinning mill, and later at a power loom. His parents and siblings subsisted on potatoes and oatcakes; he recalled that he did not lay eyes on a loaf of wheat bread until much later, when he moved to Manchester. As a young man he had been a passionate supporter of Chartism, the working-class movement calling for universal male suffrage, the abolition of property requirements for holding political office, and other reforms to the electoral system. Schulze-Gävernitz was impressed by the old man's acute critique of the conditions facing industrial workers, as well as by his continued allegiance to the principles of Chartism.

Schulze-Gävernitz's interlocutor believed that overall the lot of workers had improved greatly since those harder days. He spoke eloquently about the benefits won through trade unionism, and astonished the younger operatives gathered at the table with his tales of a time when ordinary people could not afford even the leisure to enjoy an amateur football match on the beach, let alone a day's holiday. 'But if you wish to see the true sign of this change,' continued the grey-haired veteran, with beaming eyes, 'it lies before you on the table, the strength of Lancashire.' The old man then 'raised with triumphant bearing a piece of wheaten bread'.[78]

Bread rather than a poverty-diet of potatoes: for the elderly mill-worker a wheaten loaf made an apt symbol of the struggle over the living standards of the industrial working class because for him, as for so many other working men and women, bread represented the opposite of an impoverished life subsisting on potatoes and oatcakes, tied to a spinning mill from before 'he could scarcely speak and walk', subjected to a thirteen-hour day and banned from joining a union. During the nineteenth century the contrasting resonance of wheat bread versus a meal of potatoes went straight to the heart of the tensions over industrialisation and its relationship to economic growth and political reform. Both critics of the industrial system such as the Blackpool mill-worker and enthusiastic capitalists such as Trevelyan concurred that a diet of potatoes encapsulated something about the relationship between working people and the capitalist system, even if they diverged sharply in their interpretation of the potato's role in enabling capitalism's onward march. Daily diets, and the place of potatoes within them, provided a language for talking about the relationship between workers, the state and the new industrial order.

The connections between the everyday diets of the population and the strength and wealth of the state forged in the eighteenth century laid the foundations for these nineteenth-century debates, which focused increasingly on the goal of developing a body of robust industrial workers. The challenge of feeding the urban proletariat lay in matching the nourishing food that these human machines required with the nutritional resources that their salaries could command. Balancing the equation that connected the market value of labour to the amount of energy a worker could expend was of direct importance to the nation as a whole. As Francesco Nitti insisted in 1896, a better diet for workers led directly to 'a greater and more beneficial increase of general wealth'.[79] Meat and other protein-rich foods promoted this, while a potato diet, heavy in starch and low in protein, impeded industrialisation and weakened the nation's military. (See figure 16.)

At the same time, Schulze-Gävernitz's mill-worker did not reject the warm, boiled potatoes that accompanied his dinner of mutton, ham and peas. Those potatoes existed in a different symbolic plane from the potatoes that contrasted so powerfully with the wheaten strength of Lancashire. Potatoes became a symbol of proletarian poverty at the same time as they

Provinces.	Percentage of the Productive Population to the entire Population.	Absolute Amount of Albuminoids in the Workman's food.	Proportion obtained from potatoes.	Deaths from Phthisis out of 1,000 Deaths 1851–55.	Exemptions from Military Service per Thousand.
	°/₀	grammes	°/₀		
West Flanders	58	75	11·58	194	147
East Flanders	52	62·8	18·18	226	128
Hainault	42	59·9	3·88	171	75
Limburg	40	75	25·59	240	128
Antwerp	37	74	31·43	200	156
Brabant	37	75	17·30	194	131
Liège	36	72	13·75	141	77
Namur	31	49	1·96	149	64
Luxemburg	30	79	17·26	122	82

Figure 16 Francesco Nitti's table correlating high potato consumption with illness. A potato-heavy diet reduced the energy and vitality of workers, in the view of many nineteenth-century analysts. This chart, from the Italian economist Francesco Nitti's study of 'the food and labour-power of nations', linked the prevalence of potatoes with high levels of tuberculosis. Potato-eating regions also had higher numbers of exemptions from military service, a matter of direct concern to the state.

became an ever more normal, and welcome, presence on the tables of the working classes. They were, as the anonymous letter-writer put it nearly a hundred years previously, among the '5 principel Things that poor Peple want to bye'.[80] The potato's capacity to index both the bare life of the new industrial proletariat, and also the comforts won by trade unionism and working-class action, speaks to the importance of food in thinking about the relationship between people and the modern state.

CHAPTER 6

Security Potatoes

POTATO PETE

'**F**OLLOW ME MADAM; I'LL SHOW YOU A THING OR TWO.' SO promised a cartoon potato named Potato Pete, the protagonist of a British pamphlet produced in 1940. Potato Pete was the creation of the Ministry of Food. As part of the war effort, the Ministry vigorously encouraged potato consumption; *Potato Pete's Recipe Book* aimed to help housewives incorporate potatoes into every stage of the daily diet, from breakfast to pudding. Medical advice, the pamphlet stated, recommended that everyone eat at least twelve (and ideally sixteen) ounces of potatoes every day. (This equates to about two large baking potatoes.) It offered recipes for savoury potato waffles, potato fish cakes and, inevitably, potato soup, together with information on the potato's nutritional merits. The pamphlet's practical hints about how to stretch the limited amount of fat and milk available through rationing were enlivened by Potato Pete's louche comments and double entendres. He glossed the recommendation to boil potatoes in their skins with the comment that 'good taste demands I keep my jacket on'. 'I'm a devil of a fellow', he remarked, next to the recipe for devilled potatoes. On the back cover Potato Pete walks arm-in-arm with a pair of stylish women at the head of a long parade of cheering housewives (and a few men), looking dapper in a pair of spats.[1] (See figure 17.)

As Potato Pete's escapades suggest, by the mid-twentieth century the potato was once again a welcome component of state projects to transform everyday eating habits. In Britain the Ministry of Food's interest in the potato reflected the strains on the nation's food supply imposed by the Second World War, but it was not due solely to these pressing contingencies. From the 1910s, changing conceptions of the relationship between hunger, poverty and statecraft combined with national security concerns to focus in new ways on the chains linking agriculture, the food

Figure 17 Potato Pete. Potatoes were the taste of World War Two, as the historian Lizzie Collingham put it. In Britain national campaigns were very successful in increasing production, but boosting consumption was not straightforward. *Potato Pete's Recipe Book* tried to convert a collection of recipes featuring potatoes into a small romantic drama, with Potato Pete as the unlikely hero. 'Let me be your sweetie', he implored housewives on the page offering recipes for puddings. Other recipes were accompanied by more risqué remarks.

supply, everyday eating practices and the state. This chapter charts the twentieth-century developments that reconnected potatoes to national well-being.

At the end of the nineteenth century the political and social implications of hunger were preoccupying politicians in many parts of the world. Poverty, the historian James Vernon has shown, was increasingly perceived not as an individual calamity but as a public threat demanding 'a new ethic of collective social responsibility and action'.[2] Ongoing research into the science of nutrition and the mechanisms that spread disease intersected with fears that alcoholism and illness were undermining the robustness of the working class, to create a consensus among scientists and politicians that the political challenges posed by hunger and improper diet could no longer be addressed solely by unco-ordinated private initiatives. These threats to national strength and security needed to be defused through state-level schemes.

In response, bureaucrats and officials designed an imaginative array of programmes and policies to transform national eating habits, and thereby ensure the security of the nation as a whole. In so doing, they built on the foundations laid in the eighteenth century, when political thinkers had begun to posit a connection between what ordinary people ate and the wealth and prowess of the polity. Compared to their eighteenth-century predecessors, twentieth-century states were far better able to translate these convictions into effective policies. While eighteenth-century models of statecraft maintained that the nation would benefit if working people ate more nourishing foods, politicians possessed few tools for actually modifying everyday eating habits. Eighteenth-century states lacked 'the consistent coercive power, the fine-grained administrative grid, or the detailed knowledge that would have permitted them to undertake more intrusive experiments in social engineering', as the political anthropologist James C. Scott put it.[3] Twentieth-century attention to the political importance of diet thus represented not so much a fundamental change in the goals of statecraft, as a transformation in the technologies the state could deploy to implement its goals. Twentieth-century and early modern states shared many ambitions, but the modern state possessed instruments of statecraft, from statistical bureaux to public schooling, that would, in Scott's words,

'take them farther along this road than any seventeenth-century monarch would have dreamed'.[4] Programmes to modify eating habits formed
an important element of this toolkit.

Since the early twentieth century, states in many parts of the world had
experimented with new ways of improving the health of the population
by altering how and what people ate. In some countries these programmes reflected a greatly expanded conception of the state's responsibility for ensuring the well-being of the population, which led to the
modern welfare state, but schemes to modify popular eating habits also
emerged in countries that did not adopt an explicitly welfarist approach.
Classes in 'domestic economy' taught schoolgirls around the world about
the nutritional needs of the human body, the vitamin content of ingredients, and the effects of different cooking techniques on the nutritiveness of the finished dish, in the hope that they would use this knowledge
to improve the diets of themselves and their families. School refectories
and state-supported low-cost restaurants began to offer nutritionally
balanced meals for children and workers in many countries across
Europe, Asia and the Americas.[5]

The socio-political dimensions of these programmes were clear. They
aimed to improve the health of participants so as to mould them into
better citizens. In Britain every aspect of the school dinner schemes
introduced from 1904 was carefully designed to instruct children in
proper dietary and cultural practices such as self-control and hygiene.
Such measures were, as a Liberal MP put it, 'first-class imperialism', since
a healthy population ensured Britain's military and economic success.[6]
In Mexico, the leftist government that came to power in the 1920s
created an ambitious programme of public dining halls aimed at incul-
cating nutritious eating habits and modern behaviour. Physicians associated with the recently founded Ministries of Public Assistance and
Public Health believed that the low protein content and other nutritional
failings of the working-class diet resulted in low productivity and so
weakened Mexico. In response the government established a network
of 'National Dining Halls' serving subsidised, nutritionally informed
meals to working-class families. These institutions also offered classes in
cookery and nutrition, all with the aim of transforming the clientele into
useful and modern citizens. Similar ambitions shaped the attitudes of

colonial administrations in British India and politicians in early twentieth-century Japan, who likewise hoped to increase productivity and prosperity by modifying popular diets.[7]

In linking a well-nourished population to a strong state, these schemes reveal many continuities with the recommendations of eighteenth-century political thinkers. The health and vitality of actual or potential soldiers and workers remained the objects of particular attention. Everywhere such schemes met a varied reception from working people, who often appreciated the dietary and social opportunities they offered, but also objected to their judgemental tone and disciplinary intent.

FOOD, PUBLIC HEALTH AND THE FIRST WORLD WAR

The events of the First World War proved a turning point in the creation of this politico-dietary toolkit. The mobilisation of millions of soldiers required elaborate provisioning systems to deliver the food necessary to feed these recruits, and so helped create the administrative expertise and institutional infrastructures that would enable even more sustained interventions in everyday eating practices. The war also focused attention on the political and military consequences of malnutrition.

Many officials believed that the fragile nutritional health of recruits undermined military strength. In Britain, this concern built on earlier revelations from the Boer War, when recruitment officers determined that between 40 and 60 per cent of recruits were unfit for service. The Medical Boards set up to grade potential recruits after 1916 produced equally troubling results. Prime Minister David Lloyd George believed that ill-health deprived Britain of at least a million potential recruits. Referring to the system of classification used by these boards, he insisted that 'you cannot maintain an A-1 Empire with a C-3 population'.[8] Creating an A-1 population required government action to ensure that people ate properly. Ignorance of the basic principles of healthy eating, alongside poor budgeting skills, explained the dismaying prevalence of malnutrition in military recruits, in the opinion of recruiting officers. The principal cause of 'Poor Physique' in children, opined a military commissioner in Manchester in 1918, was 'the gross ignorance of the simplest forms of domestic economy and cookery' by their mothers. He believed that the introduction of mandatory classes in domestic science for working-class girls would eliminate, or at least greatly reduce, the number of men deemed unfit for military service.[9] Just as colonists in India had blamed famine on the backwardness of locals, so working people in Britain were held responsible for the terrible conditions in which they often lived.

Others argued that poverty, rather than ignorance, was the principal cause of malnutrition, but this did not make the result any less worrisome. Seebohm Rowntree, the heir to the Rowntree chocolate manufacturers, carried out a wide-ranging survey of poverty and household expenditure in turn-of-the-century York. He carefully compiled information about household diets, which allowed him to demonstrate that in York poverty forced the labouring classes to consume 'about 25 per cent less food than has been proved by scientific experts to be necessary for the maintenance of physical efficiency'.[10] These undernourished men alarmed recruiting officers and weakened Britain's fighting strength. Mass recruitment, which shone a spotlight on the ill-health that plagued working people, highlighted the ways in which malnutrition among the poor affected the nation as a whole.

There was moreover widespread agreement that government action was required to coordinate agricultural production with wartime food needs. The contending countries established new ministries aimed explicitly at addressing these challenges. The UK created the Ministry of Food Control in 1916; Austria-Hungary established a Joint Food Committee; and the United States founded the Fuel and Food Administration on its entry to the war. Imperial Germany acquired the War Food Office, the War Wheat Corporation and the Imperial Potato Office. Alongside nationalised railways, docks and munitions industries, these new structures greatly increased the state's control over economic production and daily life. In particular, they provided a way of directing both the production and consumption of food.[11]

As the German Potato Office indicates, potatoes formed a significant part of these broader programmes.[12] Renewed state-level interest in the potato reflected both its dietary importance in many parts of Europe and also changes in scientific understandings of nutrition. In the early twentieth century, nutritionists' myopic focus on protein began to be replaced with a more complex view of the chemical components associated with good nutrition. Potatoes consequently regained some of their lustre as a healthful foodstuff. 'The plain, substantial, standard food materials, like the cheaper cuts of meat and fish, milk, flour, corn meal, oatmeal, beans, and potatoes, are as digestible and nutritious and as well fitted for the nourishment of people in good health as are any of the costlier materials,' declared Wilbur Atwater, a leading figure in the investigation of food science, shortly before the outbreak of war.[13] Potatoes, working people were assured, were just as nourishing as more expensive foodstuffs such as steak. Therefore, nutritionists insisted, the working classes need not exhaust their limited resources on this sort of food in the mistaken belief that it was healthier or more sustaining. Nor was there any reason to agitate for the higher wages that would enable a more luxurious diet.

In wartime Britain, farmers were issued with Cultivation Orders, which stipulated the acreage of wheat and potatoes they were required to grow; from 1917 the British state moreover purchased the entire annual potato harvest, which was sold at set prices. These efforts to enhance production were successful; the size of the potato harvest was nearly 50 per cent higher than pre-war levels, and per capita weekly consumption jumped from 3.67 to 5.26 pounds.[14] Other regulations restricted the use of wheat flour in bread and pastries, fixed the size of servings permitted in restaurants and hotels, and criminalised food waste. By 1918 the government's food regulations themselves weighed half a pound. Violators were taken to court; in 1917 Emily Evans for instance appeared in the dock in Pembrokeshire, charged with selling potatoes for more than the permitted maximum.[15]

In all countries, pro-war propaganda tried to encourage greater potato consumption. 'Join the Ranks and Spud the Kaiser', urged a 1918 shop-window display in the Iowa town of Maquoketa. The US government hoped increased domestic potato consumption would compensate for the export of 20 million bushels of wheat destined for allies in Europe. Potatoes therefore featured regularly in the flourless wartime 'victory recipes' distributed by the new Food Administration. 'Eat potatoes with their starch, help the fighters on their march. Each baked potato that you eat will help to fill the ships with wheat. Eat potatoes, save the wheat, drive the Kaiser to defeat,' urged the authors of one wartime cookery book.[16] The owners of the Staack & Luckiesh pharmacy in Maquoketa used their shop window to present an imaginative visual staging of this advice. Towards the front of the window a small battalion of potatoes brandished sabres and waved the stars and stripes under the leadership of a larger potato representing General Pershing, head of the US Expeditionary Forces in Europe. An explanatory label hailed the formation of 'the newest fighting corps: the Potatriots'. 'Eat potatoes and save wheat' was the overall message, proclaimed clearly on a placard. Suitable recipes could be obtained inside the shop. (See figure 18.)

In Germany, potatoes were the first food to be subject to a price ceiling, and officials viewed the maintenance of the potato supply as a matter of the highest importance. Politicians rightly feared that

Figure 18 'Spud the Kaiser' window display. 'The potato is a good soldier. Eat it uniform and all', urged a notice in the window of this Iowa pharmacy. Governments in all combatant countries promoted potatoes, although in some cases demand outpaced supply and rationing was introduced. US cooks were advised not only about eating potatoes in their jackets, but also on how to prepare potato bread and other patriotic substitutes for wheat.

a reduction would reduce the population's capacity to work, and might also trigger political unrest. As one official in Berlin put it in early 1915, 'the potato question is the most important, the most burning, since the potato plays such as important role for the poorer population'. In addition to regulating potato prices, the state required bakers to use an increasing percentage of potato in the manufacture of bread, which from January 1915 was rationed to preserve the wheat supply. The resultant loaf was known as *K-Brot*, with the K standing for both *Krieg* (war) and *Kartoffel* (potato). By March 1915, however, potatoes themselves were in such short supply that they began to be rationed alongside bread and flour. Civilians found it increasingly difficult to obtain enough food. Public canteens were established in a number of cities, with mixed success, and special programmes to provide nutritious breakfasts for schoolchildren were trialled. Factories producing munitions and other matériel likewise set up refectories. Set quantities of meat and potatoes were allocated to these kitchens to ensure that workers in key industries were adequately fed.[17]

The German state's efforts at ensuring a steady supply of potatoes and other basic foodstuffs were undermined by poorly designed policies and a series of bad harvests. The British blockade imposed from 1914 exacerbated the situation, since Germany had previously relied on imports for a third of its food. By 1917 Germans faced real hunger; the nutritionist Max Rubner, who was advising the imperial government, believed the population was experiencing 'slow starvation'.[18] Attempts to address shortages by importing potatoes from abroad merely displaced the problem to the exporting country. In neutral Sweden, the export of potatoes to Germany provoked first rationing and then serious protest over the reduction in domestic food supplies. Dissatisfaction escalated. Workers' committees began calling for the distribution of land to enable small-scale potato cultivation. Demands for legislation limiting working hours and other social policies emerged alongside campaigns for land reform. Some 250,000 people participated in protests during Sweden's 1917 'potato revolution'.[19]

Across Europe these experiences helped redefine the relationship between food, the population and the state. Civilian populations became increasingly articulate in their expectation that the state should help ensure they had access to sufficient food. 'The boundaries of every-day life had changed,' as the historian Simon Hancock noted.[20] In Germany, the shortage of potatoes, bread, butter and meat reduced public support for the war, and ultimately helped bring down the government, which collapsed in November 1918.[21] At the same time, wartime rationing, the establishment of government-run canteens, agricultural and consumer committees, and other experiments in modifying popular diets developed the instruments that would permit interventions into everyday eating practices far greater than had been possible in the eighteenth century. Ensuring an adequate supply of potatoes, and encouraging the population to eat more of them, were among the ways in which these new instruments were deployed.

BREEDING A BETTER POTATO

By the early twentieth century the techniques of plant breeding had transformed commercial agriculture in Europe and the United States. Scientific agronomy programmes at universities and research institutes created new hybrids able to produce higher yields, tolerate pests, thrive in challenging environmental conditions, and other beneficial qualities. Research laboratories devoted specifically to potato breeding also started to appear. Cambridge University set up a Potato Breeding Institute in 1912, which later released a number of commercially successful varieties such as Maris Piper. Cornell University, a leading centre for plant breeding in the United States, taught potato breeding from the early twentieth century.[22] Similar programmes were meanwhile experimenting with new varieties of maize, wheat and other crops. The result was a range of highly successful hybrids that revolutionised commercial agriculture in Europe and the United States in terms of productivity and resilience.

In the case of potatoes, breeding efforts focused particularly on yield and resistance to diseases such as the late blight that had devastated Europe eighty years earlier. One way of developing such plants was to cross established commercial potatoes with lesser known, non-commercial varieties possessing relevant qualities. For this reason, non-commercial and wild varieties were highly sought after, despite the fact that the 'traditional' agriculture associated with them was generally viewed in a dim light by trained agronomists. Breeders rightly suspected that the Andes were the best place to hunt for these overlooked landraces, or locally cultivated species. Scientists hoped to draw on the untapped breeding potential of the many wild potato species and landraces known to exist in Chile, Bolivia, Peru, Ecuador and Colombia. The traditional and wild potatoes of South America thus provided the raw material that could be converted into modern seed varieties.[23]

Efforts to utilise this resource for breeding new commercial varieties had begun in the nineteenth century, largely under the impetus of individual growers and plantsmen. The Russet Burbank, now commonly used for baked potatoes and industrial French fries in the United States, was the eventual result of one such excursion to South America.[24] By the 1930s expeditions to collect promising landraces were supported by the formal infrastructure of dedicated agronomic institutes, and enjoyed direct government funding. Erwin Baur, director of the Kaiser Wilhelm Institute for Plant Breeding in Müncheberg, travelled to South America in 1931, returning with some thousand potato specimens.[25] In the same years the Russian geneticist Nikolai Ivanovich Vavilov undertook two expeditions to Latin America, where he collected large numbers of potatoes, as well as many other crops.[26] In 1938 the British Empire Potato Collecting Expedition likewise departed for Latin America, under the leadership of the botanists E. K. Balls and W. Balfour Gourlay. Collectors visited village markets, talked with locals, and consulted scientists and breeders in the Andes.[27]

Scientists based in Europe and the United States were not alone in their renewed interest in potatoes. The Andean biologists whose expertise the European expeditions hoped to tap were themselves associated with experimental breeding stations and national research programmes established from the late 1920s. In 1940s Peru the recently created Ministry of Agriculture began a series of breeding programmes focused on traditional varieties, and subsequently launched a national potato improvement programme, together with schemes for several other crops. The biologist Carlos Ochoa studied agronomy in Bolivia and the United States before assuming the directorship of Peru's National Potato Programme. Ochoa developed many new potato hybrids, including Renacimiento, now the most commonly grown commercial variety in

Peru. The Bolivian and Colombian Ministries of Agriculture likewise funded potato collections and experimental farms from the late 1930s.[28] With the support of the nationalist government, the Chinese scientist Guan Jia-Ji set up a potato research programme in the 1930s, and later ran courses in potato breeding at the Chengdu Central Farming Experimental Station.[29] India's Central Potato Research Institute was established in 1949 at Patna, incorporating several smaller breeding stations founded in the 1930s. India has subsequently played a leading role in developing new varieties adapted to sub-tropical conditions; it is now the world's second largest producer of potatoes, just behind China.

The specimens gathered by these excursions and developed through experimentation were deposited in the national potato collections that began to be established from the 1940s. Ochoa's acquisitions were stored in the Ministry of Agriculture's Experimental Station in the Mantaro Valley, which later formed the basis of Peru's national germplasm collection. The British Empire Potato Collecting Expedition's materials were held at the British Empire Potato Collection, subsequently renamed the Commonwealth Potato Collection. Others are housed at the US Potato Genebank, the German Groß Lüsewitz Potato Collection, and collaborative collections such as the Dutch–German Potato Collection at Wageningen.[30]

The establishment of these state-level centres, like the funding of national potato-collecting expeditions, points to the importance that individual states had come to accord the potato as a resource for managing the nation's food supply. The First World War had left European countries, in particular, in no doubt about the need for robust mechanisms for ensuring this, and by the 1930s the science of plant breeding was on hand to help.[31] When war returned to Europe in 1939, governments drew on these mechanisms to address the unprecedented challenges with which they and their citizens were confronted. As before, potatoes joined the war effort.

THE TASTE OF WAR

Food lay at the heart of the global calamity of the Second World War. The desire to ensure a reliable supply of food drove German and Japanese aggression. With the outbreak of war, states were moreover confronted with the monumental challenges of feeding the nearly two billion people mobilised, as well as the millions more who worked in agriculture, manned transport ships, laboured in vital industries and contributed in other ways to the war effort. Potatoes were a central feature of both national food policies and individual survival techniques, as the historian Lizzie Collingham has demonstrated.[32]

In Britain the wartime government actively promoted potatoes as a way of reducing the reliance on food imports while at the same time improving the nation's overall health. Stagnating or even declining potato consumption during the 1920s–30s alarmed government nutritionists, who had come to view the potato as a cornerstone in a healthy diet.[33] Since 'war demands better physique and health than peace', officials were convinced of the need to effect fundamental changes in the nation's eating habits. 'The English diet', complained the journal *Public Health* in 1941, 'is haphazard and its present composition depends largely upon chance and the tastes that have developed with industrialisation and prosperity. Certain sections of the nation, both rich and poor, are known to be feeding faultily.'[34] Eating properly, which included a greatly increased consumption of potatoes, was an individual obligation and a national necessity.

In 1939, Britain was heavily dependent on imported foods such as the millions of tons of wheat brought from Canada and Argentina to manufacture bread and feed livestock. Importing grain for these purposes struck ministers as a risky and inefficient use of Britain's vulnerable shipping capacity. In place of white bread and fresh meat fed on imported grains, the government encouraged a diet based around potatoes and wholegrain bread made with home-grown wheat. (Energy-dense processed foods such as tinned meat were imported from the empire to complement this recommended dietary.) Some 2.4 million hectares of pasture were accordingly converted to arable farming in a nation-wide 'plough-up' campaign, and farmers were directed by the County War Executive Committees to increase the acreage devoted to potatoes. All households were urged to keep rabbits, raise chickens and, especially, grow potatoes, which were promoted as an excellent source of energy and vitamin C, suited to British agricultural conditions and the capabilities of the home-gardener. The Ministry of Food's Potato Division was extremely successful in its efforts to increase production. By the end of the war, acreage devoted to potatoes had doubled from 1939. Such was the success that individual consumption struggled to keep pace.[35] Potato Pete's risqué advice formed part of this larger campaign to consume the 500,000 ton surplus that had accumulated by 1940. Nutritionists reinforced Pete's message through radio broadcasts and poster campaigns. Just as it had done in previous centuries, the British state also encouraged potato cultivation in its colonies and allied territories. Potato-growing schemes were introduced in Iraq, Syria, Egypt, Palestine and Cyprus. As a result of such efforts, British bases in Kenya, for instance, were supplied with locally produced potatoes grown by Kikuyu farmers.[36]

When the Soviet Union entered the war in 1941 it faced enormous impediments to its efforts to feed itself. Agricultural production was in disarray as a result of Stalin's programme of collectivisation, which had caused the devastating 1933 Ukrainian famine, in which as many as seven million people died. Wartime mobilisation deprived the countryside of some nineteen million agricultural labourers at a moment when more rather than less food was needed. Consequently by 1942 both the grain and potato harvests fell to a third of their pre-war volume. Soldiers and civilians were hungry all the time, despite a rationing system. When German troops captured key agricultural zones in the Ukraine, the situation worsened further. At least three million Soviets – probably many more – starved to death during the war.[37] Problems with distribution as well as supply obliged soldiers to forage for themselves; gaunt factory workers collapsed from hunger on assembly lines. Soviet officials responded by urging everyone to plant potatoes. From the nineteenth century, bread and potatoes had formed the backbone of the popular diet, and unlike grain, potatoes are relatively easy to cultivate on small pieces of ground. Newspapers dispensed horticultural advice and factory administrators endeavoured to provide workers with allotments. As a result, in 1943 Moscow 'floated in a green sea of potato plants'. Many organisations, including the Soviet military, set up farms on local wastelands to supplement the meagre state rations. By 1944 such auxiliary farms were producing over 2.6 million tons of potatoes and other vegetables, enough to ensure an additional 250 calories per day for workers lucky enough to have access to them. These efforts provided an essential source of food for perhaps 25 million people.[38]

With or without top-down encouragement, people around the globe turned to potatoes to keep body and soul together. Soviet peasants, who during the war relied almost entirely on foods they grew themselves, more than doubled their potato consumption. 'They ate potatoes for breakfast, for lunch and for tea; they ate them all ways – baked, fried, in potato cakes, in soup, but most often simply boiled,' recalled one Russian.[39] The family of Giovanni Tassoni, poor labourers living in the countryside outside Rome, devoted their entire garden to potatoes after the occupying German military began requisitioning food in 1943. Jews starving in the Warsaw ghetto crept into the city's hinterland in the hope of digging up a few potatoes that they might smuggle back to feed their relatives. Twelve thousand kilometres away, in New Guinea, isolated Japanese soldiers abandoned by their high command tried to survive by stealing potatoes from villagers. Home-grown, frozen, dehydrated, rotten, mashed, boiled, stolen, rationed, potatoes were the food, and the taste, of World War Two, as Collingham put it.[40]

Japanese soldiers in the South Pacific were familiar with potatoes because, since the 1920s, the Japanese government had encouraged potato consumption as part of a broader campaign to reshape national eating habits. Drawing on the latest nutritional research, the Japanese military developed a comprehensive programme of mass catering based on the heavy use of lard, meat, potatoes and onions, which it believed offered the best (and most economical) way of nourishing soldiers. Novel dishes such as *korokke*, a deep-fried potato/meat croquette, proved popular among servicemen, and helped familiarise the Japanese population with Western-style cuisine. During the war, radio programmes and magazines reinforced this process by dispensing recipes and cooking advice, all with the overall aim of modifying the nation's eating habits so as to produce a more energetic and better-nourished population. Neighbourhood associations reiterated government messages and promoted the new ways of cooking, as did the communal dining rooms established in the 1940s.[41]

In Germany the National Socialists likewise sought to modify eating habits to create the sort of polity they desired. Nazi political philosophy viewed the health of the German state as virtually identical to the health of individual Germans. Citizens therefore had a civic obligation to look after themselves; 'health as a duty' became an official party slogan in 1939. Nazi officials contrasted this collective approach with the selfishness of Marxists, who supposedly believed that people should be allowed to do whatever they wanted with their bodies. For good Nazis, nutrition 'is not a private matter!', as the members of Hitler Youth were reminded in training manuals.[42] Wartime rationing was designed to nurture proper Germans by denying food to the unwanted sections of the population. Jews, the mentally ill, political opponents, and the many other people whom the Nazi state disowned were allotted utterly inadequate rations. Jews in occupied territories were entitled to 420 calories a day. German workers undertaking heavy labour were allocated ten times this amount.[43]

Rationing also aimed to increase Germany's 'nutritional freedom' by reducing its reliance on imports. Haunted by the memories of hunger and civil unrest during the First World War, the National Socialists were determined not to repeat the unsuccessful food policies of earlier governments, which they blamed for contributing to Germany's defeat. From 1933 the National Socialists campaigned with some success to make Germany self-sufficient in key foodstuffs; by 1939 nearly all its sugar, meat, grain and potatoes were produced domestically. This last achievement was particularly important since, as Nazi propagandists insisted, Germans were 'the people of the potato', who relied on the tuber as an essential part of their daily diet. An ample supply of potatoes was therefore seen as crucial to Germany's independence and the achievement of its military ambitions.[44] When Germany invaded the Soviet Union in 1941 the USSR's renowned plant-breeding institutes were among its most coveted assets. German scientists took charge of most Soviet institutes, and after 1943 either destroyed or took with them hundreds of thousands of plant samples, including breeding material for potatoes, justifying these actions in the name of 'national interest'.[45]

The potato was the object of intense promotion by the National Socialists. Countless radio broadcasts, magazines and training courses dispensed information on the multitude of ways in which this 'nutritious, filling and at the same time cheap' vegetable could be prepared. Over the course of the war annual consumption more than doubled, from 12 million to 32 million tons. Eating potatoes was encouraged as a patriotic gesture, and housewives were advised how to prepare them in the most healthful and economical fashion, as well as how to feed pigs with specially processed potato-peel.[46] Increased consumption was made possible by increased cultivation both in Germany and in the lands it occupied after 1939. Prisoners of war and other forced labourers were mobilised to harvest some of this bounty, which was shipped back to Germany, further reducing the supply of food available for locals. In 1942, Poland for instance was scheduled to provide Germany with 150,000 tons of potatoes, along with 600,000 tons of grain and 30,000 tons of meat.[47]

Because of the close relationship that the Nazis perceived between people and potatoes, their aim wasn't only to ensure a consistent supply of potatoes. National Socialists also hoped to amplify the German-ness of the potatoes that the population consumed. The state invested heavily in plant-breeding programmes to produce robust, locally adapted varieties resistant to potato wart, late blight and other diseases. This resulted in the Imperial List of Approved Varieties, which stipulated which seed potatoes could be sold commercially. In 1941, not only the sale but also the cultivation of potatoes not featuring on the list was outlawed. While in the 1910s German farmers were growing some 1,500 different varieties of potato, by 1941 they were permitted to cultivate a mere 74. All others were prohibited. Just as the Nazis stipulated which peoples and races could inhabit German soil, so they also specified which species of potatoes were permitted to grow. The aim was to breed uniquely national foodstuffs, which could be used to nourish the national body. By growing and eating such deeply German potatoes, individuals both increased the nation's economic autonomy and helped make their own bodies more German. Best of all was to eat these potatoes together with pork from the new, *bodenständig* ('rooted in the local soil') variety of pig, itself bred to feed on local potatoes.[48] German food policy, and its attitude towards potatoes, reflected the broader aims of Nazi ideology.

In the United States too, the approach to wartime provisioning was shaped by the broader ideological context. While in Germany the state hoped to make the potatoes and pork eaten by Germans more *bodenständig*, in the United States efforts reflected tensions between the advantages of a centrally directed, national nutrition programme and a commitment to individualism. Protecting the health and efficiency of the population was a central wartime concern and potatoes again played a role in ensuring this. US government guidelines stressed the benefits of ample helpings of potatoes, which featured prominently in nutritional charts such as the 1943 'Basic Seven' visualisation of a healthy diet. This pie-chart divided foods into seven key groups around which meals should be constructed. 'Potatoes and other vegetables and fruits' constituted an entire group on their own.

At the same time, Roosevelt's government stressed that its aim was to enable citizens to make informed dietary choices, rather than to dictate what people ate. Its advice, disseminated over the radio, in newspapers and magazines, and through promotional pamphlets, was in no way intended to undermine American 'initiative and democratic habits'.[49] 'Choice in food is one sign of being an adult in America,' the Committee on Food Habits affirmed, echoing the views of Immanuel Kant two centuries earlier. Lack of dietary choice reduced adults 'to the status of a child with the consequent development of dependency attitudes and lowering of morale'. Overly prescriptive dietary guidelines, in other words, might facilitate the US population's acceptance of fascism.[50] Any increase in potato consumption was therefore to be achieved through campaigns of education and persuasion, rather than through more direct interventions.

The extension in March 1943 of rationing from sugar and coffee to a much larger range of foods was accompanied by a media blitz aimed at convincing housewives that the measure provided an opportunity to demonstrate patriotism, rather than constituting a government intrusion into private life. The Office of Price Administration hired a consultant ('Mrs. Philip L. Crowlie from South Dakota'), while the Office of War Information lobbied successfully for advertisers to promote the rationing scheme. The Office also fed stories to the editors of the women's pages of national and regional newspapers, which stressed the freedom these measures permitted, rather than highlighting the limitations they imposed. The *New York Times* for instance explained that the programme's aim was to give housewives 'as wide a choice as possible'. The recipes it published for dinners of liver sausage, creamed potatoes and spinach were pitched as opportunities for readers to display individual culinary creativity, as well as patriotism. Beautiful presentation and attractive serving dishes, together with culinary skill, would convert wartime cooking into evidence of feminine talent for artistic home-building.[51] (See recipe for Jellied Meat and Potato Salad.)

*

During the Second World War potatoes were a key to survival for many of those caught up in the global conflict. Their importance transcended ideological differences between the Allied and Axis powers and reflects the potato's remarkable capacity to serve as a resource for ordinary people independent of larger structures of governance. Potato growers in Moscow, Berlin and Bedford were linked in their shared reliance on the tuber's starchy bounty. At the same time, the potato's varied status within national provisioning schemes reflects the different models of modernisation and statecraft advanced by the opposing countries. In the United Kingdom, potatoes underpinned the wartime socialism that authorised direct interventions in public eating habits, and resulted in dramatic improvements in public health. In Nazi Germany they formed part of the regime's blood and soil ideology, which stressed the connections between German land and German identity. In the United States, eating potatoes was framed as an opportunity to display individual creativity. In all cases, their prominence responded to the exceptional demands that wartime mobilisation placed on the food supply.

At the conclusion of the war, food was at the centre of the international discussions aimed at preventing further conflict. The World Bank, the FAO and other international institutions created after 1945 reflected this conviction that political instability was closely linked not just to poverty but specifically to hunger and malnutrition. The new world order envisioned in the hotels of Yalta and Bretton Woods, however, accorded little role to the modest potato in eradicating these evils.

Jellied Meat and Potato Salad

The New York Times *offered weekly menu plans and reported regularly on food throughout the Second World War. The paper's first food editor, Margot Murphy, used her columns to translate government recommendations into specific recipes. News from 1943 about that year's bumper potato harvest was accompanied by recipes for a variety of potato dishes, including this layered meat and potato salad. It was illustrated with step-by-step photographs culminating in an elegantly set table featuring the unmoulded dish surrounded by a garnish of eggs and salad greens. Murphy described it as a 'cool and attractive main course' for serving in hot weather.*

Jellied Meat and Potato Salad

Step One: In a bowl prepare Mixture A by combining 2 cups cubed cooked meat – beef, lamb, bologna, frankfurters, luncheon loaf, or any other kind – with 1½ cups diced celery or shredded cabbage, ½ cup thinly sliced radishes and ¼ cup chopped sweet pickle.

Step Two: In a second bowl prepare Mixture B by combining 2 cups cold cooked potatoes, cubed, with ½ cup diced cucumber, ½ teaspoon each of salt, prepared mustard and sugar, 1/3 cup mayonnaise and 1 tablespoon each of grated onion and vinegar.

Step Three: In a third bowl soften 1½ tablespoons of gelatin in 1/3 cup of cold water and add 2 cups of boiling water. Add three bouillon cubes and stir until thoroughly dissolved. Garnish bottom of a loaf pan with 5 cucumber slices, cover with a thin layer of the gelatin mixture and chill until firm. Chill remaining aspic until syrupy, then add about two-thirds of it to Mixture A and one-third of it to Mixture B.

Step Four: When gelatin in loaf pan is firm, place half of Mixture A on top of it, cover with Mixture B and then with remainder of Mixture A. Chill until very firm.

Step Five: When gelatin is set, turn out on platter and garnish with lettuce, sliced tomatoes and hard-cooked eggs. Serve with mayonnaise. This recipe is adequate for eight people: for four proceed as above, halving the ingredients.

FOOD SECURITY AND THE POTATO

The foundation in 1945 of the FAO marked the international institutionalisation of the consensus that improving the nutritional health of the world's population was an urgent political and economic goal. Members described their aims as:

> raising levels of nutrition and standards of living of the peoples under their respective jurisdictions; securing improvements in the efficiency of the production and distribution of all food and agricultural products; bettering the condition of rural populations; and thus contributing towards an expanding world economy and ensuring humanity's freedom from hunger.[52]

In subsequent decades a series of additional agencies and programmes – UNICEF (1946), World Food Programme (1961), World Food Council (1974), Food Security Assistance Programme (1975), International Fund for Agricultural Development (1976) and World Food Security Compact (1985), among others – were formed to support these goals. These institutions shared the conviction that a better-fed global population would increase political stability and fuel an expanding global economy. 'The construction of a postwar order began with food,' as the historian Nick Cullather has explained.[53]

This conviction reflected post-war developments at the same time as it built on earlier foundations. Experts in Europe and the United States were predicting that world population would soon outpace the food supply, prompting a Malthusian catastrophe of global proportions. Their fear that poverty and overpopulation threatened world stability was seemingly borne out in the rise of nationalist movements in India, China, Latin America and elsewhere. Alarmed Western governments hoped that a reduction in poverty combined with aggressive programmes of modernisation might dampen the allure of socialism.[54] Better-fed populations, in turn, would provide more effective workers, facilitating economic take-off. Modernised agriculture able to feed national populations was thus key to economic development and stability. At the same time, the belief that the health and vitality of the population affected the wealth and stability of the state dated back to the Enlightenment. 'That men in general should work better when they are ill fed than when they are well fed, when they are disheartened than when they are in good spirits, when they are frequently sick than when they are generally in good health, seems not very probable,' Adam Smith had observed in 1776.[55]

These connections between nutrition and economic and political stability underpin the concept of 'food security'. The term began to appear in UN documents in 1974, in reference to the threat of food shortages caused by recent poor harvests. Discussion focused on the need for grain reserves, and also on the importance of increasing production through development schemes. A few years later, in 1979, the FAO published *The Struggle for Food Security*, which stressed that increases in food production should be accompanied (or preceded) by social change. The concept has continued to evolve, from its initial focus on macro-economic and agricultural policies to a broader concern with issues of access, rather than the overall quantity of food. The scale at which food security is to be addressed has oscillated between the household, the region, the nation and the global economic system. Underlying these changing conceptualisations, however, is a constant conviction: that the dietary health of national populations is a matter of global political and economic importance. The Rome Declaration on World Food Security, produced at the UN's 1996 International Food Summit, captured well this policy consensus that food insecurity threatens 'the stability of the international community itself', as well as violating basic human rights.[56]

The overarching principles of food security derived from the concept of 'development'. Development was (and is) an international strategy aimed at fostering industrialisation and economic growth in poorer countries that otherwise lacked the economic resources to achieve this. The fundamental aim is to convert supposedly backward and overly large agrarian populations into industrial workforces through directed programmes of investment and intervention. From the 1950s, ambitious development schemes supported by Western governments, international bodies such as the World Bank, and private organisations including the Rockefeller Foundation, were introduced in many parts of the world. The concept was premised on the idea that technical and scientific intervention by appropriately trained advisers would succeed in stimulating these changes. Careful modelling, the creation of a corpus of knowledge derived from case studies, and the training of local experts were important elements. The practices and techniques of development, like the word itself, implied a process of maturation, or a transition from traditional to modern economic practices, although, as Cullather has noted, 'traditional' practices were in fact often the result of recent colonial intervention.[57]

Agricultural change was an essential part of development. Alongside programmes to stimulate industry, development schemes aimed to reorient rural agriculture from inefficient subsistence towards profitable commercial production. Attention focused primarily on systems of rural credit, mechanisation, and the dissemination of new seed varieties, together with the fertilisers and pesticides that were necessary for them to achieve their potential. The work of breeding these new varieties took place on many levels, between collaborators from both 'developed' and 'developing' countries. Scientists from India, China and elsewhere travelled to Europe and the United States to study, and Western scientists took up short- or longer-term positions at institutes in the developing world. This loose network of research programmes produced some dramatic successes such as the IR8 variety of semi-dwarf hybrid rice, created by a Taiwanese plant geneticist trained at Cornell University. IR8 gave significantly higher yields than existing commercial varieties, without collapsing under the weight of the increased grain. Partly as a result, food supply in developing countries grew by perhaps 12 per cent between 1960 and 1990, according to some estimates. The so-called Green Revolution made concrete contributions to reducing hunger in ways that, its advocates hoped, would increase global food security, and also reduce the appeal of left-wing political movements among the world's poorest people.[58] Food supply was thus central to the overall programme of development.

Exactly what foods people were eating, and the cultural practices that shaped diet, were not important elements of the initial conceptualisations of development and food security. Indian agronomists sometimes argued that breeders needed to take account of the 'chapati quality' of new wheat varieties, but international experts dismissed such concerns as 'minutia'.[59] Non-commercial, subsistence crops attracted even less attention. The FAO initially focused uniquely on grains. When some committee members suggested that its remit be widened to include 'other basic foodstuffs ... which play an important role in consumption', they had in mind commercially traded commodities such as sugar, powdered milk and meat, not the roots and tubers that, as the FAO's own data indicated, constituted as much as 50 per cent of the per capita caloric intake of people in developing countries.[60] As noted in Chapter 4, villagers in Maoist China pleaded with agronomists to devise improved varieties of sweet potato, rather than focusing on hybrid rice. The Colombian minister of agriculture was similarly driven to lobby the Rockefeller Foundation in 1951 to include potatoes in its regional research programme. And although yams were an essential food resource for village women in 1960s Kenya, agricultural officials did not consider these a 'priority crop'. When an elderly farmer attempted to share her expertise in yam cultivation with extension workers from the Agriculture Department, she was told that they 'had no place in their programmes for yams'. Such foods rarely featured in early discussions of food security.[61]

Agronomists associated with international development programmes acknowledged the drawbacks of this focus on commercially traded grains. Reports from the 1970s began to highlight the need to support research into tropical root crops and plantains, and admitted that these widely eaten foods had not enjoyed a level of investigation commensurate with their global dietary importance. In general, the FAO admitted in 1971, 'these crops are grown and consumed almost entirely in developing countries, and hardly enter into world trade. They have therefore received little attention from research programmes in developing countries.' While some work had been undertaken, the FAO admitted that 'much remains to be done'.[62] The very success of modern hybrids also caused alarm. Their ubiquity within commercial agriculture increased the likelihood that a single pathogen or pest could devastate a large percentage of a crop. Development agencies accordingly began to discuss the need to halt the 'erosion' of the world's 'genetic resources' by preserving local landraces that might prove useful for devising new commercial varieties. These plants – or more precisely the genetic material they contained – were thus framed as a global resource for future development projects.[63]

For these reasons development agencies provided some funding for research into potatoes. From the 1950s the Peruvian agronomist Carlos Ochoa for instance drew on grants from the Rockefeller Foundation to collect traditional varieties of potato from the Andean highlands.[64] The Foundation also gave sustained thought to establishing a potato research centre comparable to the international institutes already set up to study rice and maize. The national programmes of research into potatoes such as those headed by Ochoa in Peru also worked to put the potato on the development map. Nonetheless, international agencies persisted in viewing what they called the 'Irish potato' as largely irrelevant to the global fight against hunger. A Rockefeller Foundation report from 1970 for example classified the potato as 'not relevant' for addressing issues of food security in most regions of the world.[65] The potato, alongside tropical roots and tubers, continued to fly under the radar of international development schemes.

By the 1990s, agitation from NGOs and activists made this disregard of subsistence agriculture hard to sustain. In 1992 the UN itself acknowledged that the 'knowledge, innovations and practices' of peasant communities played an important role in conserving biodiversity and ensuring food security.[66] As a result, the international debate about food security, national programmes of potato breeding, and the continued importance of the potato as a daily staple for millions of people converged into a consensus that the potato was a vital resource in ensuring national and global food security. The potato's new status as a weapon in the fight against food insecurity is perfectly captured in the UN's decision to name 2008 'The International Year of the Potato' (IYP). The designation of an entire year devoted to a foodstuff was, if not entirely unprecedented, at least unusual. The first such 'International Year' was 1959–60, World Refugee Year. Other years were subsequently allocated to the global status of women (1975), world literacy (1990), indigenous people (1993), and a number of other themes, but before 2008 the only year dedicated to

Figure 19 International Year of the Potato 2008 logo. The potato, declared the United Nations in 2008, was a 'hidden treasure', an ideal remedy against food insecurity and hunger. It had been hiding in plain sight. Since the 1970s, United Nations analysts had recognised the importance of potatoes and other tubers to daily diets in many parts of the world, but for decades their attention had focused on globally traded commodities such as wheat and rice. The IYP sought to reverse this imbalance.

a foodstuff had been 2004, International Year of Rice. The UN justified the decision to make 2008 IYP largely on the grounds of the potato's contribution to food security. The tuber was firmly positioned within IYP literature as 'a highly recommended food security crop'. The FAO admitted that international development schemes had in the past overlooked the potato's contribution to global food security; the IYP was intended to rectify this oversight. The potato contributed to food security because it was widely eaten, and was hence 'a truly global food', because it was nutritious and easy to cultivate, and – crucially – because it was *not* an internationally traded commodity. Since potato markets were generally local, shoppers were protected from global price fluctuations. Cereal prices, in contrast, had increased markedly since 1990, causing serious hunger in the developing world. Many people moreover grew potatoes for their own consumption, and so could avoid markets altogether. Potatoes, the FAO predicted, would for these reasons form an important component of efforts to address the food needs of the world's growing population.[67] The very features that had made the potato invisible to the FAO in the 1970s were now identified as central to its importance in the fight against food insecurity. (See figure 19.)

The IYP contrasted with the FAO's previous approach not simply in its focus on the potato. The IYP reflected a very different understanding of subsistence agriculture's contribution to food security. The earlier development model had focused on commercial agriculture. Subsistence farming fits poorly into this model, which works most efficiently when fields are sown with a single crop that can be treated uniformly with pesticides and fertilisers, and harvested at an optimal moment. The cultivation of many different crops, often on multiple plots of land, that typifies small-scale farming is less amenable to the techniques of modern commercial agriculture. More than this, peasants themselves were often positioned as part of the obsolete style of agriculture that development aimed to replace. In ways that echoed early modern and colonial tendencies to undervalue the agricultural skills of small farmers, many development advisers in the post-war years bemoaned the failure of peasants to implement recommended policies. 'How to overcome the destructive conservatism of the people and generate the drastic agrarian reforms which must be effected if the country is to survive is one of the most difficult problems the political leaders of Tanzania have to face,' stated one study from 1970.[68] Small farmers were regularly chastised for being conservative or opposed to change. In addition, their agricultural knowledge was rarely viewed as relevant. In Peru, the Rockefeller Foundation struggled to insulate its potato-breeding programmes from the 'backward' and 'unscientific' practices used in the highlands. Peruvian agronomists who endorsed Andean farming techniques were criticised and did not benefit from funding. Although not all advocates of development shared this attitude, peasant farmers were often 'the problem to which the agricultural experts were the solution'.[69]

In striking contrast to this earlier vision of the peasant farmer as a problem, the FAO now celebrates the flexible, adaptive nature of peasant agriculture. FAO publications stress that smallholder farming systems play an essential role in sustaining the potato's genetic diversity, and so 'small farmers in the Andes are helping ensure world food security'. The FAO also highlights the central contribution of women to this process. The IYP website includes many photographs of farmers planting and harvesting potatoes by hand. Only one shows any mechanisation, other than a lorry into which hand-dug potatoes are being loaded.[70] Small-scale potato cultivation using simple tools has become part of the FAO's solution to the problem of food security.

A very similar message is conveyed by the Lima-based International Potato Center, or CIP (an acronym derived from its Spanish name). CIP was founded in 1971 with funding from the Rockefeller Foundation as part of a coordinated international effort to preserve the genetic diversity of major food crops through seed-banking, research, and extension programmes. CIP's initial brief was to breed improved varieties of potato. It was also to train scientists and disseminate information about up-to-date research. It is now the foremost repository of knowledge about modern potato breeding, and an important interlocutor in discussions on the potato's contributions to global food security.

CIP's early publications, like those of the FAO, focused on agronomic challenges such as the production of fungal- and nematode-resistant varieties, as well as the development of effective strategies for post-harvest storage and the importance of establishing international research collaborations. Peasant know-how and the contribution of women to global food security were not addressed, nor did the Center devote much attention to the potato's long-standing importance in the region's history, beyond its occasional use of pre-Columbian decorative motifs in its annual reports.[71] All of these dimensions now feature prominently in CIP's work. Its website, which characterises the potato as 'a critical crop in terms of food security in the face of population growth and increased hunger rates', accords Andean farmers past and present a central role in preserving the potato's biodiversity.[72] Its many publications stress the connections between potatoes and a vivid and living indigenous culture that dates back millennia. From this perspective, traditional agricultural practices are an essential part of the potato's modern relevance. (See figure 20.)

More than this, CIP now characterises Andean potato varieties as part of Peru's 'highly valued heritage'.[73] Potatoes, in other words, are celebrated as part of Peru's cultural distinctiveness as a nation. The notion of creating a UN International Year of the Potato in fact originated with the Peruvian government, which lobbied energetically for several years. At the same time as it pressed for an international potato year, it also established 30 May as National Potato Day, and set up both a National Potato Congress and various regional potato festivals. These latter endeavours emphasised that the potato was profoundly Peruvian. According to the 2005 legislation

Figure 20 Andean potato farmers from an International Potato Center publication. Villagers from Ampay, in the Peruvian highlands, gather to mark the start of the planting season with an offering to Mother Earth. Towards the right are several *chakitaqlla*, similar to those depicted in Figure 2. In contrast to its earlier focus on the 'scientific potato', CIP now celebrates the potato's deep roots in Peruvian culture and society; this photograph features on the cover of a 2001 publication.

creating National Potato Day, Peru was the principal centre of origin of the potato and continued to possess the greatest genetic diversity, factors which were quickly translated in the Peruvian media into affirmations that the potato was '100% Peruvian'.[74] This sort of gastronationalism, as the sociologist Michaela DeSoucey has observed, 'strategically weds consideration of national identity to the idea of the nation as a protector of cultural patrimony'.[75] Unsurprisingly, when neighbouring Chile attempted the next year to register nearly three hundred varieties of potato as Chilean, the Peruvian government reacted sharply. Peru's foreign minister insisted that 'it has been widely accepted that potato originated in southern Peru and therefore belongs to our nation's cultural heritage'.[76]

Such official celebration of the potato as part of Peru's national heritage resonates with growing gastronomic interest in the Andean potato as an artisanal foodstuff. Historically, potatoes and other foods associated with the indigenous population shared the low status of the Andean people who grew and ate them. Since the early 2000s, however, the status of the potato (although not necessarily of Andean farmers) has risen notably. The emergence of 'New Andean Cuisine' has helped create a market for distinctive local foods that can be sold to urban consumers and tourists eager to sample authentic Peruvian gastronomy. New Andean cuisine reinterprets older Peruvian dishes using techniques drawn from molecular gastronomy and similar international restaurant trends to produce novel dishes such as quinotto (a risotto made of quinoa) or a 'deconstructed' version of the familiar Peruvian dish *causa* (mashed potato stuffed with meat or some other filling). Gastón Acurio and other Peruvian chefs gained global renown for their imaginative use of regional ingredients and flavours; as a result Lima began to be hailed as a gastronomic powerhouse. Peru's many varieties of potato fit easily into narratives about authenticity and *terroir*, which stress the potato's deep cultural links to the region and its history.[77]

In response, CIP has launched a research programme into the brightly coloured potatoes that feature prominently in Peru's gastronomic renaissance, and collaborates with Peruvian culinary academies to develop new recipes.[78] Peru is not alone in its gastronational celebration of local potato varieties. A number of countries, from Denmark to Ecuador, have likewise established national potato days, or sought to protect specific varieties under international legislation. Comber new potatoes from Northern Ireland, Idaho potatoes, and many other varieties are now registered under trademark and European Union regulations that limit their production to specific regions. International regulatory structures thus help to nationalise potatoes by according them formal status as part of the national patrimony.[79] Its long history as an overlooked, localised food resource now enables the potato to toggle between the global food system and notions of culinary heritage, in a way that other major commodities such as sugar or maize have largely failed to do.

In Peru, indigenous communities have sought to harness this framing of the potato as part of the nation's cultural heritage in order to bolster their own claims for recognition by the state. For such groups CIP's insistence that indigenous farmers are vital custodians of the Andean potato's genetic diversity is extremely helpful. In 2004, for instance, drawing on national legislation recognising the 'collective knowledge of indigenous people', one group based in the Pisac Valley signed a 'native potato repatriation agreement' with CIP. The agreement involved the transfer of a number of potato specimens from CIP to the group in Pisac. The intention was to allow the historic communities where these potatoes were first cultivated to collaborate in research, as well as to facilitate locals in growing them for their own consumption. The agreement also provided a way for the community to generate a small income. The group's Potato Park offers tourists a five-day trek along its 'Potato Trail', as well as gastronomic experiences at a restaurant showcasing local potatoes. Gastronationalism, concerns about food security, and contestation over the ownership of the world's biological diversity combine to make the Andean potato a source of cultural and economic capital in today's Peru.[80]

CONCLUSIONS

Over the twentieth century the potato rose steadily in its importance as a political instrument. No longer blamed for generating sluggish potato blood, by the First World War potatoes were lauded as a healthful staple. National governments concerned to provide for the wartime needs of the population actively encouraged potato consumption as a patriotic effort. National programmes of potato breeding and nationally funded collecting expeditions reflected this conviction that potatoes helped ensure what by the 1970s was called food security. Many of today's commercially available potato varieties are the result of these state-supported schemes.

These twentieth-century programmes of dietary intervention differed in many ways from the vague assertions of eighteenth-century statesmen that it was important to ensure that the population was well fed. The events of the nineteenth and early twentieth centuries transformed the relationship between populations and states, which by the post-war years possessed technological capacities far beyond those enjoyed by eighteenth-century monarchs. The national rationing schemes introduced in wartime Europe bear no comparison to the earnest recommendations offered in the 1790s that working people should consider eating more potatoes. Nor would eighteenth-century potato-promoters necessarily endorse twentieth-century welfarist attempts to end hunger by reducing social and economic inequality. At the same time, the assertion that individual eating habits were the foundation of national strength and productivity would not have sounded unfamiliar to the eighteenth-century writers who insisted that for a state to flourish it was essential that its workers be well fed. These ideas were born in the eighteenth century. As the sociologist Mitchell Dean reminds us, it is possible to identify continuities between eighteenth- and twentieth-century ideas about governance 'without denying the evident reality of state transformation of the last two centuries'.[81]

Although commercial breeding and initiatives to promote consumption formed part of national programmes of food security in the twentieth century, the economic development models that emerged in the post-war years paid little attention to the agricultural practices of small-scale farmers in the developing world, including those whose expertise in growing potatoes was later identified as a vital resource in the fight against food insecurity. Only recently has smallholder and peasant agriculture been incorporated into international models of food security. The FAO's designation of 2008 as the International Year of the Potato is emblematic of this new appreciation of 'traditional' farming as a site of innovation and relevant knowledge. Just as the peasant know-how that spread potato cultivation across early modern Europe remained invisible to many mid-twentieth-century historians, so the expertise that preserved the potato's genetic diversity has only recently been appreciated by the international organisations concerned with food security.

The FAO and CIP are right to appreciate the expertise of small-scale potato farmers. Like university-trained scientists, such cultivators are often experimentalists, engaging in observation, interpretation, field-trials, evaluation and manipulation in order to identify and develop new cultivars and new methods of cultivation. They discuss their

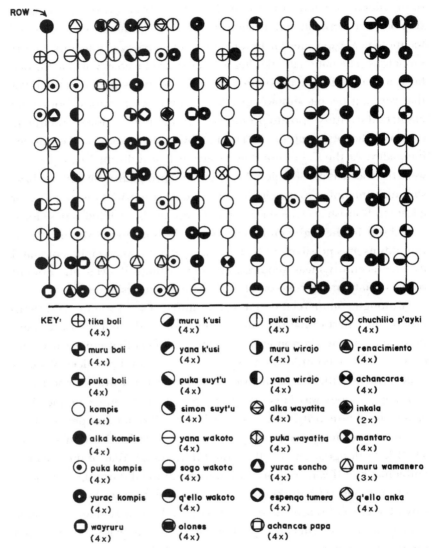

Figure 21 Schematic drawing of an Andean potato field. Andean farmers typically grow dozens of different varieties of potato; a single field may contain nearly fifty. This drawing depicts one such field. While the arrangement may appear disorderly, it is not. Planting reflects the particular requirements of the soil and altitude, and carefully matches the seed potatoes to the micro-environment. This field includes Renacimiento, an extremely successful commercial variety developed by Carlos Ochoa, director of Peru's National Potato Programme, as well as more traditional landraces.

experiences with others in their locality and adapt their own practices in light of these conversations. Most Andean potato farmers maintain between twelve and fifteen different plots in continuous cultivation; yet more are cultivated non-continuously. They may also swap both seeds and fields with neighbours. Through such exchanges it is possible for a single farmer to gain access to up to a hundred different potato cultivars. Matching particular seed potatoes to the soil and environmental requirements of specific pieces of land requires a vast body of practical agronomic knowledge, and leads to ongoing experimentation. This sort of constant evaluation and innovation is responsible for the remarkable diversity of potato varieties in the Andes. In the 1960s agronomists thought that Peru possessed some 1,400 native potato varieties; current estimates now put the figure somewhere between 2,700 and 4,500.[82] (See figure 21.)

The heritageisation of traditional potato varieties, visible in the celebration of national potato days, international geographical indication conventions and gastronationalism, melds state-level interest in the daily eating habits of the population and the recognition that traditional farming methods form part of the solution to global food security into a story about cultural heritage. Food's powerful ability to convey nationalist narratives makes the potato an apt symbol of these interconnections.[83] Potatoes, it seems, tell us both about who we are as individuals, and also about where collectively we are headed.

CONCLUSIONS

Parmentier, Peasants and Personal Responsibility

POTATO HEROES

PARIS'S BOULEVARD PARMENTIER RUNS FROM THE PLACE DE LA République eastward to the Père Lachaise Cemetery, where the remains of Marcel Proust, Frédéric Chopin and Jim Morrison are interred. The cemetery also houses the tomb of Antoine Augustin Parmentier. The eighteenth century's most famous potato-promoter lies surrounded by the tubers he helped popularise. Visitors to the cemetery often leave offerings on the tombs. On Parmentier's they leave potatoes. (See figure 22.)

Parmentier has long been credited with bringing potatoes to France. The placards lining Boulevard Parmentier state precisely this – that he 'introduced potato cultivation to France'. Parmentier was born in 1737 in a provincial town and trained in Paris as an apothecary. As he later reported, his interest in the potato dated from the 1750s, when he served in the French army during the Seven Years War. First as a prisoner of war, and subsequently while living in Frankfurt, he began to contemplate the potato's potential to supplement or even replace bread. Following his return to France he started to investigate the tuber's chemical qualities, and in 1771 won a competition (sponsored by the Besançon Academy of Science, Literature and Arts) for the best essay on alternatives to grain for use in periods of scarcity such as France was experiencing at that moment. He proposed potatoes. This was the first of many publications recommending the potato; the prize-winning 1771 essay was followed by a series of works on the myriad uses of the potato as a food for humans, as an animal feed, and as an industrial starch.[1]

Between the 1770s and his death in 1813, Parmentier experimented tirelessly with the chemical components of potatoes, alongside other foods, in an effort to understand their nutritive qualities, in order, as he repeatedly stated, to serve his country by providing it with a more secure

Figure 22 Parmentier's tomb, Père Lachaise Cemetery, decorated with potatoes. The bonds uniting Antoine Augustin Parmentier with the potato endure two hundred years after his death. His tomb in Paris's Père Lachaise Cemetery is adorned with votive potatoes, and families across France eat *hachis Parmentier*, or potato-topped shepherd's pie. His reputation for bringing potatoes to the French is secure, if not entirely deserved.

alimentary base. Parmentier devoted decades to developing ways of convert-ing potatoes into a leavened loaf that bread-loving Parisians might enjoy. Parmentier designed progressively more complex ways of extracting starch from potatoes, and also of making potato-yeast, to create a yeasted bread composed entirely of potatoes. Writers across eighteenth-century Europe lauded Parmentier's writings, thanking him for helping to reveal the pota-to's many qualities. His varied investigations are today commemorated not only along Boulevard Parmentier, but also in the French term for potato-topped shepherd's pie: *hachis Parmentier*. He would doubtless have been pleased to be remembered in this everyday dish. In his many publications he reiterated his conviction that the potato was a peerless foodstuff, America's greatest gift to humanity.[2]

Potatoes were of course well known in France prior to Parmentier's interventions. Indeed, all of the contributors to the 1771 Besançon essay competition had recommended potatoes as the best solution to problems of scarcity. Parmentier was hardly alone in recognising their potential as a supplement to wheat or oats. Neither was he unique in his efforts to reduce the potato to its chemical components. Experiments with potato starch and other processed forms of potato had been underway since the 1730s, and potato breads – whether made with mashed potato, potato starch or potato flour – were the object of prior investigation by scientists in various parts of Europe.[3] Clearly, Parmentier cannot be credited with introducing potatoes to France. Nor can he be heralded as their sole advocate. He wrote so extensively about the potato not because it was novel, but because he wanted to increase consumption as a means of strengthening the French state. As he explained, 'the type and choice of foods has a great influence on the population, so that one cannot take too many precautions to ensure that the people are well fed'.[4] Such matters, he believed, were 'worthy of the meditations of philosophers and the protec-tion of government', which is precisely why philosophers and governments devoted such attention to the potato during the Enlightenment.[5]

The potato's increased political visibility during the eighteenth cen-tury has been misread to convert figures such as Parmentier into spokes-men of a despised vegetable hitherto rejected by the population. What his story in fact reveals is the unprecedented importance that eating came to hold in eighteenth-century ideas about the wealth and power of nations. This misreading of Parmentier's role perpetuates the perception that historical change is a top-down process. More specifically, it misrepresents the contribution of ordinary people to agricultural and dietary innovation. Peasants and labourers were almost certainly the first Europeans to grow potatoes as a source of food, rather than as a botanical oddity, and in the eighteenth century they continued to possess agronomic knowledge necessary for elite experimentation. As it happens, it was from 'one Grégoire, a peasant from Jalhay, near Liège', that the great potato-promoter first learned how to grow potatoes.[6]

Today, the flexible, adaptive nature of peasant agriculture is rightly praised for its contribution to global food security. Farms of under two hectares grow a disproportionate percentage of the world's food, since smallholdings are often more productive than larger units in terms of yield per hectare. Studies from many parts of the world, and many different time periods, show that 'less advanced' agricultural practices can out-perform more complex technologies. Detailed knowledge of local conditions, combined with a pragmatic receptivity to useful ideas, facilitates effective use of resources, while the precarious conditions many small farmers face encourage innovation.[7] In highland Guatemala, smallholders maintain vegetable plots producing food for their households alongside fields with export crops of the sort encouraged by development programmes. Such farmers cannot afford to be conservative in their agricultural practices. 'Anxious for anything that can help them squeeze a little more money out of the fields', they regularly experiment with new seeds, pesticides and fertilisers, notes the anthropologist Ioulia Evgenyevna Fenton.[8]

Another anthropologist, Robert Netting, wrote extensively about the flaws in the developmentalist conviction that 'traditional intensive cultivators must be taught how to farm with machines, purchased inputs, and scientific knowledge'. Netting's analysis of smallholder practices in Nigeria, Switzerland, China, Java and elsewhere led him to conclude that this belief is 'directly contradicted by the land productivity, the reliability, the ecological sustainability, and the adaptability' of smallholder agriculture.[9] Exactly this sort of continual adjustment and adaptation was necessary to create the thousands of potato varieties that now flourish in the Andes, where farming communities draw on a vast body of practical agronomic knowledge to match particular seed potatoes to the soil and environmental requirements of specific pieces of land. Scholars refer to this practical knowledge as 'savoir-faire paysan' or the 'art de la localité' – the local know-how necessary for such forms of agriculture to succeed.[10] It was likewise in cottage gardens and peasant plots that the potato first adapted to Europe's varied growing conditions, and so took the first steps towards become a global staple.

Recognising peasant contributions to the history of the potato is not simply a matter of historical justice. It is also relevant for our future. Biodiversity is today identified as an essential component of both long-term environmental sustainability and global food security. This essential diversity, in turn, relies on the expertise of the world's small farmers, who are acknowledged to be the most important counterweight to the forces of highly homogenised large-scale commercial agriculture. Small farmers – many of them women – grow crops for many different purposes: some to sell at market, some because they are particularly tasty or suitable for specific dishes, others for use as gifts or to store as capital against future expenses. Different ends call for different varieties that possess the particular qualities needed for each purpose. In some cases storage capacity is the most important, in others yield or flavour. This sort of agriculture values, and promotes, crop diversity. It is not typically characterised by inertia and the reflexive replication of past practice. The FAO, long indifferent to subsistence agriculture, now hails the local knowledge that underpins traditional potato cultivation as key to global food security past and present. The potato's history reminds us not to overlook the contributions of small-scale agriculture to the larger history of innovation and change.

A SECOND HELPING OF POTATOES

Following the potato also reveals how our attitudes towards eating became embedded in a particular vision of statecraft. In Europe, prior to the eighteenth century what a person ate was of direct importance to that man or woman, girl or boy. It likewise mattered to the people who prepared and supplied their food, to those with whom they shared their meals, and to many others, so that what a person ate traced out a web of connections that in some ways constituted their social world. Eating is, and remains, at the heart of human culture. It lies at the core of our existence and identity. What ordinary people ate for dinner was not, however, of much *political* interest.

Today, in contrast, such matters are important enough to merit entire governmental programmes devoted to improving our eating habits. Healthy eating plates, dietary guidelines, and educational campaigns aimed at increasing our vegetable consumption or reducing our intake of salt are familiar features of our current food landscape. Providing advice about how to optimise one's diet is now an accepted component of modern governance. In Europe, the conviction that it is proper for the state to concern itself with such matters emerged in the eighteenth century, as part of a broader reconceptualisation of the relationship between the state and the population. This reconceptualisation occurred in tandem with new ways of thinking about commerce and trade. The notion that self-interest provided the most efficient way of organising economic exchange found its dietetic parallel in the conviction that the way to improve public health was by facilitating individuals in making sound dietary choices. Just as other systems were able, almost magically, to regulate themselves in ways that would provide the maximum benefit to all, so the pursuit of dietary happiness would lead to greater health and vigour for both individual eaters and the larger polity. So, at least, it was claimed.

This history helps explain the genealogy of our conviction that eating is at once a personal matter, and a legitimate arena for governmental intervention. It also helps explain our ambivalence about such intervention. Our notions of personal freedom are profoundly indebted to eighteenth-century debates about the primacy of the individual as a 'choosing subject'. Choosing what we eat provides a concrete, daily opportunity to exercise our fundamental autonomy as individuals. As the US Committee on Food Habits put it in 1942, 'choice in food is one sign of being an adult'.[11] Lack of dietary choice, whether it derives from outside intervention or from poverty, sits uneasily with the notions of liberty that we have inherited from the Enlightenment. Vincent van Gogh's painting of a peasant family huddled around a table to eat their evening meal of boiled potatoes offers a depressing image of this sort of impoverished choice landscape. 'Because choice and the freedom to choose have become part of the normative category of food,' writes John Coveney, 'not having choice is regarded as a situation in need of

Figure 23 Vincent van Gogh, *The Potato Eaters*. 'Because choice and the freedom to choose have become part of the normative category of food, not having choice is regarded as a situation in need of correction,' according to John Coveney. Exercising choice allows individuals to demonstrate responsibility for their own health, and so constitutes a fundamental part of being a modern consumer. Van Gogh's peasant family, eating their meal of home-grown potatoes, represent the antithesis of this modern vision, which is perhaps why viewers often find the painting unsettling.

correction.'[12] The urge to rebrand paupers as choosing subjects explains why the potato's enthusiastic eighteenth-century promoters tried to pretend that the hungry poor who thronged Europe's many soup kitchens genuinely enjoyed charity potato broths garnished, if they were lucky, with Count Rumford's happiness-inducing croutons. (See figure 23.)

If, today, the role of government is to provide a supportive environment for us to make informed food choices, responsibility for our decisions lies ultimately with us. 'One of the things I talk a lot about is the need to really work on cultural change in America to encourage a culture of personal responsibility,' stated George W. Bush in a lecture about the HealthierUS initiative, launched in 2002 to promote 'healthier lifestyles' through diet and exercise schemes. HealthierUS, Bush continued, 'really appeals to personal responsibility, doesn't it? It says that we are responsible to our own health.' Governments cannot, and should not, aspire to make the population healthier, declared UK Prime Minister Tony Blair in a 2004 policy document on 'Choosing Health'. In his view, 'it is for people to make the healthy choice if they wish to'. The role of modern government is to support us in 'making good choices' about what we eat, as the New Zealand Ministry of Health put it in 2018.[13]

It is up to us to follow governmental and industry guidelines by selecting plain boiled potatoes and other recommended foods, and shunning high-fat snacks such as the seventy-six pounds of fries and other highly-processed potato nibbles consumed per capita each year in the United States. And if we're ill and overweight because we've eaten too many chips, well, it's our own fault. 'Negative attitudes towards the obese are highly correlated with negative attitudes towards minorities and the poor, such as the belief that all these groups are lazy and lack self-control and will power,' notes a 2006 study.[14] Just as William Buchan had insisted in 1797 that potatoes would end poverty for everyone except 'the profligate', so the language of personal responsibility and choice implies that those who fail to thrive have only themselves to blame.

Such hapless eaters perfectly embody the surplus people identified by the French philosopher Michel Foucault as obstacles to modern forms of governance. Foucault contrasted the modern state's approach to managing the population with earlier forms of political power. For the modern state, he believed, power is not a matter of intermittent displays of authority via periodic executions of criminals or other episodic demonstrations of state might. Rather it is a continual process of fostering the well-being of some sections of the population, and removing all support from those whose well-being the state does not wish to promote. 'One might say', Foucault observed, that in modern times 'the ancient right to *take* life or *let* live was replaced by a power to *foster* life or *disallow* it to the point of death'.[15]

The population, the productive members of society, should be nurtured, helped to live and flourish. It is precisely such ideas that contributed to the rise, in the eighteenth century, of the conviction that the strength and security of the state depended on the vigour and happiness of the population. As Foucault described it, this new relationship between individuals and the state comprised:

a circle that starts from the state as a power of rational and calculated intervention on individuals and comes back to the state as a growing set of forces, or forces to be developed ... This circle ... must succeed in linking together the state's strength and individual felicity. This felicity, as the individual's better than just living, must in some way be drawn on and constituted into state utility: making men's happiness the state's utility, making men's happiness the very strength of the state.[16]

This, he argued, was the first time in the history of Western societies that 'the being and well-being of individuals really became relevant for government intervention'. This is why its eighteenth-century promoters so often insisted that the potato offered a high road to personal happiness.

From within the logic of this modern form of statecraft, however, there are others who are not part of the population. They are just people, and they are in the way. The state sees no compelling reason to encourage their existence. Modern politics, Foucault argued, is a matter both of 'making live' and also of 'letting die'. The Italian philosopher Giorgio Agamben has written evocatively about the dismal fate of those whom the state 'lets die' – the marginal, the stateless, those whose lives are deemed 'unworthy of being lived' and from whom support is withdrawn. In his view, we all teeter on the edge of this abyss, potential outsiders constantly at risk of being left to die, should we cease being of utility, should we eat too many chips and stop exercising, should we be profligate.[17]

Potatoes of all sorts were once promoted as a way to build strong populations, understood within a broad framework of personal choice and individual benefit. Today, when some 50 per cent of the US potato crop is converted into fries, crisps and other calorific and nutritionally poor snack foods, we are encouraged to reject such highly processed potatoes in favour of simpler preparations, for the sake of our own well-being. US government websites endorse plainly boiled or low-calorie stuffed potatoes as smarter dietary choices.[18] At the same time, the broad, eighteenth-century recommendations to consume more potatoes, and current advice to shun chips, share an underlying logic, which views our diets as simultaneously an important part of national well-being and also, fundamentally, a matter of individual choice, and therefore of individual responsibility. (See recipe for Wonderful Stuffed Potatoes.)

Wonderful Stuffed Potatoes

An essential part of becoming a 'Healthier You is making healthy choices' about food, according to the US Department of Health and Human Services. Its website offers a series of officially endorsed recipes, helpfully classified according to the time required for preparation. All are described as healthful, easy and fun. Alongside explanations of how to prepare 'Good for you' corn bread, and Yosemite chicken stew with dumplings, are recipes for new potato salad, black skillet beef with greens and red potatoes, and this recipe for 'Wonderful Stuffed Potatoes'. Each serving of half a potato provides 293 mg of potassium and 113 calories. If the diner chooses to consume more than half a medium potato, to the detriment of their health, that is their choice, and therefore their responsibility.

Wonderful Stuffed Potatoes

'Baked potatoes stuffed with seasoned, low-fat cottage cheese are a lavish low-fat, low-cholesterol, low-sodium treat.'

4 medium baking potatoes
¾ cup cottage cheese, low fat (1%)
¼ cup milk, low fat (1%)
2 tbsp soft (tub) margarine
1 tsp dill weed
¾ tsp herb seasoning
4–6 drops hot pepper sauce
2 tsp Parmesan cheese, grated

1. Prick potatoes with fork. Bake at 425° F for 60 minutes or until fork is easily inserted.
2. Cut potatoes in half lengthwise. Carefully scoop out potato, leaving about ½ inch of pulp inside shell. Mash pulp in large bowl.
3. Mix in by hand remaining ingredients except Parmesan cheese. Spoon mixture into potato shells.
4. Sprinkle top with ¼ teaspoon of Parmesan cheese.
5. Place on baking sheet and return to oven. Bake 15–20 minutes or until tops are golden brown.

*

Events, including the encouragement to eat potatoes, are best understood when they are seen as part of larger sets of ideas, rather than as singularities. The pan-European eighteenth-century potato vogue reflected the new political importance that eating acquired during the eighteenth century, as politicians and philosophers began to link individual diets to the strength and wealth of nations. They framed this debate within a language of choice and the individual pursuit of happiness. It is these links that explain the potato's unprecedented political visibility. The connections between everyday life, individualism and the state forged in the late eighteenth century, of which the history of the potato forms a part, continue to shape today's debates about how to balance personal dietary freedom with the health of the body politic. The seductive promise that, collectively and individually, we can somehow eat our way to health and happiness remains a powerful component of our uneasy global world.

Figure 24 Potato print of a disgruntled subject throwing a potato at Frederick the Great. Stories of benevolent monarchs bringing potatoes to the masses don't do justice to the role of ordinary people in shaping how we eat. Eating, after all, is an agricultural act, as the farmer and writer Wendell Berry put it.

Acknowledgements

'You should think about Rumford Soup': Roger Cooter's advice, offered on a balmy evening in Croatia more years ago than I care to recall, started it all off. Since then the Potato Project has accumulated many happy debts to generous colleagues, wise potato growers, and helpful interlocutors of all sorts. A full list of the potato-related information, references, and stories that I've gained through these conversations would fill many pages and tax the patience of all but the most indulgent readers. Justice, however, demands that I thank not only Roger Cooter, but also my dear Foucauldian and friend Claudia Stein, likewise present at the creation. Her influence on my thinking is palpable throughout this book, even though she would surely enjoy nothing more than arguing with me about virtually every aspect of my approach to writing history. Other colleagues also exercised a decisive influence on my thinking. Jakob Klein provided immense help in thinking about the long-standing connections between potatoes and modern forms of statecraft, and was unstinting in sharing his knowledge of contemporary Chinese history. Keith Tribe was an unbelievable font of wisdom on the history of economic thought, and one of many reasons to be grateful to the fellowship programme at the Swedish Collegium for Advanced Studies (and to Björn Wittrock's visionary approach to collegiality). Helen Curry was another reason to be grateful to SCAS. She let me read her own work-in-progress on the changing ways that scientists have sought to preserve the biodiversity of commercial food crops, and was endlessly gracious in explaining the history of plant breeding. In Uppsala I also enjoyed the luxury of regular conversations with David Cannadine, Linda Colley, Anandi Hattiangadi, Jürgen Kokka, Mika Perälä, Otto Sibaum, Jakob Starlander and Jan

Stenger, and, last but hardly least, the daily support of Pia Campeggiani's friendship, wit and wisdom. A year in Uppsala further gave me the opportunity to benefit from the expertise of Lili-Annè Aldman, Prasenjit Duara, Ylva Hasselberg, Kapil Raj, Steven Shapin and R. Bin Wong, who helped me understand early modern Swedish customs records, Chinese nutritional governmentality, Indian botanical illustrations, early modern dietetics, and more.

Several particularly selfless colleagues read and commented on entire chapters. In addition to Keith Tribe and Helen Curry, who read multiple drafts, Shrikant Botre gave enormously helpful advice about Chapter 4. Margaret Hunt commented on Chapter 1 and told me about 'stooping crops'. Kenneth Banks provided much-appreciated feedback and reassurance while this project was in its early stages. Others shared specific references; 'only you would find this interesting' was the start of many an email. I'm particularly grateful to Cheryl Butler for information about a gift of potatoes in 1590s Southampton, Bernard Capp for telling me how the Earl of Dorset died, Lizzie Collingham for potatoes in Joseph Arch's autobiography (as well as for her outstanding study of food during the Second World War), Rudi Matthee for helping me understand Iranian foodways, Kathryn Santner for details (and scans) about what nuns ate in Arequipa, and Helen Wakely for potatoes in the Wellcome Library's collection of early modern manuscript cookery books. I'd also like to thank Håkan Blomqvist for explaining Sweden's potato revolution, Ioulia Evgenyevna Fenton, Leon Sealey-Huggins and Alastair Smith for their expertise on peasant agriculture, Tiago Saravia for fascist pigs and potatoes, Xiaoping Sun for describing the role of potatoes in helping villages survive the Chinese famine of 1959–61, Joonas Tammela for telling me about Finnish potato heroes, and Iranga Tcheko for sharing her grandmother's memories of being obliged to grow potatoes in the Belgian Congo. Carolyn Steedman and Mark Philp glossed and contextualised 'The Potato Man'. It is a privilege to have such generous and knowledgeable friends and colleagues.

Because the potato has spread to so many corners of the world, its presence in the documentary record vastly exceeds my own linguistic skills. I am therefore particularly grateful to the people who helped me trace its movements through Greek, Latin, Norwegian, Swedish, Finnish,

Russian, Icelandic and Mandarin texts. For Latin and Greek I relied on Desirée Arbó, Dennis Landis, Jan Stenger and Mika Perälä. Amund Pedersen carried out careful research on potatoes in early modern Norway. Jakob Starlander and Hanna Hodacs steered me through eighteenth-century Swedish almanacs and scientific writings, while Jussipekka Luukkonen composed a virtual dissertation on Finnish potato-promoters. Colum Leckey was generous in helping me understand Russian potato-promotion, and returned repeatedly to his own notes to track down specific details – and I had no hope of understanding the potato's spread across Iceland without the guidance of Hrefna Róbertsdóttir. Anne Gerritsen, Huang Lu and Claire Tang jointly translated a challenging slogan from colloquial Mandarin in a way that drew admiration from others.

Two people who have long indulged my conviction that potatoes merit attention are my mother, Lisa Earle, and my husband Matt Western. The former knows far more about the potato's botanical complexities than I can ever hope to do. Typically, she visited the International Potato Center in Peru years – decades – before the Potato Project was even a glimmer in my eye. It has been a delight to talk potatoes with her, and to benefit in a small way from her own expertise as a biologist and scholar. The glimmer in Matt's eye has been amused indulgence, as I've soliloquised about, well, the topic should be clear by now. *Feeding the People* is dedicated to them both, with love.

Notes

INTRODUCTION: POURING OURSELVES A LARGE GIN

1. 'Woman's Hour', BBC Radio 4, 17 Mar. 2014.
2. Martin Wainwright, 'The Battle of Rawmarsh', *Guardian*, 20 Sept. 2006; *New York Times*, 2 June 2012.
3. See for instance Rebecca Smith, 'Obesity Epidemic "Could Bankrupt the NHS"', *Telegraph*, 15 Oct. 2007; Amanda Platell, 'Sorry, Why Should the NHS Treat People for Being Fat?', *Daily Mail*, 27 Feb. 2009; Runge, 'Economic Consequences of the Obese'; Business in the Community, *Healthy People=Healthy Profits*; Harvard School of Public Health, 'Public Health and the US Economy'; Sarah Boseley, 'Obesity Could Bankrupt NHS if Left Unchecked', *Guardian*, 17 Sept. 2014. On the horsemeat scandal, see Abbots and Coles, 'Horsemeat-Gate'.
4. Biltekoff, *Eating Right in America*, 45–79. Thaler and Sunstein explore these tensions in *Nudge*.
5. FAO, FAOSTAT. (To be precise, potatoes are grown in every country for which the FAO has data.)
6. Rabinbach, *The Human Motor*; Harmke Kamminga and Andrew Cunningham, 'Introduction', *The Science and Culture of Nutrition*, ed. Kamminga and Cunningham, 2; Helstocky, 'The State, Health, and Nutrition'; Zweiniger-Bargielowska, *Managing the Body*, 22; Nally, 'The Biopolitics of Food Provisioning'.
7. Vernon, 'The Ethics of Hunger and the Assembly of Society', 699 (quote); Vernon, *Hunger*; Cullather, *The Hungry World*.
8. Maxwell, 'Food Security'; Shaw, *World Food Security*; Schanbacer, *The Politics of Food*.
9. Harcout, *The Illusion of Free Markets*, 44. I owe the phrase 'nutritional governmentality' to Swislocki, 'Nutritional Governmentality'.
10. Walter, 'The Social Economy of Dearth in Early Modern England', 76. Or see Davis, 'Poor Relief, Humanism and Heresy'; and Tilly, 'Food Supply and Public Order in Modern Europe'.
11. Murra, *The Economic Organization of the Inka State*, 121–34; Rickman, *Corn Supply of Ancient Rome*; Braudel, *The Mediterranean and the Mediterranean World*, I: 328–32, 570–605; Will and Wong, *Nourish the People*; Steel, *Hungry City*.

12. Murphey, 'Provisioning Istanbul'; Will and Wong, *Nourish the People*, 511. For exemplary studies of efforts to police the French grain market see Kaplan, *Bread, Politics and Political Economy*; Miller, *Mastering the Market*; Harcout, *The Illusion of Free Markets*.

13. 'Ordinances of the Pastelers, or Piebakers', 3 Richard II. A.D. 1379, *Memorials of London and London Life*, ed. Riley, 438 (quote); Pullan, 'The Roles of the State and the Town in the General Crisis of the 1590s', *Poverty and Charity*; Sharp, *Famine and Scarcity in Late Medieval and Early Modern England*.

14. Brundage, 'Sumptuary Laws and Prostitution in Late Medieval Italy', 344; Rath, *Food and Fantasy in Early Modern Japan*, 114–16.

15. Moyer, '"The Food Police"'.

16. See for instance Pullan, *Poverty and Charity*; Safley, ed., *The Reformation of Charity*; Abreu, *The Political and Social Dynamics of Poverty*; Campbell, *At the First Table*.

17. Thompson, 'The Moral Economy of an English Crowd'; Kaplan, *Bread, Politics and Political Economy*; Khondker, 'Famine Policies in Pre-British India'; Davis, *Late Victorian Holocausts*, 286–8; Murphey, 'Provisioning Istanbul'; Will and Wong, *Nourish the People*, 2, 511.

18. Tilly, 'Food Supply and Public Order in Modern Europe', 431.

19. On the centrality of food to bodily and spiritual health see Gentilcore, *Food and Health in Early Modern Europe*.

20. Machiavelli, *The Prince*; Botero, 'The Reason of State' (1598 edition), *The Reason of State and The Greatness of Cities*, 73.

21. Hobbes, *Leviathan*. See also Pagden, *The Languages of Political Theory in Early Modern Europe*.

22. Mexico and Peru thus nourished Europe with a steady flow of 'gold and silver breast-milk': Salinas y Cordova, *Memorial, Informe y Manifiesto*, 19r. 'If the stomach does not digest the food and distribute its goodness not only do the other parts of the body starve and decay, but the stomach itself also; and in the same way a prince who takes to himself and consumes the wealth of his subjects, without digesting it and sharing it according to their needs, brings ruin upon himself no less than to his vassals', wrote Botero: 'The Greatness of Cities' (1606 Robert Peterson translation), *The Reason of State and The Greatness of Cities*, 142.

23. *Times*, 4 Nov. 1795, 2.

24. Foucault, 'The Subject and Power'; Foucault, *Security, Territory, Population*; Coveney, *Food, Morals and Meaning*. See also Stern and Wennerlind, eds., *Mercantalism Reimagined*.

25. Marquis de Chastellux, *De la félicité publique*, II: 142–3.

26. Alletz, *L'Agronome*, II: 360. See also Spary, *Feeding France*.

27. Buchan, *Domestic Medicine*, 46.

28. Hartley, *How to Feed the Children*; Rowntree, *Poverty*, 240 (second quote); Vernon, 'The Ethics of Hunger and the Assembly of Society', 719–21; Treitel, 'Max Rubner and the Biopolitics of Rational Nutrition' (first quote); Biltekoff, *Eating Right in America*; Vernon, *Hunger*.

29. 'Jamie Oliver Bemoans Chips, Cheese and Giant TVs of Modern-day Poverty', *Guardian*, 27 Aug. 2013, www.theguardian.com/lifeandstyle/2013/aug/27/jamie-oliver-chips-cheese-

modern-day-poverty; BBC News, 'Tory Peer Apologises for Saying "Poor Can't Cook"', 8 Dec. 2014; Dowler, 'Food Banks and Food Justice in "Austerity Britain"', 164. See also Wheeler, 'To Feed or to Educate?'

30. The phrase is from Smith, *Sure Guide in Sickness and Health*, 61.

31. Buchan, *Observations Concerning the Diet of the Common People*, 43; Hartley, *How to Feed the Children*, 2.

32. More, *The Cottage Cook*; Shapiro, *Perfection Salad*; Treitel, 'Max Rubner and the Biopolitics of Rational Nutrition'; BBC News, 'Cookery to be Compulsory', 22 Jan. 2008; Elliot, 'Cookery Examined'; Richardson, *The Political Worlds of Women*; Biltekoff, *Eating Right in America*; BBC News, 'Tory Peer Apologises for Saying "Poor Can't Cook"'.

33. Vernon, *Hunger*; Simmons, *Vital Minimum*.

34. Burke, *Thoughts and Details on Scarcity*, 2.

35. Ugent, Dillehay and Ramírez, 'Potato Remains from a Late Pleistocene Settlement in Southcentral Chile'; Louderback and Pavlik, 'Starch Granule Evidence for the Earliest Potato Use in North America'.

36. Earle, *The Body of the Conquistador*.

37. Kant, 'What is Enlightenment?'; Gray, *Liberalism*; Bavetta, Navarra and Maimone, *Freedom and the Pursuit of Happiness*, 43.

38. Cobbett, *Cobbett's Weekly Political Register*, 24 Mar. 1832, 786–7.

39. Moleschott, *Lehre der Nahrungsmittel*, 119.

40. Harcout, *The Illusion of Free Markets*, 50.

41. Serres, 'Theory of the Quasi-Object'; Spary, *Eating the Enlightenment*, 192 (quote).

IMMIGRANT POTATOES

1. Vicente de Valverde to Charles V, Cuzco, 20 Mar. 1539, *Cartas del Perú*, ed. Porras Barrenechea, 314.

2. Murra, 'Rite and Crop in the Inca State'; Ugent, Dillehay and Ramírez, 'Potato Remains from a Late Pleistocene Settlement in Southcentral Chile'; Coe, *America's First Cuisines*; Naranjo Vargas, 'La comida andina antes del encuentro', *Conquista y comida*; Louderback and Pavlik, 'Starch Granule Evidence for the Earliest Potato Use in North America'. It is possible that the Casma Valley potatoes were wild rather than domesticated varieties.

3. Pascual de Angagoya, 'Relación que da el Adelantado de Andagoya de las tierras y provincias que abajo se hará mención', 1545, *Pascual de Andagoya*, 138.

4. Cieza de León, *Parte primera de la Chronica del Perú*, chap. 40, 105; Zárate, *Historia del descubrimiento y conquista del Perú*, book 1, chap. 8; Santo Thomas, *Grammatica*, 159v; Molina, *Relación de las fábulas y ritos de los incas*, 62–3; 'Descripción y relación de la provincia de los Yauyos', 1586, 'Descripción de la tierra del repartimiento de San Francisco de Atunrucana y Laramanti', 1586, and 'Relación de la Provincia de los Collaguas', all in *Relaciones geográficas de las Indias*, ed. Jiménez de la Espada, I: 156, 234, 586; Purchas, *Hakluytus Posthumus*, II: 157 (quote); Acosta, *Natural and Moral History of the Indies*, 148, 201–2.

5. FAO, FAOSTAT: 'Food and Agricultural Commodities Production'; and Helgi Library, 'Potato Consumption Per Capita in the World'.

6. Salaman, *History and Social Influence of the Potato*; Slicher Van Bath, *The Agrarian History of Western Europe*, 267–8; Langer, 'American Foods and Europe's Population Growth', 53; Messer, 'Three Centuries of Changing European Tastes for the Potato', 104; Kiple, *A Moveable Feast*, 136–7 (quote); Toussaint-Samat, *A History of Food*, 646–53; Reader, *Potato*, 112–14; Galli, *La conquête alimentaire du Nouveau Monde*. See Spary, *Feeding France*, 62, 86, for illuminating comments.

7. Salaman, *History and Social Influence of the Potato*, 116.

8. Las Casas, *Apologética historia sumaria*, III: 37; Acosta, *Natural and Moral History of the Indies*, 206 (quote); Monardes, *Joyfull News out of the New-found Worlde*, 20; Galli, *La conquête alimentaire du Nouveau Monde*.

9. Bauhin, *Prodromos Theatri Botanici*, 89–90.

10. Kiple, *A Moveable Feast*, 136–7.

11. Eagle and Younge, eds., *Collection of the Reports of Cases*, II: 228; Evans, *The Contentious Tithe*.

12. Rev Charles Layfield v. Thomas Ayscough et al, Croston, 1686, LRO, PR 718; Decree in Chancery: Rev Charles Layfield, Rector of Croston, & Thomas Ayscough, Thomas Lathom, Peter Lathom, Thomas Crookham, Thomas Hodson, John Rutter, John Moore, Thomas Miller, Thomas Christophers, Henry Yate, Richard Tompson, Edward Disley, Richard Moore, & William Forshaw, all of Mawdesley & Bispham, 16 May 1686, LRO, PR 718; Elizabeth Save v. Henry Thwaites, Kirkby Malzeard 1736, TNA, E134/10Geo2/Hil3; Papers concerning the Rev. Richard Rothwell claim to Tithe Potatoes in Sefton parish, 1789, LRO, DDM 11/61 (quote); Resolutions of Inhabitants to resist the Rev. Glover Moore's claim to Tithe of potatoes, Seals, 3 Oct. 1791, LRO PR/ 284; Eagle and Younge, eds., *Collection of the Reports of Cases*, II: 91, 141, 149, 189, 258, 310, 313, 380–98, 552, 588–9, 648, 690–1; Salaman, *History and Social Influence of the Potato*, 452; Evans, *The Contentious Tithe*, 7, 47, 53; Thirsk, *The Agrarian History of England and Wales*, I: 64; Zylberberg, 'Fuel Prices, Regional Diets and Cooking Habits', 112.

13. Agreement by 162 tenants of Formby, Ainsdale, and Raven Meols to frustrate the attempt of the rector of Walton, to take tithe of Potatoes and 'Garden-Stuff', 24 Feb. 1789, LRO, DDFO 23/4.

14. Vandenbroeke, 'Cultivation and Consumption of the Potato'; Terrón, *España, encrucijada de culturas alimentarias*, 143–4; Ibáñez Rodríguez, 'El diezmo en la Rioja', 192; Olsson and Svensson, 'Agricultural Production in Southern Sweden', 117–39; Palanca Cañon, 'Introducción y Generalización del Cultivo y Consumo Alimentario y Médico de la Patata', 77, 240–50, 263, 266.

15. Contrast the narrative in Eagle and Younge, eds., *Collection of the Reports of Cases*, II: 589, with Aikin, *A Description of the Country from Thirty to Forty Miles Round Manchester*, 45–6, 204, 237–8, 285, 306, 362.

16. Cardano, *De Rerum Varietate*, 30–1; Michiel, *I cinque libri di piante*, 143, 447; Clusius, *Rariorum Plantarum Historia*, 80; Bauhin, *Prodromos Theatri Botanici*, 89–90; Gerarde, *The Herbal or General History of Plants*, 926–8; Besler, *Hortus Eystenttensis*, section on 'classis autumnalis',

plate 27; Laufer, *American Plant Migration, part 1*, 27–69; Salaman, *History and Social Influence of the Potato*, 73–100.

17. See for instance Carolus Clusius to Joachim Camerarius, Frankfurt, 18 Nov. 1589. This and many other letters are transcribed at Van Gelder, ed., *Clusius Correspondence*.

18. Clusius, *Rariorum Plantarum Historia*, 80; Gutaker et al., 'The Origins and Adaptation of European Potatoes'.

19. Jacques Plateau to Carolus Clusius, Tournai, 3 Sept. 1588, *Clusius Correspondence*.

20. Bauhin, *Prodromos Theatri Botanici*, 89–90.

21. Jacques Garet Jr. to Carolus Clusius, 19 Jan. 1589; Jacques Garet Jr. to Carolus Clusius, 28 July 1589; and Gian Vincenzo Pinelli to Carolus Clusius, Padua, 19 Sept. 1597, 8 Dec. 1597, all in *Clusius Correspondence*; Clusius, *Rariorum Plantarum Historia*, 80.

22. Bauhin, *Prodromos Theatri Botanici*, 89–90. See also Gerarde, *Herball, or General History of Plantes*, 782; Clusius, *Rariorum Plantarum Historia*, 80; Sala, *De Alimentis et Eorum Recta Administratione Liber*, 12, 54, 65, 77; Zwinger, *Theatrum Botanicum*, 893.

23. Aldini, *Exactissima Descriptio Rariorum Quarundam Plantarum*; Cienfuegos, 'Historia de las plantas', BNE, vol. 1, chap. 88: 'De las papas del Perú, que en Indias llaman chuno, al pan que dellas se haze', fols. 498–505. For more evidence of new-world roots in early sixteenth-century Rome and Tuscany see Michiel, *I Cinque Libri di Piante*, 143; Aldrete, *Del orígen y principio de la lengua castellana*, 110–11; Magazzini, *Coltivazione toscana*, 16; and Targioni-Tozzetti, *Cenni storici sulla introduzione di varie piante nell'agricoltura ed Orticoltura Toscana*, 38–9. Or see Gartner, *Horticultura* on 'papas indorum' or 'artofeler'.

24. Gentilcore, *Food and Health in Early Modern Europe*.

25. Benzo et al., *Regole della sanità et natura de cibi*. Or see Nuñez de Oria, *Regimiento y aviso de sanidad*, 41v; Elsholtz, *Diaeteticon*, 31–32; Albala, *Eating Right in the Renaissance*.

26. In her excellent 'Apunte bibliográfico acerca de la batata/patata en la literatura del siglo de oro', María Isabel Amado Doblas argues that prior to the eighteenth century the term 'patata' always refers to the sweet potato; I see no reason for this confidence.

27. Monardes, *Joyfull News out of the Newe Founde World*, 104, notes the widespread cultivation of sweet potatoes in Vélez-Málaga.

28. He described 'a plant that has recently reached us from Italy and is called Taratouphli. It grows by itself in the soil and has pretty flowers, a good smell and below on the roots it has many *tubera* (bulbs), which when cooked are very pleasant to eat. They must first be simmered in water to remove the skin. After that they are drained and braised in butter': Wilhelm IV von Hessen to Christian I von Sachsen, Kessel, 10 Mar. 1591, *Quellenbuch zur sächsischen Geschichte*, ed. Arras, 61. Or see Michiel, *I cinque libri di piante*, Libro giallo, 143, Libro rosso II, 447.

29. See for instance Rosenhane, *Oeconomia*, 130.

30. Coles, *Adam in Eden*, 33.

31. Jacques Garet Jr. to Carolus Clusius, 19 Jan. 1589, 9 Sept. 1589, 28 Aug. 1590, all in *Clusius Correspondence*; Gerarde, *The Herbal or General History of Plants. The Complete 1633 Edition*, 926; Salaman, *History and Social Influence of the Potato*, 426–39; and *The Book of Fines*, ed. Butler, 207. Gardeners at Hampton Court have succeeded in cultivating sweet

potatoes; there is little horticultural reason to doubt the evidence that they were grown there in Tudor times: Historic Royal Palaces Blog, 'The History of the Sweet Potato'.

32. Labat, *Nouveau voyage aux îles de l'Amerique*, II: 400–1; Boissier de Sauvages, *Dictionnaire languedocien-françois*, 344; 'Pomme de terre, Topinambour, Batate, Truffe blanche, Truffe rouge'; Dillon, *Travels Through Spain*, 331.

33. For the European careers of the sweet potato and Jerusalem artichoke see for instance Monardes, *Joyfull News out of the Newe Founde World*, f. 104; Benzo et al., *Regole della sanitá*, 622–3; Parkinson, *Paradisi in Sole Paradisus Terrestris*, 518; Zwinger, *Theatrum Botanicum*, 400–1; Parmentier, *Traité sur la culture et les usages des pommes de terre, de la patate, et du topinambour*; Targioni-Tozzetti, *Cenni storici sulla introduzione di varie piante*, 46; Salaman, *History and Social Influence of the Potato*; Crosby, *The Columbian Exchange*; Hawkes and Francisco-Ortega, 'The Early History of the Potato in Europe'; Amado Doblas, 'Apunte bibliográfico acerca de la batata/patata'; Galli, *La conquête alimentaire du Nouveau Monde*.

34. Terrón, *España, encrucijada de culturas alimentarias*, 169; Muldrew, *Food, Energy and the Creation of Industriousness*, 46; Nadeau, *Food Matters*, 163, 165, 168.

35. Rumpolts, *Ein new Kochbuch*, 16b, 143b. *Olla podrida* is discussed in Nadeau, *Food Matters*.

36. Casteau, *Ouverture de cuisine*, 94–5.

37. For printed cookery books see Dawson, *Good Huswife's Jewell*, 20v (quote); Murrell, *A New Book of Cookerie*, 4, 80–1; Cooper, *The Art of Cookery Refin'd and Augmented*, 36–7; Woolley, *The Queen-Like Closet*; *Accomplished Ladies Rich Closet of Rarities*; Grey, *A Choice Manual*; Astry, *Diana Astry's Recipe Book*, 95. For manuscript collections see 'Physical and Chyrurgicall Receipts', fol. 107; 'Collection of Cookery and Medical Receipts by Edward and Katherine Kidder', fol. 21; 'Recipe Book of the Godrey-Faussett Family of Heppington', fols. 19, 79; 'Anonymous Collection of Cookery and Medical Receipts', fols. 36–7; 'Cookery Receipts Collected by Johnson Family of Spalding, Lincs.', fols. 112r–v; and 'Manuscript Recipe Book', c. 1700, SL, Sophie D. Coe Manuscript Cookbook Collection, box 1, folder 1, fol. 4. See also Thirsk, *Food in Early Modern England*, 111, 115; Pennell, 'Recipes and Reception'.

38. *The Letters of John Chamberlain*, ed. McClure, II: 551; and Nadeau, *Food Matters*, 35.

39. Royer, *Eine gute Anleitung*, 104–5.

40. Elsholtz, *Diaeteticon*, 31–32 (quote); Helmhardt von Hohberg, *Herrn von Hohbergs Georgica Curiosa Aucta*, 387; and *Die Curieuse ... Köchin*, 563.

41. *Frauenzimmer-Lexikon*, cols. 1979–81; Howard, *England's Newest Way in All Sorts of Cookery*, 14; Hall, *The Queen's Royal Cookery*, 98, 100–1; Salmon, *The Family-Dictionary*, 390, 408; 'Anonymous Collection of Cookery and Medical Receipts', fols. 36–7; 'Recipe Book of the Godrey-Faussett Family of Heppington, Nackington, Kent', fols. 19, 79; Smith, *The Compleat Housewife*, 9, 132–3, 139; *Collection of Receipts in Cookery, Physick and Surgery*, 131–2; 'English Manuscript Cookbook', SL, American Institute of Wine & Food Recipe Books, box 1; Altimiras, *Nuevo arte de cocina*, 140–1; Buc'hoz, *Manuel alimentaire des plantes*, 485–6; Rigaud, *Cozinheiro moderno*, 396, 403; Pennell, 'Recipes and Reception'.

42. Serres, *Le theatre d'agriculture*, 513–14; Parkinson, *Paradisi in Sole Paradisus Terrestris*, 516 (quote); Magazzini, *Coltivazione toscana*, 16; *The Compleat Planter and Cyderist*, 245–7; Markham, *The Husbandman's Jewel*, 7; Turner, *An Almanack*, 17; Parker, *The Gardeners Almanack*, 33.

43. Evelyn, *Kalendarium Hortense*, 14, 19 (quote), 122; Helmhardt von Hohberg, *Georgica Curiosa Aucta*, 640; Switzer, *The Practical Kitchen Gardiner*, 217–19, 378.

44. Hawkes and Francisco-Ortega, 'The Early History of the Potato in Europe'.

45. Cienfuegos, 'Historia de las plantas', BNE, vol. 1, chap. 88: 'De las papas del Perú', fols. 498–505; Leon Pinelo, *Question moral si el chocolate quebranta el ayuno eclesiástico*, 63.

46. Lili-Annè Aldman, personal communication, 2015, citing material from Sweden's Landsarkiv in Vadstena, Vadstena: Drevs Församling: LIb: 1 (1635–50), 19–149, 207–65; and Långasjö Församlin: LIa: 1 (1651–67).

47. Griffith v. Allerton, 1698–9, TNA, C 6/414/31; Chamberlayne, *Angliae Notitia*, 40; *Act of Tonnage and Poundage, and Rates of Merchandize*; Salaman, *History and Social Influence of the Potato*, 224–5, 451; Hawkes and Francisco-Ortega, 'The Potato in Spain during the Late Sixteenth Century'; Hawkes and Francisco-Ortega, 'The Early History of the Potato in Europe'; Thirsk, *Agrarian History of England and Wales*, I: 64, 373; Clarkson and Crawford, *Feast and Famine*.

48. Evans, 'Some Reasons for the Growth of English Anti-Clericalism'; Barnard, 'Gardening, Diet and "Improvement"'.

49. Molinier, *Stagnations et croissance*, 266. Authorities in the Staffordshire village of Caverswell likewise determined in 1722 to levy tithes on 'potatoes, parsnips, carriots [sic], turnips and all manner of roots': Evans, 'Tithing Customs and Disputes', 25. On chestnuts and root vegetables see also Grieco, 'The Social Politics of Pre-Linnaean Botanical Classification'; Camporesi, *The Magic Harvest*.

50. Ávila, *Escritos de Santa Teresa*, II: 128, 158.

51. Rich, *True Report of a Late Practice Enterprised by a Papist*, sig. Bi. Salaman, *History and Social Influence of the Potato*, 428ff., catalogues many such works.

52. [Hamilton], *The Country-Man's Rudiments*, 31.

53. Wiegelmann, *Alltags- und Festspeisen in Mitteleuropa*; Morineau, 'The Potato in the Eighteenth Century'; Braudel, *Civilization and Capitalism*, I: 168–70; Ferrières, 'Le cas de la pomme de terre dans le Midi'; Zylberberg, 'Fuel Prices, Regional Diets and Cooking Habits', 119.

54. McNeil, 'How the Potato Changed the World's History'; Terrón, *España, encrucijada de culturas alimentarias*, 84–5; Lemire, '"Men of the World"'.

55. Magazzini, *Coltivazione toscana*, 16; Benzo et al., *Regole della sanitá et natura de cibi*, 622–3; Schuler, *Geschichte und Beschreibung des Landes Glarus*, 130; Boll, *Geschichte Meklenburgs mit besondere Berücksichtigung der Culturgeschichte*, II: 523. Berg, 'Die Kartoffel und die Rübe'; and Blum, *The End of the Old Order*, 271, discuss the role of soldiers and artisans in spreading potatoes.

56. DeLoughrey, 'Globalizing the Routes of Breadfruit and Other Bounties'. See also Ploeg, 'Potatoes and Knowledge'.

57. Vandenbroeke, 'Cultivation and Consumption of the Potato', 19.

58. Eden, *The State of the Poor*, I: 508.

59. Symner, 'Notes on Natural History in Ireland' (quote); Petty, 'The Political Anatomy of Ireland', 1672, *Tracts; Chiefly Relating to Ireland*, 319, 355, 366, 374; Clarkson and Crawford, *Feast and Famine*; Barnard, 'Gardening, Diet and "Improvement"'.

60. Baxter, 'The Reverend Richard Baxter's Last Treatise'; Overton, *Agricultural Revolution in England*, 102.

61. Elsholtz, *Diaeteticon*, 31–2.

62. Royer, *Eine gute Anleitung*, 104; Helmhardt von Hohberg, *Georgica Curiosa Aucta*, book 5, chap. 42, 639. For the early modern peasant diet see Camporesi, *Bread of Dreams*; Capatti and Montanari, *Italian Cuisine*; Fox, 'Food, Drink and Social Distinction in Early Modern England'.

63. Royer, *Eine gute Anleitung*, 104–5; Jacques Plateau to Carolus Clusius, Tournai, 3 Sept. 1588, *Clusius Correspondence*.

64. Terrón, *España, encrucijada de culturas alimentarias*, 139–42; Ferrières, 'Le cas de la pomme de terre dans le Midi', 210 (quote); Miodunka 'L'essor de la culture de la pomme de terre au sud de la Pologne'.

65. On this see Berg, 'Afterword: Things in Global History'.

66. Kaldy, 'Protein Yield of Various Crops as Related to Protein Value'; FAO, 'International Year of the Potato 2008: Potato and Water Resources'. A kilo of wheat is, however, considerably more calorific than a kilo of potatoes. See also Sauer, *Agricultural Origins and Dispersals*, 136–7.

67. Shammas, *The Pre-Industrial Consumer in England and America*, 137.

68. Terrón, *España, encrucijada de culturas alimentarias*, 139–43; Zylberberg, 'Fuel Prices, Regional Diets and Cooking Habits'.

69. Netting, *Balancing on an Alp*, 38. Bräker, *The Poor Man of Toggenburg*, offers a first-hand account of potato cultivation in the Swiss mountains.

70. For the ongoing debate about the potato's role in population growth see Komlos, 'The New World's Contribution to Food Consumption'; McNeill, 'How the Potato Changed the World's History'; Nunn and Qian, 'The Potato's Contribution to Population and Urbanization'.

71. Simonton, *A History of European Women's Work*, 19–33, 116–28. On women and hoe-culture more generally see Boserup, *Woman's Role in Economic Development*.

72. Scott, *Seeing Like a State*; Scott, *The Art of Not Being Governed*, 195–207 (196 quote); Scott, *Against the Grain*, 130.

73. Hutchison, 'Swedish Population Thought in the Eighteenth Century', 91.

74. Laurence, *The Duty of a Steward to his Lord*, 30, 119; Thirsk, *The Agrarian History of England and Wales*, I: 56.

75. Linnaeus, *Skånska resa år 1749*, 7 June 1749; Koerner, *Linnaeus*, 148–9. See also Linnaeus, *Dissertatio Academicum de Pane Diaetetico*, 20; I owe this translation to Desirée Arbó.

76. Ward, *Proyecto económico*, 72.

77. Dechambre, ed., *Dictionnaire encyclopédique des sciences médicales*, 229.

78. Slicher Van Bath, *The Agrarian History of Western Europe*, 267–8.

79. Zanon, *Della coltivazione, e dell'uso delle patate*, 71; Gasparini, *Polenta e formenton*; Galli, *La conquête alimentaire du nouveau monde*, 235–8. On maize as a peasant crop elsewhere in Europe see also Forster, 'The Noble as Landlord in the Region of Toulouse', 241; Casado Soto, 'Notas sobre la implantación del maíz en Cantabria y la sustitución de otros cultivos';

Terrón, *España, encrucijada de culturas alimentarias*, 74–91; Gentilcore, *Food and Health in Early Modern Europe*, 147.

80. Hoffman, *Growth in a Traditional Society*; Thick, 'Root Crops and the Feeding of London's Poor', 294–5.

81. McClellan III and Regourd, 'The Colonial Machine'; Raj, 'Colonial Encounters and the Forging of New Knowledges and National Identities'; Chakrabarty, *Provincializing Europe*; Cañizares-Esguerra, *Nature, Empire and Nation*; Safier, *Measuring the World*; Smith, *The Body of the Artisan*; Raj, *Relocating Modern Science*; Roberts, 'Situating Science in Global History'; and McClellan III, *Colonialism and Science*.

82. Ambrosoli, *The Wild and the Sown*, 406.

83. Toussaint-Samat, *A History of Food*, 647.

84. On maize's versatility and peasant practice see Brush, *Farmer's Bounty*. Farmers in eighteenth-century Norway both ate potatoes and smoked their leaves in place of tobacco: Wilse, *Physisk, oeconomisk og statistisk Beskrivelse*, 255–6. Amund Pedersen translated the Norwegian.

85. Forster, *Englands Happiness Increased* is one such exception.

86. Petty, 'Political Arithmetic' (1690), and 'Political Anatomy of Ireland', *Tracts*, 238, 319, 355, 366, 374. Or see Brady, 'Remedies Proposed for the Church of Ireland', 166.

ENLIGHTENED POTATOES

1. Legrand d'Aussy, *Histoire de la vie privée des Français*, I: 112.

2. Varenne de Béost, *La cuisine des pauvres*, 2 (first quote); *Journal historique & litteraire* 156 (1780), 128–9; Buchan, *Observations Concerning the Diet of the Common People*, 43 (second quote).

3. Toussaint-Samat, *A History of Food*, 646.

4. Virey, 'De la vie et des ouvrages d'Antoine-Augustin Parmentier', 60–1. See also Parmentier, *Observations on Such Nutritive Vegetables as May be Substituted in the Place of Ordinary Food*, 8–9.

5. Thomopoulos, *The History of Greece*, 71.

6. A Finnish colleague for instance explained that he had been taught how the Finnish priest Axel Laurell 'spread potatoes to his parishioners by posting a night-guard on his fields. But he ordered that this guard actually had to let the parishioners steal some potatoes from those fields at night. Laurell thought that the parishioners would actually try growing potatoes themselves if they thought that it was a kind of "forbidden" or "protected" fruit': Joonas Tammela, 16 Oct. 2017, personal communication.

7. Parker, *Global Crisis*.

8. Riley, *Population Thought in the Age of the Demographic Revolution*; Tomaselli, 'Moral Philosophy and Population Questions in Eighteenth-Century Europe'; Cole, *The Power of Large Numbers*; Rusnock, *Vital Accounts*, 95 (quote, my emphasis); Charbit, *The Classical Foundations of Population Thought*; McCormick, 'Population: Modes of Seventeenth-Century Demographic Thought'.

9. Ward, *Proyecto económico*, 70.

10. Ward, *Proyecto económico*, 70; Hutchison, 'Swedish Population Thought in the Eighteenth Century', 85–6.

11. Riley, *Population Thought in the Age of the Demographic Revolution*; Tomaselli, 'Moral Philosophy and Population Questions in Eighteenth-Century Europe'; Charbit, *The Classical Foundations of Population Thought*, 124–31.

12. G. Warde, 'An Idea for the Relief of the Poor', Bradfield, 15 Feb. 1795, *Annals of Agriculture* 24 (1795), 370. For this he relied on no less an authority than Adam Smith, who had himself affirmed that 'the most decisive mark of the prosperity of any country is the increase of the number of its inhabitants': Smith, *An Inquiry into the Nature and Causes of the Wealth of Nations*, I.viii.23.

13. Mill, 'Colony'.

14. Foucault, *Security, Territory, Population*. See also Dean, *The Constitution of Poverty*.

15. Moheau, *Recherches et considérations sur la population de la France*, 250.

16. Ward, *Proyecto económico*, 196 (my emphasis).

17. Ward, *Obra pía*; Ward, *Proyecto económico*, 'Al lector', v (quote).

18. Ward, *Proyecto económico*, 58.

19. Ward, *Proyecto económico*, 58 (my emphasis). See also Argumossa y Gandara, *Erudicción política*; Rodríguez de Campomanes, *Discurso sobre el fomento de la industria popular*, 136; Campillo y Cosío, *Nuevo sistema de gobierno económico*, 261; Cabarrús, 'Discurso sobre la libertad de comercio'; Uriz, *Causas prácticas de la muerte de los niños expósitos*. Tavárez Simó, 'La invención de un imperio comercial hispano', argues that the *Nuevo sistema de gobierno económico* should be attributed to Melchor Rafael de Macanaz.

20. Hutchison, 'Swedish Population Thought in the Eighteenth Century', 84.

21. Parmentier, *Les pommes de terre, considérées relativement à la santé & à l'économie*, 133.

22. Lagrange, 'Essai d'arithmétique politique sur les premiers besoins de l'intérieur de la république', 1796, *Oeuvres*, VII: 578 (quote); Simmons, *Vital Minimum*, 231–2.

23. Dalrymple, *The Poor Man's Friend*, 21 (appendix).

24. Becher, *Politische Discurs*, 205 (quote, my emphasis); Petyt, *Britannia Languens*, section 7; Tribe, *Governing Economy*, 85; Tribe, 'Cameralism and the Sciences of the State', 527.

25. Melon, *Essai politique sur le commerce*, 12. Or see Béguillet, *Traité des subsistances et des grains*, I: 252; and Lavoisier, 'Résultats extraits d'un oeuvrage intitulé de la richesse territoriale du royaume de France', 1784, *Oeuvres*, VI: 422.

26. Hanway, *A Candid Historical Account of the Hospital*, 10.

27. Girdler, *Observations on the Pernicious Consequences of Forestalling*, 53 (quote), 88.

28. Benavídez, *Secretos de chirurgia*, 26–7 (quote); Huarte de San Juan, *Examen de Ingenios*, 21–2; Lemnius, *The Touchstone of Complexions*, 25–31; Moffet, *Health's Improvement*, 59; Earle, *The Body of the Conquistador*; Gentilcore, *Food and Health in Early Modern Europe*.

29. Fox, 'Food, Drink and Social Distinction in Early Modern England'.

30. Smith, *An Inquiry into the Nature and Causes of the Wealth of Nations*, I.viii.45.

31. Fielding, 'An Enquiry into the Causes of the Late Increase of Robbers', 90. See also Lémery, *Traité des aliments*, I: xxix–xxx; Des-Essartz, *Traité de l'éducation corporelle des enfants*; Ballexserd, *Dissertation sur l'éducation physique des enfans*, 29; Bonells, *Perjuicios que acarrean al género humano y al estado las madres que rehusan criar a sus hijos*; Dalrymple, *The Poor Man's Friend*, 21; Girdler, *Observations on the Pernicious Consequences of Forestalling*, 53, 88; Uriz, *Causas prácticas de la muerte de los niños*

expósitos, I: 85; Arteta, *Disertacion sobre la muchdumbre de niños que mueren en la infancia*, I: 16.

32. Des-Essartz, *Traité de l'éducation corporelle des enfants*, vi (first quote); Guimarães Sá, 'Circulation of Children in Eighteenth-Century Portugal', 29 (second quote).

33. Uriz, *Causas prácticas de la muerte de los niños expósitos*, I: 85 (quote), II: 127–30, 157.

34. See for instance Bonells, *Perjuicios que acarrean al género humano*; Uriz, *Causas prácticas de la muerte de los niños expósitos*, I: 85 (quote), II: 127–30, 157; Arteta, *Disertación sobre la muchdumbre de niños que mueren en la infancia*, I: 16; Morel, 'Théories et pratiques de l'allaitement en France au XVIIIe siècle', esp. 403–4; Sherwood, *Poverty in Eighteenth-Century Spain*; Andrews, *Philanthropy and Police*; Guimarães Sá, 'Circulation of Children in Eighteenth-Century Portugal', 29 (quote); Morel, 'Children', I: 247.

35. Turnbull, *The Naval Surgeon*, 23–46; Admiral Philip Patton, 'Strictures on Naval Discipline and the Conduct of a Ship of War', c. 1807, *Shipboard Life and Organisation*, ed. Lavery, 629 (quote); Macdonald, *British Navy's Victualling Board*; Knight and Wilcox, *Sustaining the Fleet*; Macdonald, *Feeding Nelson's Navy*.

36. Buchet, *The British Navy*, 125.

37. González, *Tratado de las enfermedades de la gente de mar*.

38. Lémery, *Traité des aliments*, I: xxx; Lorry, *Essai sur les alimens*, II: 216; Poissonnier Desperrières, *Traité des maladies des gens de mer*, 11 (first quote); Poissonnier Desperrières, *Mémoire sur les avantages qu'il y aurait a changer absolument la nourriture des gens de mer*, 7 (second quote); Lebeschu de la Bastays, *L'Ami des navigateurs*, esp. iii, 60–87.

39. Post, 'Nutritional Status and Mortality in Eighteenth-Century Europe'; Gallego, *El motín de Esquilache, América y Europa*.

40. On this see Stedman Jones, *An End to Poverty?*

41. Bignami, *Le patate*, 15, 4, respectively.

42. Henry, *The Complete English Farmer*, 275–6. Or see Smith, *An Inquiry into the Nature and Causes of the Wealth of Nations*, I.xi.b.41; Parmentier, *Les pommes de terre, considérées relativement à la santé & à l'économie*, 195; Parmentier, *Traité sur la culture et les usages des pommes de terre, de la patate, et du topinambour*, 17–18; Doyle, *Tratado sobre el cultivo, uso y utilidades de las patatas* (1797), 24–5; *Feuille de cultivateur*, 10 Feb. 1799.

43. Bentham, 'Panopticon; or, the Inspection-House: Containing the Idea of a New Principle of Construction applicable to any sort of establishment, in which persons of any description are to be kept under inspection … written in the year 1787', *The Works of Jeremy Bentham*, IV: 155; and Good, *Dissertation*, 77 (quote).

44. Ferrières, 'Le cas de la pomme de terre dans le Midi'.

45. Engel, *Traité*, 45–6.

46. Cadet de Vaux, *L'Ami de l'économie*, 59.

47. *Essay on Modern Luxuries*, 7.

48. Hanway, *A Candid Historical Account of the Hospital*, 11 (quote). For complaints about alcohol see Brennan, *Public Drinking and Popular Culture in Eighteenth-Century Paris*; Kümin, *Drinking Matters*, 153; Warner, *Craze*.

49. [Lobb], *Primitive Cookery*; [Colquhoun], *An Account of a Meat and Soup Charity*, 19.

50. Eden, *The State of the Poor*, I: 491–2. See also Dean, *The Constitution of Poverty*, 50.

51. Buchan, *Domestic Medicine*, 46.

52. Buchan, *Domestic Medicine*, 67.

53. Buchan, *Observations Concerning the Diet of the Common People*, 7.

54. Buchan, *Observations Concerning the Diet of the Common People*, 31; Richard Pearson, 'Analysis of the Potatoe-Root', *Report of the Committee of the Board of Agriculture*, Board of Agriculture, 79–86.

55. Buchan, *Observations Concerning the Diet of the Common People*, 31–2. On potato gardens see Burchardt, 'Land and the Laborer'.

56. Board of Agriculture Minute Books, SR RASE A/I-II, B/I (fols. 31–4 slugs), B/II, B/VI–VII, B/X, B/XIII (fol. 266 earless sheep), MRELSC; 'Plan for Establishing a Board of Agriculture and Internal Improvement, Originally Printed in May 1793', *Communications to the Board of Agriculture*, Board of Agriculture; and Mitchison, 'The Old Board of Agriculture'.

57. An experimental supply of these dried potatoes was indeed sent on a naval vessel to Botany Bay, 'this root thus prepared being extremely salutary to the health of seamen': Board of Agriculture Minutes, 23 May 1797, SR RASE B/XIII, fol. 199, MRELSC.

58. The minutes of the Committee on Potatoes are in SR RASE B/X, MRELSC. See also Board of Agriculture, *Account of the Experiments tried by the Board of Agriculture in the Composition of Various Sorts of Bread*.

59. 'Sir John Sinclair's Address to the Board of Agriculture, on Tuesday, the Twenty-fourth of May, 1796', *Communications to the Board of Agriculture*, Board of Agriculture, lxiv.

60. Board of Agriculture, *Report of the Committee of the Board of Agriculture*, vii (quote); 'Substance of Sir John Sinclair's Address to the Board of Agriculture, on Tuesday the 14th July, 1795', *Communications to the Board of Agriculture*, Board of Agriculture, lx–lxiii.

61. Board of Agriculture, *Report of the Committee of the Board of Agriculture*, 74.

62. Board of Agriculture, *Report of the Committee of the Board of Agriculture*, 70 (quote); Board of Agriculture, *Hints Respecting the Culture and the Use of Potatoes*. The difficulty with 'panifying' potatoes is that potatoes alone do not contain sufficient gluten to allow a good rise.

63. Board of Agriculture, *Report of the Committee of the Board of Agriculture*, 73. Since the potato afforded food to a significant portion of Britain's inhabitants, 'every improvement in its culture becomes an object of national importance', agreed the president of the Horticultural Society of London: Knight, 'On Raising New and Early Varieties of the Potatoe', I: 57. Encouraging potato cultivation, observed the translator of a text by France's premier potato-promoter, was 'an object of highest national importance': Parmentier, *Observations on Such Nutritive Vegetables as May be Substituted in the Place of Ordinary Food*, vii.

64. Phillips, *The New World of Words*, entry on 'potatoes'.

65. See for instance Switzer, *The Practical Kitchen Gardiner*, 217–19, 378; Miller, *The Gardeners Dictionary*, II: lycopersicon entry; Adam, *Practical Essays on Agriculture*, essay 7, II: 1 (quote); Henriette Charlotte Gräfin von Itzenplitz, treatise on potatoes, Kew, 18 Aug. 1793, LRO, DDSc 9/47; *Annals of Agriculture* 24 (1795), *passim*; Aikin, *A Description of the Country from Thirty to Forty Miles Round Manchester*, 45–6, 362; Board of Agriculture, *Communications to the*

Board of Agriculture, Board of Agriculture, 37–45, 93; Overton, *Agricultural Revolution in England*, 102; Horrell and Oxley, 'Hasty Pudding versus Tasty Bread'; Zylberberg, 'Fuel Prices, Regional Diets and Cooking Habits'.

66. *The Gentleman's Magazine and Historical Chronicle* 34 (1764), 599; *Extractos de las Juntas Generales celebradas por la Real Sociedad Bascongada de los Amigos del País en la ciudad de Vitoria por julio de 1786*, 28; Doyle, *Tratado sobre el cultivo, uso y utilidades de las patatas* (1797). For other state-level directives see for instance *Instrucção sobre a cultura das batatas*; *El Excmo. Sr. Secretario de Estado y del Despacho de Hacienda*; Wiegelmann, *Alltags- und Festspeisen in Mitteleuropa*, 83n.40; Spary, *Feeding France*; Jones, *Provincial Development in Russia*, 154–5; Smith and Christian, *Bread and Salt*, 199–200; and Kisbán, 'The Beginnings of Potato Cultivation in Transylvania and Hungary: Government Policy and Spontaneous Process'.

67. Parmentier, *Manière de Faire le Pain de Pommes de Terre sans Mélange de Farine*; Parmentier, *Les pommes de terre, considérées relativement à la santé & à l'économie*; Baldini, *De' Pomi di terra ragionamento*; Parmentier, *Mémoire couronné le 25 aout 1784*; Parmentier, *Traité sur la culture et les usages des pommes de terre, de la patate, et du topinambour*; Berg, 'Die Kartoffel und die Rübe'; Talve, 'The Potato in Finnish Food Economy'; Gentilcore, *Italy and the Potato: A History*.

68. John Howard, Cardington, Bedfordshire, 17 Feb. 1769, RSA, RSA/PR/GE/110/26/70 and 71; *Københavnske Nye Tidende*, 1758, in *Norges landbrukshistorie*, ed. Kåre. Amund Pedersen translated the Norwegian.

69. Laurell, *Lyhykäinen kirjoitus potatesten eli maan-päronain wiljelemisestä*; Wilse, *Physisk, oeconomisk og statistisk Beskrivelse*, 255–6; 'Carta del cura del Linares sobre el cultivo y aprovechamiento de las patatas', *SAA* 2 (1797), 222–7, 245–52, 261–9, 277–82; 'Carta del cura de Linares', *SAA*, 26 Dec. 1799, 401–2; 'Carta del cura de Linares', *SAA*, 13 Aug. 1801, 97–106; Simonen, *Raivaajia ja rakentajia*, 33–6; Drake, *Population and Society in Norway*, 54–5. Amund Pedersen and Jussipekka Luukkonen interpreted the material in Norwegian and Finnish.

70. Campini, *Saggi d'Agricoltura*, 388–93.

71. Spary, *Feeding France*, 167–86.

72. *Cuisinière républicaine*; More, *The Cottage Cook*.

73. Agricultural techniques are explained for instance in Miller, *The Gardeners Dictionary*; Rudenschöld, *Almanach*; Halldórsson, *Korte Beretninger om nogle Forsög til Landvæsenets*; Zanon, *Della coltivazione, e dell'uso delle patate*; Hammer, *Afhandling om Patatos*; Engel, *Traité*; Henry, *The Complete English Farmer*; *Beskrifning om jordpärons plantering*; Hertzberg, *Underretning for Bønder*; Baldini, *De' Pomi di terra ragionamento*; Occhiolini, *Memorie sopra il meraviglioso frutto americano*; Adam, *Practical Essays on Agriculture* II; Parmentier, *Traité sur la culture et les usages des pommes de terre, de la patate, et du topinambour*; Doyle, *Tratado sobre el cultivo, uso y utilidades de las patatas* (1797); Larumbe, *Epítome cristiano de agricultura*; *Metodo facile, e sperimentato per coltivare le patate*; Gómez de Ortega, *Elementos teóricos-prácticos de agricultura*; Estéban Boutalou, 'Memoria sobre las patatas', *SAA* 19 (1806); Riera Climent and Riera Palmero, 'Los alimentos americanos en los *Extractos de la Bascongada*'. In 1797 Arthur Young indexed the articles on potatoes that had appeared

in his *Annals of Agriculture*, the index provides a good sense of the range of topics – from manures to harvesting times – addressed by one such work: *Annals of Agriculture* 29 (1797), 38–62.

74. Most of the works listed above address issues of storage. See also *Angående potaters förvarande*, M. de Bullion, 'Moyen de conserver les Pommes-de-terre', *Mémoires d'agriculture, d'économie rurale et domestique* (1789), 183–6; Board of Agriculture, *Hints Respecting the Culture and the Use of Potatoes*, *Annals of Agriculture* 24 (1795), 64–71; Amoretti, *Della coltivazione delle patate*, 40–4; 'Modo de conservar las patatas muchos años', *SAA* 17 (1805), 392–3; Virey, 'Pomme-de-terre, ou papas des Américas', 542ff.; Popplow, 'Economizing Agricultural Resources in the German Economic Enlightenment', 277; Spary, *Feeding France*.

75. Engel, *Traité*, 68; *Bibliothèque physico-économique, instructive et amusante* (1787); *Mémoires d'agriculture, d'économie rurale et domestique* (1789), 34; Adam, *Practical Essays on Agriculture*, II: 1–37; Parmentier, *Traité sur la culture et les usages des pommes de terre, de la patate, et du topinambour*; Billingsley, 'On the Culture of Potatoes, and feeding Hogs with them'; John Boys, 'Experiments on Fattening Hogs', *Annals of Agriculture* 29 (1797), 150–9; Doyle, *Tratado sobre la cría y propagación de pastos y ganados*; *SAA* 19 (1806), 249; Drake, *Population and Society in Norway*, 55.

76. Varenne de Béost, *La cuisine des pauvres*; Parmentier, *Les pommes de terre, considérées relativement à la santé & à l'économie*; 'Potatoes, by a Lancashire Man', *Annals of Agriculture* 24 (1795), 568–75; 'Modo de cocer las patatas en Irlanda', *SAA* 17 (1805), 256; and Guðmundsdóttir, 'Viðreisn garðræktar á síðari hluta 18. Aldar': Hrefna Róbertsdóttir explained the Icelandic. 'Various methods of boiling potatoes have been much extolled, but there do not seem to have been sufficiently accurate experiments made to ascertain, which is the best. Should you be able to decide the question and to form a comparative trial have the goodness to inform us of the result,' the Board of Agriculture wrote to one of their correspondents: Board of Agriculture Minutes, 8 Mar. 1796, SR RASE B/XIII, fol. 71, MRELSC.

77. Skytte, 'Ron at utaf potatoes brånna brännavin', 231–2; *Magazzino toscana* 22:1 (1775), 114; Parmentier, *Les pommes de terre, considérées relativement à la santé & à l'économie*, 32, 176–80; *Encyclopédie méthodique: Arts et métiers mécaniques* 2 (1783), 196; James Anderson, 'Of Ardent Spirits Afforded by Potatoes', *Letters and Papers on Agriculture* 4 (1788), 43–52; Board of Agriculture Committee on Potatoes, 28 Jan. 1795, SR RASE B/X, fol. 5, MRELSC; Keith, *A General View of the Agriculture of Aberdeenshire*, 266–8; Alonso de Herrera, *Agricultura general*, II: 253; Kisbán, 'The Beginnings of Potato Cultivation in Transylvania and Hungary', 180–1; Koerner, *Linnaeus*, 132, 149.

78. James Stonhouse, 'Expedients for alleviating the Distress occasioned by the present Dearness of Corn', Northampton, *Universal Magazine* 21 (1757), 270; Bolotov, 'O delanii iz tartofelia muki'; Parmentier, *Manière de Faire le Pain de Pommes de Terre*; *Extractos de las Juntas Generales celebradas por la Real Sociedad Bascongada de los Amigos del País en la villa de Vergara por setiembre de 1779*; Baldini, *De' Pomi di terra ragionamento*, 23–7; William Augustus Howard, Grays Inn Great Square, 14 July 1795, TNA, HO 42/35, fols. 157–8; Board of Agriculture Minutes of Committee on Potatoes, Committee on the Scarcity of Grain, 23

Aug. 1794–27 Nov. 1795, SR RASE B/X, fols. 1–45, MRELSC; Board of Agriculture, *Account of the Experiments tried by the Board of Agriculture in the Composition of Various Sorts of Bread*; Doyle, *Tratado sobre el cultivo, uso y utilidades de las patatas* (1797); 'Carta del cura del Linares sobre el cultivo y aprovechamiento de las patatas', *SAA* 2 (1797), 222–7, 245–52, 261–9, 277–82; 'Report from Saxon Electoral Society of Agriculture on the Cultivation of Potatoes', *Communications to the Board of Agriculture*, Board of Agriculture, 295; Kisbán, 'The Beginnings of Potato Cultivation in Transylvania and Hungary'; Koerner, *Linnaeus*, 149; Popplow, 'Economizing Agricultural Resources in the German Economic Enlightenment', 277; Hiler, 'La pomme de terre révolutionnaire'; Spary, *Feeding France*. Colum Leckey interpreted the Russian for me.

79. Doyle, *Tratado sobre el cultivo, uso y utilidades de las patatas* (1797), 8, 24, 31; Uriz, *Causas prácticas de la muerte de los niños expósitos*, II: 127.

80. Lavoisier, *Oeuvres*, II: 815; Grimaux, *Lavoisier*, 165; *SAA* 3 (1798), 61; Larriba, 'Un intento de reforma agraria'.

81. *SAA* 11 (1802), 316.

82. Doyle, *Tratado sobre el cultivo, uso y utilidades de las patatas* (1797).

83. Engel, *Traité*, 7–8, 12, 35, 42, 56, 60, 68.

84. Mr. Tschiffeli, 'An Experiment to Make Potatoes Thrive without Dung', *Foreign Essays on Agriculture and Arts*.

85. Skytte, 'Ron at utaf potatoes brånna brånnavin', 231–2; *L'Avantcoureur*, 18 Nov. 1771; *Magazzino toscana* 22:1 (1775), 114; Keith, *A General View of the Agriculture of Aberdeenshire*, 266–8; Henriette Charlotte Gräfin von Itzenplitz, treatise on potatoes, Kew, 18 Aug. 1793, LRO, DDSc 9/47; George Way on spirit from potatoe apples, 21 Dec. 1797, RSA/PR/MC/105/10/396; Koerner, *Linnaeus*, 149.

86. Miodunka 'L'essor de la culture de la pomme de terre au sud de la Pologne'. Or see Parmentier, *Mémoire couronné le 25 aout 1784*, 5; Adam, *Practical Essays on Agriculture*, II: 20–1.

87. *SAA* 18 (1805), 4 and 11 July 1805; 19 (1806), 20 Feb. and 6 Mar. 1806; Gómez de Ortega, *Elementos teóricos-prácticos de agricultura*, II: 137; Estéban Boutalou, 'Memoria sobre las patatas', *SAA* 19 (1806); and Alonso de Herrera, *Agricultura general*, II: 248 (quote).

88. Cadet de Vaux, *L'Ami de l'économie*, 58–9.

89. *Journal historique et politique des principaux événemens des différentes cours de l'Europe* 1, 10 Jan. 1779, 69.

90. Thompson, 'Of Food, and Particularly of Feeding the Poor', *Essays, Political, Economical and Philosophical*, I: 277.

91. Colum Leckey, personal communication, 3 Nov. 2015, citing material in Russian State Historical Archive, St Petersburg, fond 91, opis' 1, delo 35, ll. 191–6; Khodnev, *Istoriia Imperatorskago Vol'nago Ekonomicheskago Obshchestva*, 382.

92. Stapelbroek and Marjanen, eds., *The Rise of Economic Societies in the Eighteenth Century*.

93. *Annalen der Braunschweig Luneburgischen Churlande; Verhandlungen und Schriften*, 72; Henriette Charlotte Gräfin von Itzenplitz, treatise on potatoes, Kew, 18 Aug. 1793, LRO, DDSc 9/47; 'Report from Saxon Electoral Society of Agriculture on the Cultivation of Potatoes', *Communications to the Board of Agriculture*, Board of

Agriculture, 295–300; Eichler, 'Die Leipziger Ökonomische Sozietät', 369; Lowood, *Patriotism, Profit and the Promotion of Science*, 159–60; Popplow, 'Economizing Agricultural Resources in the German Economic Enlightenment', 277–83.

94. Talve, 'The Potato in Finnish Food Economy'. See also Kreuger, 'Mediating Progress in the Provinces', 50.

95. *Journal historique et politique de Genève*, 1 Dec. 1779, 497–8; *London Review of English and Foreign Literature* 11 (1780), 325; *Letters and Papers on Agriculture* 1 (1783), 32–3, 242–62, and 3 (1786), 292–3; *Monthly Magazine and British Register for 1797* 3 (1797) no. 13; Mackenzie, *Prize Essays and Transactions of the Highland Society of Scotland*; *Correio mercantil e economico de Portugal*, 24 Apr. 1798; White, *Natural History of Selborne*, 210.

96. Piqueras Haba, 'La difusión de la patata en España', 83–4.

97. *Extractos de las juntas generales celebradas por la Real Sociedad Bascongada de los Amigos del País en la ciudad de Vitoria por julio de 1786*, 28; Riera Climent and Riera Palmero, 'Los alimentos americanos en los Extractos de la Bascongada'. On the importance of such translations see Usoz, 'Political Economy and the Creation of the Public Sphere'. See also 'Explicación de la voz batata para incluir en un diccionario de la lengua', *Memorial literario, instructivo y curioso de la corte de Madrid*, Nov. 1790, no. 121, 365; *SAA* 7 (1800), 13 Mar. 1800, 173; *Junta Pública de la Real Sociedad Económica de Amigos del País de Valencia*; *SAA* 11 (1802), 173; Piqueras Haba, 'La difusión de la patata en España'.

98. Kisbán, 'The Beginnings of Potato Cultivation in Transylvania and Hungary', 181. For the broader contours of eighteenth-century *agromanie*, see Blum, *The End of the Old Order*, 247–304.

99. Board of Agriculture, *Report of the Committee of the Board of Agriculture*, 73; Tribe, *Land, Labour and Economic Discourse*; Tribe, *Governing Economy*; Tribe, *Strategies of Economic Order*; Tribe, 'Cameralism and the Sciences of the State', 525–6; Phillips, *Acolytes of Nature*; Spary, *Feeding France*; Serrano, 'Making *Oeconomic* People'.

100. Joseph Dombey to André Thovin, Lima, 1 Dec. 1778, *Joseph Dombey*, ed. Hamy, 42; Tabáres de Ulloa, *Observaciones prácticas sobre el cacahuete*; Targioni-Tozzetti, *Cenni storici sulla introduzione di varie piante*, 46; Koerner, *Linnaeus*; Drayton, *Nature's Government*; Spary and White, 'Food of Paradise'; Bleichmar, *Visible Empire*, 123–48; Zilberstein, 'Inured to Empire'; Earle, 'Food, Colonialism and the Quantum of Happiness'.

101. Smith, *An Inquiry into the Nature and Causes of the Wealth of Nations*, I.xi.39; *SAA* 19 (1806), 20, 27 Mar. 1806; Popplow, 'Economizing Agricultural Resources in the German Economic Enlightenment'.

102. On eighteenth-century concepts of nourishment see Earle, 'The Political Economy of Nutrition'.

103. [Colquhoun], *An Account of a Meat and Soup Charity*, 10, 15. Or see Parmentier, *Les pommes de terre, considérées relativement à la santé*; Parmentier, *Traité sur la culture et les usages des pommes de terre, de la patate, et du topinambour*; Young, *The Question of Scarcity Plainly Stated*, 65.

104. Petty, 'The Political Anatomy of Ireland', 1672, *Tracts*, 366.

105. Doyle, *Tratado sobre el cultivo, uso y utilidades de las patatas* (1797), 4–5 (quote), 78–9, 85.

106. Doyle, *Tratado sobre el cultivo, uso y utilidades de las patatas* (1797), 24–5, 33, 81.

107. Doyle, *Instrucción*, 26–7; Doyle, *Tratado sobre el cultivo, uso y utilidades de las patatas* (1797), 6 (quote), 8, 24, 31; Doyle, *Tratado sobre el cultivo, uso y utilidades de las patatas o papas, corregido y considerablemente aumentado* (1804), 7.

108. Sheehan and Wahrman, *Invisible Hands*.

FREE-MARKET POTATOES

1. Grote, *An Examination of the Utilitarian Philosophy*, 85; Tribe, 'Henry Sidgwick', 921.

2. Taylor, 'Atomism', *Philosophical Papers*, II: 187.

3. Nanny State Index. The libertarian Cato Institute, established with funding from businessman and free marketeer Charles Koch, likewise argues that 'one of the more disturbing trends in government expansion over the last 30 years has been the collection of laws, regulations, and binding court decisions that make up the "nanny state." Those laws and regulations represent government at its most arrogant': Cato Institute, 'The Nanny State'.

4. Harsanyi, *Nanny State*.

5. Brownell et al., 'The Public Health and Economic Benefits of Taxing Sugar-Sweetened Beverages'.

6. For hints and encouragement see for instance *Underrättelse om potatoës*; *Gentleman's Magazine and Historical Chronicle* 34 (1764), 599; Varenne de Béost, *La cuisine des pauvres*; Board of Agriculture, *Hints Respecting the Culture and the Use of Potatoes*; More, *The Cottage Cook*; Buchan, *Observations Concerning the Diet of the Common People*, 7; Doyle, *Tratado sobre el cultivo, uso y utilidades de las patatas* (1797); Wirilander, *Savon Historia*, 647–50; Drake, *Population and Society in Norway*, 55; Jones, *Provincial Development in Russia*, 154–5; Kisbán, 'The Beginnings of Potato Cultivation in Transylvania and Hungary'; Koerner, *Linnaeus*, 120, 132, 149; Gentilcore, *Italy and the Potato*; Spary, *Feeding France*, 167–86. Jussipekka Luukkonen interpreted the material in Finnish.

7. Coveney, *Food, Morals and Meaning*; Sarah Boseley, '"Ultra-processed" Products Now Half of all UK Family Food Purchases', *Guardian*, 3 Feb. 2018.

8. Marquis de Langle, *Voyage de Figaro en Espagne*, 60; *Joseph Dombey*, ed. Hamy, xxxiv; Adam, *Practical Essays on Agriculture*, II: 20 (quote); Parmentier, *Traité sur la culture et les usages des pommes de terre, de la patate, et du topinambour*, 26; 'Substance of Sir John Sinclair's Address to the Board of Agriculture, on Tuesday the 14th July, 1795', *Communications to the Board of Agriculture*, Board of Agriculture, lxii; Buchan, *Observations Concerning the Diet of the Common People*, 31; Doyle, *Tratado sobre el cultivo, uso y utilidades de las patatas* (1797), 27; *Feuille de cultivateur*, 10 Feb. 1799; *SAA* 6 (1799), 21 Nov. 1799; Dubroca, *Conversaciones de un padre con sus hijos*, II: 74–5; Alletz, *Agronomía*, 166; Virey, 'Pomme-de-terre, ou papas des Américas', 526, 531–3, 548; Alonso de Herrera, *Agricultura general*, II: 248.

9. Zanon, *Della coltivazione, e dell'uso delle patate*, 9; Bignami, *Le patate*, 4.

10. Eden, *The State of the Poor*, I: 505.

11. Varenne de Béost, *La cuisine des pauvres*, 11; Spary, *Feeding France*, 181.

12. James Stonhouse, 'Expedients for alleviating the Distress occasioned by the present Dearness of Corn', Northampton, *Universal Magazine* 21 (1757), 269; *Bibliothèque physico-économique, instructive et amusante* (1787), I: 201–2; Parmentier, *Les pommes de terre, considérées relativement à la santé & à l'économie*, 184–5; 'Lettre d'une fermiere de ... sur differens moyens de nourrir les pauvres', *Bibliothèque physico-économique, instructive et amusant* (1790), I: 245; Good, *Dissertation*, 79; Delle Piane, *De' pomi di terra*, 1; [Colquhoun], *An Account of a Meat and Soup Charity*, 10–15; Cadet de Vaux et al., *Recueil de rapports*, 30; Cadet de Vaux, *L'Ami de l'économie*, 56.

13. *Magazzino toscana* 22:1 (1775), 109; Marquis de Langle, *Voyage de Figaro en Espagne*, 60; Thompson, 'Of Food, and Particularly of Feeding the Poor', *Essays, Political, Economical and Philosophical*, I: 206–7. The truly obstinate were described as so gastronomically blinkered as to render their opinions irrelevant: Carta de San Lucar de Barrameda, *SAA* 3 (1798), 272 (26 Apr. 1798).

14. Smith, *An Inquiry into the Nature and Causes of the Wealth of Nations*, I.viii.43 (quote), IV. ii.4.

15. Smith, *An Inquiry into the Nature and Causes of the Wealth of Nations*, IV.ii.9.

16. Covarrubias, *En busca del hombre útil*, 26–7.

17. Mandeville, *The Fable of the Bees*, 9; Vico, *The New Science*, 62; Montesquieu, 'De l'Esprit des loix', 1748, *Oeuvres*, III: 132; Hirschman, *The Passions and the Interests*, 10, 17; Hont, *Jealousy of Trade*; Berg and Eger, 'Introduction', 2.

18. Riquetti, *Philosophie rurale*, I: xlii–xliii; and Tribe, 'Continental Political Economy', 160.

19. Hirschman, *The Passions and the Interests*; Foucault, *Security, Territory, Population*; Vardi, *The Physiocrats and the World of the Enlightenment*; Sheehan and Wahrman, *Invisible Hands*, 249–57.

20. Persson, *Grain Markets in Europe*, 1–22.

21. Kaplan, *Bread, Politics and Political Economy*; Miller, *Mastering the Market*; Gallego, *El motín de Esquilache*; Hochstrasser, 'Physiocracy and the Politics of Laissez-Faire'.

22. Quesnay, 'Fermiers'.

23. Camporesi, *The Magic Harvest*; Jütte, *Poverty and Deviance in Early Modern Europe*, 72–8.

24. Manuscript Recipe book of W. Walker, Hayes Middlesex, c.1798–1826, 'Recipes for cures and cookery, c. 1802–1826', SL, AR297, 85–6. See also Manuscript Recipe Book, LRO, DDB acc 6685 Box 179 b. 34, third folder, small notebook; English manuscript receipt book, McGL, Doncaster Recipes Collection, MSG 1230; Mason, *The Lady's Assistant*, 189; Varenne de Béost, *La cuisine des pauvres*; More, *The Cottage Cook*; *Ensayos de comidas económicas á la Rumford*; Hunter, *Culina Famulatrix Medicinae*, 37; *Housekeeper's Receipt Book*, 59.

25. *Appendix to the Scots Magazine* (1740); also James Stonhouse, 'Expedients for alleviating the Distress occasioned by the present Dearness of Corn', Northampton, *Universal Magazine* 21 (1757); Young, *Farmer's Letters to the People of England*, 193; *Bibliothèque physico-économique, instructive et amusant* (1790), 238–49; *English Review* 24 (1794), 116; *Annals of Agriculture* 24 (1795); *Gentleman's Magazine* 65:1 (1795), 15, 393; *Weekly Entertainer*, 4 Jan. 1796, 15; *Correo mercantil de España y sus Indias*, 10 Aug. 1801, 508;

SAA 11 (1802), 184; *Memorial literario, ó, Biblioteca periódica de ciencias y artes* 3 (1802), 35, 90–100; Cadet de Vaux, *L'Ami de l'économie.*

26. Zanon, *Della coltivazione, e dell'uso delle patate*; *Annals of Agriculture* 24 (1795); [Colquhoun], *An Account of a Meat and Soup Charity*; Doyle, *Tratado sobre el cultivo, uso y utilidades de las patatas* (1797), 68; Good, *Dissertation*; *European Magazine and London Review* (June 1800), 427 (quote); Cadet de Vaux et al., *Recueil de rapports*; Amoretti, *Della coltivazione delle patate*; *Junta Pública de la Real Sociedad Económica de Amigos del País de Valencia*, 36–7; *Ensayos de comidas económicas á la Rumford*; Demerson, 'La distribución de sopas económicas'; Redlich, 'Science and Charity'; Wells, *Wretched Faces*; Gonnella, 'L'assistenza pubblica a Trieste'; Valles Garrido, 'La distribución de sopas económicas del Conde Rumford'; Spary, *Feeding France*, esp. 32–4.

27. Grove, 'The Great El Niño of 1789–93'; Muldrew, *Food, Energy and the Creation of Industriousness*, 322.

28. 'High price of bread', Board of Agriculture, SR RASE B/XIII, MRELSC, fol. 2.

29. Thomas Wilson, Questionnaire for Clitheroe, Lancashire, 8 Nov. 1800, TNA H.O. 42/35, fol. 188.

30. Eden, *The State of the Poor*, I: 533. Wells, *Wretched Faces*, gives a clear account of aversion to soup.

31. Redlich, 'Science and Charity'. The city's population was roughly 24,000: 'Genève (commune)', *Dictionnaire Historique de la Suisse*.

32. [Lobb], *Primitive Cookery*, 4 (first quote); Duhamel du Monceau, *Moyens de conserver la santé aux equipages des vaisseaux*, 153–4; and 'Report respecting bread, corn, &c. &c', 10 Feb. 1800, 38 (second quote), *House of Commons Sessional Papers of the Eighteenth Century.*

33. Marquis de Chastellux, *De la félicité publique*, I: 15.

34. Tribe, *Strategies of Economic Order*; Bruni and Porta, '*Economia civile* and *pubblica felicità* in the Italian Enlightenment'; Wahnbaeck, *Luxury and Public Happiness*; McMahon, *Happiness*, 200 (first quote); Beales, 'Philosophical Kingship and Enlightened Despotism', 513 (second quote); Tribe, 'Cameralism and the Sciences of the State', 528–9; Paquette, *Enlightenment, Governance, and Reform*, 56–92; Usoz, 'Political Economy and the Creation of the Public Sphere'; Earle, 'Food, Colonialism and the Quantum of Happiness'.

35. Foucault, *Security, Territory, Population*, 327 (quote), 338–9.

36. 'Substance of Sir John Sinclair's Address to the Board of Agriculture, on Tuesday the 14th July, 1795', *Communications to the Board of Agriculture*, Board of Agriculture, lxiii.

37. On the quantifying spirit see Foucault, *Discipline and Punish*; Cohen, *A Calculating People*, 110–12; Frangsmyr et al., eds., *The Quantifying Spirit in the Eighteenth Century*, 2 (quote).

38. Hutcheson, *Inquiry into the Original of Our Ideas of Beauty and Virtue*, 163–78; Argumossa y Gandara, *Erudicción política*, 390; Marquis de Chastellux, *De la félicité publique*, II: 97–144; Bentham, *An Introduction to the Principles of Morals and Legislation*, 26–7 (for 'felicific calculus'); McMahon, *Happiness*, 205–22.

39. Sokolow, 'Count Rumford and Late Enlightenment Science, Technology and Reform', 71.

40. Thompson, 'Of Food, and Particularly of Feeding the Poor', *Essays, Political, Economical and Philosophical*, I: 192 (emphasis as in original).

41. Thompson, 'Of Food, and Particularly of Feeding the Poor', *Essays, Political, Economical and Philosophical*, I: 193–5, 202, 210–11. On saliva see Lémery, *Traité des aliments*, I: lxix–lxxii; Manetti, *Delle specie diverse di frumento e di pane siccome della panizzazione*, 55–60; Clericuzio, 'Chemical and Mechanical Theories of Digestion in Early Modern Medicine'.

42. Thompson, 'Of Food, and Particularly of Feeding the Poor', *Essays, Political, Economical and Philosophical*, I: 206–7 (quote), 256–7.

43. Cadet de Vaux, 'Variétés', 367–8 (quotes; emphasis as in original). On restaurants see Spang, *The Invention of the Restaurant*.

44. The *Bibliothèque britannique* reported extensively on Rumford's work; see for instance 'Morale Politique: An Account of an Establishment, &c. . . . par le Comte Rumford', *Bibliothèque britannique* 2: *Littérature* (1796), 137–82; and Letter of Abraham Joly, Geneva, 25 Nov. 1797, *Bibliothèque britannique, ou Recueil extrait des ouvrages anglais périodiques* 6: *Sciences et Arts* (1797), 300–1. See also *Ausfuhrlicher Unterricht zur Bereitung der rumfortschen Spaarsuppen*, 17; Bonaparte, 'Note Dictated at a Ministerial Council', Paris, 11 Mar. 1812, *Letters of Napoleon*, No. 239; Redlich, 'Science and Charity'; Jaffe, '"Noticia de la vida y obras del Conde de Rumford"'; Gentilcore, *Italy and the Potato*, 3–4.

45. *SAA* 7 (1800), 54–64, 71–80, 119–28, 132–8, 148–60, 184–8, 340–9, 393–400; 8 (1800), 120–8, 271–2, 369–76; 10 (1801), 54–8, 63–4; and 11 (1802), 284–7; [Thompson], *Ensayos, políticos, económicos y fisosóficos*; *Memorial literario, ó, Biblioteca periódica de ciencias y artes* 3 (1802), 35, 90–100; Abad-Zardoya, 'Arquitectos en los fogones', 657.

46. *Junta Pública de la Real Sociedad Económica de Amigos del País de Valencia*, 60.

47. *Ensayos de comidas económicas*, 15 (second quote); Demerson, 'La distribución', 123 (first quote).

48. *SAA* 10 (1801), 64 (quote); Cadet de Vaux et al., *Recueil de rapports*, 193, 199; *Memorial literario, ó, Biblioteca periódica de ciencias y artes* 3 (1802), 98; Gonnella, 'L'assistenza pubblica', 1595–6. The Neapolitan version, like those from Spain, included hot pepper, while Turin's incorporated chestnuts: *Correo mercantil de España y sus Indias*, 9 Feb. 1801, 90; Gentilcore, *Italy and the Potato*, 3–4. See also [Colquhoun], *An Account of a Meat and Soup Charity*, 10.

49. *Memorial literario, ó, Biblioteca periódica de ciencias y artes* 3 (1802), 35.

50. Spary, *Feeding France*, 32.

51. Varenne de Béost, *La cuisine des pauvres*, 24–34.

52. *General Report of the Committee of Subscribers*, 9; Sherman, *Imagining Poverty*.

53. Cadet de Vaux et al., *Recueil de rapports*, 46.

54. Sherman, *Imagining Poverty*, 28–9.

55. Shammas, 'The Eighteenth-Century English Diet and Economic Change'; Wells, *Wretched Faces*, 63, 66 (quotes); Muldrew, *Food, Energy and the Creation of Industriousness*; Meredith and Oxley, 'Food and Fodder'. There was of course significant regional variation: Zylberberg, 'Fuel Prices, Regional Diets and Cooking Habits'.

56. Sherman, *Imagining Poverty*, 182–3, 192 (quote).
57. Smith, *An Inquiry into the Nature and Causes of the Wealth of Nations*, IV.vii.88.
58. Smith, *An Inquiry into the Nature and Causes of the Wealth of Nations*, IV.ix.51.
59. The landed gentleman, insisted the Glaswegian academic John Millar, was 'often unmindful of his own interest as well as of every other': Hirschman, *The Passions and the Interests*, 122.
60. Smith, *An Inquiry into the Nature and Causes of the Wealth of Nations*, I.xi.9 (conclusion) (first quote), V.i.50 (third quote), V.i.53, V.i.61 (second quote); Fiori, 'Individuals and Self-Interest in Adam Smith's Wealth of Nations'; and Mehta, 'Self-Interest and Other Interests'.
61. Smith, *The Theory of Moral Sentiments*, I.i.1.1. On the broader contours of the eighteenth century's appreciation of 'self organization', see Sheehan and Wahrman, *Invisible Hands*.
62. Smith, *An Inquiry into the Nature and Causes of the Wealth of Nations*, I.viii.36.
63. Smith, *An Inquiry into the Nature and Causes of the Wealth of Nations*, I.xi.39. Rather surprisingly, these strong men and beautiful women turn out to be Irish coal-porters and prostitutes.
64. Smith, *An Inquiry into the Nature and Causes of the Wealth of Nations*, I.xi.39. For a lucid discussion of the parallel situation in late eighteenth-century France see Spary, *Feeding France*; Kaplan, *The Stakes of Regulation*.
65. Alcedo, *The Geographical and Historical Dictionary of America and the West Indies*, III: 198.
66. Turton, *An Address to the Good Sense and Candour of the People*, 85–6.
67. 'Report respecting bread, corn, &c. &c', 10 Feb. 1800, 38 (second quote), *House of Commons Sessional Papers of the Eighteenth* Century, 6.
68. Sherman, *Imagining Poverty*, 38–9, 155 (quote).
69. Tribe, *Strategies of Economic Order*, 12.
70. Kant, 'What is Enlightenment?' See also Kant, 'What Does it Mean to Orient Oneself in Thinking?'
71. Smith viewed the drive to trade as 'a certain propensity in human nature . . . common to all men'. He also believed that people were driven by an equally profound desire to be loved and esteemed by their fellows. As he explained, 'it is chiefly from this regard to the sentiments of mankind, that we pursue riches and avoid poverty': Smith, *An Inquiry into the Nature and Causes of the Wealth of Nations*, I.ii.1–2 (first quote); and Smith, *The Theory of Moral Sentiments*, I.iii.2.1 (second quote). See also Hont, *Jealousy of Trade*.
72. Kant, *Metaphysics of Morals*, 30 (quote); Bielefeldt, 'Autonomy and Republicanism'; Fleischacker, *A Third Concept of Liberty*.
73. Appleby, 'Ideology and Theory', 515.
74. Fleischacker, *A Third Concept of Liberty*.
75. Riquetti, *Philosophie rurale*, I: 138; Tribe, 'Continental Political Economy', 160.

GLOBAL POTATOES

1. Kaye, *The Life and Correspondence of Major-General Sir John Malcolm*, II: 48 (first quote); Jones, *Account of the Transactions of his Majesty's Mission to the Court of Persia*, I: vii–viii (second quote); Binning, *Journal of Two Years' Travel in Persia Ceylon, Etc.*, II: 87–8.

2. Wills, *The Land of the Lion and the Sun*, 170 (quote), 174, 300; Matthee, 'Patterns of Food Consumption in Early Modern Iran'.
3. Hamilton, *A New Account of the East Indies*, I: 92; Wills, *The Land of the Lion and the Sun*, 174, 300; Matthee, 'Patterns of Food Consumption in Early Modern Iran'.
4. Swislocki, 'Nutritional Governmentality'.
5. Jefferson, 'Summary of Public Service', spelling modernised. On rice see Dusinberre, *Them Dark Days*; Carney, *Black Rice*; Eltis et al., 'Agency and Diaspora in Atlantic History'; Carney and Rosomoff, *In the Shadow of Slavery*; '*AHR* Exchange: The Question of Black Rice'.
6. Edwards, *The History, Civil and Commercial, of the British Colonies in the West Indies*, I: 13–14.
7. The trees produce a large fruit that when baked or boiled is 'soft and white, like the inside of new baked bread': Ellis, *A Description of the Mangostan and the Bread-Fruit*, 11.
8. Bligh, *A Voyage to the South Sea*; Dening, *Mr Bligh's Bad Language*; Spary and White, 'Food of Paradise'.
9. Hinton East to Joseph Banks, Kingston, 19 July 1784, Banks, *The Indian and Pacific Correspondence of Sir Joseph Banks*, II: 62–3 (quote); Daniel Solander to John Ellis, London, 4 May 1776, Solander, *Daniel Solander*, 363–4; Ellis, *A Description of the Mangostan and the Bread-Fruit*, 11, 13.
10. West-India Planter, *Remarks on the Evidence Delivered on the Petition*; Parry, 'Plantations and Provision Grounds'; Marshall, 'Provision Ground and Plantation Labor in Four Windward Islands'; Tobin, *Colonizing Nature*.
11. Guilding, *An Account of the Botanic Garden*, 32. See also Alexander Anderson to Joseph Banks, St Vincent, 3 June 1793, James Wiles to Joseph Banks, Kingston, 14 Dec. 1793, and Alexander Anderson to Joseph Banks, St Vincent, 30 Mar. 1796, all in Banks, *The Indian and Pacific Correspondence of Sir Joseph Banks*, IV: 132, 181, 371–2; Thomas Dancer to Samuel More, Bath, Jamaica, 20 July 1794, RSA, PR/MC/104/10/240.
12. Guilding, *An Account of the Botanic Garden*, 12 (quote); DeLoughrey, 'Globalizing the Routes of Breadfruit'.
13. Sheridan, 'The Crisis of Slave Subsistence'.
14. Bligh, *A Voyage to the South Sea*, 12.
15. Collins, *Practical Rules for the Management and Medical Treatment of the Negro Slaves*, 111–12; Sheridan, 'Captain Bligh, the Breadfruit and the Botanic Gardens of Jamaica'; Earle, 'Food, Colonialism and the Quantum of Happiness'.
16. Stewart, *An Account of Jamaica and its Inhabitants*, 98.
17. Proceedings of the governor general ... relative to the establishment of a botanical garden in Calcutta, 1786, BL, IOR H/Misc/799; Robert Kyd to the Court of Directors, 1786, Banks, *The Indian and Pacific Correspondence of Sir Joseph Banks*, II: 113–16; Mackay, *In the Wake of Cook*, 177; Drayton, *Nature's Government*, 118–20.
18. Joseph Banks to Henry Dundas, 1787, Banks, *The Indian and Pacific Correspondence of Sir Joseph Banks*, II: 205.
19. Arnold, 'Hunger in the Garden of Plenty'; Davis, *Late Victorian Holocausts*.
20. Proceedings of the governor general and council relative to the establishment of a botanical garden in Calcutta, 1786, BL, IOR H/Misc/799, 59–169; *Transactions of the Agricultural and Horticultural Society of India*, I: 8, 31, 130, 220, 225.

21. Linschoten, *The Voyage of John Huyghen van Linschoten*, II: 42, 279; Collingham, *Curry*, 52–73.

22. Terry, *A Voyage to East-India*, 195–7; Mazumdar, 'The Impact of New World Food Crops'.

23. Fryer, *A New Account of East India and Persia*, II: 76; Watt, *Dictionary of the Economic Products of India*, VI: 266; Raj, *Relocating Modern Science*, 42–3.

24. Tennant, 'On the Culture of the Potatoe', 1797, *Indian Recreations*, I: iv.

25. Locke, *Second Treatise of Government*, 20 (first quote); Said, *Culture and Imperialism*, 8 (second quote, emphasis as in original); Drayton, *Nature's Government*, 229. On the discourse of improvement see Drayton, *Nature's Government*; Arnold, 'Agriculture and "Improvement" in Early Colonial India'.

26. 'On the Agriculture of India', *Friend of India* 1 (1820), 42, 46; Porter, *Religion versus Empire?*, 74.

27. Tennant, *Indian Recreations*, I: 45–51.

28. Temple, 'The Agri-Horticultural Society of India', 341 (quote), 342–50.

29. William Carey, 'Prospectus of an Agricultural and Horticultural Society in India', 1820, *Transactions of the Agricultural and Horticultural Society of India*, I: 211–21 (216, 219 quotes, emphasis as in original).

30. *Transactions of the Agricultural and Horticultural Society of India*, II: 23, 27, 36, 81, 175 (quote), 253, 264, 265.

31. *Transactions of the Agricultural and Horticultural Society of India*, I: 21, 235 (quote), 237–8, II: 30ff., 81, 253, 264, 265; Temple, 'The Agri-Horticultural Society of India', 356–8.

32. *Transactions of the Agricultural and Horticultural Society of India*, I: 8; Temple, 'The Agri-Horticultural Society of India', 354–8; Ray, *Culinary Culture in Colonial India*. On benevolence, see Tobin, *Colonizing Nature*.

33. William Carey, Prospectus of an Agricultural and Horticultural Society in India, 1820, *Transactions of the Agricultural and Horticultural Society of India*, I: 214; 'Introductory discourse, delivered by the president, 21 Sept. 1824', *Transactions of the Agricultural and Horticultural Society of India*, I: 3, 8 (quotes).

34. Proceedings of the governor general and council relative to the establishment of a botanical garden in Calcutta, 1786, BL, IOR H/Misc/799, 59–169; *Transactions of the Agricultural and Horticultural Society of India*, I: 8, 31, 130, 220, 225.

35. Davis, *Late Victorian Holocausts*, is a sobering introduction to the impact of colonial rule on India's food security.

36. Joseph Banks to the Court of Directors, 1789, and George Sinclair, 1798, both in Banks, *The Indian and Pacific Correspondence of Sir Joseph Banks*, II: 396, V: 24; Bazar prices in Calcutta, June 1791, Robert Kyd papers, BL, MSS EUR/F95/2, 193b; Tennant, *Indian Recreations*, II: 153–4 (first quote); Minute of William Bentinck, 12 Nov. 1803, BL, IOR F/4/179, 5r–6r; Benjamin Heyne to William Bentinck, Bangalore 21 Jan. 1805, BL, IOR P/242/73, 684–8; Whitelaw Ainslie, 'Treatise on the edible vegetables of India', 12 Sept. 1810, BL, IOR/F/4/379/9495; Arnold, 'Agriculture and "Improvement" in Early Colonial India', 519; Mazumdar, 'The Impact of New World Food Crops'; Lang, *Notes of a Potato Watcher*, 31–3; Narayanan, 'Cultures of Food and Gastronomy in Mughal and Post-Mughal India', 91–2 (second quote), 119–31.

37. Roy, 'Meat-Eating, Masculinity, and Renunciation in India', 66 (second quote); Gandhi, *Affective Communities*; Roy, 'A Dietetics of Virile Emergency', 258–9 (first quote); Ray, *Culinary Culture in Colonial India*.

38. Shrikant Botre, personal communication, Oct. 2018.

39. Crosby, *The Columbian Exchange*; Crosby, *Ecological Imperialism*; Foster and Cordell, eds., *Chillies to Chocolate*; Mazumdar, 'The Impact of New World Food Crops'; Carney, *Black Rice*; McCann, *Maize and Grace*; Earle, *The Body of the Conquistador*; Carney and Rosomoff, *In the Shadow of Slavery*.

40. Galloway, 'Agricultural Reform and the Enlightenment in Late Colonial Brazil'; Mackay, *In the Wake of Cook*; Osborne, *Nature, the Exotic, and the Science of French Colonialism*; Miller and Reill, eds., *Visions of Empire*; McClellan III and Regourd, 'The Colonial Machine'; Drayton, *Nature's Government*; Spary, *Utopia's Garden*; Touchet, *Botanique & Colonisation*; Castro-Gómez, *La hybris del punto cero*; Schiebinger and Swan, eds., *Colonial Botany*; Vos, 'Natural History and the Pursuit of Empire'; Schiebinger, *Plants and Empire*; McClellan III, *Colonialism and Science*; Bleichmar, *Visible Empire*; Jonsson, *Enlightenment's Frontier*.

41. Watt, *Dictionary of the Economic Products of India*, VI: 3, 266–72.

42. Frost, 'The Antipodean Exchange'; Bligh, *A Voyage to the South Sea*, 49; Malte-Brun, *Universal Geography*, 3: 551.

43. Cunningham, 'Part of Two Letters to the Publisher from Mr James Cunningham', 1203; Saint Pierre, *A Voyage to the Isle of France*, 131; *Asiatic Journal and Monthly Register for British India and its Dependencies* 18 (1824), 113, 388, 608; 22 (1826), 575; *The South African Magazine* 3 (1869), 263; Dyer, *The West Coast of Africa as Seen from the Deck of a Man-of-War*, 61, 122; Richthofen, *Ferdinand von Richthofen's Tagebücher aus China*, II: 123–39; Beinart and Middleton, 'Plant Transfers in Historical Perspective', 14 (quote).

44. McCook, *States of Nature*, 59.

45. [Butler], *The History of the Bermudaes*, 30; Hughes, *The American Physitian*, 14; Browne, *Civil and Natural History of Jamaica*, 175; Lunan, *Hortus Jamaicensis*, II: 92–3; Parry, 'Plantations and Provision Grounds', 14.

46. Penn, 'A Further Account', 74; *New London County, Selectmen, Agreeable to an Act of Assembly of the State of Connecticut, for Regulating the Prices of Labour*, London Gazette, 2 June 1778, 3; 5 July 1783, 1; Wilson, 'Americans Learn to Grow the Irish Potato' (quote 345–6); Coates, *The Metamorphosis of Landscape and Community in Early Quebec*.

47. Glaiser, 'French and Indian War Diary of Benjamin Glaiser', 84 (second quote); Washington, *The Writings of George Washington*, IV: 180; Sarah Fayerweather, Manuscript cookbook, 26 June 1764, SL; Anonymous Cookbook, *c.*1780?, SL; William Bache, 'Oration on the History, Culture and Qualities of the Potatoe. Delivered at the Publick Commencement in the University of Pennsylvania, on the 8th of July, 1790', *Massachusetts Spy*, 23 Dec. 1790; Mrs Mathew [Belinda] Clarkson, manuscript receipt book, 1793, Marion King Schlefer Recipe Collection, SL (first quote); Simmons, *American Cookery*, 10 (quote); Wilson, 'Americans Learn to Grow the Irish Potato'; Mt. Pleasant, 'The Paradoxes of Plows and Productivity', 473.

48. Ray, *Culinary Culture in Colonial India*, 45; Mackenzie, 'Contested Ground', 701.

49. Josephine, interviewed by her granddaughter Iranga Tcheko, 2017, personal communication.

50. Worboys, 'The Discovery of Colonial Malnutrition between the Wars', 222–3 (quote); Davis, *Late Victorian Holocausts*.

51. *Colonial Times and Tasmanian Advertiser*, 1 Dec. 1826.

52. Smith and Choules, *Origin and History of Missions*, II: 301; Laufer, *American Plant Migration, part 1*, 89.

53. Eastwick, *Journal of a Diplomate's (sic) Three Years' Residence in Persia*, I: 258.

54. Petrie, *Chefs of Industry*.

55. Smith and Choules, *Origin and History of Missions*, I: 438 (quote); Beinart and Middleton, 'Plant Transfers in Historical Perspective'. On the potato's uneven spread across Africa, for instance, see McCann, *Stirring the Pot*; FAO, 'Potato World: Africa'.

56. Viqueira Albán, *Propriety and Permissiveness in Bourbon Mexico*; Adelman, *Republic of Capital*; Lafuente, 'Enlightenment in an Imperial Context'; Voekel, *Alone Before God*; Silva, *La ilustración en el Virreinato de Nueva Granada*; Castro-Gómez, *La hybris del punto cero*; Nieto Olarte, *Orden Natural y orden social*; Safier, *Measuring the World*; Bleichmar et al., eds., *Science in the Spanish and Portuguese Empires*; Meléndez, *Deviant and Useful Citizens*, 45–6; Soule, *The Bishop's Utopia*; Paquette, ed., *Enlightened Reform*.

57. Zeta Quinde, *El pensamiento ilustrado en el Mercurio peruano*.

58. Gerbi, *The Dispute of the New World*; Pagden, *Spanish Imperialism and the Political Imagination*; Brading, *The First America*; Cañizares-Esguerra, *How to Write the History of the New World*. On the prize essay see Caradonna, *The Enlightenment in Practice*, 156–9.

59. Bowles, *Introducción a la historia natural y de la geografía física de España*, 230–1; 'Explicación de la voz batata para incluir en un diccionario de la lengua', *Memorial literatio, instructivo y curioso de la corte de Madrid* 21 (1790), 362; Francisco González Laguna, 'Memoria de las plants extrañas que se cultivan en Lima introducidas en los últimos 30 años hasta el de 1794', *MP* 11 (1794), 10 June 1794 and 13 June 1794, 163, 165–77; Doyle, *Tratado sobre el cultivo, uso y utilidades de las patatas o papas, corregido y considerablemente aumentado* (1804), 105; *SAA*, 30 Mar. 1797, 28 Mar. 1805, 4 and 11 July 1805, 20 Feb. and 6 Mar., 1806; Gómez de Ortega, *Elementos teóricos-prácticos de agricultura*, II: 137; Estéban Boutalou, 'Memoria sobre las patatas', *SAA* 19 (1806); Alonso de Herrera, *Agricultura general*, II: 248.

60. *Coup d'oeil sur les quatre concours*, 14. Cochineal is a red dye derived from a Central American beetle.

61. Santo Thomas, *Grammatica*, 159v.

62. Andagoya, 'Relación que da el Adelantado de Andagoya de las tierras y provincias que abajo se hará mención', 1545, *Pascual de Andagoya*, 138–9; Cieza de León, *Parte primera de la chrónica del Perú*, book 1, chap. 40; 'Descripción y relación de la Provincia de los Yauyos', 1586, 'Descripción de la tierra del repartimiento de San Francisco de Atunrucana y Laramanti', 1586, and 'Relación de la Provincia de los Collaguas', all in *Relaciones geográficas de las Indias*, ed. Jiménez de la Espada, I: 156, 234, 586; Acosta, *Natural and*

Moral History of the Indies, 148, 201–2; Molina, *Compendio de la historia civil del reyno de Chile*, 120–1, 213; Naranjo Vargas, 'La comida andina antes del encuentro'.

63. Molina, *Relación de las fábulas y ritos de los incas*, 62–3; Acosta, *Natural and Moral History*, 262; García, *Orígen de los indios del Nuevo Mundo*, 59–169; Guaman Poma de Ayala, 'El primer nueva corónica y buen gobierno', esp. chaps. 11, 12, 37; Spalding, *Huarochirí*, 63, 262; Silverblatt, *Moon, Sun, and Witches*; Weismantel, *Food, Gender and Poverty in the Ecuadorian Andes*; Salomon and Urioste, *The Huarochirí Manuscript*, 54–73, 120, 131; Harrison, *Signs, Songs and Memory in the Andes*.

64. Apuntes de los gastos del Monasterio de Santa Tereza de Jesús … desde 19 de abril de 1794, año 2; and Sobre seglares de Santa Catalina, y alimentos de religiosas, refectorio, etc., 1 Mar. 1796; both in AAA, Santa Teresa legajo 2, and Santa Catalina legajo 8 respectively; Leon Pinelo, *Question moral si el chocolate quebranta el ayuno elesiástico*, 57, 63; Pilcher, *¡Que Vivan los Tamales!*; Earle, *The Body of the Conquistador*.

65. 'Idea general del Perú', *MP* 1 (1791); 'La Province of Caxatambo' and 'Descripción de la Provincia de Chachapoyas'; both in *MP* 5 (1792), 6, 190, 194, 225; Carrió de la Vandera, *El lazarillo de ciegos caminantes desde Buenos Aires*, 301, 335; Joseph Ignacio Lequanda, 'Descripción de Caxamarca', *MP* 10 (1794), 202; Francisco López, 'Descripción de Porco', *MP* 11 (1794), 19, 29–30, 37–8, 63, 68–72, 77, 87–9, 92.

66. Davalos, *De morbis nonnullis Limae, grassantibus ipsorumque therapeia*, 11–12. Davalos was obliged to matriculate in France because Peruvian universities would not accept those who like Davalos were classified as mulattos. Dennis Landis translated the Latin.

67. Panacio Montano, 'Medicina práctica', *MP* 1 (1791), 45–7.

68. Unanue, *Observaciones sobre el clima del Lima*, 153. On wind, see also Valle y Caviedes, 'Defensas que hace un ventoso al pedo', *Obra completa*, 277.

69. Chambers, 'Little Middle Ground', 45.

70. Francisco López, 'Descripción de Porco', *MP* 11 (1794), 101–2; *MP* 11 (1794), 106; Manuel Espinavete López, 'Descripción de la Provincia de Abancay', *MP* 12 (1795), 131, 137, 145–6, 156–7; Spalding, *Huarochirí*, 134, 163, 196–7; Haitin, 'Prices, the Lima Market, and the Cultural Crisis of the Late Eighteenth Century in Peru'.

71. Withers, *Placing the Enlightenment*, 14 (quote); Conrad, 'The Enlightenment in Global History; Conrad, *What is Global History?*, 76; Premo, *The Enlightenment on Trial*.

72. Laufer, *American Plant Migration*, part 1, 74; Jia, 'Weather Shocks, Sweet Potatoes and Peasant Revolts'.

73. Struys, *Drie aanmerkelyke en zeer rampspoedige Reizen*, 58; Richthofen, *Ferdinand von Richthofen's Tagebücher aus China*, II: 117, 156, 165, 174, 230, 244; Davies, *Yün-nan*, 233; Laufer, *American Plant Migration*, part 1, 69–79; Ho, 'The Introduction of American Food Plants into China', 191–201; Murray, 'New World Food Crops in China', 320–68 (346 quote); Gitomer, *Potato and Sweetpotato in China*, 7–12; Lo and Barrett, 'Cooking up Fine Remedies', 416.

74. Will and Wong, *Nourish the People*; Bray, *Technology and Gender*, 36–7; Bray, 'Chinese Literati and the Transmission of Technological Knowledge'.

75. Swislocki, 'Nutritional Governmentality'.

76. Lee, 'Taste in Numbers'; Swislocki, 'Nutritional Governmentality'.

77. Schmalzer, *Red Revolution, Green Revolution*.

78. Jansky et al., 'Potato Production and Breeding in China'. The nationalist government of Chiang Kai-shek also sponsored potato research: Van de Ven, *War and Nationalism in China*, 260–2.

79. Gitomer, *Potato and Sweetpotato in China*, 21; Schmalzer, *Red Revolution, Green Revolution*, 88, 114.

80. Gitomer, *Potato and Sweetpotato in China*; Xiaoping Sun, personal communication, 29 Sept. 2017.

81. See for instance Klein, 'Connecting with the Countryside?', 121; Ingebretson, 'The *Tuhao* and the Bureaucrat', 246.

82. Gitomer, *Potato and Sweetpotato in China*; Reader, *Potato*, 267–78; Jansky et al., 'Potato Production and Breeding in China'; China News Service, 'China to Boost Potato Cultivation'. Jing, 'Introduction' discusses 'population quality'.

83. Garnett and Wilkes, *Appetite for Change*.

84. Jansky et al., 'Potato Production and Breeding in China'; Ministry of Agriculture and Rural Affairs, 'China to Position Potato as Staple Food'; China News Service, 'China to Boost Potato Cultivation'; Ying, 'The Great Potato Debate'; 'Vice Minister of the Party at Ministry of Agriculture Emphasizes: Strengthen Potato Industry'.

85. Sala, 'Tudou for the Tuhao'. Anne Gerritsen, Huang Lu and Claire Tang helpfully translated this slogan.

86. Chen, 'Pushing the Potato'.

87. Qu and Xie, eds., *How the Chinese Eat Potatoes*, 23.

88. See for instance Wang, 'The Post-Communist Personality'; Yan, 'The Chinese Path to Individualization'.

89. *Asiatic Journal and Monthly Register for British India and its Dependencies* 18 (1824), 113, 389.

90. Beinart and Middleton, 'Plant Transfers in Historical Perspective'.

91. Trentmann, *Empire of Things*.

CAPITALIST POTATOES

1. *London Gazette*, 27 Dec. 1800. A quartern loaf of bread weighed about four pounds.

2. Cobbett, *Cobbett's Weekly Political Register*, 24 Mar. 1832, 786–7.

3. Salaman, *History and Social Influence of the Potato*, 601–2; Thompson, 'The Moral Economy of an English Crowd'; Gallagher and Greenblatt, 'The Potato in the Materialist Imagination'.

4. Salaman, *History and Social Influence of the Potato*, 521–2; Booth, 'Food Riots in the North-West of England', 90; Wells, *Wretched Faces*, 95, 98, 164, 167 (quote), 312; Bohstedt, 'The Myth of the Feminine Food Riot', 24, 41, 49; Rule and Wells, *Crime, Protest and Popular Politics in Southern England*, 32; Bohstedt, *The Politics of Provisions*, 184, 203–4, 241.

5. Styles, 'Custom or Consumption?', 103.

6. Skytte, 'Ron at utaf potatoes brånna brånnavin', 231–2; James Stonhouse, 'Expedients for alleviating the Distress occasioned by the present Dearness of Corn', Northampton,

Universal Magazine 21 (1757), 270; Young, *Farmer's Letters to the People of England*, 193–4; Engel, *Traité*; Henry, *The Complete English Farmer*, 114; Corrado, *Il credenziere di bueon gusto*, 39–40; Béguillet, *Traité des subsistances*, VI: 507–12; Parmentier, *Les pommes de terre, considérées relativement à la santé & à l'économie*, 32, 176–80; James Anderson, 'Of Ardent Spirits Afforded by Potatoes', *Letters and Papers on Agriculture* 4 (1788), 43–52; *Verhandlungen und Schriften*, 72; Lindroth, *Kungl. Svenska vetenskapsakademiens historia*, 261–3; Kisbán, 'The Beginnings of Potato Cultivation in Transylvania and Hungary', 180–1; Spary, *Feeding France*.

7. Webb and Webb, 'The Assize of Bread'; Stern, 'The Bread Crisis in Britain'; Wells, *Wretched Faces*, 210; Petersen, *Bread and the British Economy*.

8. Committee on Doctor Gordon's Discoveries in the Art of Dying, & Making Potatoe Bread, 23 Aug. 1794, SR RASE B/X, fols. 2–3, MRELSC. See also *European Magazine and London Review*, Aug. 1790; Board of Agriculture Minutes of Committee on Potatoes, Committee on the Scarcity of Grain, and the High price of Provisions, and Committee of Correspondence and Expenditure, 23 Aug. 1794–27 Nov. 1795, SR RASE B/X, fols. 1–45, MRELSC; *Annals of Agriculture* 24 (1795); *Account of the Experiments tried by the Board of Agriculture in the Composition of Various sorts of Bread*, Board of Agriculture; William Augustus Howard, Grays Inn Great Square, 14 July 1795, TNA, HO 42/35, fols. 157–8; Board of Agriculture, *Hints Respecting the Culture and the Use of Potatoes*.

9. Parmentier, *Traité sur la culture et les usages des pommes de terre, de la patate, et du topinambour*; Delle Piane, *De' pomi di terra*; 'Report from Saxon Electoral Society of Agriculture on the Cultivation of Potatoes', *Communications to the Board of Agriculture*, Board of Agriculture, 295; Doyle, *Instrucción formada de orden del Consejo por D. Enrique Doyle*; Doyle, *Tratado sobre el cultivo, uso y utilidades de las patatas* (1797); Dionisio Escudo, Ampudia, 20 Feb. 1798, *SAA* 3, 19 Apr. 1798 (1798), 253; *Instrucção sobre a cultura das batatas*; Amoretti, *Della coltivazione delle patate*; Birembaut, 'L'École gratuite de boulangerie'; Kaplan, *Bread, Politics and Political Economy*; Spary, *Feeding France*.

10. Lord Sheffield, Sheffield, 28 June 1795, TNA, HO 42/35, fols. 51–2. See also Henry Shelley to Duke of Richmond, Lewes, 28 June 1795, TNA, HO 42/35, fols. 57–8.

11. More, *The Way to Plenty*; Webb and Webb, 'The Assize of Bread', 208–9 (second quote); Webb, 'Not So Pleasant to the Taste', 7 (first quote). For examples see the printed declarations made at the Staffordshire quarter sessions, 16 July 1795, the circular published in Newmarket-upon-Trent, 22 July 1795, the printed 'engagement entered into by the lords of his majesty's privy council, and others, in order to diminish the consumption of wheat in their respective families', Manchester, 6 July 1795, and the Minute from Hamilton, 4 Aug. 1795; all in TNA, HO 42/35, fols. 255, 264, 312, 401.

12. 'Plain Man', *Times*, 11 July 1795, 3.

13. Thompson, *The Making of the English Working Class*; Wells, *Wretched Faces*, 406–57.

14. *Times*, 4 Nov. 1795, 2.

15. *Annals of Agriculture* 24 (1795), 204.

16. *Annals of Agriculture* 24 (1795), 137.

17. *Annals of Agriculture* 24 (1795), 284–6. See also Henry Curzon, Waterperry House, Wheatley, Oxon, 5 July 1795, TNA, HO 42/35, fol. 96; Webb and Webb, 'The Assize

of Bread', 210; Salaman, *History and Social Influence of the Potato*, 504–6; Rule and Wells, *Crime, Protest and Popular Politics*, 22–4; Earle, 'The Political Economy of Nutrition'.

18. Holland Watson to War Office, Stockport, 5 Aug. 1795, TNA, WO 1/1094.
19. Sir Charles Willoughby to my lord Duke, Baldon House, 5 July 1795, TNA, HO 42/35, fols. 91–3. See also Tapwell, *A Friendly Address to the Poor of Great Britain*.
20. Mr Peacock's Evidence as to the bread, and Mr Smith's Evidence, both in GL, Ms 7801, box 2; *Times*, 4 Nov. 1795; Eden, *The State of the Poor*, I: 526; Thomas Turton to Duke of Portland, Starborough Castle, 7 Feb. 1801, TNA, HO 42/61, fol. 118 (quote); Fourth Report, 17 Dec. 1800, *House of Commons Sessional Papers the Eighteenth Century*, 402–3; Hanway, *The Great Advantage of Eating Pure and Genuine Bread*, 10–11; *Parliamentary History of England, from the Earliest Period to the Year 1803*, 238; Petersen, *Bread and the British Economy*, 15–35 (33, quote); Fox, 'Food, Drink and Social Distinction in Early Modern England', 180; Earle, 'The Political Economy of Nutrition'.
21. On potato/meat versus all-bread diets, see Koenker, 'Was Bread Giffen?'
22. *London Gazette*, 27 Dec. 1800.
23. Cobbett, *Cobbett's Weekly Register*, 14 Dec. 1822, 686 (quote); Dyck, *William Cobbett and Rural Popular Culture*; and Dyck, 'William Cobbett and the Rural Radical Platform', 191.
24. Cobbett, *Cottage Economy*, para. 80.
25. Cobbett, *Cottage Economy*, para. 77; Cobbett, *Cobbett's Two-Penny Trash* 1 (1831), 200; Gallagher and Greenblatt, 'The Potato in the Materialist Imagination'.
26. Cobbett, *Cottage Economy*, para. 79.
27. Cobbett, *Cottage Economy*, para. 99; Cobbett, *Cobbett in Ireland*, esp. 82, 92–5, 125.
28. Cobbett, *Cottage Economy*; Dyck, *William Cobbett and Rural Popular Culture*.
29. Dyck, *William Cobbett and Rural Popular Culture*, 98–106. Or see Cobbett, *Cobbett in Ireland*, 110.
30. *Annals of Agriculture* 32 (1799), 602 (quote); Cobbett, *Cottage Economy*, para. 77; Dyck, *William Cobbett and Rural Popular Culture*, 116–17. For an analysis of potato gardens as 'part of a fundamentally exploitative agrarian regime that subjected agricultural laborers even further to their employers' see Burchardt, 'Land and the Laborer', 684.
31. Cobbett, *Cobbett in Ireland*, 108–9.
32. Cobbett, *Cottage Economy*, para. 99; Cobbett, *Cobbett in Ireland*, 95, 125 (the ban exempted potatoes intended for stuffing geese); Dyck, *William Cobbett and Rural Popular Culture*, 210–11.
33. Hobsbawm and Rudé, *Captain Swing*, 15 (quote), 47; Holland, 'Swing Revisited'.
34. Cobbett, *Cobbett's Weekly Political Register*, 16 June 1832, 652; Rule and Wells, *Crime, Protest and Popular Politics*, 11.
35. Cobbett, *Cobbett's Weekly Political Register*, 20 Nov. 1830, 787, 11 Dec. 1830, 956, 24 Mar. 1832, 786–7, 14 Apr. 1832, 93; Hammond and Hammond, *The Village Labourer*, 227–9; Dyck, *William Cobbett and Rural Popular Culture*, 166.
36. *Times*, 17 Sept. 1830, 3, 22 Nov. 1830, 3, 23 Nov. 1830, 3, 30 Dec. 1830, 3; Hobsbawm and Rudé, *Captain Swing*, 99, 123.
37. Arch, *From Ploughtail to Parliament*, 12–13. See also Zylberberg, 'Fuel Prices, Regional Diets and Cooking Habits'.

38. 'If you still hanker after that accursed root without which Ireland could not have been brought to its present state, and which has *banished bread* from the labourer's house here, if you still hanker after this "COARSER" food, you shall go elsewhere to get it,' he wrote to one of his farm workers: Cobbett, *Cobbett in Ireland*, 95.

39. Rule and Wells, *Crime, Protest and Popular Politics*, 117.

40. Gurney, '"Rejoicing in Potatoes"'.

41. Young, *Farmer's Letters to the People of England*, 202–3; Young, *A Tour in Ireland*, II: 112–14 (quote); Young, *The Question of Scarcity Plainly Stated*, 77; Lloyd, 'The Political Economy of the Potato'.

42. Tribe, *Land, Labour and Economic Discourse*; Lloyd, 'The Political Economy of the Potato', 313 (quote).

43. Dean, *The Constitution of Poverty*; Vernon, *Hunger*.

44. Roncaglia, *The Wealth of Ideas*, 163; and for a somewhat different interpretation, Bashford and Chaplin, *The New Worlds of Thomas Robert Malthus*.

45. Malthus, *An Essay on the Principle of Population* (1798), 38–9.

46. Malthus, *An Essay on the Principle of Population. The 1803 Edition*, 453.

47. Malthus, *An Essay on the Principle of Population. The 1803 Edition*, 265, 454, 450, respectively.

48. Malthus, 'Newenham on the State of Ireland', 164; Lloyd, 'The Political Economy of the Potato'.

49. McCulloch, 'Cottage System', 382–3, 386.

50. Vanhaute et al., 'The European Subsistence Crisis of 1848–1850', 26.

51. Clarkson and Crawford, *Feast and Famine*, 59, 93; Vanhaute et al., 'The European Subsistence Crisis of 1848–1850', 22–3.

52. For an overview see Ó Gráda, 'Ireland's Great Famine: An Overview', and Daly, 'Something Old and Something New'.

53. Trevelyan, *The Irish Crisis*, 2; Gray, *Famine, Land and Politics*; Gray, 'The European Food Crisis and the Relief of Irish Famine, 1845–1850'; Lloyd, 'The Political Economy of the Potato'.

54. Trevelyan, *The Irish Crisis*, 229–320. 'The Fleming clings to his plot of ground with the same desperate obstinacy as the cottier tenant in Ireland, and is equally unable or unwilling to perceive that his condition can only be ameliorated by his becoming a paid labourer, and ceasing to be a pauper proprietor', insisted the *Times*: 'Flanders and Ireland', *Times*, 29 Nov. 1847, 5; Gray, 'The European Food Crisis and the Relief of Irish Famine, 1845–1850', 104.

55. Gray, *Famine, Land and Politics*, 103, 119.

56. Marx, 'The Eighteenth Brumaire of Louis Napoleon', 101. Marx viewed his own consumption of potatoes as evidence of extreme poverty: Stedman Jones, *Karl Marx*.

57. Dechambre, ed., *Dictionnaire encyclopédique des sciences medicales*, 229–31.

58. Broadberry et al., 'Industry', 169–70; Malanima, 'Urbanization', 244.

59. Nitti, 'The Food and Labour-Power of Nations', 35, 38.

60. Rabinbach, *The Human Motor*.

61. Rabinbach, *The Human Motor*; Carpenter, *Protein and Energy*; Kamminga and Cunningham, eds., *The Science and Culture of Nutrition*; Cullather, 'The Foreign Policy of the Calorie'; Treitel, 'Max Rubner and the Biopolitics of Rational Nutrition'; Biltekoff, *Eating Right in America*; Simmons, *Vital Minimum*.

62. Hildesheim, *Die Normal-Diät*; Meinert, *Armee- und Volks-Ernährung*; Rabinbach, *The Human Motor*, 128–30.

63. Rubner, *Volksernährungsfragen*, 48–52 (48, quote); Rabinbach, *The Human Motor*, 262–4; Treitel, 'Max Rubner and the Biopolitics of Rational Nutrition', 14 (trans.); Treitel, 'Food Science/Food Politics'.

64. Meinert, *Armee- und Volks-Ernährung*; Wiegelmann, *Alltags- und Festspeisen in Mitteleuropa*, 87–90; Dickler, 'Organization and Change in Productivity in Eastern Prussia'; Teuteberg, 'Der Verzehr von Nahrungsmitteln in Deutschland pro Kopf und Jahr'; Komlos, 'The New World's Contribution to Food Consumption', 68–74; Bass, 'The Crisis in Prussia', 187–9; Mahlerwein, 'The Consequences of the Potato Blight in Southern Germany', 214–16.

65. Blum, *The End of the Old Order*, 271–6; Bekaert, 'Caloric Consumption in Industrializing Belgium'; Vanhaute, '"So Worthy an Example to Ireland"', 123; Paping and Tassenaar, 'The Consequences of the Potato Disease in the Netherlands 1845–1860', 157 (quote).

66. Morell, 'Diet in Sweden during Industrialization, 1870–1939'; Henriksen, 'A Disaster Seen from the Periphery', 297–8; Gadd, 'On the Edge of a Crisis', 321–2.

67. Smith and Christian, *Bread and Salt*, 254–5 (quote), 278–87.

68. Caird, *Our Daily Food*, 35; Burnett, *Plenty and Want*, 113 (quote), 151; Overton, *Agricultural Revolution in England*, 102–3.

69. Tiedemann, *Geschichte des Tabaks und anderer ähnlicher Genußmittel*, 388–9; Meinert, *Armee- und Volks-Ernährung*, I: 139, II: 186–8, 358.

70. Moleschott, *Der Kreislauf des Lebens*, II: 570.

71. Moleschott, *Lehre der Nahrungsmittel*, 115–20, 184; Moleschott, *Der Kreislauf des Lebens*, II: 568–70.

72. Moleschott, *Der Kreislauf des Lebens*, II: 268–70; Moleschott, *Lehre der Nahrungsmittel*, 80, 115–20 (119 quote), 184; Meinert, *Armee- und Volks-Ernährung*, II: 189; Kamminga, 'Nutrition for the People, or the Fate of Jacob Moleschott's Contest for a Humanist Science', 26; Meneghello, *Jacob Moleschott*, 63, 67, 83, 117, 133–7, 309.

73. Rabinbach, *The Human Motor*, 129. Or see Pissling, *Gesundheitslehre für das Volk*, 68; Hildesheim, *Die Normal-Diät*, 37; Meinert, *Armee- und Volks-Ernährung*, II: 188.

74. Current recommendations are about half that amount.

75. Nitti, 'The Food and Labour-Power of Nations', 41, 57.

76. Nitti, 'The Food and Labour-Power of Nations'.

77. Schulze-Gävernitz, *The Cotton Trade in England and on the Continent*, 135–8 (quote), 176–89; Rabinbach, *The Human Motor*, 129.

78. Schulze-Gävernitz, *The Cotton Trade in England and on the Continent*, 200–1.

79. Nitti, 'The Food and Labour-Power of Nations', 60–1.

80. Styles, 'Custom or Consumption?', 103.

SECURITY POTATOES

1. *Potato Pete's Recipe Book.*
2. Vernon, 'The Ethics of Hunger and the Assembly of Society', 723; Vernon, *Hunger.*
3. Scott, *Seeing Like a State*, 88.
4. Scott, *Seeing Like a State*, 343; Helstocky, 'The State, Health, and Nutrition'.
5. Thane, 'The Working Class and State "Welfare" in Britain'; Shapiro, *Perfection Salad*, 137–8; Pedersen, *Family Dependence, and the Origins of the Welfare State*; Daunton, *Wealth and Welfare*; Kaufmann, *Variations of the Welfare State*; Aguilar, 'Cooking Modernity'; Pohl-Valero, 'Food Science, Race, and the Nation in Colombia'.
6. Pedersen, *Family Dependence, and the Origins of the Welfare State*, 53 (quote); Vernon, 'The Ethics of Hunger and the Assembly of Society'.
7. Worboys, 'The Discovery of Colonial Malnutrition between the Wars'; Arnold, 'The "Discovery" of Malnutrition and Diet in Colonial India'; Kamminga and Cunningham, eds., *The Science and Culture of Nutrition*; Davis, *Home Fires Burning*; Helstocky, 'The State, Health, and Nutrition'; Drinot, 'Food, Race and Working-Class Identity'; Cwiertka, 'Militarization of Nutrition in Wartime Japan'; Andresen and Elvbakken, 'From Poor Law Society to the Welfare State'; Aguilar, 'Cooking Modernity'; Cullather, 'The Foreign Policy of the Calorie', 359; Nally, 'The Biopolitics of Food Provisioning'; Swislocki, 'Nutritional Governmentality'; Pohl-Valero, '"La raza entra por la boca"'.
8. Winter, 'Military Fitness and Civilian Health in Britain', 212.
9. Ministry of National Service, 1917–19, *Report upon the Physical Examination of Men of Military Age by National Service Medical Boards*, 43–4 (quote). 'It is not lack of food from which the children suffer, but wrong food, bad housing and ventilation, want of personal cleanliness, irregularity of habits, insufficient sleep, and, lastly, lack of self-control,' insisted a delegate at the 1905 conference of the National Union of Women Workers. 'Ignorance on the part of mothers' was the core problem: Pedersen, *Family Dependence, and the Origins of the Welfare State*, 52. See also Zweiniger-Bargielowska, *Managing the Body*.
10. Rowntree, *Poverty*, 303–4.
11. Beckett, 'Total War'.
12. Burnett, *Plenty and Want*, 255; Petránová, 'The Rationing System in Bohemia during the First World War'; Essemyr, 'Food Policies in Sweden during the World Wars'; Scholliers, 'The Policy of Survival'; Davis, *Home Fires Burning*; Bonzon, 'Consumption and Total Warfare in Paris (1914–1918)'; De Nijs, 'Food Provision and Food Retailing in The Hague, 1914–1930'.
13. Langworthy, *Potatoes and Other Root Crops as Food*; Atwater, *Principles of Nutrition and Nutritive Value of Food*, 44 (quote).
14. Salaman, *History and Social Influence of the Potato*, 576–7; Dewey, *British Agriculture in the First World War*, 206, 244–8; Crowe, 'Profitable Ploughing of the Uplands?', 209.
15. Hancock, 'The Social Impact of the First World War in Pembrokeshire', 61.
16. Cullather, *The Hungry World*, 21; Farnham et al., eds., *Choice War Time Recipes*, 56.
17. Davis, *Home Fires Burning*, 59.
18. Davis, *Home Fires Burning*, 169.

19. Blomqvist, 'Sweden's Potato Revolution'; Håkan Blomqvist, personal communication, May 2018.

20. Hancock, 'The Social Impact of the First World War in Pembrokeshire', 61.

21. Davis, *Home Fires Burning*.

22. Murphy and Kass, *Evolution of Plant Breeding at Cornell University*; Brown, 'Notes on the History of the Potato Breeding Institute, Trumpington'.

23. Ochoa, 'Potato Collecting Expeditions in Chile, Bolivia and Peru'.

24. Bethke et al., 'History and Origin of Russet Burbank (Netted Gem)'. Russet Burbanks originate in a potato collected by C. E. Goodrich in 1851, which he called the Rough Purple Chili.

25. Elina et al., 'Plant Breeding on the Front', 165.

26. Hawkes, 'N.I. Vavilov – The Man and his Work', 3–6.

27. Hawkes, *Potato Collecting Expeditions in Mexico and South America*, 8; Christiansen González, *El cultivo de la papa en el Perú*; Shepherd, 'Imperial Science'; Reader, *Potato*, 231–9; Scott, 'Plants, People, and the Conservation of Biodiversity of Potatoes in Peru'.

28. Hawkes, *Potato Collecting Expeditions in Mexico and South America*, 8; Christiansen González, *El cultivo de la papa en el Perú*; Shepherd, 'Imperial Science'; Scott, 'Plants, People, and the Conservation of Biodiversity of Potatoes in Peru'.

29. Qu and Xie, eds., *How the Chinese Eat Potatoes*, 374–8.

30. Scott, 'Plants, People, and the Conservation of Biodiversity of Potatoes in Peru', 25; Sood et al., 'History of Potato Breeding'.

31. Helstocky, 'The State, Health, and Nutrition', 1582–3; Davis, *Home Fires Burning*; Daunton, *Wealth and Welfare*; Leisering, 'Nation State and Social Policy'.

32. Collingham, *The Taste of War*, 8.

33. Boyd-Orr, *Food, Health and Income*.

34. 'Review of *The Nation's Larder*', 14–15.

35. Salaman, *History and Social Influence of the Potato*, 578–81; Hammond, *Food and Agriculture in Britain*, 33–7, 79–86; Burnett, *Plenty and Want*, 307; Martin, *The Development of Modern Agriculture*, 40; Collingham, *The Taste of War*, 29, 90, 101, 361–3, 384–414.

36. Collingham, *The Taste of War*, 137, 404.

37. Moskoff, *The Bread of Affliction*; Collingham, *The Taste of War*, 219–27, 317.

38. Moskoff, *The Bread of Affliction*; Barber and Harrison, *The Soviet Home Front*, 77–93; Ries, 'Potato Ontology'; Collingham, *The Taste of War*, 220–5, 323, 334, 337 (quote), 341.

39. Barber and Harrison, *The Soviet Home Front*, 85–6.

40. Piktin, *The House that Giacomo Built*, 57; Collingham, *The Taste of War*, 14, 70, 173–4, 207, 296–7, 501.

41. Pauer, 'Neighbourhood Associations and Food Distribution in Japanese Cities'; Cwiertka, 'Popularizing a Military Diet in Wartime and Postwar Japan'; Collingham, *The Taste of War*, 277–81.

42. Procter, *The Nazi War on Cancer*, 124.

43. Collingham, *The Taste of War*, 193, 357–9.

44. Procter, *The Nazi War on Cancer*; Cole, 'Feeding the Volk', 160.

45. Elina et al., 'Plant Breeding on the Front'. Potatoes were the object of the first experiments at the Biologisches Reichanstalt für Land- und Forstwirtschaft, which in 1905 became part of the German Ministry of Interior: Saraiva, *Fascist Pigs*, 74–5.

46. Reagin, *Sweeping the German Nation*, 158–9; Cole, 'Feeding the Volk', 160–83 (160 quote); Saraiva, *Fascist Pigs*, 128–9.

47. Ninety per cent of the potatoes consumed by Army Group Centre, based in Belorussia between September 1941 and August 1942, were acquired in this way, for instance: Collingham, *The Taste of War*, 29, 156–64, 186, 211–13.

48. Saraiva, *Fascist Pigs*, 7.

49. Bentley, *Eating for Victory*, 68 (quote); Collingham, *The Taste of War*, 416–29; Biltekoff, *Eating Right in America*.

50. Bentley, *Eating for Victory*, 63–4.

51. Yang, 'Creating the Kitchen Patriot', 62.

52. FAO, 'Constitution'.

53. Whitaker, 'Food Entitlements', 1589–90; Staples, *The Birth of Development*; Shaw, *World Food Security*; Schanbacer, *The Politics of Food*; Cullather, *The Hungry World*, 34 (quote); Gibson, *The Feeding of Nations*.

54. For a classic statement of the links between communism and hunger in the developing world see Truman, 'Inaugural Address'.

55. Smith, *An Inquiry into the Nature and Causes of the Wealth of Nations*, I.viii.45.

56. United Nations, *Report of the Forty-Ninth Session of the Committee on Commodity Problems*, paras. 41–67; FAO, *Report of the Council of FAO*; FAO, *Approaches to World Food Security*; Pottier, *The Anthropology of Food*; Carr, 'Postmodern Conceptualizations, Modernist Applications'; Jarosz, 'Defining World Hunger'; FAO, Rome Declaration on World Food Security (quote).

57. Cullather, 'Development? It's History'; Cullather, *The Hungry World*.

58. George, *How the Other Half Dies*; Escobar, 'Power and Visibility'; Cullather, *The Hungry World*; Pingali, 'Green Revolution', 12303.

59. Cullather, *The Hungry World*, 201.

60. United Nations, *Report of the Forty-Ninth Session of the Committee on Commodity Problems*, paras. 41–67; FAO, *Roots, Tubers, Plantains and Bananas in Human Nutrition*, table 3.6.

61. Jacob George Harrar, 'Notes on meeting with Colombian Minister of Agriculture [Antonio Angel Escobar]', Bogotá, 9 Aug. 1951, RF, Rockefeller Foundation Records, Officers Diaries, PG 12, 1951 February 11–1952 February 6, 90; Moris, *Extension Alternatives in Tropical Africa*, 55 (quote).

62. FAO, 'FAO Overview'.

63. Ochoa, 'Potato Collecting Expeditions in Chile, Bolivia and Peru'; Fenzi and Bonneuil, 'From "Genetic Resources" to "Ecosystems Services"'.

64. Shepherd, 'Imperial Science'; Scott, 'Plants, People, and the Conservation of Biodiversity of Potatoes in Peru', 25.

65. Rockefeller Foundation, 'Accelerating Agricultural Modernization in Developing Nations'; FAO, 'FAO Overview' (quote).

66. Fenzi and Bonneuil, 'From "Genetic Resources" to "Ecosystems Services"', 78.

67. FAO, 'Why Potato?'; FAO, International Year of the Potato 2008.

68. Escobar, 'Power and Visibility'; Scott, *Seeing Like a State*, 241; Mackenzie, 'Contested Ground'; Beinart, 'African History and Environmental History'; Watts, 'Development and Governmentality'; Nally, 'The Biopolitics of Food Provisioning'; Coulson, *Tanzania*, 124–5 (quote).

69. Netting, *Smallholders, Householders*; Scott, *Seeing Like a State*, 241 (quote); Pottier, *The Anthropology of Food*; Shepherd, 'Imperial Science'; Cullather, *The Hungry World*.

70. FAO, 'Potato and Biodiversity' and 'Potato and Gender'.

71. See for instance Centro Internacional de la Papa, *Informe anual 1975*; Centro Internacional de la Papa, *Informe anual 1979*.

72. Centro Internacional de la Papa, 'Potato' (quote); Scott, 'Plants, People, and the Conservation of Biodiversity of Potatoes in Peru'.

73. Centro Internacional de la Papa, 'Native Potato Varieties'.

74. Congreso de la República, Resolución Suprema, 287,797; 'Perú: Hoy se celebra el Día Nacional de la Papa', SERVINDI; FAO, 'Background'; Scott, 'Plants, People, and the Conservation of Biodiversity of Potatoes in Peru'.

75. DeSoucey, 'Gastronationalism', 447.

76. BBC News, 'Potatoes Spark Chile–Peru Dispute'.

77. Matta, 'Valuing Native Eating'.

78. Scott, 'Plants, People, and the Conservation of Biodiversity of Potatoes in Peru'; Schlüter, 'Promoting Regional Cuisine as Intangible Cultural Heritage in Latin America; Palomino Gonzales, 'Gourmetización del alimento andino'.

79. Faulhaber, 'Cured Meat and Idaho Potatoes'; DeSoucey, 'Gastronationalism'; Cassidy, 'Comber Spuds get European Protected Status'.

80. Pottier, *Anthropology of Food*, 176–9; Carneiro Dias and da Costa, 'Indigenous Claims to Native Crops and Plant Genebanks'; Scott, 'Plants, People, and the Conservation of Biodiversity of Potatoes in Peru', 30; Parque de la Papa.

81. Dean, *The Constitution of Poverty*, 6.

82. Ploeg, 'Potatoes and Knowledge'; Mayer, *The Articulated Peasant*; De Jong et al., *The Complete Book of Potatoes*; Scott, 'Plants, People, and the Conservation of Biodiversity of Potatoes in Peru', 22.

83. See for instance Wilk, 'Beauty and the Feast', 296; Palmer, 'From Theory to Practice'; Helstosky, 'Recipe for the Nation'; O'Connor, 'The King's Christmas Pudding'; DeSoucey, 'Gastronationalism'.

CONCLUSIONS : PARMENTIER, PEASANTS AND PERSONAL RESPONSIBILITY

1. See for instance Parmentier, *Manière de Faire le Pain de Pommes de Terre sans Mélange de Farine*; Parmentier, *Les pommes de terre, considérées relativement à la santé & à l'économie*; Parmentier, *Traité sur la culture et les usages des pommes de terre, de la patate, et du topinambour*; Spary, *Feeding France*.

2. 'The vegetable kingdom', he declared, 'offers no plant capable of supplying a more healthful, more convenient and less expensive food than potatoes ... I do not allow myself to be blinded by enthusiasm, but in view of this plant's almost miraculous fecundity, who could fail to admire it?': Parmentier, *Les pommes de terre, considérées relativement à la santé*, 184, 195.

3. 'Farine & farineux'; *Universal Magazine* 21 (1757); *Underrättelse om potatoës eller jordpärons plantering*; Duhamel du Monceau, *Moyens de conserver la santé aux equipages des vaisseaux*, 188; Zanon, *Della coltivaziones, e dell'uso delle patate*; Young, *Farmer's Letters to the People of England*; Varenne de Béost, *La cuisine des pauvres*; Parmentier, *Les pommes de terre, considérées relativement à la santé*, 44; Parmentier, *Traité sur la culture et les usages des pommes de terre, de la patate, et du topinambour*, 18; Koerner, *Linnaeus*, 149; Spary, *Feeding France*, 61–88.

4. Parmentier, *Les pommes de terre, considérées relativement à la santé*, 133

5. Parmentier, *Les pommes de terre, considérées relativement à la santé*, 3–4.

6. Morren, *Belgique Horticole*, III: 14.

7. See for instance Scott, *Seeing Like a State*, 189, 264; Prain et al., eds., *Biological and Cultural Diversity*; Mt. Pleasant, 'The Paradoxes of Plows and Productivity'; FAO, 'Smallholders and Family Farmers'; FAO, *The State of Food and Agriculture*; Ricciardi et al., 'How Much of the World's Food do Smallholders Produce?'

8. Ioulia Evgenyevna Fenton, personal communication, 9 Jan. 2018.

9. Netting, *Smallholders, Householders*, 8–9.

10. Lacroix, *Transformations du procès de travail agricole*, 95 (first quote); Ploeg, 'Potatoes and Knowledge', 209 (second quote).

11. Bentley, *Eating for Victory*, 63–4.

12. Pollock, 'Van Gogh and the Poor Slaves'; and Coveney, *Food, Morals and Meaning*, 92–3 (quote). Van Gogh, in contrast, believed his painting was an uplifting illustration of the integrity of peasant life: Vincent van Gogh to Theo van Gogh, Nuenen, 30 Apr. 1885, Vincent van Gogh: The Letters.

13. Bush, 'Remarks on the HealthierUS Initiative in Dallas, Texas' (first quote); UK Department of Health, 'Choosing Health: Making Healthy Choices Easier' (second quote); Biltekoff, *Eating Right in America*, 127; New Zealand Ministry of Health, 'Eating and Activity Guidelines'.

14. Campos et al., 'The Epidemiology of Overweight and Obesity', 58. Or see Lang and Heasman, *Food Wars*; Guthman and Allen, 'From "Old School" to "Farm-to-School"'; Crawford, 'Health as a Meaningful Social Practice'; Jarosz, 'Defining World Hunger'; Biltekoff, *Eating Right in America*; Dowler, 'Food Banks and Food Justice in "Austerity Britain"'.

15. Foucault, *History of Sexuality*, I: 138.

16. Foucault, *Security, Territory, Population*, 327 (quote), 338–9.

17. Agamben, *Homo Sacer*, 123.

18. See for instance King and Slavin, 'White Potatoes, Human Health, and Dietary Guidance'; US Department of Health and Human Services, 'A Healthier You'.

Bibliography

ARCHIVES

Archivo Arzobispal de Arequipa, Arequipa

Santa Catalina leg. 8.
Santa Teresa leg. 2.

Biblioteca Nacional de España, Madrid

Bernardo de Cienfuegos, 'Historia de las plantas', 7 vols., c.1627–31, Mss/3357–63.

British Library, London

IOR F/4/179.
IOR H/Misc/799, 59–169.
IOR P/242/73.
IOR/F/4/379/9495.
MSS EUR/F95/2.

Guildhall Library, London

Ms 7801, box 2.

Lancashire Record Office, Preston

DDB acc 6685 box 179.
DDFO 23/4.
DDM 11/61.
DDSc 9/47.
PR 718.
PR/284.

McGill University Library, Montreal

Doncaster Recipes Collection, MSG 1230.

Museum of English Rural Life Special Collections, University of Reading, Reading

SR RASE A/I–II.
SR RASE B/I, B/II, B/VI–VII. B/X, B/XIII.

Rockefeller Foundation Archives Online

Officers Diaries, PG 12.

Royal Society of Arts Archive, London

PR/MC/104/10/240.
RSA/PR/GE/110/26/70–71.
RSA/PR/MC/105/10/396.

Schlesinger Library, Radcliffe College, Cambridge, MA

American Institute of Wine & Food Recipe Books, *c.*1690–*c.*1830, MC 675, box 1.
Manuscript recipe book of W. Walker, Hayes Middlesex, *c.*1798–1826, Recipes for Cures and Cookery, AR297.
Marion King Schlefer Recipe Collection, A/S33.
Sarah Fayerweather Cookbook, 1764, A/F283.
Sophie D. Coe Manuscript Cookbook Collection, MC 844, box 1.

The National Archives, Kew

C 6/414/31.
E134/10Geo2/Hil3.
HO 42/35, 42/61.
WO 1/1094.

Wellcome Library, London

Collection of Cookery and Medical Receipts by Edward and Katherine Kidder, 1699, Ms 3107.
Collection of Cookery and Medical Receipts, *c.*1685–*c.*1725, Ms 1796.

Cookery Receipts Collected by Johnson Family of Spalding, Lincs., 1694–1831, Ms 3082.

Physical and Chyrurgicall Receipts. Cookery and Preserves. Collected by Elizabeth Jacob and Others, 1654–*c*.1685, Ms 3009.

Recipe Book of the Godrey-Faussett Family of Heppington, Nackington, Kent, late 17th century to mid 18th century, Ms 7998.

NEWSPAPERS AND JOURNALS

Annals of Agriculture and Other Useful Arts, London (1795, 1797, 1799).

Appendix to the Scots Magazine, Edinburgh (1740).

Asiatic Journal and Monthly Register for British India and its Dependencies, London (1824, 1826).

Bibliothèque britannique: Littérature, Geneva (1796).

Bibliothèque britannique, ou Recueil extrait des ouvrages anglais périodiques: Sciences et Arts, Geneva (1797).

Bibliothèque physico-économique, instructive et amusant, Paris (1787, 1790).

Colonial Times and Tasmanian Advertiser, Tasmania (1826).

Correio mercantil e economico de Portugal, Lisbon (1798).

Correo mercantil de España y sus Indias, Madrid (1801).

English Review, London (1794).

European Magazine and London Review, London (1790, 1800).

Feuille de cultivateur, Paris (1799).

Friend of India, Serampore (1820).

Gentleman's Magazine and Historical Chronicle, London (1764, 1795).

Guardian, London (2006, 2013, 2014, 2018).

Journal historique & litteraire, Luxembourg (1780).

Journal historique et politique de Genève, Geneva (1779).

Journal historique et politique des principaux événemens des différentes cours de l'Europe, Geneva (1779).

L'Avantcoureur, Paris (1771).

London Gazette, London (1778, 1800).

London Review of English and Foreign Literature, London (1780).

Magazzino toscana, Florence (1775).

Massachusetts Spy, or the Worcester Gazette, Worcester, MA (1790).

Mémoires d'agriculture, d'économie rurale et domestique, Paris (1789).

Memorial literario, ó, Biblioteca periódica de ciencias y artes, Madrid (1802).

Memorial literatio, instructivo y curioso de la corte de Madrid, Madrid (1790).

Mercurio peruano de historia, literatura, y noticias públicas que da á luz la Sociedad Academica de Amantes de Lima, Lima (1792, 1794).

Monthly Magazine and British Register, London (1797).

New York Times, New York (1943, 2012).

Semanario de agricultura y artes dirigido a los párrocos, Madrid (1797, 1799, 1800, 1801, 1802, 1805, 1806).

South African Magazine, A Contribution to Colonial Literature, Cape Town (1869).

Telegraph, London (2007).

The Struggle; Devoted to the Advocacy of Free Trade and the Repeal of the Corn Laws, Preston (1843).

Times, London (1795, 1830, 1847).

Universal Magazine, London (1757).

Weekly Entertainer, London (1796).

OTHER SOURCES

Abad-Zardoya, Carmen, 'Arquitectos en los fogones: del *theatrum machinarum* a los proyectos ilustrados para una cocina económica', *Artigrama* 26 (2011), 649–68.

Abbots, Emma-Jayne and Benjamin Coles, 'Horsemeat-Gate: The Discursive Production of a Neoliberal Food Scandal', *Food, Culture and Society* 16:4 (2013), 535–50.

Abreu, Laurinda, *The Political and Social Dynamics of Poverty, Poor Relief and Health Care in Early-Modern Portugal,* Routledge (London, 2016).

Accomplished Ladies Rich Closet of Rarities (London, 1687).

Acosta, José de, *Natural and Moral History of the Indies,* trans. Frances López-Morillas, Duke University Press (Durham, 2002 [1590]).

Act of Tonnage and Poundage, and Rates of Merchandize (Edinburgh, 1705).

Adam, James, *Practical Essays on Agriculture,* 2 vols. (London, 1789).

Adelman, Jeremy, *Republic of Capital: Buenos Aires and the Legal Transformation of the Atlantic World,* Stanford University Press (Stanford, 1999).

Africa and America Described with Anecdotes and Numerous Illustrations, 2 vols. (London, 1856).

Agamben, Georgio, *Homo Sacer: Sovereign Power and Bare Life,* trans. Daniel Heller-Roazen, Stanford University Press (Stanford, 1998).

Aguilar, Sandra, 'Cooking Modernity: Nutrition Policies, Class, and Gender in 1940s and 1950s Mexico City', *The Americas* 64:2 (2007), 177–205.

'*AHR* Exchange: The Question of Black Rice', *American Historical Review* 1115:1 (2010), 123–71.

Aikin, John, *A Description of the Country from Thirty to Forty Miles Round Manchester* (London, 1795).

Albala, Kenneth, *Eating Right in the Renaissance,* University of California Press (Berkeley, 2002).

Alcedo, Antonio de, *The Geographical and Historical Dictionary of America and the West Indies Containing an Entire Translation of the Spanish Work of Colonel Don Antonio de Alcedo,* ed. G. A. Thompson, 5 vols. (London, 1812).

Aldini, Tobias, *Exactissima Descriptio Rariorum Quarundam Plantarum, que continentur Rome in Horto Farnesiano* (Rome, 1625).

Aldrete, Bernardo, *Del orígen y principio de la lengua castellana o romance que oi usa en España* (Rome, 1606).

Alletz, Pons Augustin, *Agronomía, ó diccionario manual del labrador,* trans. Pedro Charro de Lorenzana (Madrid, 1817).

Alletz, Pons Augustin, *L'Agronome, ou Dictionnaire portatif du cultivateur,* 2 vols. (Paris, 1799).

Alonso de Herrera, Gabriel, *Agricultura general de Gabriel Alonso de Herrera, corregida según el texto original de la primera edición publicada en 1513 por el mismo autor y adicionada por la Real Sociedad Económica Matritense*, 2 vols. (Madrid, 1819).

Altimiras, Juan, *Nuevo arte de cocina, sacado de la escuela de la esperiencia económica* (Barcelona, 1758).

Amado Doblas, María Isabel, 'Apunte bibliográfico acerca de la batata/patata en la literatura del siglo de oro', *Isla de Arriarán* 18 (2001), 275–87.

Ambrosoli, Mauro, *The Wild and the Sown: Botany and Agriculture in Western Europe: 1350–1850*, trans. Mary McCann Salvatorelli, Cambridge University Press (Cambridge, 1997).

Amoretti, Carlo, *Della coltivazione delle patate e loro uso. Instruzione* (Milan, 1801).

Andagoya, Pascual de, *Pascual de Andagoya, Relación y documentos*, ed. Adrian Blázquez, Historia 16 (Madrid, 1986).

Andresen, Astri and Kari Tove Elvbakken, 'From Poor Law Society to the Welfare State: School Meals in Norway, 1890–1950s', *Journal of Epidemiology & Community Health* 61:5 (2007), 374–7.

Andrews, Donna, *Philanthropy and Police: London Charity in the Eighteenth Century*, Princeton University Press (Princeton, 1989).

Angående potaters förvarande (Stockholm, 1788).

Annalen der Braunschweig Luneburgischen Churlande 9:1 (Hanover, 1795).

Appleby, Joyce, 'Ideology and Theory: The Tension between Political and Economic Liberalism in Seventeenth-Century England', *American Historical Review* 81:3 (1976), 499–515.

Arch, Joseph, *From Ploughtail to Parliament. An Autobiography*, Cresset Library (London, 1986 [*c.*1896]).

Argumossa y Gandara, Theodoro Ventura de, *Erudicción política despertador sobre el comercio, agricultura, y manufacturas, con avisos de buena policía, y aumento del real erario* (Madrid, 1743).

Arnold, David, 'Agriculture and "Improvement" in Early Colonial India: A Pre-History', *Journal of Agrarian Change* 5:4 (2005), 505–25.

Arnold, David, 'Hunger in the Garden of Plenty: The Bengal Famine of 1770', in *Dreadful Visitations: Confronting Natural Catastrophe in the Age of Enlightenment*, ed. Alessa Johns, Routledge (London, 1999), 81–112.

Arnold, David, 'The "Discovery" of Malnutrition and Diet in Colonial India', *Indian Economic and Social History Review* 31:1 (1994), 1–26.

Arras, Paul, ed., *Quellenbuch zur sächsischen Geschichte*, Europäisscher Geschichtsverlag (Paderborn, 2015 [1912]).

Arteta, Antonio, *Disertacion sobre la muchdumbre de niños que mueren en la infancia, y modo de remediarla, y de procurar en sus cuerpos la conformidad de sus miembros, robustez, agilidad y fuerzas competentes*, 2 vols. (Zaragoza, 1801–2).

Astry, Diana, *Diana Astry's Recipe Book*, ed. Betty Stitt, Bedfordshire Historical Society (Streatley, 1957).

Atwater, W. O., *Principles of Nutrition and Nutritive Value of Food*, Government Printing Office (Washington, 1910).

Ausfuhrlicher Unterricht zur Bereitung der rumfortschen Spaarsuppen (Leipzig, [1805?]).

Ávila, Teresa de, *Escritos de Santa Teresa*, ed. Vicente de la Fuente, 2 vols. (Madrid, 1862).

Baldini, Filippo, *De' Pomi di terra ragionamento* (Naples, 1783).

Ballexserd, Jacques, *Dissertation sur l'éducation physique des enfans* (Paris, 1762).

Banks, Joseph, *The Indian and Pacific Correspondence of Sir Joseph Banks, 1768–1820*, ed. Neil Chambers, 5 vols., Pickering & Chatto (London, 2008).

Barber, John and Mark Harrison, *The Soviet Home Front, 1941–1945: A Social and Economic History of the USSR in World War II*, Longman (New York, 1993).

Barnard, T. C., 'Gardening, Diet and "Improvement" in Later Seventeenth-Century Ireland', *Journal of Garden History* 10:1 (1990), 71–85.

Bashford, Alison and Joyce Chaplin, *The New Worlds of Thomas Robert Malthus: Rereading the Principle of Population*, Princeton University Press (Princeton, 2016).

Bass, Hans, 'The Crisis in Prussia', in *When the Potato Failed: Causes and Effects of the 'Last' European Subsistence Crisis, 1845–1850*, ed. Cormac Ó Gráda, Richard Paping and Eric Vanhaute, Brepols (Turnhout, 2007), 185–212.

Batmanglij, Najmieh, *Food of Life: Ancient Persian and Modern Iranian Cooking and Ceremonies*, Mage Publishers (Washington, 2016).

Bauhin, Gaspard, *Prodromos Theatri Botanici* (Frankfurt, 1620).

Bavetta, Sebastiano, Pietro Navarra and Dario Maimone, *Freedom and the Pursuit of Happiness: An Economic and Political Perspective*, Cambridge University Press (Cambridge, 2014).

Baxter, Richard, 'The Reverend Richard Baxter's Last Treatise', ed. Frederick J. Powicke, *Bulletin of the John Rylands Library*, 10 (1926), 163–218.

BBC News, 'Cookery to be Compulsory', 22 Jan. 2008, http://news.bbc.co.uk/1/hi/education/7200949.stm.

BBC News, 'Potatoes Spark Chile–Peru Dispute', 29 Mar. 2006, http://news.bbc.co.uk/go/pr/fr/-/2/hi/americas/4856154.stm.

BBC News, 'Tory Peer Apologises for Saying "Poor Can't Cook"', 8 Dec. 2014, www.bbc.co.uk/news/uk-politics-30379431.

BBC Radio 4, 'Woman's Hour', 17 Mar. 2014.

Beales, Derek, 'Philosophical Kingship and Enlightened Despotism', in *The Cambridge History of Eighteenth-Century Political Thought*, ed. Mark Goldie and Robert Wokler, Cambridge University Press (Cambridge, 2006), 495–524.

Becher, Johann Joachim, *Politische Discurs von den eigentlichen Ursachen deß Auff- und Abnehmens der Städt, Länder und Republicken* (Frankfurt, 1688).

Beckett, Ian, 'Total War', in *War, Peace and Social Change in Twentieth-Century Europe*, ed. Clive Emsley, Arthur Warwick and Wendy Simpson, Open University Press (Milton Keynes, 1989), 26–44.

Béguillet, Edme, *Traité des subsistances et des grains, qui servent a la nourriture de l'homme*, 6 vols. (Paris, 1780).

Beinart, William, 'African History and Environmental History', *African Affairs* 99:395 (2000), 269–302.

Beinart, William and Karen Middleton, 'Plant Transfers in Historical Perspective: A Review Article', *Environmental History* 10:1 (2004), 3–29.

Bekaert, Geert, 'Caloric Consumption in Industrializing Belgium', *Journal of Economic History* 51:3 (1991), 633–55.

Benavídez, Pedrarias de, *Secretos de chirurgia, especial de las enfermedades de morbo gallico y lamparones y mirrarchia* (Valladolid, 1567).

Bentham, Jeremy, *An Introduction to the Principles of Morals and Legislation* (London, 1789).

Bentham, Jeremy, *The Works of Jeremy Bentham*, ed. John Bowring (Edinburgh, 1843).

Bentley, Amy, *Eating for Victory: Food Rationing and the Politics of Domesticity*, University of Illinois Press (Urbana, 1998).

Benzo, Ugo, Lodovico Bertaldi and Baldassar Pisanelli, *Regole della sanitá et natura de cibi* (Turin, 1620).

Berg, Gösta, 'Die Kartoffel und die Rübe', *Ethnologia Scandinavica* (1971), 158–66.

Berg, Maxine, 'Afterword: Things in Global History', in *The Global Lives of Things: The Material Culture of Connections in the Early Modern World*, ed. Anne Gerritsen and Giorgio Riello, Routledge (London, 2016), 253–8.

Berg, Maxine and Elizabeth Eger, 'Introduction', in *Luxury in the Eighteenth Century: Debates, Desires and Delectable Goods*, ed. Maxine Berg and Elizabeth Eger, Palgrave Macmillan (Basingstoke, 2003), 1–4.

Beskrifning om jordpärons plantering (Stockholm, 1773).

Besler, Basilius, *Hortus Eystenttensis* (Nuremberg, 1640).

Bethke, Paul C., Atef M. K. Nassar, Stan Kubow, Yves N. Leclerc, Xiu-Qing Li, Muhammad Haroon, Teresa Molen, John Bamberg, Max Martin, and Danielle J. Donnelly, 'History and Origin of Russet Burbank (Netted Gem): A Sport of Burbank', *American Journal of Potato Research* 91:6 (2014), 594–609.

Bielefeldt, Heiner, 'Autonomy and Republicanism: Immanuel Kant's Philosophy of Freedom', *Political Theory* 25:4 (1997), 524–58.

Bignami, Pietro Maria, *Le patate* (Bologna, 1773).

Billingsley, John, 'On the Culture of Potatoes, and feeding Hogs with them, during Seven Years', in *Letters and Papers on Agriculture, Planting, & Selected from the Correspondence of the Bath and West of England Society for the Encouragement of Agriculture, Arts, Manufactures and Commerce* 6 (London, 1792), 339–94.

Biltekoff, Charlotte, *Eating Right in America: The Cultural Politics of Food and Health*, Duke University Press (Durham, 2013).

Binning, Robert B. M., *Journal of Two Years' Travel in Persia Ceylon, Etc.*, 2 vols. (London, 1857).

Birembaut, Arthur, 'L'École gratuite de boulangerie', in *Enseignement et diffusion des sciences en France au XVIIIe siècle*, ed. René Taton, Hermann (Paris, 1964), 493–509.

Bleichmar, Daniela, *Visible Empire: Botanical Expeditions and Visual Culture in the Hispanic Enlightenment*, University of Chicago Press (Chicago, 2012).

Bleichmar, Daniela, Paula De Vos, Kristin Huffine and Kevin Sheehan, eds., *Science in the Spanish and Portuguese Empires, 1500–1800*, Stanford University Press (Stanford, 2009).

Bligh, William, *A Voyage to the South Sea for the Purpose of Conveying the Bread-fruit Tree to the West Indies* (Cambridge, 2013 [1792]).

Blomqvist, Håkan, 'Sweden's Potato Revolution', *Solidarity*, Nov.–Dec. 2017, https://solidarity-us.org/atc/191/p5131/.

Blum, Jerome, *The End of the Old Order in Rural Europe*, Princeton University Press (Princeton, 1978).

Board of Agriculture, *Account of the Experiments tried by the Board of Agriculture in the Composition of Various Sorts of Bread* (London, 1795).

Board of Agriculture, *Communications to the Board of Agriculture on Subjects Relative to the Husbandry, and Internal Improvement, of the Country* 1: I–II (London, 1797).

Board of Agriculture, *Hints Respecting the Culture and the Use of Potatoes* (London, 1795).

Board of Agriculture, *Report of the Committee of the Board of Agriculture Appointed to Extract Information from the County Reports and other Authorities Concerning the Culture and Use of Potatoes* (London, 1795).

Bohstedt, John, 'The Myth of the Feminine Food Riot: Women as Proto-Citizens in English Community Politics, 1790–1810', in *Women and Politics in the Age of the Democratic Revolution*, ed. Harriet Applewhite and Darline Levy, University of Michigan Press (Ann Arbor, 1993), 21–60.

Bohstedt, John, *The Politics of Provisions: Food Riots, Moral Economy, and Market Transition in England, c.1550–1850*, Ashgate (Farnham, 2010).

Boissier de Sauvages, François, *Dictionnaire languedocien-françois* (Nimes, 1756).

Boll, Ernst, *Geschichte Meklenburgs mit besondere Berücksichtigung der Culturgeschichte* (Neubrandenburg, 1856).

Bolotov, Andrei, 'O delanii iz tartofelia muki', *Trudy Vol'nago Ekonomicheskago Obshchestva* 14 (1770), 33–63.

Bonaparte, Napoleon, *Letters of Napoleon*, ed. J. M. Thompson, Dent (London, 1954).

Bonells, Jaime, *Perjuicios que acarrean al género humano y al estado las madres que rehusan criar a sus hijos* (Madrid, 1786).

Bonzon, Thierry, 'Consumption and Total Warfare in Paris (1914–1918)', in *Food and Conflict in Europe in the Age of the Two World Wars*, ed. Frank Trentmann and Flemming Just, Palgrave Macmillan (Basingstoke, 2006), 49–64.

Booth, Alan, 'Food Riots in the North-West of England, 1790–1801', *Past & Present* 77 (1977), 84–107.

Boserup, Ester, *Woman's Role in Economic Development*, intro. Nazneen Kanji, Su Fei Tan and Camilla Toulmin, Earthscan (London, 2007).

Botero, Giovanni, *The Reason of State and The Greatness of Cities*, ed. and trans. P. J. Waley and D. P. Waley, Yale University Press (New Haven, 1956).

Bowles, Guillermo, *Introducción a la historia natural y de la geografía física de España*, trans. José Nicolás de Azara (Madrid, 1775).

Boyd-Orr, John, *Food, Health and Income: Report on a Survey of Adequacy of Diet in Relation to Income*, Macmillan (London, 1936).

Brading, David John, *The First America, the Spanish Monarchy, Creole Patriots, and the Liberal State, 1492–1867*, Cambridge University Press (Cambridge, 1991).

Brady, John, 'Remedies Proposed for the Church of Ireland (1697)', *Archivium Hibernicum* 22 (1959), 163–73.

Bräker, Ulrich, *The Poor Man of Toggenburg*, 1789, trans. Margaret Clare Britton, www.keithsayers.id.au/Toggenburg/Cover.htm.

Braudel, Fernand, *Civilization and Capitalism, 15th–18th Century, vol. I: The Structure of Everyday Life*, trans. Siân Reynolds, University of California Press (Berkeley, 1982).

Braudel, Fernand, *The Mediterranean and the Mediterranean World in the Age of Philip II*, trans. Siân Reynolds, 2 vols., University of California Press (Berkeley, 1995).

Bray, Francesca, 'Chinese Literati and the Transmission of Technological Knowledge: The Case of Agriculture', in *Cultures of Knowledge: Technology in Chinese History*, ed. Dagmar Schäfer, Brill (Leiden, 2011), 299–325.

Bray, Francesca, *Technology and Gender: Fabrics of Power in Late Imperial China*, University of California Press (Berkeley, 1997).

Brennan, Thomas, *Public Drinking and Popular Culture in Eighteenth-Century Paris*, Princeton University Press (Princeton, 1988).

Broadberry, Stephen, Rainer Fremdling and Peter Solar, 'Industry', in *The Cambridge Economic History of Modern Europe*, vol. I: *1700–1850*, ed. Stephen Broadberry and K. O'Rourke, Cambridge University Press (Cambridge, 2010), 164–86.

Broadberry, Stephen and K. O'Rourke, eds., *The Cambridge Economic History of Modern Europe*, 3 vols., Cambridge University Press (Cambridge, 2010).

Brown, Stephen, 'Notes on the History of the Potato Breeding Institute, Trumpington', Jan. 2011, Trumpington Local History Group, www.trumpingtonlocalhistorygroup.org/subjects_PBIhistory.html.

Browne, Patrick, *Civil and Natural History of Jamaica* (London, 1789).

Brownell, Kelly D., Thomas Farley, Walter C. Willett, Barry M. Popkin, Frank J. Chaloupka, Joseph W. Thompson and David S. Ludwig, 'The Public Health and Economic Benefits of Taxing Sugar-Sweetened Beverages', *New England Journal of Medicine* 361 (2009), 1599–605.

Brundage, James, 'Sumptuary Laws and Prostitution in Late Medieval Italy', *Journal of Medieval History* 13:4 (1987), 343–55.

Bruni, Luigino and Pier Luigi Porta, '*Economia civile* and *pubblica felicità* in the Italian Enlightenment', in *Oeconomies in the Age of Newton*, ed. Margaret Schabas and Neil de Marchi, Duke University Press (Durham, 2003), 361–85.

Brush, Stephen, *Farmer's Bounty: Locating Crop Diversity in the Contemporary World*, Yale University Press (New Haven, 2004).

Brush, Stephen, Heath Carney and Zósimo Huamán, 'Dynamics of Andean Potato Agriculture', *Economic Botany* 35:1 (1981), 70–88.

Buchan, William, *Domestic Medicine: or, a Treatise on the Prevention and Cure of Diseases by Regimen and Simple Medicines* (London, 1776).

Buchan, William, *Observations Concerning the Diet of the Common People, Recommending a Method of Living Less Expensive, and More Conducive to Health, than the Present* (London, 1797).

Buchet, Christian, *The British Navy, Economy and Society in the Seven Years War*, trans. Anita Higgie and Michael Duffy, Boydell & Brewer (Woodbridge, 2013).

Buc'hoz, Pierre-Joseph, *Manuel alimentaire des plantes* (Paris, 1771).

Burchardt, Jeremy, 'Land and the Laborer: Potato Grounds and Allotments in Nineteenth-Century Southern England', *Agricultural History* 74:3 (2000), 667–84.

Burke, Edmund, *Thoughts and Details on Scarcity Originally Presented to the Right Hon. William Pitt, in the Month of November 1795* (London, 1800).

Burnett, John, *Plenty and Want: A Social History of Food in England from 1815 to the Present Day*, Routledge (London, 1989).

Burnett, John and Derek Oddy, eds., *The Origins and Development of Food Policies in Europe*, Leicester University Press (London, 1994).

Bush, George W., 'Remarks on the HealthierUS Initiative in Dallas, Texas', 18 July 2003, *Public Papers of the Presidents of the United States* III: 893, The US

National Archives and Records Administration, www.gpo.gov/fdsys/pkg/PPP-2003-book2/html/PPP-2003-book2-doc-pg889-2.htm.

Business in the Community, *Healthy People=Healthy Profits* (London, 2009).

Butler, Cheryl, ed., *The Book of Fines: The Annual Accounts of the Mayors of Southampton, vol. III: 1572–1594*, Southampton Records Series 44 (Southampton, 2010).

[Butler, Nathaniel], *The History of the Bermudaes or Summer Islands*, ed. John Henry Lefroy (London, 1882).

Cabarrús, Francisco, 'Discurso sobre la libertad de comercio', 1778, reproduced in Santos Manuel Coronas González, 'Espíritu ilustrado y liberación del tráfico comercial con Indias', *Anuario de historia del derecho español* (1992), 102–11.

Cadet de Vaux, Antoine-Alexis, *L'Ami de l'économie aux amis de l'humanité sur les pains divers dans la composition desquels entre le pomme-de-terre* (Paris, 1816).

Cadet de Vaux, Antoine-Alexis, 'Variétés', *La Décade philosophique, littéraire et politique* 24 (Paris, 1800), 367–71.

Cadet de Vaux, Antoine-Alexis, [Augustin Pyramus] Decandolle, [Benjamin-Jules-Paul] Delessert, Money and Antoine Augustin Parmentier, *Recueil de rapports, de mémoires et d'expériences sur les soupes économiques et les fourneaux a la Rumford* (Paris, 1801).

Caird, James, *Our Daily Food, Its Price, and Sources of Supply* (London, 1868).

Campbell, Jodi, *At the First Table: Food and Social Identity in Early Modern Spain*, University of Nebraska Press (Lincoln, 2017).

Campillo y Cosío, José del, *Nuevo sistema de gobierno económico para la América, con los males y daños que le causa el que hoy tiene, de los que participa copiosamente España y remedios universales para que la primera tenga considerables ventajas, y al segunda mayores intereses* (Madrid, 1789).

Campini, Antonio, *Saggi d'Agricoltura del medico Antonio Campini* (Turin, 1774).

Camporesi, Piero, *Bread of Dreams: Food and Fantasy in Early Modern Europe*, trans. David Gentilcore, Polity Press (Cambridge, 1989).

Camporesi, Piero, *The Magic Harvest: Food, Folklore and Society*, trans. Joan Hall, Polity Press (Cambridge, 1993).

Campos, Paul, Abigail Saguy, Paul Ernsberger, Eric Oliver and Glenn Gaesser, 'The Epidemiology of Overweight and Obesity: Public Health Crisis or Moral Panic?', *International Journal of Epidemiology* 35:1 (2006), 55–60.

Cañizares-Esguerra, Jorge, *How to Write the History of the New World: Histories, Epistomologies and Identities in the Eighteenth-Century Atlantic World*, Stanford University Press (Stanford, 2001).

Cañizares-Esguerra, Jorge, *Nature, Empire and Nation: Explorations of the History of Science in the Iberian World*, Stanford University Press (Stanford, 2006).

Capatti, Alberto and Massimo Montanari, *Italian Cuisine: A Cultural History*, trans. Aine O'Healy, Columbia University Press (New York, 2003).

Caradonna, Jeremy L., *The Enlightenment in Practice: Academic Prize Contests and Intellectual Culture in France, 1670–1794*, Cornell University Press (Ithaca, 2012).

Cardano, Geronimo, *De Rerum Varietate* (Basle, 1557).

Carneiro Dias, Camila and Maria Conceição da Costa, 'Indigenous Claims to Native Crops and Plant Genebanks: A Case Study from Peru', unpublished conference paper, IV Globelics Conference, Mexico City, 2008.

Carney, Judith, *Black Rice: The African Origins of Rice Cultivation in the Americas*, Harvard University Press (Cambridge, MA, 2001).

Carney, Judith and Richard Rosomoff, *In the Shadow of Slavery: Africa's Botanical Legacy in the Atlantic World*, University of California Press (Berkeley, 2009).

Carpenter, Kenneth, *Protein and Energy: A Study of Changing Ideas in Nutrition*, Cambridge University Press (Cambridge, 1994).

Carr, Edward, 'Postmodern Conceptualizations, Modernist Applications: Rethinking the Role of Society in Food Security', *Food Policy* 31 (2006), 14–29.

Carrió de la Vandera, Alonso, *El lazarillo de ciegos caminantes desde Buenos Aires, hasta Lima*, 1773, Biblioteca Virtual Miguel de Cervantes, www.cervantesvirtual.com.

Casado Soto and José Luis, 'Notas sobre la implantación del maíz en Cantabria y la sustitución de otros cultivos', in *Población y sociedad en la España cantábrica durante el siglo XVII*, Institución Cultural de Cantabria (Santander, 1985), 159–73.

Cassidy, Martin, 'Comber Spuds get European Protected Status', 25 Jan. 2012, BBC News, www.bbc.com/news/uk-northern-ireland-16727411.

Casteau, Lancelot de, *Ouverture de cuisine* (Liège 1604).

Castro-Gómez, Santiago, *La hybris del punto cero: ciencia, raza e ilustración en la Nueva Granada (1750–1816)*, Pontificia Universidad Javeriana (Bogotá, 2005).

Centro Internacional de la Papa, *Informe anual 1975*, Centro Internacional de la Papa (Lima, 1975).

Centro Internacional de la Papa, *Informe anual 1979*, Centro Internacional de la Papa (Lima, 1979).

Centro Internacional de la Papa, 'Potato', https://cipotato.org/crops/potato/.

Chakrabarty, Dipesh, *Provincializing Europe: Postcolonial Thought and Historical Difference*, Princeton University Press (Princeton, 2000).

Chamberlayne, Edward, *Angliae Notitia: or the Present State of England* (London, 1702).

Chambers, Sarah, 'Little Middle Ground: The Instability of a Mestizo Identity in the Andes, Eighteenth and Nineteenth Centuries', in *Race and Nation in Modern Latin America*, ed. Nancy Appelbaum, Anne Macpherson and Karin Alejandra Rosemblatt, University of North Carolina Press (Chapel Hill, 2003), 32–55.

Charbit, Yves, *The Classical Foundations of Population Thought from Plato to Quesnay*, Springer (London, 2011).

Chen, Te-Ping, 'Pushing the Potato: China Wants People to Eat More "Earth Beans"', *Wall Street Journal Online*, 11 Jan. 2015, https://blogs.wsj.com/chinar ealtime/2015/01/09/pushing-the-potato-china-wants-people-to-eat-more-earth-beans/.

China News Service, 'China to Boost Potato Cultivation', 6 Jan. 2015, www.china-news.co.jp/node?page=1433.

Christiansen González, Jorge, *El cultivo de la papa en el Perú*, Editorial Jurídica (Lima, 1967).

Cieza de León, Pedro de, *Parte primera de la Chronica del Perú* (Antwerp, 1554).

Clarkson, L. A. and E. Margaret Crawford, *Feast and Famine: Food and Nutrition in Ireland 1500–1920*, Oxford University Press (Oxford, 2001).

Clericuzio, Antonio, 'Chemical and Mechanical Theories of Digestion in Early Modern Medicine', *Studies in History and Philosophy of Biological and Biomedical Sciences* 43 (2012), 329–37.

Clusius, Carolus (Charles de L'Écluse), *Clusius Correspondence: A Digital Edition-in-Progress*, ed. Esther van Gelder, http://clusiuscorrespondence.huygens.knaw.nl.

Clusius, Carolus, *Rariorum Plantarum Historia* (Antwerp, 1601).

Coates, Colin, *The Metamorphosis of Landscape and Community in Early Quebec*, McGill-Queen's University Press (Montreal and Kingston, 2000).

Cobbett, William, *Cobbett in Ireland: A Warning to England*, ed. Denis Knight, Lawrence & Wishart (London, 1984).

Cobbett, William, *Cobbett's Two-Penny Trash or, Politics for the Poor* 1 (London, 1831).

Cobbett, William, *Cobbett's Weekly Political Register* (London, 1822–32).

Cobbett, William, *Cottage Economy* (London, 1826).

Coe, Sophie, *America's First Cuisines*, University of Texas Press (Austin, 1994).

Cohen, Patricia Cline, *A Calculating People: The Spread of Numeracy in Early America*, University of Chicago Press (Chicago, 1982).

Cole, Joshua, *The Power of Large Numbers: Population, Politics, and Gender in Nineteenth-Century France*, Cornell University Press (Ithaca, 2000).

Cole, Mark, 'Feeding the Volk: Food, Culture and the Politics of Nazi Consumption, 1933–1945', DPhil, University of Florida, 2011.

Coles, William, *Adam in Eden: or, Natures Paradise. The History of Plants, Fruits, Herbs and Flowers* (London, 1657).

Collection of Receipts in Cookery, Physick and Surgery (London, 1746).

Collingham, Lizzie, *Curry: A Biography*, Chatto & Windus (London, 2005).

Collingham, Lizzie, *The Taste of War: World War Two and the Battle for Food*, Penguin (London, 2011).

Collins, David John, *Practical Rules for the Management and Medical Treatment of the Negro Slaves in the Sugar Colonies* (London, 1803).

[Colquhoun, Patrick], *An Account of a Meat and Soup Charity* (London, 1797).

Compleat Planter and Cyderist (London, 1690).

Congreso de la República, Resolución Suprema N. 009–2005-AG, 23 Feb. 2005, *Normas legales: El peruano: Diario Oficial* 22: 9018(Lima, 2005).

Conrad, Sebastian, 'The Enlightenment in Global History: A Historiographical Critique', *American Historical Review* 117:4 (2012), 999–1027.

Conrad, Sebastian, *What is Global History?*, Princeton University Press (Princeton, 2016).

Cooper, Joseph, *The Art of Cookery Refin'd and Augmented* (London, 1654).

Corrado, Vincenzo, *Il credenziere di bueon gusto* (Naples, 1820 [1778]).

Coulson, Andrew, *Tanzania: A Political Economy*, Oxford University Press (Oxford, 2013).

Coup d'oeil sur les quatre concours (Lyon, 1791).

Covarrubias, José Enrique, *En busca del hombre útil: Un estudio comparativo del utilitarianismo neomercantilista en México y Europa, 1748–1833*, Universidad Nacional Autónoma de México (Mexico City, 2005).

Coveney, John, *Food, Morals and Meaning: The Pleasure and Anxiety of Eating*, Routledge (London, 2006).

Crawford, Robert, 'Health as a Meaningful Social Practice', *Health* 10:4 (2006), 401–20.

Crosby, Alfred, *The Columbian Exchange: Biological and Cultural Consequences of 1492*, Greenwood Press (Westport, 1972).

Crosby, Alfred, *Ecological Imperialism: The Biological Expansion of Europe, 900–1900*, Canto (Cambridge, 1986).

Crowe, Hilary, 'Profitable Ploughing of the Uplands? The Food Production Campaign in the First World War', *Agricultural History Review* 55:2 (2007), 205–28.

Cuisinière républicaine, qui enseigne la manière simple d'accomoder les Pommes de terre avec quelques avis fur les soins nécessaires pour les conserver (Paris, year III [1794/5]), facsimile edition of Daniel Morcrette (Luzarches, 1976).

Cullather, Nick, 'Development? It's History', *Diplomatic History* 24:4 (2000), 641–53.

Cullather, Nick, 'The Foreign Policy of the Calorie', *American Historical Review* 112:2 (2007), 337–64.

Cullather, Nick, *The Hungry World: America's Cold War Battle Against Poverty in Asia*, Harvard University Press (Cambridge, MA, 2010).

Cunningham, James, 'Part of Two Letters to the Publisher from Mr James Cunningham, F.R.S. and Physician to the English at Chusan in China, Giving an Account of his Voyage Thither', *Philosophical Transactions* 23 (1703), 1201–9.

Die Curieuse... Köchin (Nürnberg, 1706).

Cwiertka, Katarzyna, 'Militarization of Nutrition in Wartime Japan', *ILAS Newsletter* 38 (2005), 15.

Cwiertka, Katarzyna, 'Popularizing a Military Diet in Wartime and Postwar Japan', *Asian Anthropology* 1:1 (2002), 1–30.

Dalrymple, Alexander, *The Poor Man's Friend* (London, 1795).

Daly, Mary, 'Something Old and Something New: Recent Research on the Great Irish Famine', in *When the Potato Failed: Causes and Effects of the 'Last' European Subsistence Crisis, 1845–1850*, ed. Cormac Ó Gráda, Richard Paping and Eric Vanhaute, Brepols (Turnhout, 2007), 59–78.

Daunton, Martin, *Wealth and Welfare: An Economic and Social History of Britain 1851–1951*, Oxford University Press (Oxford, 2007).

Davalos, José Manuel, *De morbis nonnullis Limae, grassantibus ipsorumque therapeia* (Montpellier, 1787).

Davies, H. R., *Yün-nan: The Link between Indian and the Yangtze*, Cambridge University Press (Cambridge, 1909 [2010 digital edition]).

Davis, Belinda, *Home Fires Burning: Food, Politics, and Everyday Life in World War I Berlin*, University of North Carolina Press (Chapel Hill, 2000).

Davis, Mike, *Late Victorian Holocausts: El Niño and the Making of the Third World*, Verso (London, 2001).

Davis, Natalie Zemon, 'Poor Relief, Humanism and Heresy', in *Society and Culture in Early Modern France*, Stanford University Press (Stanford, 1975), 17–64.

Dawson, Thomas, *Good Huswife's Jewell* (London, 1596).

De Jong, Hielke, Joseph B. Sieczka and Walter de Jong, *The Complete Book of Potatoes: What Every Grower and Gardener Needs to Know*, Timber Press (Portland, 2011).

De Nijs, Thimo, 'Food Provision and Food Retailing in The Hague, 1914–1930', in *Food and Conflict in Europe in the Age of the Two World Wars*, ed. Frank Trentmann and Flemming Just,Palgrave Macmillan (Basingstoke, 2006), 65–87.

Dean, Mitchell, *The Constitution of Poverty: Toward a Genealogy of Liberal Governance*, Routledge (London, 1991).

Dechambre, Amédée, ed., *Dictionnaire encyclopédique des sciences medicales* (Paris, 1877), fourth series, FAA-FET.

Delle Piane, Niccolò, *De' pomi di terra, ossia patate* (Genoa, 1793).

DeLoughrey, Elizabeth, 'Globalizing the Routes of Breadfruit and Other Bounties', *Journal of Colonialism and Colonial History* 8:3 (2007).

Demerson, Paula, 'La distribución de sopas económicas por la Real Sociedad Matritense en 1803–1804', *Boletín de la Real Academia de Historia* 164 (1969), 119–35.

Dening, Greg, *Mr Bligh's Bad Language: Passion, Power and Theatre on the Bounty*, Cambridge University Press (Cambridge, 1992).

Des-Essartz, Jean-Charles, *Traité de l'éducation corporelle des enfants en bas âge, ou réflexions-pratiques sur les moyens de procurer une meilleure constitution aux citoyens* (Paris, 1760).

DeSoucey, Michaela, 'Gastronationalism: Food Traditions and Authenticity Politics in the European Union', *American Sociological Review* 75:3 (2010), 432–55.

Dewey, P. E., *British Agriculture in the First World War*, Routledge (London, 1989).

Dickler, Robert, 'Organization and Change in Productivity in Eastern Prussia', in *European Peasants and Their Markets: Essays in Agrarian Economic History*, ed. William Parker and Eric Jones, Princeton University Press (Princeton, 1975), 269–92.

Dillon, John Talbot, *Travels Through Spain, with a View to Illustrate the Natural History and Physical Geography of that Kingdom* (London, 1782).

Dombey, Joseph, *Joseph Dombey: Médecin, naturaliste, archéologue, exploratuer du Pérou, du chili et du Brésil (1778–1785): Sa vie, son oeuvre, sa correspondence*, ed. Ernest-Théodore Hamy (Paris, 1905).

Dowler, Elizabeth, 'Food Banks and Food Justice in "Austerity Britain"', in *First World Hunger Revisited: Food Charity or the Right to Food*, ed. Graham Riches and Tiina Silvasti, Palgrave Macmillan (London, 2014), 160–75.

Doyle, Enrique, *Instrucción formada de orden del Consejo por D. Enrique Doyle, para el cultivo y uso de las patatas* (Madrid, 1785).

Doyle, Enrique, *Tratado sobre el cultivo, uso y utilidades de las patatas o papas, corregido y considerablemente aumentado* (Madrid, 1804).

Doyle, Enrique, *Tratado sobre el cultivo, uso y utilidades de las patatas ó papas, é instrucción para su mejor propagación* (Madrid, 1797).

Doyle, Enrique, *Tratado sobre la cría y propagación de pastos y ganados*, 2 vols. (Madrid, 1799).

Drake, Michael, *Population and Society in Norway, 1735–1865*, Cambridge University Press (Cambridge, 1969).

Drayton, Richard, *Nature's Government: Science, Imperial Britain, and the 'Improvement' of the World*, Yale University Press (New Haven, 2000).

Drinot, Paulo, 'Food, Race and Working-Class Identity: Restaurantes Populares and Populism in 1930s Peru', *The Americas* 62:2 (2005), 425–70.

Dubroca, Jean François, *Conversaciones de un padre con sus hijos sobre la historia natural*, trad. Manuel Maria de Ascargorta y Ramírez (Madrid, 1802).

Duhamel du Monceau, Henri Louis, *Moyens de conserver la santé aux equipages des vaisseaux* (Paris, 1759).

Dusinberre, William, *Them Dark Days: Slavery in the American Rice Swamps*, Oxford University Press (Oxford, 1996).

Dyck, Ian, *William Cobbett and Rural Popular Culture*, Cambridge University Press (Cambridge, 1992).

Dyck, Ian, 'William Cobbett and the Rural Radical Platform', *Social History* 18:2 (1993), 185–204.

Dyer, Hugh McNeile, *The West Coast of Africa as Seen from the Deck of a Man-of-War* (London, 1876).

Eagle, F. K. and Edward Younge, eds., *Collection of the Reports of Cases, the Statutes, and Ecclesiastical Laws Relating to Tithes*, 4 vols. (London, 1826).

Earle, Rebecca, *The Body of the Conquistador: Food, Race and the Colonial Experience in Spanish America, 1492–1700*, Cambridge University Press (Cambridge, 2012).

Earle, Rebecca, 'Food, Colonialism and the Quantum of Happiness', *History Workshop Journal* 84 (2017), 170–93.

Earle, Rebecca, 'The Political Economy of Nutrition in the Eighteenth Century', *Past & Present* 242:1 (2019), 79–117.

Eastwick, Edward, *Journal of a Diplomate's Three Years' Residence in Persia* (London, 1864), 79–117.

Eden, Frederick Morton, *The State of the Poor, or a History of the Labouring Classes in England, from the Conquest to the Present Period*, 3 vols., Cambridge University Press (Cambridge, 2011 [1797]).

Edwards, Bryan, *The History, Civil and Commercial, of the British Colonies in the West Indies*, 2 vols. (London, 1793).

Eichler, Helga, 'Die Leipziger Ökonomische Sozietät im 18. Jahrhundert', *Jahrbuch für Geschichte des Feudalismus* 2 (1978), 357–86.

El Excmo. Sr. Secretario de Estado y del Despacho de Hacienda dice a esta Junta Superior con fecha del de 19 de marzo próximo pasado lo que sigue (La Coruña, 27 April 1812).

Elina, Olga, Susanne Heim and Nils Roll-Hansen, 'Plant Breeding on the Front: Imperialism, War, and Exploitation', *Osiris* 20 (2005), 161–79.

Elliot, Gill, 'Cookery Examined – 1937–2007: Evidence from Examination Questions of the Development of a Subject over Time', *Research Matters* 6 (2008), 24–30.

Ellis, John, *A Description of the Mangostan and the Bread-Fruit: the First, Esteemed one of the Most Delicious, the Other, the Most Useful of all the Fruits of the Eat Indies, to which are added Directions to Voyagers, or Bringing over these and other Vegetable Productions, which would be extremely beneficial to the Inhabitants of our West India Islands* (London, 1775).

Elsholtz, Johann Sigismund, *Diaeteticon* (Cölln an der Spree, 1682).

Eltis, David John, Philip Morgan and David Richardson, 'Agency and Diaspora in Atlantic History: Reassessing the African Contribution to Rice Cultivation in the Americas', *American Historical Review* 112:5 (2007), 1329–58.

Encyclopédie méthodique: Arts et métiers mécaniques 2 (Paris, 1783).

Engel, Samuel, *Traité de la nature, de la culture et de l'utilité des pommes de terre par un Ami des Hommes* (Lausanne, 1771).

Ensayos de comidas económicas á la Rumford hechos por una comisión nombrada á este fin por la Real Sociedad Económica Matritense (Oviedo, 1803).

Escobar, Arturo, 'Power and Visibility: Development and the Invention and Management of the Third World', *Cultural Anthropology* 3:4 (1988), 428–43.

Essay on Modern Luxuries: An Essay on Tea, Sugar, White Bread and Butter, Country Alehouses, Strong Beer and Geneva, and other Modern Luxuries (Salisbury, 1777).

Essemyr, Mats, 'Food Policies in Sweden during the World Wars', in *The Origins and Development of Food Policies in Europe*, ed. John Burnett and Derek Oddy, Leicester University Press (London, 1994), 161–77.

Evans, E. J., 'Tithing Customs and Disputes: The Evidence of Glebe Terriers', *Agricultural History Review* 18:1 (1970), 17–35.

Evans, Eric, *The Contentious Tithe: The Tithe Problem and English Agriculture, 1750–1850*, Routledge (London, 1976).

Evans, Eric, 'Some Reasons for the Growth of English Anti-Clericalism, c. 1750–c. 1830', *Past & Present* 66 (1975), 84–109.

Evelyn, John, *Kalendarium Hortense* (London, 1666).

Extractos de las Juntas Generales celebradas por la Real Sociedad Bascongada de los Amigos del País en la ciudad de Vitoria por julio de 1786 (Vitoria, 1786).

Extractos de las Juntas Generales celebradas por la Real Sociedad Bascongada de los Amigos del País en la villa de Vergara por setiembre de 1779 (Vitoria, [1779]).

FAO, *Approaches to World Food Security: Selected Working Papers of the Commodities and Trade Division*, United Nations (Rome, 1983).

FAO, 'Background', International Year of the Potato, www.fao.org/potato-2008/en/aboutiyp/background.html#fao.

FAO, 'Constitution of the United Nations Food and Agriculture Organization', Québec, 16 Oct. 1945, University of Oslo, www.jus.uio.no/english/services/library/treaties/14/14–01/food-organization.xml.

FAO, 'FAO Overview: Major Weaknesses in Present Agricultural Production and Related Research Efforts in Developing Countries', Rome, 12 Jan. 1971, 6, AGR-RES/71–5, CGSpace, https://cgspace.cgiar.org/bitstream/handle/10947/519/cg7101b.pdf?sequence=1&isAllowed=y.

FAO, 'New Light on a Hidden Treasure. An End-of-Year Review', *International Year of the Potato 2008* (Rome, 2008).

FAO, 'Potato and Biodiversity', International Year of the Potato, www.fao.org/potato-2008/en/potato/biodiversity.html.

FAO, 'Potato and Gender', International Year of the Potato, www.fao.org/potato-2008/en/potato/gender.html.

FAO, 'Potato and Water Resources', International Year of the Potato, www.fao.org/potato-2008/en/potato/water.html.

FAO, 'Potato World: Africa', International Year of the Potato, www.fao.org/potato-2008/en/world/africa.html.

FAO, *Report of the Council of FAO*, 64th Session, Rome, 18–29 Nov. 1974, www .fao.org/docrep/meeting/007/F5340E/F5340E03.htm#ch2.4.

FAO, Rome Declaration on World Food Security, Rome, 13 Nov. 1996.

FAO, *Roots, Tubers, Plantains and Bananas in Human Nutrition* (Rome, 1990).

FAO, 'Smallholders and Family Farmers' (2012), www.fao.org/fileadmin/tem plates/nr/sustainability_pathways/docs/Factsheet_SMALLHOLDERS.pdf.

FAO, *The State of Food and Agriculture: Innovation in Food and Agriculture* (Rome, 2014).

FAO, 'Why Potato?', International Year of the Potato, www.fao.org/potato-2008/ en/aboutiyp/index.html.

FAO, FAOSTAT, www.fao.org/faostat/en/#data.

'Farine & farineux', 1756, *Encyclopédie, ou dictionnaire raisonné des sciences, des arts et des métiers, etc.*, ed. Denis Diderot and Jean le Rond d'Alembert, University of Chicago: ARTFL Encyclopédie Project (Spring 2013 Edition), ed. Robert Morrissey, http://encyclopedie.uchicago.edu/.

Farnham, Mrs. Frank, Mrs. Francis Harding, Mrs. Roland Hopkins, Mrs. Henry Prout and Mrs. Howard Rogers, eds., *Choice War Time Recipes* (Chestnut Hill, 1918).

Faulhaber, Lilian, 'Cured Meat and Idaho Potatoes: A Comparative Analysis of European and American Protection and Enforcement of Geographic Indications of Foodstuffs', *Columbia Journal of European Law* 11 (2005), 623–64.

Fenzi, Marianna and Christophe Bonneuil, 'From "Genetic Resources" to "Ecosystems Services": A Century of Science and Global Policies for Crop Diversity Conservation', *Culture, Agriculture, Food and Environment* 38:2 (2016), 72–83.

Ferrières, Madeleine, 'Le cas de la pomme de terre dans le Midi', in *L'échec a-t-il des vertus économiques?*, ed. Natacha Coquery and Matthieu de Oliveira, OpenEdition (Paris, 2015), 205–15.

Fielding, Henry, 'An Enquiry into the Causes of the Late Increase of Robbers', 1751, in *An Enquiry into the Causes of the Late Increase of Robbers and Related Writings*, ed. Malvin Zirker, Oxford University Press (Oxford, 1988), 75–174.

Fiori, Stefano, 'Individuals and Self-Interest in Adam Smith's Wealth of Nations', *Cahiers d'économie politique* 49 (2005), 19–31.

Fleischacker, Samuel, *A Third Concept of Liberty: Judgment and Freedom in Kant and Adam Smith*, Princeton University Press (Princeton, 1999).

Foreign Essays on Agriculture and Arts consisting chiefly of the Most Curious Discoveries made in the Several Provinces of France, Flanders, Germany, Switzerland, etc. and Communicated to the Learned in those Countries for the Improvement of British Husbandry (London, 1766).

Forster, John, *Englands Happiness Increased, or, A Sure and Easie Remedy against all Succeeding Dear Years* (London, 1664).

Forster, Robert, 'The Noble as Landlord in the Region of Toulouse at the End of the Old Regime', *Journal of Economic History* 17 (1957), 224–44.

Foster, Nelson and Linda S. Cordell, eds., *Chillies to Chocolate: Food the Americas Gave the World*, University of Arizona Press (Tucson, 1992).

Foucault, Michel, *Discipline and Punish: The Birth of the Prison*, trans. Alan Sheridan, Penguin (London, 1991).

Foucault, Michel, *History of Sexuality*, trans. Robert Hurley, Random House (New York, 1978).

Foucault, Michel, *Security, Territory, Population: Lectures at the Collège de France, 1977–1978*, ed. Michel Senellart, trans. Graham Burchell, Palgrave Macmillan (New York, 2009).

Foucault, Michel, 'The Subject and Power', *Critical Inquiry* 8:4 (1982), 777–95.

Fox, Adam, 'Food, Drink and Social Distinction in Early Modern England', in *Remaking English Society: Social Relations and Social Change in Early Modern England*, ed. S. Hindle, A. Shepard and J. Walter, Boydell & Brewer (Woodbridge, 2013), 165–87.

Frangsmyr, Tore, J. L. Heilbron and Robin Rider, eds., *The Quantifying Spirit in the Eighteenth Century*, University of California Press (Berkeley, 1990).

Frauenzimmer-Lexikon (Leipzig, 1715).

Frost, Alan, 'The Antipodean Exchange: European Horticulture and Imperial Designs', in *Visions of Empire: Voyages, Botany, and Representations of Nature*, ed. David Philip Miller and Peter Hanns Reill, Cambridge University Press (Cambridge, 1996), 58–79.

Frost, John, *The Book of Travels in Africa, from the Earliest Ages to the Present Time* (New York, 1848).

Fryer, John, *A New Account of East India and Persia being Nine Years' Travels, 1672–1681*, ed. W. Crooke, 3 vols., Hakluyt Society (London, 1909–15).

Gadd, Carl-Johan, 'On the Edge of a Crisis: Sweden in the 1840s', in *When the Potato Failed: Causes and Effects of the 'Last' European Subsistence Crisis, 1845–1850*, ed. Cormac Ó Gráda, Richard Paping and Eric Vanhaute, Brepols (Turnhout, 2007), 313–42.

Gallagher, Catherine and Stephen Greenblatt, 'The Potato in the Materialist Imagination', in *Practicing New Historicism*, University of Chicago Press (Chicago, 2000), 110–35.

Gallego, José Andrés, *El motín de Esquilache, América y Europa*, Consejo Superior de Investigaciones Científicas (Madrid, 2003).

Galli, Marika, *La conquête alimentaire du Nouveau Monde. Pratiques et représentations franco-italiennes des nouveaux produits du XVIe au XVIIIe siècle*, L'Harmattan (Paris, 2016).

Galloway, J. H., 'Agricultural Reform and the Enlightenment in Late Colonial Brazil', *Agricultural History* 53:4 (1979), 763–79.

Gandhi, Leela, *Affective Communities: Anticolonial Thought, Fin-de-Siècle Radicalism, and the Politics of Friendship*, Duke University Press (Durham, 2005).

García, Gregorio, *Orígen de los indios del Nuevo Mundo*, ed. Franklin Pease, Fondo de Cultura Economica (Mexico City, 1981 [1607]).

Garnett, T. and A. Wilkes, *Appetite for Change: Social, Economic and Environmental Transformations in China's Food System*, Food Climate Research Network, University of Oxford (Oxford, 2014), www.fcrn.org.uk/sites/default/files/fcrn_china_mapping_study_final_pdf_2014.pdf.

Gartner, Christian, *Horticultura* (Trondheim, 1694).

Gasparini, Danilo, *Polenta e formenton. Il mais nelle campagne venete tra XVI e XX secolo*, Cierre (Verona, 2002).

General Report of the Committee of Subscribers, to a Fund for the Relief of the Industrious Poor, Resident in the Cities of London and Westminster, the Borough of Southwark, and the Several Out Parishes of the Metropolis (London, 1800).

'Genève (commune)', *Dictionnaire Historique de la Suisse*, www.hls-dhs-dss.ch/tex tes/f/F2903.php.

Gentilcore, David, *Food and Health in Early Modern Europe: Diet, Medicine, and Society, 1450–1800*, Bloomsbury (London, 2016).

Gentilcore, David, *Italy and the Potato: A History, 1550–2000*, Bloomsbury (London, 2012).

George, Susan, *How the Other Half Dies: The Real Reasons for World Hunger*, Penguin (Harmondsworth, 1986 [1976]).

Gerarde, John, *Herball, or General History of Plantes* (London, 1597).

Gerarde, John, *The Herbal or General History of Plants. The Complete 1633 Edition as Revised and Enlarged by Thomas Johnson*, Dover (New York, 1975).

Gerbi, Antonello, *The Dispute of the New World: The History of a Polemic, 1750–1900*, trans. Jeremy Moyle, University of Pittsburgh Press (Pittsburgh, 1973 [1955]).

Gibson, Mark, *The Feeding of Nations: Redefining Food Security for the 21st Century*, CRC Press (Boca Raton, 2012).

Girdler, J. S., *Observations on the Pernicious Consequences of Forestalling, Regrating, and Ingrossing* (London, 1800).

Gitomer, Charles, *Potato and Sweetpotato in China: Systems, Constraints, and Potential*, International Potato Center (Lima, 1996).

Glaiser, Benjamin, 'French and Indian War Diary of Benjamin Glaiser of Ipswich, 1758–1760', *Essex Institute Historical Collections* 86 (1950), 65–92.

Goldie, Mark and Robert Wokler, eds., *The Cambridge History of Eighteenth-Century Political Thought*, Cambridge University Press (Cambridge, 2006).

Gómez de Ortega, Casimiro, *Elementos teóricos-prácticos de agricultura . . . traducidos del francés del célebre Mr. Duhamel de Monceau*, 2 vols. (Madrid, 1805).

Gonnella, Anna, 'L'assistenza pubblica a Trieste: l'alimentazione nell'Istituto dei Poveri (1818–1918)', in *Archivi per la stories dell'alimentazione*, ed. Paola Carucci, 3 vols. (Rome, 1995), III, 1590–1608.

González, Pedro María, *Tratado de las enfermedades de la gente de mar, en que se exponen sus causas, y los medios de precaverlas* (Madrid, 1805).

Good, John Mason, *Dissertation on the Best Means of Maintaining and Employing the Poor in Parish Work-Houses* (London, 1798).

Graves, Christine, *The Potato Treasure of the Andes: From Agriculture to Culture*, International Potato Center (Lima, 2001).

Gray, John, *Liberalism*, Open University Press (Milton Keynes, 1986).

Gray, Peter, 'The European Food Crisis and the Relief of Irish Famine, 1845–1850', in *When the Potato Failed: Causes and Effects of the 'Last' European Subsistence Crisis, 1845–1850*, ed. Cormac Ó Gráda, Richard Paping and Eric Vanhaute, Brepols (Turnhout, 2007), 95–107.

Gray, Peter, *Famine, Land and Politics: British Government and Irish Society, 1843–50*, Irish Academic Press (Dublin, 1999).

Grey, Elizabeth, Countess of Kent, *A Choice Manual* (London, 1687).

Grieco, Allen, 'The Social Politics of Pre-Linnaean Botanical Classification', *I Tatti Studies* 4 (1991), 131–49.

Grimaux, Éduard, *Lavoisier, 1743–1794* (Paris, 1888).

Grote, John, *An Examination of the Utilitarian Philosophy*, ed. Joseph Bickersteth Mayor (Cambridge, 1870).

Grove, Richard, 'The Great El Niño of 1789–93 and Its Global Consequences: Reconstructing an Extreme Climate Event in World Environmental History', *Medieval History Journal* 10:1–2 (2007), 75–98.

Guaman Poma de Ayala, Felipe, 'El primer nueva corónica y buen gobierno', 1615–16, The Guaman Poma Website, Det Kongelige Bibliotek, Copenhagen, www.kb.dk/permalink/2006/poma/info/en/frontpage.htm.

Guðmundsdóttir, Jóhanna Þ., 'Viðreisn garðræktar á síðari hluta 18. aldar: viðbrögð og viðhorf almennings á Íslandi', *Saga* 52:1 (2014), 9–41.

Guilding, Landsdown, *An Account of the Botanic Garden in the Island of St. Vincent from its Establishment to the Present Time* (Glasgow, 1825).

Guimarães Sá, Isabel dos, 'Circulation of Children in Eighteenth-Century Portugal', in *Abandoned Children*, ed. Catherine Panter-Brick and Malcolm Smith, Cambridge University Press (Cambridge, 2000), 27–40.

Gurney, Peter, '"Rejoicing in Potatoes": The Politics of Consumption in England during the "Hungry Forties"', *Past & Present* 203 (2009), 99–136.

Gutaker, Rafael, Clemens Weiß, David Ellis, Noelle Anglin, Sandra Knapp, José Luis Fernández-Alonso, Salomé Prat and Hernán Burbano, 'The Origins and Adaptation of European Potatoes Reconstructed from Historical Genomes', *Nature, Ecology & Evolution* 3 (2019), 1093–101.

Guthman, Julie and Patricia Allen, 'From "Old School" to "Farm-to-School": Neoliberalism from the Ground Up', *Agriculture and Human Values* 23 (2006), 401–15.

Haitin, Marcel, 'Prices, the Lima Market, and the Cultural Crisis of the Late Eighteenth Century in Peru', *Jahrbuch für Geschichte von Staat, Wirtschaft und Gesellschaft Latein-amerikas* 22 (1985), 167–99.

Hall, T., *The Queen's Royal Cookery* (London, 1709).

Halldórsson, Björn, *Korte Beretninger om nogle Forsög til Landvæsenets og i sær Havedyrkningens Forbedring i Island* (Copenhagen, 1765).

Hamilton, Alexander, *A New Account of the East Indies*, 2 vols. (London, 1744).

[Hamilton, John], *The Country-Man's Rudiments, or an Advice to the Farmers of East-Lothian* (Edinburgh, 1713 [1699]).

Hammer, Christopher, *Afhandling om Patatos: med endeel Tanker i Land-Huusholdningen* (Christiania, 1766).

Hammond, J. L. and Barbara Hammond, *The Village Labourer: A Study in the Government of England before the Reform Bill*, Longmans, Green and Co. (London, 1920).

Hammond, R. J., *Food and Agriculture in Britain, 1939–45: Aspects of Wartime Control*, Stanford University Press (Stanford, 1954).

Hancock, Simon, 'The Social Impact of the First World War in Pembrokeshire', DPhil, Cardiff University, 2015.

Hanway, Jonas, *A Candid Historical Account of the Hospital for the Reception of Exposed and Deserted Young Children* (London, 1759).

Hanway, Jonas, *The Great Advantage of Eating Pure and Genuine Bread, Comprehending the Heart of the Wheat* (London, 1773).

Harcout, Bernard, *The Illusion of Free Markets: Punishment and the Myth of Natural Order*, Harvard University Press (Cambridge, MA, 2011).

Harrison, Regina, *Signs, Songs and Memory in the Andes*, University of Texas Press (Austin, 1989).

Harsanyi, David John, *Nanny State: How Food Fascists, Teetotaling Do-Gooders, Priggish Moralists, and Other Boneheaded Bureaucrats are Turning America into a Nation of Children*, Broadway Books (New York, 2007).

Hartley, E. R., *How to Feed the Children* (Bradford, 1908).

Harvard School of Public Health, 'Public Health and the US Economy', 2012, www.hsph.harvard.edu/news/magazine/public-health-economy-election/.

Hawkes, J. G., 'N.I. Vavilov – The Man and his Work', *Biological Journal of the Linnaean Society* 39 (1990), 3–6.

Hawkes, J. G., *Potato Collecting Expeditions in Mexico and South America*, Imperial Bureau of Plant Breeding and Genetics, School of Agriculture (Cambridge, 1941).

Hawkes, J. G. and J. Francisco-Ortega, 'The Early History of the Potato in Europe', *Euphytica* 70 (1993), 1–7.

Hawkes, J. G. and J. Francisco-Ortega, 'The Potato in Spain during the Late Sixteenth Century,' *Economic Botany* 46:1 (1992), 86–97.

Helgi Library, 'Potato Consumption Per Capita in the World', 2011, www.helgilibrary.com/indicators/potato-consumption-per-capita/world/.

Helmhardt von Hohberg, Wolf, *Georgica Curiosa Aucta. Das ist, Umständlicher Bericht und klarer Unterricht von dem vermehrten und Verbesserten Adelichen Land- und Feld-Leben*, c.1688 (Nürnberg, 1716).

Helmhardt von Hohberg, Wolf, *Herrn von Hohbergs Georgica Curiosa Aucta. Oder: Adelichen Land und Feld-Lebens*, c.1688 (Nürnberg, 1715).

Helstocky, Carol, 'Recipe for the Nation: Reading Italian History through *La scienza in cucina* and *La cucina futurista*', *Food and Foodways* 11 (2003), 113–40.

Helstocky, Carol, 'The State, Health, and Nutrition', in *The Cambridge World History of Food*, ed. Kenneth Kiple and Kriemhild Coneè Ornelas, 2 vols. Cambridge University Press (Cambridge, 2001), II, 1577–84.

Henriksen, Ingrid, 'A Disaster Seen from the Periphery: The Case of Denmark', in *When the Potato Failed: Causes and Effects of the 'Last' European Subsistence Crisis, 1845–1850*, ed. Cormac Ó Gráda, Richard Paping and Eric Vanhaute, Brepols (Turnhout, 2007), 293–312.

Henry, David John, *The Complete English Farmer, or, A Practical System of Husbandry* (London, 1771).

Hertzberg, Peter Harboe, *Underretning for Bønder i Norge om den meget nyttige Jord-Frukt Potatos: at plante og bruge* (Bergen, 1774).

Hildesheim, Wilhelm, *Die Normal-Diät. Physiologisch-chemischer Versuch zu Ermittlung des normalen Nahrungsbedürfnisse der Menschen, behufs Aufstellung einer Normal-Diät, mit besonderer Rücksicht auf das Diät-Regulative des neuen Reglements für die Friedens-Garnison-Lazarethe, und die Natural-Verpflegung des Soldaten sowie auf die Verpflegung der Armen* (Berlin, 1856).

Hiler, David, 'La pomme de terre révolutionnaire', in *Regards sur la Révolution genevoise, 1792–1798*, ed. Louis Binz, Société d'Histoire et d'Archéologie de Genève (Geneva, 1992), 91–117.

Hirschman, Albert O., *The Passions and the Interests: Political Arguments for Capitalism before Its Triumph*, Princeton University Press (Princeton, 1997).

Historic Royal Palaces Blog, 'History of the Sweet Potato', 26 Nov. 2015, http://blog.hrp.org.uk/gardeners/history-of-sweet-potato.

Ho, Ping-Ti, 'The Introduction of American Food Plants into China', *American Anthropologist* 57:2 (1955), 191–201.

Hobbes, Thomas, *Leviathan, or, The Matter, Forme, and Power of a Common Wealth, Ecclesiasticall and Civil* (London, 1651).

Hobsbawm, E. J. and George Rudé, *Captain Swing*, Lawrence & Wishart (Woking, 1969).

Hochstrasser, T. J., 'Physiocracy and the Politics of Laissez-Faire', in *The Cambridge History of Eighteenth-Century Political Thought*, ed. Mark Goldie and Robert Wokler, Cambridge University Press (Cambridge, 2006), 419–42.

Hoffman, Philip T., *Growth in a Traditional Society: The French Countryside 1450–1815*, Princeton University Press (Princeton, 1996).

Holland, Michael, 'Swing Revisited: The Swing Project', *Family & Community History* 7:2 (2004), 87–100.

Hont, Istvan, *Jealousy of Trade: International Competition and the Nation-State in Historical Perspective*, Harvard University Press (Cambridge, MA, 2005).

Horrell, Sara and Deborah Oxley, 'Hasty Pudding versus Tasty Bread: Regional Variations in Diet and Nutrition during the Industrial Revolution', *Local Population Studies* 88:1 (2012), 9–30.

House of Commons Sessional Papers of the Eighteenth Century 1715–1800, House of Commons Parliamentary Papers, Parlipapers.chadwyck.co.uk.

Housekeeper's Receipt Book, or, Repository of Domestic Knowledge (London, 1813).

Howard, Henry, *England's Newest Way in All Sorts of Cookery* (London, 1708).

Huarte de San Juan, Juan, *Examen de Ingenios, or The Examination of Mens Wits* (London, 1594).

Hughes, William, *The American Physitian, or, A Treatise of the Roots, Plants, Trees, Shrubs, Fruit, Herbs, &c. Growing in the English Plantations in America* (London, 1672).

Hunter, Alexander, *Culina Famulatrix Medicinae: Or, Receipts in Cookery, Worthy the Notice of those Medical Practitioners, who Ride in their Chariots with a Footman Behind and who Receive Two-guinea Fees from their Rich and Luxurious Patients* (York, 1804).

Hutcheson, Francis, *Inquiry into the Original of Our Ideas of Beauty and Virtue* (London, 1725).

Hutchison, E. P., 'Swedish Population Thought in the Eighteenth Century', *Population Studies* 12:1 (1959), 81–102.

Ibáñez Rodríguez, Santiago, 'El diezmo en la Rioja (XVI–XVIII)', *Brocar* 18 (1994), 189–222.

Ingebretson, Britta, 'The *Tuhao* and the Bureaucrat: The Qualia of "Quality" in Rural China', *Signs and Society* 5:2 (2017), 243–68.

Instrucção sobre a cultura das batatas, traduzida do inglez por ordem superior (Lisbon, 1800).

Jaffe, Catherine, '"Noticia de la vida y obras del Conde de Rumford" (1802) by María Lorenza de los Ríos, Marquesa de Fuerte-Híjar: Authorizing a Space for Female Charity', *Studies in Eighteenth Century Culture* 38 (2009), 91–115.

Jansky, S. H., L. P. Jin, K. Y. Xie, C. H. Xie and D. M. Spooner, 'Potato Production and Breeding in China', *Potato Research* 52:57 (2009), 57–65.

Jarosz, Lucy, 'Defining World Hunger: Scale and Neoliberal Ideology in International Food Security Policy Discourse, *Food, Culture & Society* 14:1 (2011), 117–39.

Jefferson, Thomas, 'Summary of Public Service', after 2 Sept. 1800, *The Papers of Thomas Jefferson Digital Edition* 32: *1 June 1800–16 February 1801*, ed. Barbara Oberg and J. Jefferson Looney, University of Virginia Press (Charlottesville, 2008–16), 124, http://rotunda.upress.virginia.edu/founders/TSJN-01–32-02–0080.

Jia, Ruixue, 'Weather Shocks, Sweet Potatoes and Peasant Revolts in Historical China', *Economic Journal* 124:575 (2013), 92–118.

Jiménez de la Espada, Marcos, ed., *Relaciones geográficas de las Indias: Perú*, 3 vols., Biblioteca de Autores Españoles (Madrid, 1965).

Jing, Jun, 'Introduction: Food, Children, and Social Change in Contemporary China', in *Feeding China's Little Emperors: Food, Children, and Social Change*, ed. Jun Jing, Stanford University Press (Stanford, 2000), 1–26.

Jones-Brydges, Harford, *Account of the Transactions of his Majesty's Mission to the Court of Persia in the Years 1807–11* (London, 1834).

Jones, Robert, *Provincial Development in Russia: Catherine II and Jacob Sievers*, Rutgers University Press (New Brunswick, 1984).

Jonsson, Fredrik, *Enlightenment's Frontier: The Scottish Highlands and the Origins of Environmentalism*, Yale University Press (New Haven, 2013).

Junta Pública de la Real Sociedad Económica de Amigos del País de Valencia (Valencia, 1801).

Jütte, Robert, *Poverty and Deviance in Early Modern Europe*, Cambridge University Press (Cambridge,1994).

Kaldy, M. S., 'Protein Yield of Various Crops as Related to Protein Value', *Economic Botany* 26:2 (1972), 142–4.

Kamminga, Harmke, 'Nutrition for the People, or the Fate of Jacob Moleschott's Contest for a Humanist Science', in *The Science and Culture of Nutrition, 1840–1940*, ed. Harmke Kamminga and Andrew Cunningham, Rodopi (Amsterdam, 1995), 15–47.

Kamminga, Harmke and Andrew Cunningham, eds., *The Science and Culture of Nutrition, 1840–1940*, Rodopi (Amsterdam, 1995).

Kant, Immanuel, *Metaphysics of Morals*, trans. and ed. Mary Gregor, intro. Roger Sullivan, Cambridge University Press (Cambridge, 1996).

Kant, Immanuel, 'What Does it Mean to Orient Oneself in Thinking?', 1786, in *Religion and Rational Theology, The Cambridge Edition of the Works of Immanuel Kant*, ed. A. Wood and G. di Giovanni, Cambridge University Press (Cambridge, 1996), 1–18.

Kant, Immanuel, 'What is Enlightenment?', 1784, German History in Documents and Images, http://ghdi.ghi-dc.org/sub_document.cfm?document_id=3589.

Kaplan, Steven, *Bread, Politics and Political Economy in the Reign of Louis XV*, 2 vols., Springer (The Hague, 1976).

Kaplan, Steven, *The Stakes of Regulation: Perspectives on Bread, Politics and Political Economy Forty Years Later*, Anthem Press (London, 2015).

Kåre, Lunden, ed., *Norges landbrukshistorie II: 1350–1814: Frå svartedauden til 17. Mai*, Samlaget (Oslo, 2002).

Kaufmann, Franz-Xavier, *Variations of the Welfare State: Great Britain, Sweden, France and Germany between Capitalism and Socialism*, trans. Thomas Dunlap, Springer (Heidelberg, 2013).

Kaye, John William, *The Life and Correspondence of Major-General Sir John Malcolm*, 2 vols. (London, 1856).

Keith, George Skene, *A General View of the Agriculture of Aberdeenshire* (Aberdeen, 1811).

Khodnev, A. I., *Istoriia Imperatorskago Vol'nago Ekonomicheskago Obshchestva s 1765 do 1865* (St. Petersburg, 1865).

Khondker, Habibul, 'Famine Policies in Pre-British India and the Question of Moral Economy', *South Asia: Journal of South Asian Studies* 9:1 (1986), 25–40.

King, Janet and Joanne Slavin, 'White Potatoes, Human Health, and Dietary Guidance', *Advances in Nutrition* 4:3 (2013), 393S–401S.

Kiple, Kenneth, *A Moveable Feast: Ten Millennia of Food Globalization*, Cambridge University Press (Cambridge, 2007).

Kiple, Kenneth and Kriemhild Coneè Ornelas, eds., *The Cambridge World History of Food*, 2 vols., Cambridge University Press (Cambridge, 2001).

Kisbán, Eszter, 'The Beginnings of Potato Cultivation in Transylvania and Hungary: Government Policy and Spontaneous Process', in *The Origins and Development of Food Policies in Europe*, ed. John Burnett and Derek Oddy, Leicester University Press (London, 1994), 178–93.

Klein, Jakob, 'Connecting with the Countryside? "Alternative" Food Movements with Chinese Characteristics', in *Ethical Eating in the Postsocialist and Socialist World*, ed. Yuson Jung, Jakob Klein and Melissa Caldwell, University of California Press (Berkeley, 2014), 116–43.

Knight, Roger and Martin Wilcox, *Sustaining the Fleet, 1793–1815: War, the British Navy and the Contractor State*, Boydell & Brewer (Woodbridge, 2010).

Knight, Thomas Andrew, 'On Raising New and Early Varieties of the Potatoe (*Solanum Tuberosum*)', 6 Jan. 1807, *Transactions of the Horticultural Society of London* (London, 1812), 57–9.

Koenker, Roger, 'Was Bread Giffen? The Demand for Food in England Circa 1790', *Review of Economics and Statistics* 59:2 (1977), 225–9.

Koerner, Lisbet, *Linnaeus: Nature and Nation*, Harvard University Press (Cambridge, MA, 1999).

Komlos, John, 'The New World's Contribution to Food Consumption during the Industrial Revolution', *Journal of European Economic History* 27:1 (1998), 67–82.

Kreuger, Rita, 'Mediating Progress in the Provinces: Central Authority, Local Elites, and Agrarian Societies in Bohemia and Moravia', *Austrian History Yearbook* 35 (2004), 49–79.

Kümin, Beat, *Drinking Matters: Public Houses and Social Exchange in Early Modern Central Europe*, Palgrave Macmillan (Basingstoke, 2007).

Labat, Jean-Baptiste, *Nouveau voyage aux îles de l'Amerique* (Paris, 1722).

Lacroix, Anne, *Transformations du procès de travail agricole: incidences de l'industrialisation sur les conditions de travail paysannes*, Institut de Recherche Économique et de Planification (Grenoble, 1981).

Lafuente, Antonio, 'Enlightenment in an Imperial Context: Local Science in the Late Eighteenth-Century Hispanic World, *Osiris* 15 (2000), 155–73.

Lagrange, Joseph-Louis, 'Essai d'arithmétique politique sur les premiers besoins de l'intérieur de la république', 1796, in *Oeuvres de Lagrange*, ed. J.-A. Serret, 14 vols. (Paris, 1867–92), VII, 571–82.

Lang, James, *Notes of a Potato Watcher*, Texas A&M University Press (College Station, 2001).

Lang, Tim and Michael Heasman, *Food Wars: The Global Battle for Mouths, Minds and Markets*, Earthscan (London, 2004).

Langer, William, 'American Foods and Europe's Population Growth 1750–1850', *Journal of Social History* 8:2 (1975), 51–66.

Langworthy, C. F., *Potatoes and Other Root Crops as Food*, Government Printing Office (Washington, 1907).

Larriba, Elisabel, 'Un intento de reforma agraria por y para las clases productoras: el *Semanario de Agricultura y Artes Dirigido a los Párrocos* (1797–1808)', *Brocar* 23 (1999), 87–117.

Larumbe, Josef María, *Epítome cristiano de agricultura* (Pamplona, 1800).

Las Casas, Bartolomé de, *Apologética historia sumaria*, c.1552, in *Obras escogidas*, ed. Juan Pérez de Tudela Bueso, 5 vols., Biblioteca de Autores Españoles (Madrid, 1958), III.

Laufer, Berthold, *American Plant Migration, part 1: The Potato*, Field Museum of Natural History Anthropological Series Publication 418 (Chicago, 1938).

Laurell, Axel, *Lyhykäinen kirjoitus potatesten eli maan-päronain wiljelemisestä*, Säilyttämisestä ja hyödytyxestä huonen hallituxesa (Turku, 1773).

Laurence, Edward, *The Duty of a Steward to his Lord* (London, 1727).

Lavery, Brian, ed., *Shipboard Life and Organisation, 1731–1815*, Ashgate (Aldershot, 1998).

Lavoisier, Antoine Laurent, *Oeuvres de Lavoisier*, 6 vols. (Paris, 1864–93).

Lebeschu de la Bastays, M., *L'Ami des navigateurs, ou Instruction destinée à préserver les gens de mer des maladies qui sont propres à leur état, & à les faire jouir d'une aussi bonne santé sur les vaisseaux qu'à terre* (Nantes, 1787).

Lee, Seung-joon, 'Taste in Numbers: Science and the Food Problem in Republican Guangzhou, 1927–1937', *Twentieth-Century China* 35:2 (2010), 81–103.

Legrand d'Aussy, Pierre-Jean-Baptiste, *Histoire de la vie privée des Français*, 3 vols. (Paris, 1782).

Leisering, Lutz, 'Nation State and Social Policy: An Ideational and Political History', introductory chapter to Franz-Xavier Kaufmann, *Variations of the Welfare State: Great Britain, Sweden, France and Germany between Capitalism and Socialism*, trans. Thomas Dunlap, Springer (Heidelberg, 2013), 1–22.

Lémery, Louis, *Traité des aliments, où l'on trouve la différence, & le choix qu'on en doit faire*, ed. Jacques Jean Bruhier, third edition, 2 vols. (Paris, 1755).

Lemire, Beverly, '"Men of the World": British Mariners, Consumer Practice, and Material Culture in the Era of Global Trade, c. 1660–1800', *Journal of British Studies* 54:2 (2015), 288–319.

Lemnius, Levinus, *The Touchstone of Complexions*, trans. T.N. (London, 1633).

Leon Pinelo, Antonio, *Question moral si el chocolate quebranta el ayuno elesiástico* (Madrid, 1638).

Letters and Papers on Agriculture, Planting, &c. Selected from the Correspondence-Book of the Society Instituted at Bath for the Encouragement of Agriculture, Arts, Manufactures, and Commerce (Bath and London, 1783–8).

Lindroth. Sten, *Kungl. Svenska vetenskapsakademiens historia 1739–1818*, part I, vol. I: *Tiden intill Wargentins död (1783)*, Almquist & Wiksell (Stockholm, 1967).

Linnaeus, Carl, *Dissertatio Academicum de Pane Diaetetico* (Uppsala, 1757).

Linnaeus, Carl, *Skånska resa år 1749* (Stockholm, 1751).

Linschoten, J. H., *The Voyage of John Huyghen van Linschoten to the East Indies. From the Old English Translation of 1598*, ed. A. C. Burnell and P. A. Tiele, 2 vols., Hakluyt Society (London, 1885).

Liu, Jiancheng, Hu Lianquan, Yang Jingwu and Shu Xiaojun, *Sichuan Cuisine for the Masses* [大众川菜 *Dazhong Chuancai*], Sichuan Science and Technology Publishing House (Chengdu, 1995).

Lloyd, David, 'The Political Economy of the Potato', *Nineteenth-Century Contexts* 29:2–3 (2007), 311–35.

Lo, Vivienne and Penelope Barrett, 'Cooking up Fine Remedies: On the Culinary Aesthetic in a Sixteenth-Century Chinese Materia Medica', *Medical History* 49:4 (2005), 395–422.

[Lobb, Theophilus], *Primitive Cookery: or the Kitchen Garden Display'd* (London, 1767).

Locke, John, *Second Treatise of Government*, ed. Joseph Carrig, Barnes & Noble (New York, 2004 [1690]).

Long, Janet, ed., *Conquista y comida: consecuencias del encuentro de dos mundos*, Universidad Nacional Autónoma de México (Mexico City, 1997).

Lorry, Anne-Charles, *Essai sur les alimens, pour servir de commentaire aux livres diététiques d'Hippocrate* (Paris, 1757).

Louderback, Lisbeth and Bruce Pavlik, 'Starch Granule Evidence for the Earliest Potato Use in North America', *Proceedings of the National Academy of Sciences* 114:29 (2017), 7606–10.

Lowood, Henry, *Patriotism, Profit and the Promotion of Science in the German Enlightenment: The Economic and Scientific Societies, 1760–1815*, Garland (New York, 1991).

Lunan, John, *Hortus Jamaicensis, or a Botanical Description, (According to the Linnean System) and an Account of the Virtues, &c. of its Indigenous Plants Hitherto Known, as also of the Most Useful Exotics*, 2 vols. (Jamaica, 1814).

Macdonald, Janet, *British Navy's Victualling Board, 1793–1815: Management Competence and Incompetence*, Boydell & Brewer (Woodbridge, 2010).

Macdonald, Janet, *Feeding Nelson's Navy: The True Story of Food at Sea in the Georgian Era*, Frontline (London, 2014).

Machiavelli, Niccolò, *The Prince*, trans. and ed. Peter Bondanella, intro. Maurizio Viroli, Oxford University Press (Oxford, 2005 [1532]).

Mackay, David, *In the Wake of Cook: Exploration, Science and Empire, 1780–1801*, St. Martin's Press (New York, 1985).

Mackenzie, Fiona, 'Contested Ground: Colonial Narratives and the Kenyan Environment, 1920–1945', *Journal of Southern African Studies* 26:4 (2000), 697–718.

Mackenzie, Henry, *Prize Essays and Transactions of the Highland Society of Scotland* 1 (Edinburgh, 1799).

Magazzini, Vitale, *Coltivazione toscana del molto rever. P.D. Vitale Magazzini Monaco Vallombrosano*, third edition (Florence, 1669).

Mahlerwein, Gunter, 'The Consequences of the Potato Blight in Southern Germany', in *When the Potato Failed: Causes and Effects of the 'Last' European Subsistence Crisis, 1845–1850*, ed. Cormac Ó Gráda, Richard Paping and Eric Vanhaute, Brepols (Turnhout, 2007), 213–21.

Malanima, Paolo, 'Urbanization', in *The Cambridge Economic History of Modern Europe*, vol. I: *1700–1850*, ed. Stephen Broadberry and K. O'Rourke, Cambridge University Press (Cambridge, 2010), 235–63.

Malte-Brun, Conrad, *Universal Geography, or a Description of all the Parts of the World, on a New Plan, According to the Great Natural Divisions of the Globe*, 6 vols. (Edinburgh, 1822).

Malthus, Thomas Robert, *An Essay on the Principle of Population*, 1798, ed. Philip Appleman, Norton (New York, 1974).

Malthus, Thomas Robert, *An Essay on the Principle of Population. The 1803 Edition*, ed. Shannon Stimson, Yale University Press (New Haven, 2018).

Malthus, Thomas Robert, 'Newenham on the State of Ireland', *Edinburgh Review or Critical Journal* 14 (Edinburgh, 1809).

Mandeville, Bernard, *The Fable of the Bees: Or, Private Vices, Publick Benefits* (London, 1714).

Manetti, Saverio, *Delle specie diverse di frumento e di pane siccome della panizzazione* (Florence, 1765).

Markham, Gervase, *The Husbandman's Jewel* (London, 1695).

Marquis de Chastellux, *De la félicité publique, ou Considérations sur le sort des hommes*, 2 vols. (Amsterdam, 1772).

Marquis de Langle (Jean Marie Jérome Fleuriot), *Voyage de Figaro en Espagne* (Seville, 1785).

Marshall, Woodville, 'Provision Ground and Plantation Labor in Four Windward Islands: Competition for Resources during Slavery', in *Cultivation and Culture: Labor and the Shaping of Slave Life in the Americas*, ed. Ira Berlin and Philip Morgan, University Press of Virginia (Charlottesville, 1993), 203–20.

Martin, John, *The Development of Modern Agriculture: British Farming since 1931*, Palgrave Macmillan (Basingstoke, 2000).

Marx, Karl, 'The Eighteenth Brumaire of Louis Napoleon', 1852, in *Marx's Eighteenth Brumaire: (Post)modern Interpretations*, ed. Mark Cowling and James Martin, trans. Terrell Carver, Pluto Press (London, 2002), 19–110.

Mason, Charlotte, *The Lady's Assistant for Regulating and Supplying the Table: Being a Complete System of Cookery* (London, 1787).

Matta, Raúl, 'Valuing Native Eating: The Modern Roots of Peruvian Food Heritage', *Anthropology of Food* (2013), https://journals.openedition.org/aof/7361.

Matthee, Rudolph, 'Patterns of Food Consumption in Early Modern Iran' (2016), *Oxford Handbooks Online*, www.oxfordhandbooks.com/view/10.1093/oxfordhb/9780199935369.001.0001/oxfordhb-9780199935369-e-13.

Maxwell, Simon, 'Food Security: A Post-Modern Perspective', *Food Policy* 21:2 (1996), 155–70.

Mayer, E., *The Articulated Peasant*, Westview (Boulder, 2002).

Mazumdar, Sucheta, 'The Impact of New World Food Crops on the Diet and Economy of China and India, 1600–1900', in *Food in Global History*, ed. Raymond Grew, Westview (Boulder, 1999), 58–78.

McCann, James, *Maize and Grace: Africa's Encounter with a New World Crop, 1500–2000*, Harvard University Press (Cambridge, MA, 2005).

McCann, James, *Stirring the Pot: A History of African Cuisine*, Ohio State University Press (Athens, 2009).

McClellan III, James, *Colonialism and Science: Saint Domingue in the Old Regime*, University of Chicago Press (Chicago, 2010).

McClellan III, James and François Regourd, 'The Colonial Machine: French Science and Colonization in the Ancien Regime', *Osiris* 15 (2000), 31–50.

McClure, Norman, ed., *The Letters of John Chamberlain*, 2 vols., American Philosophical Society (Philadelphia, 1939).

McCook, Stuart, *States of Nature: Science, Agriculture, and Environment in the Spanish Caribbean, 1760–1940*, University of Texas Press (Austin, 2002).

McCormick, Ted, 'Population: Modes of Seventeenth-Century Demographic Thought', in *Mercantalism Reimagined: Political Economy in Early Modern Britain and its Empire*, ed. Philip Stern and Carl Wennerlind, Oxford University Press (Oxford, 2014), 25–45.

McCulloch, John Ramsay, 'Cottage System', *Supplement to the Fourth, Fifth, and Sixth Editions of the Encyclopaedia Britannica* (Edinburgh, 1824), III, 378–87.

McMahon, Darrin, *Happiness: A History*, Atlantic Monthly (New York, 2006).

McNeil, William, 'How the Potato Changed the World's History', *Social Research* 66:1 (1999), 67–83.

Mehta, Pratap Bhanu, 'Self-Interest and Other Interests', in *The Cambridge Companion to Adam Smith*, ed. Knud Haakonssen, Cambridge University Press (Cambridge, 2006), 246–69.

Meinert, C. A., *Armee- und Volks-Ernährung. Ein Versuch Professor C. von Voit's Ernährungstheorie für die Praxis zu verwerthen*, 2 vols. (Berlin, 1880).

Meléndez, Mariselle, *Deviant and Useful Citizens: The Cultural Production of the Female Body in Eighteenth-Century Peru*, Vanderbilt University Press (Nashville, 2011).

Melon, Jean-François, *Essai politique sur le commerce* (n.p., 1736).

Meneghello, Laura, *Jacob Moleschott: A Transnational Biography – Science, Politics, and Popularization in Nineteenth-Century Europe*, Transcript (Bielefeld, 2017).

Meredith, David and Deborah Oxley, 'Food and Fodder: Feeding England, 1700–1900', *Past & Present* 222:1 (2013), 163–214.

Messer, Ellen, 'Three Centuries of Changing European Tastes for the Potato', in *Food Preferences and Tastes: Continuity and Change*, ed. Helen MacBeth, Berghahn Books (New York, 1997), 101–14.

Metodo facile, e sperimentato per coltivare le patate (Florence, 1801).

Michiel, Pietro Antonio, *I cinque libri di piante*, Real Instituto Veneto di Scienze, Lettere ed Arti (Venice, 1940 [*c*.1570]).

Mill, James, 'Colony', *Supplement to the Encyclopaedia Britannica* (London, 1825), 257–73.

Miller, David Philip and Peter Hanns Reill, eds., *Visions of Empire: Voyages, Botany, and Representations of Nature*, Cambridge University Press (Cambridge, 1996).

Miller, Judith, *Mastering the Market: The State and the Grain Trade in Northern France, 1700–1860*, Cambridge University Press (Cambridge, 1999).

Miller, Philip, *The Gardeners Dictionary*, 3 vols. (London, 1754).

Ministry of Agriculture and Rural Affairs of the People's Republic of China, 'China to Position Potato as Staple Food', 8 Jan. 2015, http://english.agri.gov.cn/news/dqnf/201501/t20150109_24781.htm.

Ministry of National Service, 1917–1919, Report upon the Physical Examination of Men of Military Age by National Service Medical Boards from November 1st 1917–October 31st 1918, *Parliamentary Papers*, 1919, 26:307, Cmd. 504.

Miodunka, Piotr, 'L'essor de la culture de la pomme de terre au sud de la Pologne jusqu'au mileau du XIXe siècle', *Histoire & Sociétés Rurales* 41:2 (2014), 67–84.

Mitchison, Rosalind, 'The Old Board of Agriculture (1793–1822)', *English Historical Review* 74:290 (1959), 41–69.

Moffet, Thomas, *Health's Improvement, or, Rule Comprizing and Discovering the Nature, Method, and Manner of Preparing all sorts of Food Used in this Nation* (London, 1655).

Moheau, Jean-Baptiste, *Recherches et considérations sur la population de la France* (Paris, 1778).

Moleschott, Jacob, *Der Kreislauf des Lebens*, 2 vols. (Gießen, 1887).

Moleschott, Jacob, *Lehre der Nahrungsmittel: Für das Volk* (Erlangen, 1858).

Molina, Cristóbal de, *Relación de las fábulas y ritos de los incas*, ed. Paloma Jiménez del Campo, Verveurt (Madrid, 2010 [*c*.1573]).

Molina, Juan Ignacio, *Compendio de la historia civil del reyno de Chile* (Madrid, 1795).

Molinier, Alain, *Stagnations et croissance: Le Vivarais aux XVIIe–SVIIIe siècles*, L'École des Hautes Études en Sciences Sociales (Paris, 1985).

Molokhovets, Elena, *Classic Russian Cooking: Elena Molokhovets' A Gift to Young Housewives*, ed. and trans. Joyce Toomre, Indiana University Press (Bloomington, 1992).

Monardes, Nicolás, *Joyfull News out of the New-found Worlde* (London, 1596).

Montesquieu (Charles-Louis de Secondat), *De l'Esprit des loix*, 1748, in *Oeuvres complètes de Montesquieu*, ed. Édouard Laboulaye (Paris, 1876), III.

More, Hannah, *The Cottage Cook or, Mrs. Jones's Cheap Dishes: Shewing the Way to do Much Good with Little Money* (London, [1795]).

More, Hannah, *The Way to Plenty, Or, the Second Part of Tom White* (London, 1796).

Morel, Marie-France, 'Children', in *Encyclopedia of the Enlightenment*, ed. Michel Delon and Philip Stewart, trans. Gwen Wells, Routledge (London, 2001), 243–7.

Morel, Marie-France, 'Théories et pratiques de l'allaitement en France au XVIIIe siècle', *Annales de démographie historique* 1 (1976), 393–427.

Morell, Mats L. W., 'Diet in Sweden during Industrialization, 1870–1939: Changing Trends and the Emergence of Food Policy', in *The Origins and Development of Food Policies in Europe*, ed. John Burnett and Derek Oddy, Leicester University Press (London, 1994), 232–48.

Morineau, Michel, 'The Potato in the Eighteenth Century', in *Food and Drink in History*, ed. Robert Forster and Orest Ranum, trans. Elborg Forster and Patricia Ranum, Johns Hopkins University Press (Baltimore, 1979), 17–36.

Moris, Jon, *Extension Alternatives in Tropical Africa*, Overseas Development Institute (London, 1991).

Morren, Charles, *Belgique Horticole*, 35 vols. (Liège, 1853).

Moskoff, William, *The Bread of Affliction: The Food Supply in the USSR during World War II*, Cambridge University Press (Cambridge, 1990).

Moyer, Johanna, '"The Food Police": Sumptuary Prohibitions on Food in the Reformation', in *Food and Faith in Christian Culture*, ed. Ken Albala and Trudy Eden, Columbia University Press (New York, 2011), 59–81.

Mt. Pleasant, Jane, 'The Paradoxes of Plows and Productivity: An Agronomic Comparison of Cereal Grain Production under Iroquois Hoe Culture and European Plow Culture in the Seventeenth and Eighteenth Centuries', *Agricultural History* 85:4 (2011), 460–92.

Muldrew, Craig, *Food, Energy and the Creation of Industriousness: Work and Material Culture in Agrarian England, 1550–1780*, Cambridge University Press (Cambridge, 2011).

Murphey, Rhoads, 'Provisioning Istanbul: The State and Subsistence in the Early Modern Middle East', *Food and Foodways*, 2:1 (1988), 217–63.

Murphy, Rose and Lee Kass, *Evolution of Plant Breeding at Cornell University*, Internet-First University Press (Ithaca, 2007).

Murra, John V., *The Economic Organization of the Inka State, Research in Economic Anthropology, Supplement 1*, JAI Press (Greenwich, CT, 1980).

Murra, John V., 'Rite and Crop in the Inca State', in *Culture in History: Essays in Honor of Paul Radin*, ed. Stanley Diamond, Octagon (New York, 1960), 393–407.

Murray, Laura May Kaplan, 'New World Food Crops in China: Farms, Food, and Families in the Wei River Valley, 1650–1910', DPhil., University of Pennsylvania, 1985.

Murrell, John, *A New Book of Cookerie* (London, 1617).

Nadeau, Carolyn, *Food Matters: Alonso Quijano's Diet and the Discourse of Food in Early Modern Spain*, University of Toronto Press (Toronto, 2016).

Nally, David, 'The Biopolitics of Food Provisioning', *Transactions of the Institute of British Geographers* 36 (2011), 37–53.

Nanny State Index, http://nannystateindex.org/.

Naranjo Vargas, Plutarco, 'La comida andina antes del encuentro', in *Conquista y comida: consecuencias del encuentro de dos mundos*, ed. Janet Long, Universidad Nacional Autónoma de México (Mexico City, 1997), 31–43.

Narayanan, Divya, 'Cultures of Food and Gastronomy in Mughal and Post-Mughal India', Inaugural dissertation, Ruprecht-Karls-Universität Heidelberg, 2015.

National Cancer Institute, 'Acrylamide and Cancer Risk', 2017, www.cancer.gov /about-cancer/causes-prevention/risk/diet/acrylamide-fact-sheet.

Netting, Robert McC., *Balancing on an Alp: Ecological Change & Continuity in a Swiss Mountain Community*, Cambridge University Press (Cambridge, 1981).

Netting, Robert McC., *Smallholders, Householders: Farm Families and the Ecology of Intensive, Sustainable Agriculture*, Stanford University Press (Stanford, 1993).

New London County Selectmen, *Agreeable to an Act of Assembly of the State of Connecticut, for Regulating the Prices of Labour, etc.* (New London, 1778).

New Zealand Ministry of Health, 'Eating and Activity Guidelines', 2 Aug. 2018, www.health.govt.nz/our-work/eating-and-activity-guidelines.

Nieto Olarte, Mauricio, *Orden Natural y orden social: Ciencia y política en el Semanario del Nuevo Reino de Granada*, Instituto Colombiano de Antropología e Historia (Madrid, 2007).

Nitti, Francesco S., 'The Food and Labour-Power of Nations', *Economic Journal* 6:21 (1896), 30–63.

Nuñez de Oria, Francisco, *Regimiento y aviso de sanidad, que trata de todos los generos de alimentos y del regimiento della* (Medina del Campo, 1586).

Nunn, Nathan and Nancy Qian, 'The Potato's Contribution to Population and Urbanization: Evidence from a Historical Experiment', *Quarterly Journal of Economics* 126 (2011), 593–650.

O'Connor, Kaori, 'The King's Christmas Pudding: Globalization, Recipes, and the Commodities of Empire', *Journal of Global History* 4 (2009), 127–55.

Ó Gráda, Cormac, 'Ireland's Great Famine: An Overview', in *When the Potato Failed: Causes and Effects of the 'Last' European Subsistence Crisis, 1845–1850*, ed. Cormac Ó Gráda, Richard Paping and Eric Vanhaute, Brepols (Turnhout, 2007), 43–57.

Ó Gráda, Cormac, Richard Paping and Eric Vanhaute, eds., *When the Potato Failed: Causes and Effects of the 'Last' European Subsistence Crisis, 1845–1850*, Brepols (Turnhout, 2007).

Occhiolini, Giovanni Battista, *Memorie sopra il meraviglioso frutto americano chiamato volgarmente patata* (Rome, 1784).

Ochoa, Carlos, 'Potato Collecting Expeditions in Chile, Bolivia and Peru, and the Genetic Erosion of Indigenous Cultivars', in *Crop Genetic Resources for Today and Tomorrow*, ed. O. H. Frankel and J. G. Hawkes, Cambridge University Press (Cambridge, 1975), 167–72.

Olsson, Mats and Patrick Svensson, 'Agricultural Production in Southern Sweden 1702–1864', in *Growth and Stagnation in European Historical Agriculture*, ed. Mats Olsson and Patrick Svensson, Brepols (Turnhout, 2011), 117–39.

Osborne, Michael, *Nature, the Exotic, and the Science of French Colonialism*, University of Indiana Press (Bloomington, 1994).

Overton, Mark, *Agricultural Revolution in England: The Transformation of the Agrarian Economy 1500–1850*, Cambridge University Press (Cambridge, 1996).

Pagden, Anthony, *The Languages of Political Theory in Early Modern Europe*, Cambridge University Press (Cambridge, 1987).

Pagden, Anthony, *Spanish Imperialism and the Political Imagination*, Yale University Press (New Haven, 1990).

Palanca Cañon, J. David, 'Introducción y Generalización del Cultivo y Consumo Alimentario y Médico de la Patata en el País Vasco', DPhil, Universidad del País Vasco, 2011.

Palmer, Catherine, 'From Theory to Practice: Experiencing the Nation in Everyday Life', *Journal of Material Culture* 3:2 (1998), 175–99.

Palomino Gonzales, María Mercedes, 'Gourmetización del alimento andino y la estetización del agricultor como parte del Boom Gastronómico Peruano', *Razón y Palabra* 20:94 (2016), 581–95.

Paping, Richard and Vincent Tassenaar, 'The Consequences of the Potato Disease in the Netherlands 1845–1860: A Regional Approach', in *When the Potato Failed: Causes and Effects of the 'Last' European Subsistence Crisis, 1845–1850*, ed. Cormac Ó Gráda, Richard Paping and Eric Vanhaute, Brepols (Turnhout, 2007), 149–84.

Paquette, Gabriel, ed., *Enlightened Reform in Southern Europe and Its Atlantic Colonies, c.1750–1830*, Palgrave Macmillan (London, 2016).

Paquette, Gabriel, *Enlightenment, Governance, and Reform in Spain and its Empire, 1759–1808*, Palgrave Macmillan (Basingstoke, 2008).

Parker, Geoffrey, *Global Crisis: War, Climate Change and Catastrophe in the Seventeenth Century*, Yale University Press (New Haven, 2013).

Parker, George, *The Gardeners Almanack* (London, 1702).

Parkinson, John, *Paradisi in Sole Paradisus Terrestris* (London, 1629).

Parliamentary History of England, from the Earliest Period to the Year 1803 (London, 1818).

Parmentier, Antoine Augustin, *Manière de Faire le Pain de Pommes de Terre sans Mélange de Farine* (Paris, 1779).

Parmentier, Antoine Augustin, *Mémoire couronné le 25 aout 1784, par l'Académie Royale des Sciences, Belles Lettres et Arts de Bordeaux, sur cette question: Quel seroit le meilleur procédé pour conserver, le plus long-temps possible, ou en grain ou en farine, le maïs ou blé de Turquie, plus connu dans la Guienne sous le nom de blé d'Espagne? Et quels seroient les différens moyens d'en tirer parti, dans les années abondantes, indépendamment des usages connus & ordinaires dans cette province?* (Bordeaux, 1785).

Parmentier, Antoine Augustin, *Observations on Such Nutritive Vegetables as May be Substituted in the Place of Ordinary Food, in Times of Scarcity* (London, 1783).

Parmentier, Antoine Augustin, *Les pommes de terre, considérées relativement à la santé & à l'économie: ouvrage dans lequel on traite aussi du froment & du riz* (Paris, 1781).

Parmentier, Antoine Augustin, *Traité sur la culture et les usages des pommes de terre, de la patate, et du topinambour* (Paris, 1789).

Parque de la Papa, www.parquedelapapa.org/esp/03parke_01.html.

Parry, John, 'Plantations and Provision Grounds: An Historical Sketch of the Introduction of Food Crops to Jamaica', *Revista de historia de América* 19 (1955), 1–20.

Pauer, Erich, 'Neighbourhood Associations and Food Distribution in Japanese Cities in World War II', in *Agriculture and Food Supply in the Second World War*, ed. Bernd Martin and Alan Milward, Scripta Mercaturae Verlag (Ostfildern, 1985), 219–41.

Pedersen, Susan, *Family Dependence, and the Origins of the Welfare State: Britain and France, 1914–1945*, Cambridge University Press (Cambridge, 1993).

Penn, William, 'A Further Account of the Province of Pennsylvania and its Improvements,' *Pennsylvania Magazine of History and Biography* 9:1 (1885), 62–81.

Pennell, Sara, 'Recipes and Reception: Tracking New World Foodstuffs in Early Modern British Culinary Texts, c.1650–1750', *Food and History* 7:1 (2010), 11–33.

Persson, Karl Gunnar, *Grain Markets in Europe, 1500–1900: Integration and Deregulation*, Cambridge University Press (Cambridge, 2009).

Petersen, Christian, *Bread and the British Economy, c.1770–1870*, ed. Andrew Jenkins, Scholar Press (Aldershot, 1995).

Petránová, Lydia, 'The Rationing System in Bohemia during the First World War', in *The Origins and Development of Food Policies in Europe*, ed. John Burnett and Derek Oddy, Leicester University Press (London, 1994), 23–38.

Petrie, Hazel, *Chefs of Industry: Maori Tribal Enterprise in Early Colonial New Zealand*, Auckland University Press (Auckland, 2013).

Petty, William, *Tracts; Chiefly Relating to Ireland* (Dublin, 1769).

Petyt, William, *Britannia Languens: or, a Discourse of Trade* (London, 1689).

Phillips, Denise, *Acolytes of Nature: Defining Natural Science in Germany, 1770–1850*, University of Chicago Press (Chicago, 2012).

Phillips, Edward, *The New World of Words, or A General English Dictionary* (London, 1678).

Piktin, Donald, *The House that Giacomo Built: History of an Italian Family, 1898–1978*, Cambridge University Press (Cambridge, 1985).

Pilcher, Jeffrey, *¡Que Vivan los Tamales! Food and the Making of Mexican Identity*, University of New Mexico Press (Albuquerque, 1998).

Pingali, P. L., 'Green Revolution: Impacts, Limits, and the Path Ahead', *Proceedings of the National Academy of Sciences* 109:31 (2012), 12302–8.

Piqueras Haba, Juan, 'La difusión de la patata en España (1750–1850): El papel de las Sociedades Económicas y del clero rural', *Ería: revista cuatrimestral de geografía* 27 (1992), 80–9.

Pissling, Wilhelm Franz, *Gesundheitslehre für das Volk* (Vienna, 1856).

Platell, Amanda, 'Sorry, Why Should the NHS Treat People for Being Fat?', *Mail Online*, 27 Feb. 2009, www.dailymail.co.uk/debate/article-1156678/AMANDA-PLATELL-Sorry-NHS-treat-people-fat.html.

Ploeg, Jan Douwe van der, 'Potatoes and Knowledge', in *An Anthropological Critique of Development: The Growth of Ignorance*, ed. Mark Hobart, Routledge (London, 1993), 209–27.

Pohl-Valero, Stefan, 'Food Science, Race, and the Nation in Colombia', *Oxford Research Encyclopedia of Latin American History* (2016), http://oxfordre.com/lati namericanhistory/view/10.1093/acrefore/9780199366439.001.0001/acrefore-9780199366439-e-321?print=pdf.

Pohl-Valero, Stefan, '"La raza entra por la boca": Energy, Diet, and Eugenics in Colombia, 1890–1940', *Hispanic American Historical Review* 94:3 (2014), 455–86.

Poissonnier Desperrières, [Antoine], *Mémoire sur les avantages qu'il y aurait a changer absolument la nourriture des gens de mer* (Versailles, 1772).

Poissonnier Desperrières, Antoine, *Traité des maladies des gens de mer* (Paris, 1767).

Pollock, Griselda, 'Van Gogh and the Poor Slaves: Images of Rural Labour as Modern Art', *Art History* 11:3 (1988), 408–32.

'Pomme de terre, Topinambour, Batate, Truffe blanche, Truffe rouge', 1765, in *Encyclopédie, ou dictionnaire raisonné des sciences, des artes et des métiers, etc.*, ed. Denis Diderot and Jean le Rond d'Alembert, University of Chicago: ARTFL Encyclopédie Project, ed. Robert Morrissey, http://encyclopedie.uchicago.edu.

Popplow, Marcus, 'Economizing Agricultural Resources in the German Economic Enlightenment', in *Materials and Expertise in Early Modern Europe:*

Between Market and Laboratory, ed. Ursula Klein and E. C. Spary, University of Chicago Press (Chicago, 2010), 261–87.

Porras Barrenechea, Raúl, ed., *Cartas del Perú (1524–1543)*, Colección de Documentos Inéditos para la Historia del Perú (Lima, 1959).

Porter, Andrew, *Religion versus Empire? British Protestant Missionaries and Overseas Expansion, 1700–1914*, Manchester University Press (Manchester, 2004).

Post, John, 'Nutritional Status and Mortality in Eighteenth-Century Europe', in *Hunger in History: Food Shortage, Poverty and Deprivation*, ed. Lucille Newman, Wiley-Blackwell (Oxford, 1995), 241–80.

Potato Pete's Recipe Book, Ministry of Food ([London], [1940?]).

Pottier, Johan, *The Anthropology of Food: The Social Dynamics of Food Security*, Polity Press (Cambridge, 1999).

Prain, Gordon, Sam Fujisaka and Michael Warren, eds., *Biological and Cultural Diversity: The Role of Indigenous Agricultural Experimentation in Development*, Intermediate Technology Publications (London, 1999).

Premo, Bianca, *The Enlightenment on Trial: Ordinary Litigants and Colonialism in the Spanish Empire*, Oxford University Press (Oxford, 2017).

Procter, Robert, *The Nazi War on Cancer*, Princeton University Press (Princeton, 1999).

Pullan, Brian, *Poverty and Charity: Europe, Italy, Venice, 1400–1700*, Variorum (Aldershot, 1994).

Purchas, Samuel, *Hakluytus Posthumus or Purchas his Pilgrimes* (Glasgow, 1905).

Qu, Dongyu and Kaiyun Xie, eds., *How the Chinese Eat Potatoes*, World Scientific (Hackensack, NJ, 2008).

Quesnay, François, 'Fermiers', 1756, in *Encyclopédie, ou dictionnaire raisonné des sciences, des arts et des métiers*, ed. Denis Diderot and Jean le Rond d'Alembert, VI: 537, University of Chicago, ARTFL Encyclopédie Project (Autumn 2017 Edition), ed. Robert Morrissey and Glenn Roe, http://encyclopedie.uchicago.edu.

Rabinbach, Anson, *The Human Motor: Energy, Fatigue and the Origins of Modernity*, University of California Press (Berkeley, 1992).

Raj, Kapil, 'Colonial Encounters and the Forging of New Knowledges and National Identities: Great Britain and India, 1760–1850', *Osiris* 15 (2000), 119–34.

Raj, Kapil, *Relocating Modern Science: Circulation and the Construction of Knowledge in South Asia and Europe, 1650–1900*, Palgrave Macmillan (Basingstoke, 2007).

Rath, Eric, *Food and Fantasy in Early Modern Japan*, University of California Press (Berkeley, 2010).

Ray, Utsa, *Culinary Culture in Colonial India: A Cosmopolitan Platter and the Middle-Class*, Cambridge University Press (Delhi, 2015).

Reader, John, *Potato: The History of the Propitious Esculent*, Yale University Press (New Haven, 2008).

Reagin, Nancy, *Sweeping the German Nation: Domesticity and National Identity in Germany, 1870–1945*, Cambridge University Press (Cambridge, 2007).

Redlich, Fritz, 'Science and Charity: Count Rumford and his Followers', *International Review of Social History* 16:2 (1971), 184–216.

'Review of *The Nation's Larder*', *Public Health* 54 (Oct. 1940–Sept. 1941), 14–16.

Ricciardi, V., N. Ramankutty, Z. Mehrabi, L. Jarvis and B. Chookolingo, 'How Much of the World's Food do Smallholders Produce?', *Global Food Security* 17 (2018), 64–72.

Rich, Barnabe, *True Report of a Late Practice Enterprised by a Papist* (London, 1582).

Richardson, Sarah, *The Political Worlds of Women: Gender and Politics in Nineteenth Century Britain*, Routledge (New York, 2013).

Richthofen, Ferdinand von, *Ferdinand von Richthofen's Tagebücher aus China*, ed. E. von Tiessen, 2 vols., Dietrich Reimer (Berlin, 1907).

Rickman, Geoffrey, *Corn Supply of Ancient Rome*, Clarendon Press (Oxford, 1980).

Riera Climent, Luis and Juan Riera Palmero, 'Los alimentos americanos en los Extractos de la Bascongada (1768–1793): el maíz y la patata', *Llull* 30 (2007), 525–40.

Ries, Nancy, 'Potato Ontology: Surviving Postsocialism in Russia', *Cultural Anthropology* 24:2 (2009), 181–212.

Rigaud, Lucas, *Cozinheiro moderno ou nova arte de cozinha* (Lisbon, 1785).

Riley, H. T., ed., *Memorials of London and London Life in the 13th, 14th and 15th Centuries* (London, 1868), British History Online, www.british-history.ac.uk.

Riley, James, *Population Thought in the Age of the Demographic Revolution*, Carolina Academic Press (Durham, 1985).

Riquetti, Victor de, *Philosophie rurale: ou, Économie générale et politique de l'agriculture*, 3 vols. (Amsterdam, 1763).

Roberts, Lissa, 'Situating Science in Global History: Local Exchanges and Networks of Circulation', *Itinerario* 33:1 (2009), 9–30.

Rockefeller Foundation, 'Accelerating Agricultural Modernization in Developing Nations', Bellagio, 2–6 Feb. 1970.

Rodríguez de Campomanes, Pedro, *Discurso sobre el fomento de la industria popular* (Madrid, 1774).

Roncaglia, Alessandro, *The Wealth of Ideas: A History of Economic Thought*, Cambridge University Press (Cambridge, 2001).

Rosenhane, Schering, *Oeconomia*, ed. Torsten Lagerstedt, Almqvist & Wiksells Boktryckeri (Uppsala, 1944 [1662]).

Rowntree, B. Seebohm, *Poverty: A Study of Town Life*, Macmillan (London, 1908).

Roy, Parama, 'A Dietetics of Virile Emergency', *Women's Studies International Forum* 44 (2014), 255–65.

Roy, Parama, 'Meat-Eating, Masculinity, and Renunciation in India: A Gandhian Grammar of Diet', *Gender & History* 14 (2002), 62–91

Royer, Johann, *Eine gute Anleitung wie man ... Garten-Gewächse ... nützen solle* (Braunschweig, 1651).

Rubner, Max, *Volksernährungsfragen* (Leipzig, 1908).

Rudenschöld, Ulrik, *Almanach* (Gothenburg, 1750).

Rule, John and John Wells, *Crime, Protest and Popular Politics in Southern England, 1740–1850*, Hambledon Press (London, 1997).

Rumpolts, Marx, *Ein new Kochbuch* (Frankfurt am Main, 1581).

Runge, C. Fore, 'Economic Consequences of the Obese', *Medscape* 56:11 (2007), 2668–72.

Rusnock, Andrea, *Vital Accounts: Quantifying Health and Population in Eighteenth-Century England and France*, Cambridge University Press (Cambridge, 2002).

Safier, Neil, *Measuring the World: Enlightenment Science and South America*, University of Chicago Press (Chicago, 2008).

Safley, Thomas Max, ed., *The Reformation of Charity: The Secular and the Religious in Early Modern Poor Relief*, Brill (Boston, 2003).

Said, Edward, *Culture and Imperialism*, Vintage (London, 1994).

Saint Pierre, J. H. B. de, *A Voyage to the Isle of France, the Isle of Bourbon, and the Cape of Good Hope: with Observations and Reflections upon Nature and Mankind* (London, 1800).

Sala, Giovanni Dominici, *De Alimentis et Eorum Recta Administratione Liber* (Padua, 1628).

Sala, Ilaria María, 'Tudou for the Tuhao: Can "Sister Potato," a Singing Peasant, Convince the Chinese to Eat More of the Lowly Spud?', *Quartz*, 24 Feb. 2016, https://qz.com/622594/can-potato-sister-a-singing-peasant-convince-the-chinese-to-eat-more-of-the-lowly-spud/.

Salaman, Redcliffe, *History and Social Influence of the Potato*, ed. J. G. Hawkes, Cambridge University Press (Cambridge, 2000 [1949]).

Salinas y Cordova, Buenaventura de, *Memorial, Informe y Manifiesto* ([Madrid?], c.1646).

Salmon, William, *The Family-Dictionary, or, Household Companion* (London, 1710).

Salomon, Frank and George Urioste, *The Huarochirí Manuscript: A Testament of Ancient and Colonial Andean Religion*, University of Texas Press (Austin, 1991).

Santo Thomas, Domingo de, *Grammatica, o Arte, que ha compuesto de la lengua general de los indios, del Peru* (Valladolid, 1560).

Saraiva, Tiago, *Fascist Pigs: Technoscientific Organisms and the History of Fascism*, MIT Press (Cambridge, MA, 2016).

Sauer, Carl O., *Agricultural Origins and Dispersals: The Domestication of Animals and Foodstuffs*, MIT Press (Cambridge, MA, 1969 [1952]).

Schanbacer, William, *The Politics of Food: The Global Conflict between Food Security and Food Sovereignty*, Praeger (Santa Barbara, 2010).

Schiebinger, Londa, *Plants and Empire: Colonial Bio-prospecting in the Atlantic World*, Harvard University Press (Cambridge, MA, 2009).

Schiebinger, Londa and Claudia Swan, eds., *Colonial Botany: Science, Commerce and Politics in the Early Modern World*, University of Pennsylvania Press (Philadelphia, 2005).

Schlüter, Regina G., 'Promoting Regional Cuisine as Intangible Cultural Heritage in Latin America', in *Food and the Tourism Experience: The OECD–Korea Workshop*, Organisation for Economic Co-operation and Development Publishing (Paris, 2012), 89–99.

Schmalzer, Sigrid, *Red Revolution, Green Revolution: Scientific Farming in Socialist China*, University of Chicago Press (Chicago, 2016).

Scholliers, Peter, 'The Policy of Survival: Food, the State and Social Relations in Belgium, 1914–1921, in *The Origins and Development of Food Policies in Europe*, ed. John Burnett and Derek Oddy, Leicester University Press (London, 1994), 39–53.

Schuler, Johann Melchior, *Geschichte und Beschreibung des Landes Glarus* (Zurich, 1837).

Schulze-Gävernitz, Gerhart von, *The Cotton Trade in England and on the Continent: A Study in the Field of the Cotton Industry*, trans. Oscar Hall (London, 1895).

Scott, Gregory, 'Plants, People, and the Conservation of Biodiversity of Potatoes in Peru', *Natureza & Conservação: Brazilian Journal of Nature Conservation* 9:1 (2011), 21–38.

Scott, James C., *Against the Grain: A Deep History of the Earliest States*, Yale University Press (New Haven, 2017).

Scott, James C., *The Art of Not Being Governed: An Anarchist History of Upland Southeast Asia*, Yale University Press (New Haven, 2009).

Scott, James C., *Seeing Like a State: How Certain Schemes to Improve the Human Condition Have Failed*, Yale University Press (New Haven, 1998).

Serrano, Elena, 'Making *Oeconomic* People: The Spanish *Magazine of Agriculture and Arts for Parish Rectors* (1797–1808)', *History and Technology* 30:3 (2014), 149–76.

Serres, Michel, 'Theory of the Quasi-Object', in *The Parasite*, trans. Lawrence Schehr, intro. Cary Wolfe, University of Minnesota Press (Minneapolis, 2007), 224–34.

Serres, Olivier de, *Le theatre d'agriculture et mesnage des champs* (Paris, 1603).

SERVINDI, 'Perú: Hoy se celebra el Día Nacional de la Papa', SERVINDI, 31 May 2006, www.servindi.org/actualidad/686.

Shammas, Carole, 'The Eighteenth-Century English Diet and Economic Change', *Explorations in Economic History* 21 (1984), 254–69.

Shammas, Carole, *The Pre-Industrial Consumer in England and America*, Clarendon Press (Oxford, 1990).

Shapiro, Laura, *Perfection Salad: Women and Cooking at the Turn of the Century*, Farrar, Straus & Giroux (New York, 1986).

Sharp, Buchanan, *Famine and Scarcity in Late Medieval and Early Modern England: The Regulation of Grain Marketing, 1256–1631*, Cambridge University Press (Cambridge, 2016).

Shaw, David John, *World Food Security: A History since 1945*, Palgrave Macmillan (Basingstoke, 2007).

Sheehan, Jonathan and Dror Wahrman, *Invisible Hands: Self-Organization and the Eighteenth Century*, University of Chicago Press (Chicago, 2015).

Shepherd, Chris, 'Imperial Science: The Rockefeller Foundation and Agricultural Science in Peru, 1940–1960', *Science as Culture* 14:2 (2005), 113–37.

Sheridan, Richard, 'Captain Bligh, the Breadfruit and the Botanic Gardens of Jamaica', *Journal of Caribbean History* 23:1 (1989), 28–50.

Sheridan, Richard, 'The Crisis of Slave Subsistence in the British West Indies during and after the American Revolution', *William and Mary Quarterly* 33:4 (1976), 615–41.

Sherman, Sandra, *Imagining Poverty: Quantification and the Decline of Paternalism*, Ohio State University Press (Columbus, 2001).

Sherwood, Joan, *Poverty in Eighteenth-Century Spain: The Women and Children of the Inclusa*, University of Toronto Press (Toronto, 1988).

Silva, Renan, *La ilustración en el Virreinato de Nueva Granada*, La Carreta (Bogotá, 2005).

Silverblatt, Irene, *Moon, Sun, and Witches: Gender Ideologies and Class in Inca and Colonial Peru*, Princeton University Press (Princeton, 1987).

Simmons, Amelia, *American Cookery* (Hartford, 1796).

Simmons, Dana, *Vital Minimum: Need, Science and Politics in Modern France*, University of Chicago Press (Chicago, 2015).

Simonen, Seppo, *Raivaajia ja rakentajia. Suomen maatalouden historiaa*, Kirjayhtymä (Helsinki, 1964).

Simonton, Deborah, *A History of European Women's Work: 1700 to the Present*, Routledge (London, 2003).

Skytte, Carl, 'Ron at utaf potatoes brånna brånnavin', in *Konglig Svenska Vetenskaps Academiens Handlingar* 8 (Stockholm, 1747), 252–3.

Slicher Van Bath, B. H., *The Agrarian History of Western Europe. A.D. 500–1850*, trans. Olive Ordish, Edward Arnold (London, 1966).

Smith, Adam, *An Inquiry into the Nature and Causes of the Wealth of Nations* (1776), *The Glasgow Edition of the Works and Correspondence of Adam Smith*, vol. II, ed. William B. Todd, Oxford University Press (Oxford, 1975).

Smith, Adam, *The Theory of Moral Sentiments* (1759), *The Glasgow Edition of the Works and Correspondence of Adam Smith*, vol. I, ed. D. D. Raphael and A. L. Macfie, Oxford University Press (Oxford, 1976).

Smith, E., *The Compleat Housewife* (London, 1739).

Smith, Pamela, *The Body of the Artisan: Art and Experience in the Scientific Revolution*, University of Chicago Press (Chicago, 2004).

Smith, R. E. F. and David Christian, *Bread and Salt: A Social and Economic History of Food and Drink in Russia*, Cambridge University Press (Cambridge, 1984).

Smith, Thomas and John Choules, *Origin and History of Missions; Containing Faithful Accounts of the Voyages, Travels, Labors and Successes of the Various Missionaries, Who Have Been Sent Forth to Evangelize the Heathen*, 2 vols. (Boston, 1832).

Smith, William, *Sure Guide in Sickness and Health, in the Choice of Food, and Use of Medicine* (London, 1779).

Sokolow, Jayme, 'Count Rumford and Late Enlightenment Science, Technology and Reform', *The Eighteenth Century: Theory and Interpretation* 21:1 (1980), 76–86.

Solander, Daniel, *Daniel Solander: Selected Correspondence, 1753–1782*, ed. Edward Duyker and Per Tingbrand, Miegunyah Press (Melbourne, 1995).

Sood, S., V. Bhardwaj, S. K. Pandey and S. K. Chakrabarti, 'History of Potato Breeding: Improvement, Diversification, and Diversity', in *The Potato Genome: Compendium of Plant Genomes*, ed. S. Kumar Chakrabarti, C. Xie and J. Kumar Tiwari, Springer (Cham, 2017), 31–72.

Soule, Emily Berquist, *The Bishop's Utopia: Envisioning Improvement in Colonial Peru*, University of Pennsylvania Press (Philadelphia, 2014).

Spalding, Karen, *Huarochirí: An Andean Society under Inca and Spanish Rule*, Stanford University Press (Stanford, 1984).

Spang, Rebecca, *The Invention of the Restaurant: Paris and Modern Gastronomic Culture*, Harvard University Press (Cambridge, MA, 2000).

Spary, Emma, *Eating the Enlightenment: Food and the Sciences in Paris, 1670–1760*, University of Chicago Press (Chicago, 2012).

Spary, Emma, *Feeding France: New Sciences of Food, 1760–1815*, Cambridge University Press (Cambridge, 2014).

Spary, Emma, *Utopia's Garden: French Natural History from Old Regime to Revolution*, University of Chicago Press (Chicago, 2000).

Spary, Emma and Paul White, 'Food of Paradise: Tahitian Breadfruit and the Autocritique of European Consumption', *Endeavour* 28:2 (2004), 75–80.

Stapelbroek, Koen and Jani Marjanen, eds., *The Rise of Economic Societies in the Eighteenth Century*, Palgrave Macmillan (Basingstoke, 2012).

Staples, Amy L. S., *The Birth of Development: How the World Bank, Food and Agriculture Organization, and the World Health Organization Changed the World, 1945–1965*, Kent State University Press (Kent, OH, 2006).

Stedman Jones, Gareth, *An End to Poverty? A Historical Debate*, Columbia University Press (New York, 2004).

Stedman Jones, Gareth, *Karl Marx: Greatness and Illusion*, Penguin (London, 2016).

Steel, Carolyn, *Hungry City: How Food Shapes Our Lives*, Vintage (London, 2013).

Stern, Philip and Carl Wennerlind, eds., *Mercantilism Reimagined: Political Economy in Early Modern Britain and its Empire*, Oxford University Press (Oxford, 2014).

Stern, Walter, 'The Bread Crisis in Britain, 1795–96', *Economica*, new series, 31:122 (1964), 168–87.

Stewart, John, *An Account of Jamaica and its Inhabitants* (London, 1808).

Struys, Jan Janszoon, *Drie aanmerkelyke en zeer rampspoedige Reizen, door Italien, Griekenland, Lystland, Moscovien, Tartaryen, Meden, Persien, Oostindien, Japan, en verscheiden andere Gewesten* (Amsterdam, 1676).

Styles, John, 'Custom or Consumption? Plebeian Fashion in Eighteenth-Century England', in *Luxury in the Eighteenth Century: Debates, Desires and Delectable Goods*, ed. Maxine Berg and Elizabeth Eger, Palgrave Macmillan (Basingstoke, 2003), 103–15.

Swislocki, Mark, 'Nutritional Governmentality: Food and the Politics of Health in Late Imperial and Republican China', *Radical History Review* 110 (2011), 9–35.

Switzer, Stephen, *The Practical Kitchen Gardiner* (London, 1727).

Symner, Miles, 'Notes on Natural History in Ireland', *c.*1656–60, University of Sheffield, Hartlib Papers 62/45/6A, www.hrionline.ac.uk/hartlib/context.

Tabáres de Ulloa, Francisco, *Observaciones prácticas sobre el cacahuete, o maní de América: su producción en España, bondad del fruto, y sus varios usos, particularmente para la extracción de aceyte; modo de cultivarle y beneficiarle para bien de la nación* (Valencia, 1800).

Talve, Ilmar, 'The Potato in Finnish Food Economy', in *Food in Perspective: Proceedings of the Third International Conference on Ethnological Food Research, Cardiff, Wales, 1977*, ed. Alexander Fenton and Trefor Owen (Edinburgh, 1981), 277–82.

Tapwell, Thomas, *A Friendly Address to the Poor of Great Britain on the Present Scarcity of Wheat and Dearness of Wheaten Bread* (London, 1796).

Targioni-Tozzetti, Antonio, *Cenni storici sulla introduzione di varie piante nell'agricoltura ed Orticoltura Toscana* (Florence, 1853).

Tavárez Simó, Fidel José, 'La invención de un imperio comercial hispano, 1740–1765', *Magallánica, Revista de Historia Moderna* 3 (2015), 56–76.

Taylor, Charles, 'Atomism', in *Philosophical Papers*, Cambridge University Press (Cambridge, 1985), II, 187–210.

Temple, Richard, 'The Agri-Horticultural Society of India', *Calcutta Review* 22 (1854), 341–59.

Tennant, William, *Indian Recreations; Consisting Chiefly of Strictures on the Domestic and Rural Economy of the Mahommedans & Hindoos*, 2 vols. (Edinburgh, 1803–4).

Terrón, Eloy, *España, encrucijada de culturas alimentarias: su papel en la difusión de los cultivos americanos*, Ministerio de Agricultura, Pesca y Alimentación, Secretaría General Técnica (Madrid, 1992).

Terry, Edward, *A Voyage to East-India, &c.* (London, 1777).

Teuteberg, Hans Jürgen, 'Der Verzehr von Nahrungsmitteln in Deutschland pro Kopf und Jahr seit Beginn der Industrialisierung (1850–1975). Versuch einer quantitativen Langzeitanalyse', *Archiv für Sozialgeschichte* 19 (1979), 331–88.

Thaler, Richard and Cass Sunstein *Nudge: Improving Decisions about Health, Wealth and Happiness*, Yale University Press (New Haven, 2008).

Thane, Pat, 'The Working Class and State "Welfare" in Britain, 1890–1914', *Historical Journal*, 27:2 (1984), 877–900.

Thick, Malcolm, 'Root Crops and the Feeding of London's Poor in the Late Sixteenth and Early Seventeenth Centuries', in *English Rural Society, 1500–1800: Essays in Honour of Joan Thirsk*, ed. John Chartres and David Hey, Cambridge University Press (Cambridge, 1990), 279–96.

Thirsk, Joan, *The Agrarian History of England and Wales, 1640–1750*, Cambridge University Press (Cambridge, 2011).

Thirsk, Joan, *Food in Early Modern England: Phases, Fads, Fashions 1500–1760*, Hambledon (London, 2007).

Thomopoulos, Elaine, *The History of Greece*, Greenwood (Santa Barbara, 2012).

[Thompson, Benjamin], *Ensayos, políticos, económicos y fisosóficos del Conde de Rumford, traducidos de órden de la Real Sociedad Económica de esta corte*, trans. Domingo Agüero y Neira, 2 vols. (Madrid, 1800–1).

Thompson, Benjamin, *Essays, Political, Economical and Philosophical*, 3 vols. (London, 1797–1803).

Thompson, E. P., *The Making of the English Working Class*, Penguin (Harmondsworth, 1984).

Thompson, E. P., 'The Moral Economy of an English Crowd in the Eighteenth Century', *Past & Present* 50:1 (1971), 76–136.

Tiedemann, Friedrich, *Geschichte des Tabaks und anderer ähnlicher Genußmittel* (Frankfurt, 1854).

Tilly, Charles, 'Food Supply and Public Order in Modern Europe', in *The Formation of National States in Western Europe*, ed. Charles Tilly, Princeton University Press (Princeton, 1975), 380–455.

Tobin, Beth, *Colonizing Nature: The Tropics in British Arts and Letters, 1760–1820*, University of Pennsylvania Press (Philadelphia, 2004).

Tomaselli, Sylvana, 'Moral Philosophy and Population Questions in Eighteenth-Century Europe', *Population and Development Review* 14 (1988), 7–29.

Touchet, Julien, *Botanique & Colonisation en Guyane française (1720–1848)*, Ibis Rouge (Cahors, 2004).

Toussaint-Samat, Maguelonne, *A History of Food: A New Expanded Edition*, trans. Anthea Bell, Blackwell (Oxford, 2009).

Transactions of the Agricultural and Horticultural Society of India, 2 vols. (Calcutta, 1838).

Treitel, Corinna, 'Food Science/Food Politics: Max Rubner and "Rational Nutrition" in Fin-de-Siècle Berlin', in *Food and the City in Europe since 1800*, ed. Peter Lummel, Derek Oddy and Peter Atkins, Ashgate (Aldershot, 2012), 51–62.

Treitel, Corinna, 'Max Rubner and the Biopolitics of Rational Nutrition', *Central European History* 41 (2008), 1–25.

Trentmann, Frank, *Empire of Things: How We Became a World of Consumers, from the Fifteenth Century to the Twenty-First*, Allen Lane (Milton Keynes, 2016).

Trentmann, Frank and Flemming Just, eds., *Food and Conflict in Europe in the Age of the Two World Wars*, Palgrave Macmillan (Basingstoke, 2006).

Trevelyan, Charles, *The Irish Crisis* (London, 1848).

Tribe, Keith, 'Cameralism and the Sciences of the State', in *The Cambridge History of Eighteenth-Century Political Thought*, ed. Mark Goldie and Robert Wokler, Cambridge University Press (Cambridge, 2006), 525–46.

Tribe, Keith, 'Continental Political Economy from the Physiocrats to the Marginal Revolution', in *The Cambridge History of Science*, vol. VII: *The Modern Social Sciences*, ed. Roy Porter, Theodore M. Porter and Dorothy Ross, Cambridge University Press (Cambridge, 2003), 154–70.

Tribe, Keith, *Governing Economy: The Reformation of German Economic Discourse, 1750–1840*, Cambridge University Press (Cambridge, 1988).

Tribe, Keith, 'Henry Sidgwick, Moral Order and Utilitarianism', *Journal of the History of Economic Thought* 24:4 (2017), 907–30.

Tribe, Keith, *Land, Labour and Economic Discourse*, Routledge (London, 1978).

Tribe, Keith, *Strategies of Economic Order: German Economic Discourse, 1750–1950*, Cambridge University Press (Cambridge, 1995).

Truman, Harry S., 'Inaugural Address', 20 Jan. 1949, Harry S. Truman Presidential Library & Museum, https://trumanlibrary.org/whistlestop/50yr_archive/inagural20jan1949.htm.

Turnbull, William, *The Naval Surgeon Comprising the Entire Duties of Professional Men at Sea. To Which are Subjoined, a System of Naval Surgery and a Compendious Pharmacopoeia* (London, 1806).

Turner, William, *An Almanack for the Year of our Lord God 1701* (London, 1701).

Turton, Thomas, *An Address to the Good Sense and Candour of the People in behalf of the Dealers in Corn: with Some Observations on a Late Trial for Regrating* (London, 1800).

Ugent, Donald, Tom Dillehay and Carlos Ramírez, 'Potato Remains from a Late Pleistocene Settlement in Southcentral Chile', *Economic Botany* 41:1 (1987), 17–27.

UK Department of Health, 'Choosing Health: Making Healthy Choices Easier', 16 Nov. 2004, http://webarchive.nationalarchives.gov.uk and www.dh.gov.uk/en/Publicationsandstatistics/Publications/PublicationsPolicyAndGuidance/DH_4094550.

Unanue, Hipólito, *Observaciones sobre el clima del Lima y sus influencias en los seres organizados* (Lima, 1806).

Underrättelse om potatoës eller jord-pärons plantering och bruk, hämtad af flere årens försök, uti Rambergs bergslag (Stockholm, 1757).

United Nations, *Report of the Forty-Ninth Session of the Committee on Commodity Problems*, Rome, 14–25 Oct. 1974.

Uriz, Joaquín Xavier de, *Causas prácticas de la muerte de los niños expósitos en sus primeros años: remedio en su origen de un tan grave mal: y modo de formarlos útiles a la religión y al estado con notable aumento de la población, fuerzas, y riqueza de España*, 2 vols. (Pamplona, 1801).

US Department of Health and Human Services, 'A Healthier You', 2005, https://health.gov/dietaryguidelines/dga2005/healthieryou/contents.htm.

Usoz, Javier, 'Political Economy and the Creation of the Public Sphere during the Spanish Enlightenment', in *The Spanish Enlightenment Revisited*, ed. Jesús Astigarraga, Voltaire Foundation (Oxford, 2015), 117–22.

Valle y Caviedes, Juan del, *Obra completa*, ed. Daniel Reedy, Ayacucho (Caracas, 1984).

Valles Garrido, J. M., 'La distribución de sopas económicas del Conde Rumford en la Segovia de comienzos del siglo XIX', *Estudios Segovianos* 92 (1995), 143–76.

Van de Ven, Hans J., *War and Nationalism in China, 1925–1945*, Routledge (Abingdon, 2003).

Van Gogh, Vincent, Vincent van Gogh: The Letters, www.vangoghletters.org.

Vandenbroeke, Christian, 'Cultivation and Consumption of the Potato in the 17th and 18th Century,' *Acta Historiae Neerlandica* 5 (1971), 15–39.

Vanhaute, Eric, '"So Worthy an Example to Ireland": The Subsistence and Industrial Crisis of 1845–1850 in Flanders', in *When the Potato Failed: Causes and Effects of the 'Last' European Subsistence Crisis, 1845–1850*, ed. Cormac Ó Gráda, Richard Paping and Eric Vanhaute, Brepols (Turnhout, 2007), 123–48.

Vanhaute, Eric, Richard Paping and Cormac Ó Gráda, 'The European Subsistence Crisis of 1848–1850: A Comparative Perspective', in *When the Potato Failed: Causes and Effects of the 'Last' European Subsistence Crisis, 1845–1850*, ed. Cormac Ó Gráda, Richard Paping and Eric Vanhaute, Brepols (Turnhout, 2007), 1–31.

Vardi, Liana, *The Physiocrats and the World of the Enlightenment*, Cambridge University Press (Cambridge, 2012).

Varenne de Béost, Claude-Marc-Antoine, *La cuisine des pauvres ou Collection des meilleurs Mémoires qui ont parus depuis peu* (Dijon, 1772).

Verhandlungen und Schriften der hamburgischen Gesellschaft zur Beförderung der Künste und nützlichen Gewerbe 1 (Hamburg, 1790).

Vernon, James, 'The Ethics of Hunger and the Assembly of Society: The Techno-Politics of the School Meal in Modern Britain', *American Historical Review* 110:3 (2005), 693–725.

Vernon, James, *Hunger: A Modern History*, Harvard University Press (Cambridge, MA, 2007).

'Vice Minister of the Party at Ministry of Agriculture Emphasizes: Strengthen Potato Industry and Make it the Aircraft Carrier to Protect Food Safety of the Country', Institute of Food Science and Technology (CASS), 2017, http://iappst.caas.cn/en/news/74612.htm.

Vico, Giambattista, *The New Science of Giambattista Vico. Unabridged Translation of the Third Edition, 1744*, trans. Thomas Goddard Bergin and Max Harold Fisch, Cornell University Press (Ithaca, 1984).

Viqueira Albán, Juan Pedro, *Propriety and Permissiveness in Bourbon Mexico*, trans. Sonya Lipsett-Rivera and Sergio Rivera Ayala, SR Books (Wilmington, 1999).

Virey, Julien Joseph, 'De la vie et des ouvrages d'Antoine-Augustin Parmentier', *Bulletin de Pharmacie et des Sciences Accessoires* 2 (1814), 60–1.

Virey, Julien Joseph, 'Pomme-de-terre, ou papas des Américas: Recherches sur son origine et l'epoque de son introduction en Europe', in *Nouveau dictionnaire d'histoire naturelle, appliquée aux arts, a l'agriculture, a l'économie rural et domistique, a la médecine, etc, par une société de naturalistes et d'agriculteurs* (Paris, 1818), XXVII, 526–49.

Voekel, Pamela, *Alone before God: The Religious Origins of Modernity in Mexico*, Duke University Press (Durham, 2002).

Vos, Paula de, 'Natural History and the Pursuit of Empire in Eighteenth-Century Spain', *Eighteenth-Century Studies* 40:2 (2007), 209–39.

Wahnbaeck, Till, *Luxury and Public Happiness: Political Economy in the Italian Enlightenment*, Oxford University Press (Oxford, 2004).

Walter, John, 'The Social Economy of Dearth in Early Modern England', in *Famine, Disease and the Social Order in Early Modern Society*, ed. John Walter and Roger Schofield, Cambridge University Press (Cambridge, 1989), 75–128.

Wang, Xiaoying, 'The Post-Communist Personality: The Spectre of China's Capitalist Market Reforms', *China Journal* 47 (2002), 1–17.

Ward, Bernardo, *Obra pía y eficaz modo para remediar la miseria de la gente pobre de España* (Madrid, 1787 [1750]).

Ward, Bernardo, *Proyecto económico, en que se proponen varias providencias, dirigidas á promover los intereses de España, con los medios y fondos necesarios para su plantificación* (Madrid, 1779).

Warner, Jessica, *Craze: Gin and Debauchery in an Age of Reason*, Random House (New York, 2003).

Washington, George, *The Writings of George Washington from the Original Manuscript Sources, 1745–1799*, ed. John Fitzpatrick, Government Printing Office (Washington, DC, 1931–44).

Watt, George, *Dictionary of the Economic Products of India*, 6 vols. (London and Calcutta, 1891).

Watts, Michael, 'Development and Governmentality', *Singapore Journal of Tropical Geography* 24:1 (2003), 6–34.

Webb, Samantha, 'Not So Pleasant to the Taste: Coleridge in Bristol during the Mixed Bread Campaign of 1795', *Romanticism* 12:1 (2006), 5–14.

Webb, Sidney and Beatrice Webb, 'The Assize of Bread', *The Economic Journal* 14:54 (1904), 196–218.

Weismantel, Mary, *Food, Gender and Poverty in the Ecuadorian Andes*, University of Pennsylvania Press (Philadelphia, 1988).

Wells, Roger, *Wretched Faces: Famine in Wartime England, 1793–1801*, Sutton Press (Gloucester, 1988).

West-India Planter, *Remarks on the Evidence Delivered on the Petition presented by the West-India Planters and Merchants, to the Hon. the House of Commons, on the 16th of March 1775* (London, 1777).

Wheeler, Erica, 'To Feed or to Educate? Labelling in Targeted Nutrition Intervention', *Development and Change* 16 (1985), 475–83.

Whitaker, William, 'Food Entitlements', in *The Cambridge World History of Food*, ed. Kenneth Kiple and Kriemhild Coneè Ornelas, 2 vols. Cambridge University Press (Cambridge, 2001), II, 1585–92.

White, Gilbert, *Natural History of Selborne* (Edinburgh, 1833).

Wiegelmann, Günter, *Alltags- und Festspeisen in Mitteleuropa. Innovation, Strukturen und Regionen vom späten Mittelalter bis zum 20. Jahrhundert*, Waxmann (Marburg 1967).

Wilk, Richard, 'Beauty and the Feast: Official and Visceral Nationalism, in Belize', *Ethnos* 58 (1993), 294–316.

Will, Pierre-Etienne and R. Bin Wong, *Nourish the People: The State Civilian Granary System in China, 1650–1850*, University of Michigan Press (Ann Arbor, 1991).

Wills, C. J., *The Land of the Lion and the Sun, or Modern Persia, Being Experiences of Life in Persia from 1866 to 1881* (London, 1891).

Wilse, J. N., *Physisk, oeconomisk og statistisk Beskrivelse over Spydeberg Præstegield og Egn i Aggershuus-Stift udi Norge* (Christiania, 1779).

Wilson, Mary Tolford, 'Americans Learn to Grow the Irish Potato', *New England Quarterly* 32:3 (1959), 333–50.

Winter, J. M., 'Military Fitness and Civilian Health in Britain during the First World War', *Journal of Contemporary History* 15 (1980), 211–44.

Wirilander, Kaarlo, *Savon Historia: Savo Kaskisavujen Kautena 1721–1870*, Kustannuskiila Oy (Kuopio,1960).

Withers, Charles, *Placing the Enlightenment: Thinking Geographically about the Age of Reason*, University of Chicago Press (Chicago, 2007).

Woolley, Hannah, *The Queen-Like Closet* (London, 1672).

Worboys, Michael, 'The Discovery of Colonial Malnutrition between the Wars', in *Imperial Medicine and Indigenous Societies*, ed. David Arnold, Manchester University Press (Manchester, 1988), 208–25.

Yan, Yunxiang, 'The Chinese Path to Individualization', *British Journal of Sociology* 61:3 (2010), 489–512.

Yang, Mei-ling, 'Creating the Kitchen Patriot: Media Promotion of Food Rationing and Nutrition Campaigns on the American Home Front during World War II', *American Journalism* 22:3 (2005), 55–75.

Ying, Li, 'The Great Potato Debate', *Global Times*, 22 Jan. 2015, www.globaltimes.cn/content/903438.shtml.

Young, Arthur, *Farmer's Letters to the People of England*, second edition (London, 1768).

Young, Arthur, *The Question of Scarcity Plainly Stated, and Remedies Considered* (London, 1800).

Young, Arthur, *A Tour in Ireland; with General Observations on the Present State of that Kingdom: Made in the Years 1776, 1777, and 1778. And Brought Down to the End of 1779*, 2 vols. (London, 1780).

Zanon, Antonio, *Della coltivazione, e dell'uso delle patate e d'altre piante commestibili* (Venice, 1767).

Zárate, Agustín de, *Historia del descubrimiento y conquista del Perú*, ed. Franklin Pease and Teodoro Hampe Martínez, Pontífica Universidad Católica del Perú (Lima, 1995 [1555]).

Zeta Quinde, Rosa, *El pensamiento ilustrado en el Mercurio peruano, 1791–1794*, Universidad de Piura (Piura, 2000).

Zilberstein, Anya, 'Inured to Empire: Wild Rice and Climate Change', *William and Mary Quarterly* 72:1 (2015), 127–58.

Zweiniger-Bargielowska, Ina, *Managing the Body: Beauty, Health and Fitness in Britain, 1880–1939*, Oxford University Press (Oxford, 2010).

Zwinger, Theodor, *Theatrum Botanicum* (Basle, 1696).

Zylberberg, David, 'Fuel Prices, Regional Diets and Cooking Habits in the English Industrial Revolution (1750–1830)', *Past & Present* 229:1 (2015), 91–122.

Index